The Economics
of Political Violence

The Economics
of Political Violence

The Effect of Political Instability on Economic Growth

Dipak K. Gupta

New York
Westport, Connecticut
London

Library of Congress Cataloging-in-Publication Data

Gupta, D. K.
    The economics of political violence : the effect of political
instability on economic growth / Dipak K. Gupta.
      p.   cm.
    Includes bibliographical references.
    ISBN 0-275-93256-7 (alk. paper)
    1. Violence. 2. Political stability. 3. Economic development.
I. Title.
    JC328.6.G87   1990
    322.4'2—dc20   89-23019

Library of Congress Catalog Card Number: 89-23019
ISBN: 0-275-93256-7

First published in 1990

Praeger Publishers, One Madison Avenue, New York, NY 10010
An imprint of Greenwood Publishing Group, Inc.

Printed in the United States of America

The paper used in this book complies with the
Permanent Paper Standard issued by the National
Information Standards Organization (Z39.48-1984).

10 9 8 7 6 5 4 3 2 1

To the loving memory of my father Dilip K. Gupta
and to
Kanika Gupta, Achyutananda Das Gupta, Anjali Das Gupta, and Sunil K. Gupta

Contents

Tables and Figures

FIGURES

TABLES

Acknowledgments

It has been an audacious attempt. In my effort to understand the causes of political violence and its effect on the aggregate economy, I had to trespass the rigid boundaries of the social sciences. In my travel across the disciplines, I have faced numerous problems, the most troublesome of which has been the lack of uniformity of methodology, paradigm, and even the language. The academic equivalent of the destruction of the tower of Babel since the breakup of political economy has caused duplicacy of effort, lack of mutual understanding, and a serious gap in the analysis of social events, the dimensions of which cannot be captured within the confines of any one branch of social science. However, in my effort to be comprehensive, I have often had to treat important matters with cursory attention. I can only hope that in the process I have not committed serious errors.

During years of study across the unknown territories, I have incurred intellectual debts from many friends and colleagues. The completion of this work, to a large extent, has been the result of their thoughtful comments, suggestions, and encouragement. I gratefully acknowledge the help of Professors Amartya K. Sen and Paul Streeten, who on many occasions have given thoughtful comments and much needed encouragement. I am also grateful to Professor Amitai Etzioni, Chalmers Johnson, and Jeffrey Nugent for their help on several occasions. Many other friends and colleagues have helped me along the way to formulate my ideas. Among them I should mention Edmund Acosta, George Babilot, James Gazell, Joel Henderson, Sam Lehman-Wilzig, Morris Mottale, Prem Pillai, Anindya Ray, Marco Walshok, Yiannis P. Venieris and James Wood. I am especially indebted to Professor Harinder Singh for his help in formulating some of the most difficult concepts in my study.

My thanks also go to Susan Archer, James Edwards, Rachael Littonjua, Stephanie Pierce, Betty Snyder, and Ellaine Wansowicz for their many technical assistance during the preparation of this manuscript. I am also particularly indebted to Ms. Susan Badger and Bert Yaeger for an excellent job in editing the manuscript.

My gratitude is also to the Louis M. Rea, Director, School of Public Administration and Urban Studies, and to the Dean's office of the college of Professional Studies and Fine Arts at San Diego State University. Without their help this work would have been much delayed.

Writing a book is a lonesome experience. And the completion of this one took much longer than I had anticipated. During these trying years, I am grateful to my wife Sumitra, my daughter Shalini, and my son, Rohan for creating some of the most delightful diversions. Without their interference this book surely would have taken even longer to complete.

The Economics
of Political Violence

1

The Scope of the Study

The end of World War II marked a distinct break in the history of human civilization. For the first time in the millennia of recorded history, war between nations increasingly started to take a backseat. Owing to the establishment of a world forum, the United Nations, the overwhelming influence of the superpower hegemony, and the threat of nuclear war dampened the nationalistic fervor for physical conquer of other countries. Instead, what we see is a virtual explosion of conflict within nations. Few countries in the world, if any, are completely free of violence caused by conflicting group aspirations in zero-sum societies.

      Indeed, as one picks up a newspaper or watches television, the images of groups of people taking part in collective political action are virtually impossible to escape. These actions are sometimes peaceful, sometimes violent, and always directed against an established political order. Sitting in the relative calm of a living room or a classroom with little moral imperative, it is difficult to relate to those wild-eyed revolutionaries in distant lands. Therefore, the temptation to brand such behavior as "fanatical," "irrational," or beyond the scope of explanation is rather strong. In fact, until quite recently the vast literature of Western (or nonMarxist) social science has had precious little to say about such behavior. However, quite interestingly, the classical eighteenth- and nineteenth-century writers were keenly aware of the role of collective rebellion in shaping the destiny of social evolution.   Karl Marx based his theory of societal evolution on conflicts generated from what he called the "inherent contradictions" within the capitalist society. The social contract theorists such as Hobbes, Locke, and Rousseau theorized about the birth of modern political structure through social strife and recognized the need to find a structure that would prevent the society from falling into the grip of anarchy. Historians such as de Tocqueville, organizational theorists like Max Weber,[1] and Social Darwinians such as Herbert Spencer paid particular attention to the role collective rebellion plays in the evolution of a nation. Even economists like Malthus linked unrestricted population growth to wide-scale social turmoil, violence, and conflict.

However, with the birth of modern social science the analysis of collective rebellion was largely abandoned. It would indeed seem absurd to think that after two great wars, several revolutions, and numerous rebellions the inquiry into the causes of political violence and its impact on the economy will be overlooked. But possibly to draw a contrast with the conflict-based Marxist theory, Western social science paradigm sought reasons for the society to adapt and ameliorate conflict and the economy to attain equilibrium. So powerful was the assumption of this centripetal force that any curiosity about the factors that can blow a society asunder from within was considered superfluous and not worthy of intellectual curiosity. This view was further bolstered by Freudian psychology, which argued that human aggressive behavior was a reflection of a subconscious death wish, a remnant of our animal past. Therefore, by placing aggression squarely on the side of instinct, there was hardly any reason to look for behavioral explanation of such action.

However, facing the frequent eruptions of political violence, especially in the Third World countries, a happy compromise between reality and the conflict-free paradigm was reached by assuming such outbursts of collective emotion to be the products of social and economic transformation. It was therefore argued that these conflicts are symptomatic of the transitional societies and they are to dissipate with the attainment of "development." Unfortunately, again reality stood in the way of a cogent theory. The events of the late 1960s and early 1970s proved that even the developed nations were not immune to collective violence.

This latest bout with reality prompted sociologists and political scientists to cast a fresh look at the causes of social conflict. The outcome was a plethora of studies exploring the structural causes of collective rebellion. These studies, like Marx's, looked for the causes of revolution in the imbalances in the basic socioeconomic structure of a nation. They argued that the changes, brought about mostly by the external forces, cause people or groups, who have so far been content within the traditional system, to demand more than what the society, the polity, or the economy can provide. The mismatch or lack of equilibrium between demand and supply of sociopolitical and economic goods causes political unrest.

Even though the social structural theorists provided some significant insights into the causes of collective rebellion, the important link between cause and effect was provided by the sociopsychologists. They argued that people take up violent resistance when they feel frustrated by the gap between what they actually have and what they feel they *should* have had. The importance of this jump that linked frustration caused by external factors with acts of aggression goes far beyond the advantage of the ability to formulate explicit, empirically testable hypotheses and, indeed, strikes at the heart of the traditional notion of an irrational and instinctive explanation of collective violent behavior. By linking external factors with the acts of violence, we assume behavioral explanation and "rational" behavior on the part of the participants. The inevitable outcome of such linkage is the policy implication that by altering the external environment one can influence the level of collective violence. The alternative to this behavioral hypothesis is the uniform policy prescription of brutal repression to keep the animal instinct under control or to keep the deviants secluded from the rest of the society.

However, the problem with linking just frustration with aggressive behavior is the fact that it offers an incomplete explanation. That is, while the frustration-aggression hypothesis is quite explicit about why people should revolt, it fails to say why they should not.

The reason for this shortcoming is twofold. First, the frustration-aggression hypothesis fails to incorporate other aspects of rational decision-making calculus, the expectations of future rewards as opposed to the fear of loosing what one already has. Second, while examining the logic of collective action, it was found to have certain theoretical problems. For example, even granting the fact that I am frustrated by the present situation, the question remains: Why should I participate in an act of collective revolt, knowing full well that if and when the movement succeeds, the resulting benefits will be shared by all the members of the group irrespective of the individual level of participation? That is, if independence from a colonial rule or the overthrow of a tyrant results from a mass movement, presumably every member of the opposition group will benefit. In that case, what rational person will risk loss of property, freedom, or life itself for something that will benefit everybody if it comes, but that will cause problems mostly for the participants if it fails?

The problem of explaining basically selfless acts (or the attempts to achieve for the collectivity rather than for the individual self) with purely selfish rule of individual profit maximization proved to be a fertile ground for research as various solutions were advanced to provide justification for such actions. From the outset, however, it became clear that we needed to consider one important element - *ideology*. The meaning of ideology can be varied. As the term is commonly understood, it can mean a religious faith or a political dogma. However, for the purpose of this book, we are defining *ideology* simply as a preference for collective goods.

The problem is, of course, that the term ideology has been an anathema to the paradigm of the rationality of individual profit maximization. Since ideology masks the behavior of individual profit maximization, which is considered to be the cornerstone of economic paradigm, how can we consider behavior based on ideology as rational? On the other hand, if we do not, how can we even attempt to explain something irrational and therefore random? Fortunately, again reality prevailed and forced a number of political scientists and even economists to consider ideology explicitly or implicitly in their behavioral framework. Therefore, we modify the basic assumption of the rational economic man, the *homoeconomicus*, whose perception of the world is through his self-interest alone. Instead, we accept the view that an individual derives utility from satisfying his own needs as well as the needs of the larger group in which he belongs. This expanded behavioral assumption, as we demonstrate in Chapter 4, explains a much wider range of behavior than is possible under the narrow definition of *economic_rationality*.

So by including ideology into the scheme of maximization of individual net benefit, we can solve two vexing problems of the two approaches. Thus, as an improvement over the frustration-aggression hypothesis, the explicit inclusion of cost factor allows us to demonstrate when an otherwise frustrated individual may not take part in a collective movement. Second, the consideration of ideology enables us to analyze conceptually the rationality of human behavior when it comes to acts of selflessness.

If the causes of political violence have received a great deal of attention during the last 30 years or so, of late the other side of the picture has begun to unfold. It is fairly obvious that economic progress cannot take place with a high degree of political instability in the nation. Adam Smith, in his *Theory of Moral Sentiments* made it abundantly clear that for the market economy to function properly the political state must (1) provide the stability and balance of institutions needed to assume justice and security and (2) incorporate ethical standards in the culture as a whole. In other words, the polity is to provide the economy with stability and generate confidence in the fairness of the institutions before economic expansion can take place. Yet, departing from this classical tradition of political economy, neoclassical economics has taken political stability and the economic actor's faith in the fairness of the system for granted. This restrictive and unrealistic assumption regarding human motivation has generated certain analytical weakness in neoclassical economics, which in some cases can indeed make its relevance open to question. For instance, important policy measures have been suggested under questionable assumptions, resulting in an increased level of confrontation in certain societies. We can, therefore, argue that the result of this social science paradigm, which considers aggressive collective behavior against an established political order irrational, or lumps it with ordinary criminal behavior, can lead to serious faults with the formulation of domestic as well as foreign policies.

Thus, in this book we take a broad view of looking at collective rebellion within a simultaneously determined system where socioeconomic conditions pave the way for a wideranging participation in collective violence. The resulting instability, in its turn, impacts the economic performance of the nation.

Before proceeding any further, we should mention that we are using the terms *political violence*, *collective violence*, and *collective rebellion* interchangeably.[2] We should also note that despite the fact that the legal distinction between activities of political violence or collective rebellion and ordinary criminal activity is indeed problematic, for us the conceptual distinction lies in the former's ultimate goal of bringing about a change in the social, political, or economic order that benefits all members of the community. In contrast, the ordinary criminal activities aim at economic betterment of the perpetrator alone and contain no political or social goals. Therefore, collective rebellion is characterized by two factors: First, it is antisystemic (against the present sociopolitical system) in nature, and second, it intends to provide a public good.[3]

THE PLAN OF THE BOOK

The book is divided essentially into three parts. By taking a historical perspective, Part One of the book looks into the reasons for the disregard of conflict in the Western social science and its subsequent inclusion of collective rebellion in the recent years. Part Two analyzes the individual motivations for joining an act of collective rebellion, and attempts to discern the impacts of socioeconomic and political environment on an individual's participatory decision. In Part Three, we attempt to construct a political economic model of growth, which treats political instability as an endogeneous variable. We test our hypotheses, first for the explanation of political instability, and then within the context of a simultaneous model of mutual causation.[4]

Chapter 2 explores the historical reasons for the exclusion of collective rebellious behavior from the mainstream social sciences. By drawing parallel to the traditional neoclassical economic paradigm, which - despite criticisms from the institutional economists - is based on the inexorable market force toward equilibrium, we discuss development of structural functionalism and Parsonian sociology with its emphasis on social harmony. Also, in this chapter we look into the postulates of Freudian psychology, which categorizes violent behavior as an instinctive reaction. In Chapter 3, we attempt to provide an up-to-date and comprehensive review of literature on the various social structural theories of collective rebellion. Starting with the theories of Marx and Smelser, which can be called "comprehensive" by their scope of explanation, we go into the various middle-range social structural theories, which generally concentrate on a limited number of explanatory variables for political violence.

The second part of the book consists of Chapters 4 and 5. In Chapter 4, we offer an explanation as to why people do and do not participate in violent actions against an established political system to achieve a collective good, that is, independence from colonial rule, end of discrimination, or a more egalitarian economic system. The failure of the social structural theories to provide the necessary causal link gave birth to the sociopsychological explanation. The sociopsychologists, by taking a quantum jump from micro to macro, used the same set of psychological variables reserved for the explanation of individual aggressive behavior to the collectivity or the group. However, we argue that the existence of systemic frustration can provide us with only the necessary condition for participation in collective violence. For sufficient condition, we must look at the broader picture of individual decision-making. The use of rational expectation theory, by which an individual maximizes his expected net gains (benefits minus costs), offers a useful explanatory tool. Culling the recent literature, in this chapter, we offer our hypothesis for the explanation of participatory motivation in a collective action. Further, we posit that the added advantage of a generalized expected utility model over the frustration-aggression theory lies in its ability to distinguish among the various kinds of political violence an individual is likely to engage in. Thus, while the frustration-aggression theory suggests that if a person is sufficiently frustrated by his present situation he will react in an aggressive manner, it fails to ascertain whether he is likely to be a terrorist, bent on acts of symbolic importance (what is known as "propaganda by deed"), or to participate in a riot. The choice of aggressive action based on our expected utility model is discussed in Chapter 5.

Chapter 5 also provides a link between the factors of individual motivations and the structural variables. Thus, we examine the relationship between our behavioral hypothesis and the other structural theories of political violence. The discussion of participation based on rational expectation theory begs the question of rationality on the part of the participants. Indeed, the question of rationality is frequently raised not only by the casual observers of collective rebellious behavior but also by the scholars engaged in its analysis. Reflecting the sentiment of the former group, a Nobel laureate economist commented in a private letter to the present author:

I am strongly reminded of (Sir Alfred) Marshall's dictum that some parts of economics should be approached through biology rather than through physics. I find it inconceivable that political disturbance can be plotted as a part of a mechanical system. For example, political disturbance may be likened to a big and dangerous dog that is peaceful most of the time, but occasionally barks shyly, or gets very angry or even bites a member of the family. What you are asking is what causes these changes of mood. This is a problem of psychology.

Quite curiously, similar sentiments were also expressed in private conversations or letters even by some of the most prominent sociologists and political scientists whose names are closely associated with the development of theories of collective rebellious behavior. Therefore, we felt the necessity to discuss the question of rationality of choice before closing Chapter 5.

The third part of the book deals with the macroeconomics of political violence. The results of the individual decisions to take part in political actions generate political instability in the aggregate. Chapter 6 looks into the impact of political instability on the aggregate economy.

The occurrence of political instability impacts the economy of a nation in two different ways. First, the lack of stability introduces uncertainty in the naturally skittish marketplace. For example, the *London Times* of April 15, 1986, reported that the British stock market lost nearly five billion pounds on the day of the American attack on Libya. The added dose of uncertainty impacts people's consumption, saving, and investment, as well as import and export behavior. Second, apart from the market risk factor, the economy of a nation experiencing political instability faces loss from the direct interference in its production process. Thus, as a result of a political strife, fields may not be plowed, factories may remain locked, or the infrastructure may break down through acts of sabotage. Chapter 6 explores this area with the help of a standard macroeconomic model of general equilibrium.

The next three chapters are devoted to the empirical verification of our hypotheses. We estimate an index of political instability in Chapter 7. The data for political violence are obtained from the Inter-University Consortium. These data series provide us with the frequencies of incidences of political violence on nine different categories. However, for conceptual as well as computational ease, we need to have but one composite index for political instability. We define political instability as a function of these incidents of political violence. We recognize that the term *political instability* is a subjective one, and in order to define the term empirically, we must start with a conceptual notion of political stability. Therefore, in this study, we went the opposite direction from the prevailing studies that use in "adhoc-ish" manner one or more incidents of political violence as surrogates for political instability, without first considering whether the index captures the essence of political instability. To establish a direct linkage between the notion of political instability and its various manifest variables, we first provided a conceptual definition of political stability and then proceeded to construct an index for instability.

We derive our index of political instability by using a two step method. In the first step, owing to our inability to define political instability, we define what we mean by *political stability*. Thus, we maintain that a nation will be called politically stable if it has experienced no incidents of political violence during the sample time period and if it is a democracy. Having provided this definition of political stability, we used cluster analysis to measure the difference in the standardized values of the various incidents of violence for each country in our sample from this hypothetical country, which represents the epitome of political stability. Therefore, we hypothesize that the further away a country is from this definition of stability, the more unstable it is. In the second step, we classified the countries into groups by their distance from the hypothetical country. Then, by using a discriminant analysis and a cumulative probability function of Logit specification, we derived two functional forms, which provided the weights for the absolute frequencies of the various incidents of violence toward the construction of a composite index of political instability.

In our study, we include 104 noncommunist countries.[5] Since it is well recognized that the data on internal strife variables are severely under-reported in the communist countries, we exclude them to minimize systematic biases in the data set. At this point, we should mention that the data on political violence were collected by the Inter University Consortium by using reports published in the *New York Times*. Therefore, it goes without saying that the exclusion of the communist countries will not eliminate the problem of systematic biases in the data set, as the data from the strategically less important Third World countries and countries with a strict authoritarian rule will be underreported. On the other hand, the data from the democratic nations in Europe and North America, especially the United States, in comparison, will be overrepresented[6]. However, despite these important shortcomings, this is the only comprehensive data set we have at present. Also, we should point out that good data never precede good analysis. The empirical investigation of political instability is still in its adolescence, and more investigations into it will certainly improve the quality of the data. In the meantime we are left with the choice between conducting analysis with some systematic errors in the variables and the problem of misspecification resulting from estimating aggregate economic relationships by ignoring important political variables. Between these two alternatives our choice is for the former.

Our empirical study concentrates around the period 1967. This choice of time period is defended by the fact that a significant number of empirical studies were undertaken at this point, when the United States and many European nations were experiencing the occurrence of political instability. Therefore, our results can be compared with the other studies of a similar nature. Based on our computation of a political instability index for the 104 noncommunist countries, we provide future researchers with a complete series based on the discriminant score of yearly indicators of political instability for the 35 year period spanning from 1948 to 1982. This data series is reproduced in the Appendix: Index for Political Instability, at the end of the book.

Having empirically defined political instability, in Chapter 8 we test various hypotheses on the structural explanation of political violence. Since it is not possible to test the behavioral formulation developed in Chapter 4 with aggregate data, we interpret the estimated results in light of our model. We derive the estimated coefficients by using the ordinary least squares method.

However, it is obvious that the environment of political stability of a nation is part of a larger system of simultaneous relationships. Therefore, in Chapter 9 we develop an impressionistic model of economic growth. The purpose of this simple, impressionistic model is to demonstrate that the process of economic growth does not take place in a world fragmented by the branches of social science. Specifically, the model shows how political violence is created by structural imbalances resulting from modernization and economic transformation, which in turn impacts the growth potential of a nation. The coefficients of the system of simultaneous equations are estimated with the help of the three stage least squares method.

The outcome of such a model is thowfold. First, by employing computer simulation, the loss of income from prolonged political instability is demonstrated. Second, neoclassical economics makes the assumption of a strict distinction between normative and positive economics - or in other words, between ethics (equality considerations) and efficiency. This schism between ethics and efficiency is nowhere more prominent than in the study of economic development and growth. The ethical norms in welfare economics are derived from the concept of Pareto optimality. However, a closer scrutiny reveals that Pareto optimality is not an ethical criterion, but a condition of efficiency. Despite its high ambitions, Pareto optimality sheds no light on the important question of the ethics of income distribution.[7] In contrast, our simultaneous model indicates that no such formal distinction between ethics and efficiency is possible within an integrated system. Our model demonstrates that if the distribution of income resulting from an efficient (defined in terms of the rate of growth of income) allocation of national resources is deemed unethical by a significant portion of the populace, who would be willing to oppose it violently, the resulting political instability may cause a tremendous loss of economic efficiency. Therefore, we posit that the theories of economic growth should recognize that while the political stability of a nation provides the necessary condition, the economic factors, such as the high rate of saving and investment, provide the sufficient condition for economic growth. We argue that by including the larger sociopolitical environment in its consideration, it is about time neoclassical economics abandons its Newtonian order for the complexity of the quantum system.

In Chapter 10 the public policy implications of the model are explored.Although the fervor of the 1950s and 1960s has been considerably tempered by reality, Third World countries still engage in national planning in a major way. Under strict economic planning, policies are spewed out under unrealistic assumptions about the world around us. By accepting the existence of a behavioral explanation of participation in collective political action, we pave the way for rethinking economic policy analysis. Also, a broader understanding of the human motivation for joining collective rebellion may influence the domestic political policies of governments who would rather treat political violence as a simple problem of law and order. The same is equally applicable to foreign policies, especially those of superpowers, as policies regarding how to deal with political opposition in Third World client states are often formulated without a clear understanding of the motivation behind the uprisings, leading to painful mistakes.

Looking around the world today, we find every reason to be concerned about political violence. In a world shrunken by technological progress in transportation and communication, violence, even in the most distant parts, touches us increasingly at a personal level. With violence drawn closer, its intensity is also likely to increase owing to the everexpanding expectations of the populace and the knowledge that one does not need to accept the social and economic constraints imposed by authorities. Therefore, tolerance for inequities and injustices due to fear, ignorance, or faith in tradition is on the wane. The proper management of collective violence comes with understanding. With the hope that this book contributes at least marginally toward the understanding of the causes of political violence and the extent of its damage on the aggregate economy, this effort has been undertaken.

NOTES

1. It is interesting to note that in contrast to the other classical writers, Weber was less interested in the causes of revolution. Rather, he foresaw the strengthening of bureaucratic structure as a result of a revolution. He argued that authority in a bureaucratic system emanates from legally defined offices rather than from hereditary privilege, or individual charisma. Therefore, Weber argued that when a revolution destroys the old structure of hereditary privilege, the new era will be characterized by a legal- based bureaucratic system, which will ultimately strengthen the power of the state.

2. We acknowledge the shortcomings of each of these terms, as participation in a protest movement may not be considered as an act of "political violence" or "collectove violence," especially, if its very purpose is to stage a peaceful, non-violent demonstration. Similarly, if an assassination is carried on by an extremely small group of people there may not be much of a "mass" or "collective nature in the act. Therefore, in order to capture the essence of anti-systemic acts to achieve a political good, we have decided to use the terms political violence, collective violence, and collective rebellion interchangeably.

3. A *public good* is distinguished from a *private good* by nonexcludability and nonrivalrousness. (R. A. Musgrave and P. B. Musgrave, 1980, pp. 55-58). Non-excludability means that none of the members of the group can be excluded from the benefit of the public good. For example, no one can be excluded from using a highway, breathing clean air, or being protected by the national military force from foreign invasion. Similarly, when a social or political change takes place as a result of a revolution or a successful political movement, all the members of the community enjoy the benefits of such a change. The second characteristic of public good- nonrivalrousness - implies that the good is to be consumed jointly. That is, the utility of a particular public good for an individual will not go down as result of another person's use of the same good. Thus, a ship captain's utility derived from a lighthouse does not decline because another ship is also using the same light signal for its navigation. In terms of a social change brought about

by a revolutionary movement, the utility of such a change for an individual will be independent of the size of the group benefiting from the end of the previous sociopolitical order.

4. It should, however, be noted that political instability impacts not only the economy but also the society and the polity, and as such, its ultimate impact on the economy may not always be detrimental, especially in the long run. For instance, as a result of a succeful political movement, discrimination can be reduced or a dictatorship can be replaced with a democracy.

5. Owing to the relative openness of the political system, we have included Yugoslavia in our sample set.

6. For a more comprehensive discussion of the short-comings of the Inter-University Consortium data set, see Sam Lehman-Wilzig (1990).

7. The concept of Pareto optimality is derived from the work of Vilfredo Pareto. Pareto suggests that the peak welfare of a nation is reached when it is no longer possible to make anyone better off without making someone else worse off. Theoretically, this point is reached in a perfectly competitive market condition, under certain specific conditions. However, the actual position of this point of optimality remains devoid of any ethical judgment about the initial distribution of wealth. Thus, in the world of Robinson Crusoe, if the initial distribution had almost all the resources going to Crusoe, and virtually none to the hapless Friday, welfare economics based on Pareto principles can pass no judgment about the distributive ethics of the situation. For a discussion on the ethics of distributive justice and neoclassical welfare economics, see Sen (1973).

Part One:

The Study of Political Violence in Perspective

2

The Conflict-Free World of Western Social Science: Paradigm Lost

I take up the standpoint that the tendency to aggression is an innate, independent, instinctual disposition in man.

Sigmund Freud[1]

In April 1985 the *Christian Science Monitor*, reporting on the riots and the eventual overthrow of President Jaafar Nemeiry of Sudan, stated that if the policymakers learned anything from these events, it was the fact that bad economic conditions bring about political unrest. To most people this association of acts of political violence with poor economic condition would not be a "scoop." Indeed, from the earliest time of recorded scholarship the correlation between the two has been accepted as self evident. The recent examples of Iran, Nicaragua, Lebanon, Nigeria, and Bangladesh provide strong enough evidence for this close relationship between economics and political stability.

Yet, contrary to this obvious reality, mainstream social sciences chose to assume collective violence away from their paradigms. In the process, they found epistemological justification for keeping political violence out of their consideration. This theoretical rationalization was further bolstered by the Freudian claim of aggressive behavior being linked to instinctive reactions. Not having any rational explanation of participation in the acts of collective rebellion connotes the sole policy prescription of coercion rather than cooperation (requiring understanding) or cooption (requiring sharing of wealth, power, and position). The rest of this chapter explains the paradigm of exclusion of conflict from the mainstream social sciences.

NEOCLASSICAL ECONOMICS: THE INEVITABILITY OF MARKET EQUILIBRIUM

It is indeed ironic that while Adam Smith, the father of modern economics, recognized the need for the political system of the nation to provide stability and generate confidence concerning the fairness of the institutions, for economic expansion, later development in economics took them for granted. Neoclassical economics pursued the question of optimum allocation of resources, holding the issues of sociopolitical environment in abeyance, under the ubiquitous assumption of ceteris paribus. Along the way, the one-dimensional economic man, the *homoeconomicus*, was assumed to possess the rationality of maximizing his profits within the set social and political constraints. However, his ability to rationally question the legitimacy of the constraints themselves was assumed away.

Going back in history, we find that until the middle of the previous century, analysis of macrosocietal conflict was part and parcel of the theories of political economy, social philosophy, and history. Conflict assumed a pivotal role in the writings of the political thinkers like Hobbes, Locke, and Rousseau; the Social Darwinians like Spencer; the historians such as de Tocqueville; and political economists such as Ricardo, Malthus, and Marx. However, with the emergence of logical empiricism, conflict disappeared from the mainstream social science.[2] A new social philosophy was born, inspired by the rapid technological progress; epistemologically, neoclassical economic theory felt justified in analyzing the economic process holding the sociopolitical environment constant.[3] While the forces that lead to market equilibrium were fully explored, the exclusive emphasis on equilibrium analysis resulted in the disregard of the study of disequilibria. The unquestioned assumption of the existence of an overwhelming centripetal force rendered the analysis of a supposedly transitory disequilibrium situation redundant.[4]

The eighteenth century, with its important scientific discoveries, witnessed the decline of the religious views of human nature, social and political institutions. The replacement of faith with reason demanded more scientific explanations amenable to empirical verification. The attack on the divine theory left a vacuum for a *supra structural*, moral philosophical framework as a point of reference. The denial of the divine theory and the quest for an alternative ethical structure gave birth to the Scottish Moralists. For the Scottish Moralists, God as the ultimate authority in specifying the social code of conduct was replaced with "nature" - the philosophy that if left to the natural course, all social ills will be cured. The corollary to it was the notion that any interference with nature inevitably led to inefficiency and human misery. Adam Smith, the best known of the Scottish

Moralists, found the "invisible hand" of the market mechanism to be the greatest equalizer and the panacea to all socioeconomic ills (Bryson, 1945). It was argued that without outside (government) interference the market would allocate resources not only *optimally* but also *ethically*, since the resulting allocation would be dictated by the relative merits of the individual actors.

The rapid acceptance of the laissez-faire philosophy can be traced to its conceptual similarity with the Darwinian "laws of nature" in general (Oberschall, 1973), as well as to its implicit political implication of maintaining a status quo.[5] Since conflict was considered to be the result of unwise interference with the laws of nature and the market force, the outcome of this new philosophy of nature was the elimination of antisystemic conflict from its theoretical framework. Further, owing to its very nature, this conflict could be assumed to be only a temporary phenomenon, which could be expected to die down in the course of time with the attainment of the point of market equilibrium. Therefore, antisystemic conflict could be considered to be "unnatural" and acts of emotion rather than of reason. As an outcome, neoclassical economists assumed complementarity of omniscience (necessary for the functioning of a perfectly competitive market), perfect rationality, and "ethically positive" behavior. Thus, economist Weisskopf (1949) aptly remarked:

Omniscience and perfect rationality are closely interrelated because both imply the knowledge of the laws that govern the universe. According to rationalistic philosophy of the Enlightenment, which underlies economic thought, the laws of nature are intelligible to man; if he acts on the basis of his insights into these laws, *he will also act in an ethically positive way* (p. 305) (emphasis added).

Hence, a rational economic man would compete for his personal gains using any means available to him without resorting to activities that attempt to change the rules of the game; a rational economic man would maximize his utilities under a *given* set of constraints (social, political, economic, or legal) without questioning the legitimacy of the constraints. Thus, the possibility that at some point a large segment of the population might take up antisystemic acts of violence as the most rational action was ignored.

The development of economics during the last quarter of the nineteenth century was guided, above all, by the emergence of a new socioeconomic order in western Europe. The transition from essentially feudalistic structure to an industrial society in which the macro question of distribution of resources among the landed aristocracy (rent), labor (wages), and the entrepreneur (interest and profit) was now complete and did not interest the economists. Rather, by the late nineteenth century the major thrust of economic inquiries was devoted to the search for the conditions under which a *given* set of productive services were allocated among competing uses to maximize consumers' satisfaction or the producers' production. With attention shifting from the aggregate distribution of resources to the problems of maximization of consumer satisfaction or firm production, for the neoclassical writers the focus of economic theory descended to a large extent from macro to micro - from aggregate to individual - and was to remain there for about 50 years until the publication of *The General Theory of Employment, Interest, and Money* by Keynes (1936).[6] In the process the question of the ethics (or even the efficiency) of aggregate resource allocation was pushed outside the realm of consideration by the neoclassical economists; it was universally assumed that there exists a tradeoff between ethics and efficiency. That is, if we are to pursue an ethical course in public policy (which means a move toward a more equal distribution of resources, ostensibly by going against the flow of market forces), we would have to do so at the cost of efficiency (measured in terms of the rate of growth of per capita national income). However, in the process the possibility of the complementarity of the two, where ethics promotes efficiency by reducing social tension and market fragmentation, was uniformly disregarded.

Therefore, with this "sanitized" version of the rational economic man, and the accompanying exclusionary assumptions, economics could claim to be a "science" (Blaug, 1980). In *Poverty of Historicism*, an exuberant Karl Popper (1960) remarked, "The success of mathematical economics shows that one social science at least has gone through its Newtonian revolution" (p.60). Thus, economics - no longer political economy - could boast being a true science. As a science the marginalist theory could claim "value neutrality" and, consequently, sterility from the sociopolitical environment.

Needless to say, economists were not oblivious to the sociopolitical reality. Rather, in support of the exclusion of sociopolitical and institutional variables from economic analysis, it was argued that (1) as long as the assumptions did not undermine the predictive powers of a model, they could be maintained safely, and (2) that if reality dictated the introduction of variables not included in the analysis, necessary amendment(s) could be made by relaxing the relevant constraint(s).

Elaborating on the necessity of the reductionistic assumptions, Milton Friedman (1953), in his famous essay "On the Methodology of Positive Economics," stated:

Truly important and significant hypothesis will be found to have assumptions that are wildly inaccurate descriptive representations of reality, and, in general the more significant the theory, the more unrealistic the assumptions [P. 3].

Friedman went on to claim that the true test of a theory lies not in its assumptions but in the extent to which its predictions are at variance with the facts.[7]

To be sure, the question is not whether general theories need exclusionary assumptions. In fact, as Brodbeck (1973, p. 296-98) pointed out, the assumptions of ceteris paribus are not endemic to the disciplines of social science; with the possible exceptions of celestial mechanics and nonatomic thermodynamics, no other theory can boast of perfect closure and completeness. Hence, the question is whether the present level of abstraction in social science in general and economics in particular is capable of providing us with explanations that approximate the reality with a tolerable level of confidence.

The criticisms of some of the basic assumptions of neoclassical economics have been leveled from the very beginning of the discipline. However, the chorus of criticism seems to have reached a crescendo during the last two decades.[8] Increasingly, some of the most prominent economists are showing their disaffection with the overall trend in economics, which tends to neglect the sociopolitical and institutional factors. The prevalence of stagflation in the developed nations and the slowing down of growth rates in many of the developing nations have painfully demonstrated the lack of explanatory and predictive capabilities of traditional neoclassical economic theories and, consequently, the need to expand their horizon to include some of these previously neglected variables.

This lack of realism is nowhere more apparent than in the theories of economic growth and development, since the analytical advantage of abstraction dissipates in the face of the problem of deviation from reality in the long run.[9] Reviewing the state of the art of growth economics in 1970, Sen (1970) lamented:

With [the] immensely practical motivation it would have been natural for growth theory to take a fairly practice-oriented shape. This, however, has not happened and much of modern growth theory is concerned with rather esoteric issues. Its link with public policy is often very remote. It is as if a poor man collected money for his food and blew it all on alcohol [p. 9].

Rather poignantly he further noted that

[i]t is partly a measure of the complexity of economic growth that the phenomenon of growth should remain, after three decades of intensive intellectual study, such an enigma. It is, however, also a reflection of our sense of values, particularly of the preoccupation with the braintwisters.. [p. 33].

Looking around 20 years since Sen's evaluation, we find little to cheer about. The college textbooks are still busy tracing the hypothetical optimal growth paths without any mention of the social, political, or institutional environment or of the actor's motivations, aspirations, and values as he faces a changing world. The most telling effect of this omission and the consequent divorce between economic theory and reality has been in the field of national planning. Major public policies have been - and still are being - studied, and recommendations are being implemented on the basis of unrealistic behavioral assumptions, with often devastating results. This led a noted scholar on national planning to observe:

Economic development takes place within a social framework of political and historical conditions and a regime of institutions, but plan models fail completely to take any account of these factors. The models put preponderant emphasis on technological constraints, but the satisfaction of these constraints constitutes only necessary and not sufficient conditions of development. [Rudra, 1974, p. 179]

The Institutional Challenge

Even though the seed of rational economic man was sown by Adam Smith, curiously the analysis of systemic conflict in its embryonic form can also be traced to his somewhat vague labor theory of value. The labor theory of value, more than any other concept in economics, has been the stepping stone of the analysis and justification of conflict. It was developed into its final form in the hands of Karl Marx via the work of Smith and Ricardo. We will have a chance to look into the Marxian theory later in the following chapter.

In Marxian analysis, labor is the sole producer of value. This assertion, therefore, leads to the theory of exploitation and hence to conflict between the classes. Ricardo, in contrast, did not credit only labor for creating value; he also included the "original and indestructible" power of land[10]. Although he elaborated on the changing distribution of income between the three classes (laborers, renters, and profiteers), Ricardo did not explicitly mention any conflict resulting from such a change. It is, however, interesting to note that despite Ricardo's adherence to the labor theory of value (which, like Adam Smith's, came from the interest of social accounting rather than ideology), his victory in the famous debate with Malthus on the applicability of Say's Identity and the possibility of overproduction paved the way for development of economic science. We may speculate that a victory for the Malthus-Sismondi-Chalmer school might have contributed toward a greater acceptance of institutional economics and a broader, if not less systematic, view of economics (Gruchy, 1971).

Being leery of the political implications, neoclassical economists rejected Marxian analysis along with Marx's insights into the causes of societal conflict. Rather, in their studies, conflict took some interesting twists. Noting that conflict underlies any competitive situation, theories of what we may call "prosystemic" or "system neutral" conflict or conflict within the rules of the market, flourished in abundance. The strategies of competition were analyzed by Cournot, Edgeworth, Richardson, Neumann, Morgenstern, Duncan, and others based upon behavioral assumptions about reactions to a conflict situation. The work of Kenneth Boulding (1962, 1970) is most valuable in his application of these micro-economic tools in analyzing some aggregate conflict situations.

    At the macrolevel, on the other hand, neoclassical economics incorporated what we may call "creative conflict," through the work of Schumpeter (1955) and later Hirschman (1970). In Schumpeter's analysis the entrepreneur assumes the role of a catalyst by introducing innovations that fundamentally alter the techno-economic relationship in the society. However, while Schumpeter's entrepreneur generated conflict in the prevalent techno-economic structure, his role in the long run was to enhance the collective well-being of the economy. Hirschman similarly welcomed conflict created by the "exit" of firms resulting from negative votes cast by the consumers in the anonymity of a supermarket, as well as "voice" raised by them to resort to political pressures to make the economic system more responsive to consumer needs. Hirschman, needless to say, did not ponder the possibilities of "scream" as opposed to "voice" when dissatisfaction is rampant and cannot be mitigated under the present socioeconomic and political system through legal channels open to the economic actors. Mancur Olson, in a similar fashion, considered the costs and benefits of voice as opposed to exit and came out in favor of exit.[11] Like Hirschman, Olson did not consider situations where someone might find violent political action to be more effective.

    Among the nonMarxian economists, only in the work of American institutional economists, and especially Veblen (1899), was the concept of antisystemic conflict germane. However, despite the centrality of the notion of a class conflict between businessmen or producers (or variously, between "pecuniary employments" and "industrial employments" or between "business enterprise" and the "machine process," or between "vendibility" and "serviceability" or between "acquisition" and "production"), Veblen made little effort at relating this to economic growth. Further, despite the cogency of his criticisms of the reductionistic, atomizing assumptions of neoclassical economics, he failed to provide us with an alternative theoretical structure to analyze the conflict-prone, dialectical process of development (Watkins, 1958). Veblen objected to the traditional neoclassical economists' assumption of the rational nature of human behavior, their approach toward the analysis of technology, their static view of the social institutional framework, and their assumption that there were forces at work driving the economic system always toward an equilibrium.

Other institutional economists, such as Wesley C. Mitchell (1910), like Veblen were critical of the marginalist analysis and the assumption of economic rationality. Instead, Mitchell argued for more realistic behavioral assumptions based on the theories of social psychology. However, he did not share Veblen's view of the instinctive nature of human behavior and believed that it was shaped by man's socioeconomic and institutional environment.[12]

Among the American institutional economists, J. M. Clark came the closest in incorporating societal conflict directly into his frame of analysis. Clark rejected the theory of social organization sublime in the neoclassical economics, which took society to be a harmonious scheme of human relations in which aggregate behavior was merely a sum of individual behaviors and in which conflict or friction automatically dissolved. A student of the pragmatic philosopher John Dewey and sociologist Charles A. Cooley, Clark viewed society to be an evolving process in which collective action dominated individual actions, and conflict, rather than harmony, prevailed among social groups. Consequently, to him disequilibrium - rather than equilibrium - was the natural state of affairs. Thus, unlike the neoclassical economists who took social harmony as a given, Clark regarded cohesion as a goal to be achieved by conscious planning (Commons, 1943).

The criticism of the basic assumptions of neoclassical economics by Veblen was further echoed in the work of Simon N. Patten (1912) and Rexford G. Tugwell (1924). They differed from Veblen, however, in two main points. First, they rejected Veblen's dualistic view of society in favor of a pluralistic one. That is, without analyzing economic activity in terms of a struggle between two classes, these later institutionalists observed conflict among a number of classes. Second, they did not share Veblen's pessimistic view regarding the future of the capitalist system; rather they asserted that the exploratory and cooperative nature of human beings will find a way toward a more harmonious social system.

Based on this world view, Tugwell explained the historical development process as a cyclical movement in which periods of cultural equilibrium are followed by periods of cultural disequilibrium, in an endless series. After the establishment of cultural equilibrium, the time comes when the forces of disequilibrium through man's restive and exploratory nature make him dissatisfied and the society, conflict prone. At this point new institutional arrangements are sought, in the process of which the old equilibriums are destroyed and replaced by a transitional period of cultural disequilibrium.

The modern-day neo-institutionalists, such as Clarence Ayers (1952), John Kenneth Galbraith (1958), and Gunnar Myrdal (1968), have also utilized a much broader horizon to include sociocultural variables in their analysis. Among these authors, the work of Myrdal in the area of economic development is most significant. Taught in the Wicksellian tradition of disequilibria, Myrdal rejected the assumption of the attainment of automatic socioeconomic equilibrium. However, unfortunately, none of the neo-institutionalists have taken political violence explicitly into account. It is indeed curious that Myrdal, one of the most prolific writers of our time, failed to analyze directly the causes or effects of sociopolitical instability on the national economy while dealing with the problems of poverty, racial discrimination and economic stagnation in his study of the politically volatile Asian region.

Finally, no discussion on the resynthesis of social sciences to broaden the horizon of neoclassical economics can be complete without considering the work done by Irma Adelman, Cynthia Morris, and their associates (I. Adelman and C. T. Morris, 1967, 1968, 1973). Their efforts over the years have been diverse and quite extensive. However, although these pioneering research endeavors were the stepping stones for a unique multidisciplinary approach to national development, they differ from ours in two important ways: First, their work is mainly static and lacks the dynamic predictive capabilities of growth models; second, and more important, despite the fact that they make use of many social, political, and institutional factors, their analyses do not consider political instability.

To conclude, therefore, apart from the Marxian economists, only some of the American institutional economists have questioned the basic assumptions of the orthodox economics and have attempted to incorporate conflict into their analysis. However, their contribution was never assimilated into the mainstream of economic thought, especially across the Atlantic. Probably the main reason for this is the failure of the institutional economists to provide us with empirically verifiable hypotheses to be included in an expanded, compelling theoretical scheme. Hence, their arguments, however cogent, were pushed into the fringes of economics and were largely forgotten or conveniently overlooked.

SOCIOLOGY: THE ADAPTIVE SOCIETY

The early non-Marxian sociological writings of the mid and late nineteenth century were dominated by the work of de Tocqueville and Max Weber. Writing approximately the same time as Marx and Engles, de Tocqueville, in his famous book *The Old Regime and the French Revolution* (1848; see 1955 translated edition), approached revolutionary change and its effect on the political system of a nation with a significantly different motivation and outlook from Marx. He agreed with Marx that the revolution in France caused a major change in the sociopolitical structure of the country; it destroyed the power of the aristocracy and the church. However, while Marx hailed the change[13] as an end to the feudal structure - a step toward the establishment of a socialist system de Tocqueville approached it with caution and suspicion. Instead of a victory for the less privileged, in the French Revolution, he saw a triumph of the centralized state. de Tocqueville reasoned that since revolutions eliminate the powerful elites, who keep a balance of power, the new society, characterized by a powerless mass, would make the state power centralized and absolute. Therefore, while Marx saw revolution as a progressive movement, ushering in a new era of equality, fairness, and freedom from the exploitation by the feudal lords, de Tocqueville saw even more reason to be fearful of the state and the newly formed social structure.

Sociologist and organizational theorist Max Weber built on de Tocqueville's predictions of the strengthening of state power as a result of a successful revolution. However, while de Tocqueville was generally suspicious of the new revolutionary order, Weber was at best ambivalent. Weber's views on revolution were, of course, peripheral to his analysis of bureaucracy. Weber saw bureaucracy based on established law, rather than ascription or charisma, as the basis of social equality and governmental efficiency. He argued that a legally constituted bureaucracy, with clear lines of organizational structure, thrives when a government recognizes merits and efficiency in distributing official positions and abolishes hereditary privileges. He agreed with de Tocqueville by reasoning that a revolutionary change against a feudalistic social structure, by promoting equality, will establish a perfect bureaucratic order. With time, Weber predicted, the superior efficiency of bureaucracy would lead to its growing entrenchment. Therefore, one of the outcomes of a revolution was a permanent bureaucracy.

It is interesting to note that in his earlier writings Weber saw in bureaucracy the desirable qualities of order, stability, and efficiency. To him it was bureaucracy, which firmly anchored an otherwise volatile society. The resulting stability in the administrative structure makes it possible to have the every day lives of ordinary citizens to remain largely unaffected even by the changes of national rulers. Thus, he cited the example of the success of German bureaucracy, which was scarcely affected by the retirement of Bismark. Thus, with a firm bureaucratic grip on the society, even a revolutionary change will appear to be only a coup d'état, with a change in the facade of the top level of administration, leaving little impact on the day to day lives of ordinary citizens. However, Weber's enthusiasm for the rock solid bureaucratic structure was tempered in his later life.

Western sociological thinking on rebellious behavior was also profoundly influenced by the writings of Gustav Le Bon. Le Bon personified the revulsion that the feudal upper class felt toward their loosing grip over their world. The sight of a violent mob frenzied with emotion has worried observers throughout the ages. Hence, it is hardly surprising that Shakespeare depicted crowds as vengeful, cruel, unpredictable, volatile, and devoid of rational thinking. The social psychologist in the Bard would show how a mass of seemingly peaceful people, originally relieved at the removal of a potential dictator, Julius Caesar, could easily turn into a murderous mob, bent on avenging his death at the suggestion of Mark Anthony, a masterful orator. In fact, time and time again the mastery of Shakespeare reveals itself through his understanding of the volatility of collective behavior.

The perception of a crowd as a dangerous force when unleashed is no more powerfully presented than by Gustav Le Bon. His classic study *Psychologie des foules*, first published in 1895, stirred a great deal of public interest with his dramatic portrayal of the "crowd-man." Already jittery about the advent of technology pushing the society inexorably to the destruction of the old societal order, along with the spread of the intellectual appeal of Marx and Marxism, a weary Le Bon looked at the rebellious crowd with awe, fear, and revulsion. Le Bon repeatedly compared the impulsiveness, "incapacity to reason, absence of judgment, and exaggeration of the sentiments" that characterize a crowd, regressing the logical individuals that comprise it back to the same tendencies "belonging in inferior [sic] forms of evolution--in women, savages and children, for instance" [p. 15].

Le Bon studied the rapid alteration of feelings in a group, vacillating between extremes of love and hate. He asserted that the "fundamental facts" of group psychology lie on the "intensification of the emotions" and the "inhibition of the intellect." Le Bon, contrary to the later criticism of him by Freud, was not oblivious to the importance of leadership in forming crowd behavior and noted its unique "thirst for obedience." This observed behavior prompted the subsequent Freudian argument that crowd followers are libidinally attached to crowd leaders, who also serve as surrogate fathers to their followers.

Le Bon was deeply disturbed by his observation of the crowd and predicted the end of the existing "civilized world," which would be replaced by what he called "the era of crowds." Taking a historical perspective, he argued that crowds act as agents of destruction (as they are unable to create anything) to the dissolutionment of weak and worn-out civilizations. He further pointed out the imperative need to study crowd behavior, especiall by the rulers of the society, arguing that "a knowledge of the psychology of crowds is today the last resource of the statesman who wishes not to govern them - that is becoming a very difficult matter - but at any rate not to be too much governed by them" (p. 19). Based on his observations of the frightful crowd, Le Bon, a pessimist, predicted the end of the civilized world, as the power would shift from the cultured elites to the unruly mass through the introduction of democracy and socialism.

Although the study of conflict was central to the Social Darwinians like Herbert Spencer,[14] twentieth-century sociological thought came to be dominated by the structural functionalist school, which shared the neoclassical economic philosophy of basic harmony in social relationships.[15]

The structural functionalist school of sociology claims its heritage in the scholarship of Talcott Parsons, which spanned over half a century. In contrast to Marxian theory, where social behavior and social structure emanated from production relationships, functionalism attempts to explain individual behavior, ideologies, and social institutions, in terms of the role individuals play within a society. In the broadest sense,

[Functionalism] seeks to do no more than assay the place of a particular element of culture or societal institutions in relation to other elements. The question may then be posed as to whether an institution leads to or assists in the perpetuation of the social entity in which it appears [R. Spencer, 1965: 1].

Parsons and his associates postulated that any social system has three prime motives - harmony, integration, and stability. A social system attempts to satisfy those motives by (1) pattern maintenance and tension management, (2) goal attainment, (3) adaptation, and (4) integration. Therefore, Parsons and his followers saw within the society the primacy of a centripetal force, which will inexorably tend to bring it back to stability and harmony. However, despite some extremely relevant criticism of this harmony theory, which emphasizes status quo (Gouldner, 1970), in all fairness, it should be pointed out that the structural functionalists did not entirely ignore conflict and societal change (see Sherman and Wood, 1979). They simply had no theory to deal with it. Thus, in his book *The Social Systems* (1951), Talcott Parsons, laconically drawing a parallel to Marx, writes:

A general theory of the processes of change of social systems is not possible in the present state of knowledge. ... We do not have a complete theory of the processes of change in social systems. ... When such a theory is available the millennium of social science will have arrived. This will not come in our time and most probably never [p. 534].

Parsons's emphasis on harmony and stability mirrors the ubiquitous assumption of equilibrating tendencies in neoclassical economics. Parsons was well aware of complementarity of the basic behavioral assumptions of the two branches of social sciences and argued for an integration of the two in his joint work with Smelser (Parsons and Smelser, 1956).

FREUD AND THE FREUDIANS: THE BIOLOGY OF AGGRESSIVE BEHAVIOR

The traditional social science paradigm of a conflict-free rational world was significantly influenced by Freud and his followers. Although his contributions are largely viewed in the context of individual psychoanalysis, Freud, in his later life, attempted to extend this individual psychological framework to the society at large. His views on aggregate societal topics are demonstrated in his book *Civilization and Its Discontents* (1929). In contrast to Marx, Freud viewed societal evolution as resulting from a dialectical process, not between the economic classes but between love and death, eros and destruction. This constant conflict, he argued, is the one that fuels the evolution of culture and society. Therefore, for Freud the dialectical force works within every individual. From this complex psychological framework, men relate to the society at large. The relationship among sex, culture, and society is interactive; that is, each is influenced by the others. Freud observed:

We see that [culture] endeavors to bind the members of the community to one another by libidinal ties as well, that it makes use of every means and favours every avenue by which powerful identification can be created among them, and that it exacts a heavy toll of aim-inhibited libido in order to strengthen communities by bonds of friendship between members. Restrictions upon sexual life are unavoidable if this object is attained [pp. 80 - 81].

Freud criticized Marx and his followers for assuming, like Rousseau, that men are instinctively good. He also found no reason to believe that aggression at the societal level was the product of private property and that violence will disappear once private property is abolished. Freud generally agreed that aggressive behavior is linked to a feeling of frustration or provocation by the external forces. However, above all, to him aggression is instinctive, it is buried deep inside the subconscious as a secret "death wish," and it is often related to suppressed sexuality.[16] He argued that while private property and factors of economic privation are important factors, they are not the strongest. Aggression resulting from repressed sexuality will prevail even in a classless society. Thus, he claimed that:

men are not gentle, friendly creatures wishing for love, who simply defend themselves if they are attacked, but that a powerful measure of desire for aggression has to be reckoned as part of their instinctual endowment [p. 85].

In the final analysis, Freud unequivocally asserts, "I take the standpoint that the tendency to aggression is an innate, independent, instinctual disposition in a man [p. 102]." As a logical consequence of this point of view, Freud had little policy recommendations. In fact, he confessed to having "no consolation to offer" in curbing violence in society.   Needless to say, the impact of Freud on the intellectual development of the Western social science paradigm has been overwhelming. Therefore, it is hardly surprising that following Freud, the vast majority of the intellectual society will dismiss conflict behavior as "irrational" or purely "instinctive."[17]

The later development of psychological theories resulted from Freud's criticism of Le Bon. Freud, however, in contrast to Le Bon, did not view the behavior of the individual within a crowd as totally irrational and found a instinctive reason for his madness. Drawing on this hypothesis, anthropologist Konrad Lorenz (1966) asserted that societal conflict tends to occur with "rhythmic regularity." This biological explanation of aggregate violent behavior can be found in the later analysis of Ralph Holloway (1968).

The second line of Freudian explanation of mass violence carries a two pronged explanation. First, on the part of the crowd followers, he hypothesized that they are libidinally attached to the crowd leaders, who serve as their surrogate fathers. By comparison, the male leaders of the crowd are motivated by their unresolved Oedipal complex, which prompts them to identify the authority figure (within the existing system) with their own fathers, to whom they feel antagonistic. The actions of the female leaders, however, are explained with the help of their subconscious penis envy of their fathers. This second strain of Freudian argument regarding unresolved sexual problems has been picked up especially by the biographers of the revolutionary leaders, who attempt to show these psychological forces influencing the policies of their subjects (see, for example, Wolfenstein, 1967).

A prime example of using Freudian psychoanalysis in the explanation of mass movements may be found in the controversial work of Lewis Feuer (1969). Feuer saw youth movements throughout history as a struggle between the generations. He argued that the unresolved sexual problems of the younger members of the society periodically take on the form of irrational violent protests against the older generation. Feuer, however, makes the distinction between "rational" and "irrational" forms of movements. He generally attributes irrationality to political movements, and rationality to economic struggles, such as the trade union movements.

Feuer sees the complex process of conflict generation within the society as follows:

1. Hostile parent-child relationship
2. Actual conflict and struggle between parents and children
3. Distant relations between parents and children
4. Rejection of parental values by their children
5. "Deauthorization" of the older generation by the younger generation
6. Alienation by the younger generation from the older generation
7. Unresolved Oedipal crises on the part of the younger generation
8. Subjection of the younger generation to harsh child-bearing practices
9. Emotional (irrational) rebellion of the younger generation against the older generation[18]

As a result of this complex interactive process between parents and children, argues Feuer, the revolutionaries are born with latent irrational, emotional hostility toward their parents' generation, who control the social establishment. Hence, to Feuer, the socioeconomic environment takes on but a secondary position to the generation of mass conflict behavior. Feuer used this analysis to explain the student movements in the United States during the 1960s as an attempt to discard the values and mores of their parents; German Nazi movements during the 1930s as a reaction to the unique Teutonic relationship between father and son; and the Russian youth movement during the revolutionary period, where the killing of the Czar was the symbolic act of patricide on the part of the youthful Russians. Feuer similarly used the hostile father-son relationship, coupled with strong bonds with their mothers, to explain the personality traits and subsequent actions of diverse revolutionary leaders such as Serbian nationalist Gavrilo Princep, Mao, and several other student leaders of the Berkeley student movement in the United States.

Not surprisingly, Feuer's analysis brought criticism on methodological, contextual, and empirical grounds. Several studies pointed out the absence of intergenerational hostility on the part of the participants as well as the leadership in the United States. student movement (Lipset and Wolin, 1965; Lyonns, 1965; Somers, 1965). Also, empirical studies failed to establish the link between activism and hostile family environment (Keniston, 1968; Block, Haan, and Smith, 1969; Wood, 1974). As a result of some of these criticisms, fortunately, this line of analysis of Freudian psychological analysis of mass movements has largely disappeared from the domain of the social sciences and has been confined primarily to the biographical analyses of individual revolutionary personalities.

NOTES

1. See Freud, 1930 p. 102.

2.. The recent epistemological trend in social science, in general, and economics, in particular, can be traced to what we can call " a state of physics envy." Gerard Radnitzki (1970), for example, explains it the best:

Logical empiricism primarily wants to *articulate an ideal of science* for a group of disciplines [emphasis G.R]. The group in question includes the natural sciences and the so called behavioral sciences -- e.g., what is the English equivalent to "science" or "science like" disciplines. In *lenea massima* this ideal of science is monistic, reductionistic, and "physicallistic." All "scientific" disciplines should form part of one basic discipline (monism). Among the scientific disciplines now in existence physics approximates the ideal best ("physicallism"). Other disciplines may be reduced to physics by making a language that has been designed for an idealized physical science, the common language of all "science-like" disciplines, and by making physical concepts the fundamental concepts of the ideal unified science ("reductionism") [p. xvi].

3. Sen (1987) seperates the origin of modern economics into two categories. The first one is based on "ethics and an ethical view of politics," and the second one is based upon "engineering" (p. 4). He contends that the ethical questions have a more prominent role in the writings of Adam Smith, John Stuart Mill, Karl Marx, and Francis Egdeworth than in the writings of the proponents of the engineering based approach such as William Petty, Françoise Quesnay, David Ricardo, Augustine Cournot, and Leon Walras.

4. For a discussion of the epistemological linkage between equilibrium analysis and the study of political violence, see Chalmers Johnson (1964).

5. On the question of the link between the epistemological development of economics science and the need to maintain the social and political status quo, see John Kenneth Galbraith (1977).

6. For an excellent discussion of the descendence of emphasis from the aggregate questions of growth to the micro question of resource utilization by the neo-classical economists from the classical tradition, see A. K. Dasgupta (1985).

7. In his famous essay on positive economics, Milton Friedman started a lively methodological controversy that has lasted for nearly 30 years, and is commonly known as the F-twist theory ("F" - after "Friedman"). See Blaug (1980) for an excellent discussion. Also see A. Musgrave (1981) for one of the later contributions to the controversy.

8. The disappointment with the recent paradigm of neoclassical economics is being shared by some of the most prominent economists of our time, which is reflected in the very titles of some of their work. For example, see Walter Heller (1975), "What's Right with Economics?"; F. H. Hahn (1970), "Some Adjustment Problems"; Harry Johnson (1971), "Keynesian Revolution and Monetarist Counterrevolution;" E. Phelps-Brown (1972), "The Underdevelopment of Economics"; Robert Gordon (1971), " Rigor and Relevance in a Changing Institutional Setting"; N. Goergescu-Roegan (1979), "Methods in Economic Science"; and Robert Solow (1986), "Economics, Is Something Missing?" For discussions of the various related problems of economics, see Akerlof (1984), Bell and Kristol (1981), Blaug (1980), Das Gupta (1985), Dyke (1981), Elster (1978, 1979, 1983), Hahn and Hollis (1979), Helm (1984, 1985), Hicks (1983), Kornai (1971, 1985), Latsis (1976), Matthews (1984), McClosky (1985), Nelson and Winter (1982), Pitt (1981), Robinson (1962), Schelling (1978), Simon (1979), Steedman and Kraus (1986), Ward (1972), and Woo (1986).

9. It is indeed interesting to note that while the respectability of economic development as an analytical discipline is being impugned from scholars in and out of the field, a noted economist characteristically rationalized it by stating: "Those among economists who can not make the grade as mathematical economists, statisticians, monetary or trade economists or economic historians, usually end up as labor economists or worse still as development economists." Quoted in Yotopoulos and Nugent (1976, p. 3).

10.   Ricardo's inclusion of land along with labor as the producer of economic value has led to a discussion as to whether his theory is only "93 percent labor theory of value." For an interesting discussion, see Stiegler (1958) and Tucker (1961).

11.   See Hirchman (1970), P. 211.

12. For an excellent commentary on the work of Wesley Mitchell, see Kuznets (1963).

13. For a discussion of Marx's view on social change and the French Revolution, see Shlomo Avinery (1969).

14.   For a concise explanation of Herbert Spencer's theory of societal evolution, see H. Spencer (1967).

15.   We should mention that structural functionalism has come under intense fire for ignoring individuals' arbitrations and the resulting conflict within the society. For example, see the blustery criticism by Alvin Gouldner (1970).   However, the intellectual influence of structural functionalism in the development of present sociological thought remains substantial. For a detailed discussion of the recent developments of functionalism, see J. Alexander (1985).

16.   Freud asserts that "(t)his instinct of aggression is the derivative main representative of the death instinct we have found along side of Eros, sharing his rule over the Earth" (Freud, 1929, pp. 102-03).

17. Another interesting aspect of Freud that has a lingering effect on the intellectual development of the western corpus of belief is inability to confront conflict. Thus, Paul Johnson (1983) points out that: "internal critics like Jung were treated as heretics; external ones, like Havelock Ellis, as infidels. Freud betrayed signs, namely, a persistent tendency to regard those who diverge from him as themselves unstable and in need of treatment" (p. 6). Thus, Johnson argues, was born the notion of regarding dissent as a form of mental sickness, especially in the Soviet Union. In parallel development, we may also add that in the Western world what blossomed was the concept that somehow taking part in antisystemic conflict is fanatical, emotional, and totally devoid of rationality.

18.   For an excellent discussion on this, see Wood and Jackson (1982).

3

Theories of Collective Rebellious Behavior: Paradigm Regained

REBEL WITH A CAUSE

The parallel to the paradigm of nonexplanation and exclusion of collective violence is the Marxist paradigm. The fundamental difference between the two paradigms is the perception of the nature of the ubiquitous social trend. The nonMarxists found reasons for society to reach the stability of market equilibrium as a part of an inexorable natural process. They, of course, did not deny the existence of forces that can destabilize a society. However, they theorized that in the long run the overwhelming strength of the stabilizing forces would prevail over the destabilizing forces. Marx and his followers, by contrast, theorized that the capitalist system by its very nature was unstable. To the Marxists, the capitalist society carries within itself the seeds of self-destruction. This preprograming for self-destruction is so strong that all the other countervailing forces, in the end, will be inadequate to stop the ultimate collaps of the market system.

NonMarxist social science, needless to say, had to contend with the reality, where incidents of collective violence were taking place all around. Facing this contradiction between their theory and reality, a compromise was reached by which it was hypothesized that antisystemic conflict was only a temporary situation. This situation, they argued, would be symptomatic of the Third World nations going through a structural change. Structural change caused by the introduction of "economic development" and a new production relationship calls for the end to the traditional social and economic relationship. This transformation, in turn, creates consternation in a society. However, these tendencies tend to disappear after the attainment of development, when the populace, by and large, accepts the norms, values, and mores of industrialization. The work of Kerr et al. (1960) on industrial disputes elaborates this point.

The discontent of workers, reflected in the disruptive forms of protest,tends to be greatest in the early stages of industrialization and tends to decline as workers become more accustomed to industrialization. The partially committed industrial worker, with strong ties to the extended family and village, unaccustomed to urban life and to the discipline and mores of factory, is more likely to reflect open revolt against industrial life than the seasoned worker more familiar with the ways of the factory, more understanding of the reasons for the web of factory rules, more reconcile to factory life [p. 30].

Therefore, Kerr reasoned that prolonged industrial disputes, wildcat strikes, and other disruptive collective behavior were symptomatic of transitional societies (or, as they are known in development economics, dual economies).[1] Similar reasonings were offered by sociologists Lucien Pye (1966) and Ralph Dahrendorf (1958), economist Mancur Olson (1968), political scientists Seymor Lipset (1959) and Samuel Huntington (1965). Lipset (1959) and Dahrendorf (1958) hypothesized that the relationship between the levels of political instability and economic development is a parabolic one. Nations with little economic development remain relatively conflict free, as they stay steeped in their old traditional relationships. However, the countries in transition face a contradiction in values as the old social system comes into conflict with the new. As this process of modernization becomes complete, the countries settle down with their new but widely accepted values, reflecting a high level of political stability. Olson (1968) echoed this view by suggesting that despite the fact that a rapid rate of growth is accepted as a desired economic goal, it may generate sociopolitical conflict in the Third World countries. Huntington (1965, 1968) similarly argued that with the advent of modernization the traditional societies face the problem of demand for social, political, and economic goods that the political system is unable to provide. This disparity between demand and supply will cause political strife.

However, the rosy prediction of political stability by the Western scholars of the 1950s and early 1960s fell short of the reality. The riots of the mid 1960s in the U.S. and some of the most affluent countries of western Europe prompted the academic community to cast a fresh look into the causes of political violence.[2] As a result, new theories cropped up in sociology and social psychology offering rationales for participation in the acts of political violence. These theories broke an important methodological barrier. By offering a behavioral (as opposed to instinctive) explanation, they assumed a rational actor. In this chapter we will discuss the paradigm of explanation of collective rebellious behavior.

We have argued in the previous chapter that in the haste to repudiate Marx and to avoid some important but disturbing value judgments, the nonMarxist writers, by and large, scrupulously avoided the inclusion of societal conflict in their paradigm. This reluctance was also rooted in their explicit or implicit belief that conflict was in fact a phenomenon of social and economic disequilibrium and was therefore but a temporary condition to be healed with time. Also, it was believed that the incidents of mass violence were irrational or emotive expressions of deep down anger (e.g., Le Bon) or some unresolved personal psychological problems of the perpetrators (e.g., Freud, Alexander, Lorenz, etc.). Yet conflict at the macrosocietal level could not be just wished away. This intellectual contradiction was amply reflected in the early attempts to explain political violence, some were unsystematic, merely taxonomic in nature, whereas others assumed that the participants in the acts of rebellion were simply maladjusted deviants or otherwise irrational people.[3] In fact, it may be safe to state that the first systematic analysis into the causes of collective violence by the nonMarxist writers began with Smelser's *Theory of Collective Behavior* (1963), which received a further boost with the publication of Gurr's *Why Men Rebel* (1970).

Smelser had a profound impact on Western sociological thinking. In contrast to the Parsonian theory of society as the ultimate resolver of conflict, Smelser, like Marx, argued that social movements in fact emanated from disequilibrium in the structure of the larger society. In his turn, Gurr demonstrated that there was a strong correlation between the acts of collective rebellion and the perception in the aggregate of persons' achievements in relation to their expectations. In other words, with a quantum leap from individual psychology to the societal level, aggressive acts were seen as responses to situations of frustrations. Inspired by the theoretical advances, and prodded by reality where societal conflict and political violence became increasingly commonplace after a couple of decades of calm in the postwar era in the Western world, sociologists and political scientists felt compelled to study the origins of mass conflict, producing a plethora of books and articles.

For a systematic evaluation of this vast literature, we will classify it according to the scheme shown in Figure 3.1. To begin with, we find that the literature on the theories of collective rebellious behavior can be broadly classified into two categories. The first category views collective rebellious behavior within a macro or aggregate context. In this group of studies, broad social, political, and economic trends are correlated with the level of political stability of a nation. The micro - or individual based - theories, in contrast, concentrate on the individual and attempt to explain an individual's motivations for joining an act of collective rebellion against an established political system.[4]

The aggregate theories can again be differentiated into comprehensive and middle range, according to the scope of the study. Both Marx and Smelser hypothesized that conflict was generated from the

imbalance in the structure of the society. Hence, these theories can be
called structural theories. Also, since both of them aimed at comprehensive explanations of societal conflict, we may classify these two
theories as comprehensive.

FIGURE   3.1

Classification of Theories on the Origin of Collective Rebellious Behavior

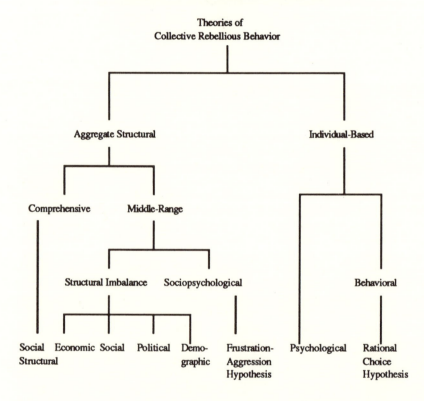

The other group of theories may be classified under what
Merton (1957, pp. 3-10) calls the middle-range theories. These theories may be defined as those that emphasize only a few variables and
attempt to explain a limited range of behavioral responses (Kuhn,
1970). Within the broad category of middle-range theories, we can
also find two subcategories of explanation: factors of structural imbalance and sociopsychological theories.

The middle-range structural imbalance theories concentrate on the various factors within the societal structure that generate collective violence. These factors are usually seen as imbalances or disequilibria within the sociopolitical and economic structure. It may be noted that we have created a separate category for demographic strain factors. This has been done because of the importance of demographic factors such as urban concentration and the size and the rate of growth of population on the generation of sociopolitical strife. Since these factors cannot be readily included in the other three categories, they have been classified separately.

The variables of economic disequilibrium are the familiar factors of unemployment, income inequality, inflation, and the like, which generate economic hardship on the populace. The political factors could include the ability of the government to meet the political demands (e.g., a greater democracy or regional autonomy, etc.) of its citizens. The disequilibrium within the society is manifested by the existence of discrimination based on ethnic, linguistic, racial, or religious backgrounds, which give rise to a heightened sense of emotion and hostility within a society. Structural imbalance resulting from changing demographic patterns, such as urbanization, and a high rate of growth of population have been found to have strong correlation with collective rebellious behavior.

Sociopsychological theories hypothesize the interrelationship among socioeconomic conditions, psychological disposition, and behavior. Sociopsychologists generally postulate the causal link between frustration felt by the actors, resulting from the environmental conditions, with aggressive collective behavior. Within a social context, frustration felt at the collective level is called *systemic frustration*.[5] Sociopsychologists maintain that this systemic frustration finds its expression through the acts of collective violence against the prevailing social and political order.

The micro - or individual based - theories scrutinize an individual's reasons for joining a rebellion. This group of theories, again, can be divided into two classes: the psychological theories and the behavioral theories. The psychological theories usually draw their inspiration from the work of Sigmund Freud. The behavioral explanations of collective rebellious behavior, on the other hand, attempt a behavioral explanation of the action of the potential participants. In their pursuit of the explanation of participatory behavior, the behavioral theorists, unlike the Freudian psychologists, do not depend upon factors, which are instinctive, learned, or subconscious. Instead, they build their hypotheses on the factors of motivation, such as pleasure and pain, profit and loss, or reward and punishment. Since an actor takes his participatory decision under the condition of uncertainty, this approach is often based upon the explicit consideration of a utility function and is known as the *rational choice approach*.

COMPREHENSIVE THEORIES

Karl Marx and the Marxists

Before delving into the Marxian insight into the causes of collective violence, it is important to note the difference in the nature of such movements in the writings of Marx and the nonMarxist writers. Without a proper distinction in the definition, one is liable to confuse the two. The Marxian inquiry into the origins of societal protest is rooted in class conflict and hence purports to explain the revolutionary move-ments of the proletariat against the bourgeoisie, whereas the non-Marxist writers attempt to explain all different kinds of collective actions without discussing class conflict. In other words, in Marx's view, every protest movement is rooted in the class struggle, and the intrinsic nature of the capitalist society, which will inevitably lead to the overthrow of the system. For the nonMarxists, collective movements are not assumed to be the expressions of class hatred and are hypothesized to be the outcomes of unbalanced social structure, norms, and values. This distinction is fundamental to our understanding of the two theories, which goes far beyond the discussions of the sets of independent variables offered by the two theories (Piven, 1976). The vast and many-faceted work of Marx on the process of the revolution-ary change of the production relationship from capitalism to socialism may be summarized with the help of the Figure 3.2.

Marx (1906) analyzed the process of a revolutionary change with the help of three major factors: economic, psychological, and leadership. The economic factor, the production   relationship, provides reasons for the psychological alienation of the working class. Together they determine the objective condition suitable for revolution, whereas the leaders of the proletarian movement bring about the ultimate destruction of the capitalist system. In the Marxian scheme the first two factors provide the necessary conditions and the third factor constitutes the sufficient condition for a successful proletarian revolution.

To Marx the chain of reasoning was simple. The capitalists make profits by depriving the laborers. In their zeal to maximize profits the capitalists enlarge their share of the pie by resorting to an ever-increasing level of labor-saving mechanization. This leads to extreme concentration of income. With the mechanized and increas-ingly more productive industries spewing out more and more goods, the market inevitably experiences over-supply, as the unemployed and highly exploited labor force fails to generate sufficient consumption capability. This lack of aggregate demand brings down the capitalist system as it plunges into the abyss of a devastating economic depression. This decline, admits Marx, is thwarted, albeit temporarily, through the intervention of the counteracting forces, such as foreign trade.

On the psychological front, the Marxist explanation includes exploitation by the bourgeoisie and the dissociation of the worker from his own fruits of labor, giving rise to a sense of alienation on the part of the worker. This feeling of alienation and deprivation deepens with the growth of capitalism, thereby generating conditions for spontaneous rebellions and other forms of social unrest.

Finally, with the correct leadership provided by the revolutionary communist parties, capitalism meets its violent death with the formation of socialistic societies. Let us look into this complex reasoning at a greater depth.

To understand Marx, one must start, like he himself did, with production of commodities and the theory of value. In any society, goods are produced for their use values. However, the distribution of these use values in production, that is, the relative levels of production of various goods, in contrast to the neoclassical economics, is not based on the market with its private utility functions, factor endowments, and a neutral government, but is determined by a plethora of ideological, technological, and economic factors - hence, for Marx the difference between the use value and the exchange value. He emphasized that while exchange value is quantifiable, the use value is not. Thus, every commodity has a use value, but not the other way around. That is, there are commodities that have use values but that are not commodities of exchange because of their abundance. Hence, the paradox that while water has a higher use value than diamonds, the latter is much more valuable than the former. For Marx, something is not defined as a commodity unless it embodies labor time and is exchanged. Therefore, the basis of the Marxian labor theory of value, all commodities are products of labor. A commodity embodies a social relationship, and can only be theoretically quantified by analyzing its exchange value from the viewpoint of the labor-time necessary to produce it.

The divergence between labor value and the market or exchange value takes place under capitalism through its ability to purchase and sell the laborers' singular commodity, their ability to work. The price of this labor power is of course wages. The use value to the purchasers of labor power is its ability to create further use value. In the Marxian analysis - the unique quality of labor as the sole creator of use value - this mode of buying and selling of labor power distinguishes itself from all other kinds of exchange.[6] This is the very kingpin of the subsequent Marxian analysis of exploitation, alienation, falling rate of profit, and the inevitable crisis of the capitalist system of society.

Figure 3.2

Marxian Scheme of the Revolutionary Process

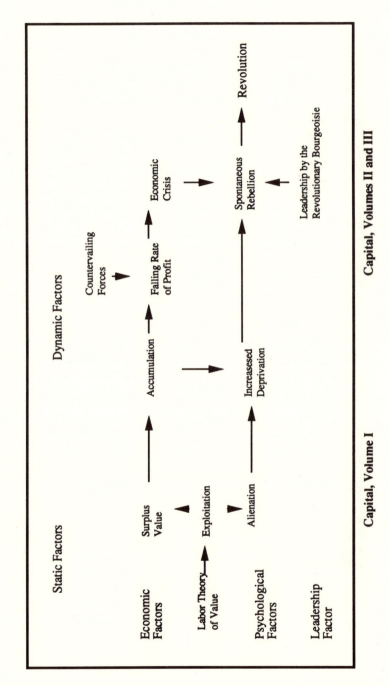

The exchange of commodities, especially intangible labor power, calls for the use of money, which acts as a unit of account, a means of payment, and a store of value.[7] Marx demonstrated the basic irony of capitalism where the exploitation of labor by the capitalist becomes the cause of his ultimate downfall. This process can be described as follows.

Under a simple exchange, a typical laborer starts with the commodity (C) he has to offer, his labor power. This labor power is exchanged for money (M). Marx expressed this exchange as C-M. With money, the laborer purchases commodities (C). Given no cheating, the commodities that he buys will have the same value as his own offering of labor power and in principle can be reversed. The cycle of exchange C-M-C starts and ends with the same values of two different commodities (otherwise, the exchange will be meaningless).

The capitalist, in contrast, starts with money, with which he purchases commodities of a special type, means of production, raw materials, and labor power (M-C). The produced commodity (C') then is exchanged (sold) for money (M'). However, since the capitalist wants to make profits, the amount of money he receives by selling his product - produced by his purchase of labor power, the real creator of value - is greater than his original outlay. That is, this cycle of exchange, M-C-M', where M' > M. The difference, M' – M = m, is what Marx calls the "surplus value" or "exploitation." In this case money acts as a capital when it is used to generate more. Marx assumed that the purpose and the unique nature of capital is to act as a self-expanding value.

The crisis of the capitalist system is deepened in two different fronts, both emanating from the capitalists' constant need (the "animal spirit") to expand by exploiting the workers: economic and psychological. Indeed, the most valuable contribution of Marx, lost on the later social scientists, in analyzing societal evolution lies in his bringing together the simultaneous interaction between economic conditions and the factors of societal frustrations and the consequent expressions of anger.

Setting the stage for dynamic analysis with his basic theoretical paradigm in the first volume of *Capital*, Marx proceeded in the two subsequent volumes to elaborate on the production process of the capitalist system. In symbolic terms he depicted this by:

$$M - C \left| \begin{array}{l} lp \\ mp \end{array} \right. - P - C' - M' \tag{3.1}$$

The capitalist starts with money (M) which he exchanges for commodity (C). Marx takes pain to explain that this commodity is divided into labor power (lp) and other means of production (mp). It is important to note this distinction, as the capitalist system forces the laborer to part with his means of production. It should, however, be noted that it is not money as means of payment or in its function as the store of value that allows it to operate as capital; it is the separation in the ownership of labor power that produces a definite class relation in the production process. This separation generates alienation and frustration among the working class.

On the economic side, this process continues with the purchase of inputs (C) to form productive capital (P). With the intervention of the productive capital (P), the input is transformed into C', which embodies not only the original inputs but also the value added of surplus value. That is, C' = C + c. This C' is exchanged for M'. It may be noted that the nominal aspect of m is the real equivalent of c, the surplus value (S):

$$m = c = S \tag{3.2}$$

Now, this added m, acting as a store of value, repeats the cycle with a larger outlay for production. Since the workers have no share in m, this depiction not only shows capital as self-expanding and points to the inevitability of overproduction within the capitalist system but also graphically portrays the basic social relationship within the capitalist mode of production.

From the analysis of the generation of surplus value, Marx derives his law of falling rate of profit. He defines the average rate of profit (r) as:

$$r = \frac{S}{(K + V)} \tag{3.3}$$

where K and V are the capitalists' expenditure on constant and variable capital. By dividing both the numerator and the denominator of the right-hand side of equation (3.3), Marx derives his famous transfor-mation equation:

$$\frac{\dfrac{S}{V}}{\dfrac{K}{V} + 1} = \frac{e}{k + 1} \tag{3.4}$$

where Marx defined e as the rate of exploitation and k as the organic composition of capital (capital-labor ratio). From this equation, Marx argued that as a consequence of accumulation, the technological advantages of economies of scale, and the capitalists' ever increasing need to generate more profit by replacing labor with capital, k will rise, and with e remaining basically unchanged, r must fall.[8]

Marx, of course, did not predict a monotonous downward movement of the average profit rate in the capitalist economy. By borrowing the term *counteracting causes* and some analysis from Mill's *Principles of Political Economy* (1884) he showed the reasons for reversal of the downward trend.

By looking at transformation equation (3.4), it is clear that such counteracting forces may come either in the form of increasing the rate of exploitation (e) or decreasing the organic composition of capital. Any increase in e must incorporate a steeper increase in m (= S = c). However, given the fact that the working hours are physically constrained and the workers are assumed to be operating at a subsistence level of wages, Marx considered this to be an unlikely scenario.

A much more plausible case may be made for a decrease in the level of capital utilization with respect to labor. This may happen if the rates of return on capital decrease, or if the marginal returns on capital fall short of the marginal productivity of labor. Another important scenario is where the import of cheap wage goods, through foreign trade, or colonization, reduces the organic composition of capital (Fine, 1975).[9] The later Marxists, in similar vein, have accused the conspicuous spending and expenditures on nonproductive items, that is, advertisement, or military expenditure of temporarily injecting a multiplier effect on the economy to keep the level of profit high in the capitalist economies.[10]

Needless to say, Marx considered these counteracting forces to be of a temporary nature and held that owing to its very nature capitalism was destined to fail. However, alongside the economic troubles of the bourgeoisie, the system of a capitalist mode of production also was a potent generator of ill will on the part of the proletariat.

The sociopsychologist in Marx (1961) argued that the separation of man from the ownership of his labor creates a situation of alienation where: "activity is experienced as suffering, strength as powerlessness, and creation as emasculation" (pp. 99 - 100). This alienation and frustration lie at the root of class enmity and class struggle. Marx admitted the possibility that even for lengthy periods of time the class relation may remain relatively stable. However, even during these periods, owing to the aforementioned inherent tendencies of capitalist production process, the economic misery of the working class will exacerbate, and consequently, the sense of psychological deprivation and frustration will deepen. Marx noted that the capitalist stage of societal history is the most productive and the most exploitative. This deepening of exploitation will intensify the class struggle.

Marx felt that in the early stages of capitalism, the capitalists had the upper hand in terms of power and control over the working class. However, with time and the increased realization by the workers that their interests were opposed to those of the capitalists, the process will reverse. It is then, he argued, that a society will be ripe for spontaneous acts of collective violence and rebellion by the workers. As a prime example, Marx cited the Luddite movement in Great Britain. Around 1811-16 a group of unemployed British factory workers organized themselves to attack the factories and destroy the machinery. Marx saw in their action a primitive class awakening and a vain attempt to resist the demands of the capitalist system. He also saw in the increasing activities of the trade unions similar desires being manifested.

However, despite the crisis in the economic front for the capitalists and the deepening of frustration, alienation, and class antagonism on the part of the working class, Marx was emphatic that this would not be enough to bring about a revolutionary movment successful enough to bring down the capitalist system. He emphasized that left to themselves the workers will get bogged down in petty issues of what Lenin decades later called "economism." Hence, for a revolution to take place there must be a revolutionary leadership provided by the Communist party, the leaders of which, Marx predicted, will come from the ranks of the bourgeoisie. These are the people who are armed with the knowledge of history and societal evolution. Thus, he noted: (in Fernbach, 1974), "when the class struggle nears the decisive hour ... a small section of the ruling class cuts itself adrift, and joins the revolutionary class" (p. 77).

The issue of leadership was taken up by his later followers such as Lenin and Mao. In fact, this is best exemplified in a lengthy passage from Karl Kautsky, quoted by Lenin in his *What Is To Be Done* (1969):

Many of our revisionist critics believe that Marx asserted that economic development and the class struggle create, not only the conditions for Socialist production, but also, and directly, the *consciousness* (K. K.'s italics) of its necessity. And these critics advance the argument that the most highly capitalistically developed country, England, is more remote than any other from this consciousness.... (by assuming that) the more capitalist development increases the number of the proletariat, the more the proletariat is compelled, and obtains the opportunity to fight against capitalism.... But this is absolutely untrue... Modern Socialist consciousness can arise only on the basis of profound scientific knowledge... The vehicle of science are not the proletariat, but the bourgeois *intelligentsia* (K. K's italics) [p. 40].[11]

Neil Smelser and Collective Violence

Among the nonMarxist social scientists Neil Smelser was one of the first to attempt to formulate a comprehensive theory of collective rebellion. Pivotal to the understanding of Smelser's theory of collective movements are the classification of six conditions and characterization of two types of movements.   Smelser developed his theory of collective behavior with the help of six conditions and contended that the presence of each of them in high-level intensity would provide sufficient cause for social movements. He argued that these conditions add to a given historical situation.   Borrowing the term from economics, he called the process "value added."   This value-added process leads to the development of a social mass movement. The Smelserian scheme, along with the factors of generation of social movement, is depicted in Figure 3.3.

Figure   3.3

Smelser's Scheme of Collective Social Movement

Conditions

1. Structural Conduciveness
2. Structural Strain
3. Growth of Generalized Beliefs
4. Precipitating Events
5. Mobilization of Participants
6. Ineffective Social Control

Value Added ➡ Collective Social Movement

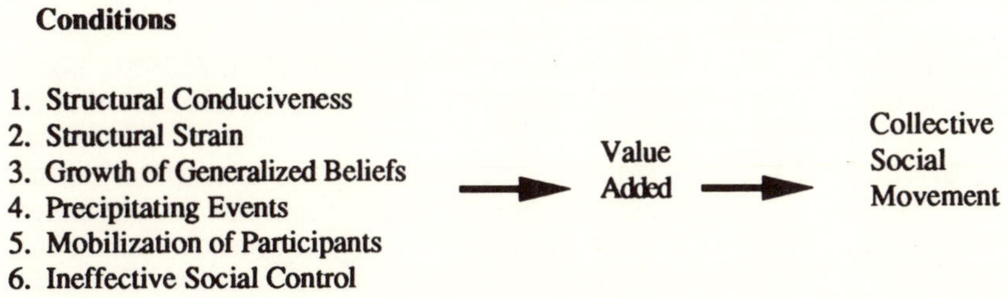

Smelser also distinguishes between two types of movements: norm-oriented movement and value-oriented movement. The norm-oriented movements are concerned with producing limited changes within the confines of an existing sociopolitical structure. In contrast, value-oriented movements aim at a much larger and more fundamental change in the value structure of a society (G. T. Marx and Wood, 1975). Norm-oriented movements attempt to change some specific regulations within the bureaucratic system, social custom, or economic policies without attempting to change the system itself in any drastic or fundamental way. Examples of norm-oriented movements would be the antinuclear movement, movement to bring about a constitutional amendment to protect equal rights for women or homosexuals.

In contrast, value-oriented movements aim at changing the basic social, political, and economic structure. Examples of this kind of movement would be the Marxist revolutions experienced in Russia, China, Vietnam, and Cuba and the many other communist insurgency movements seen in many of the Third World countries. The value-oriented movement would also include the fundamentalist Islamic movement in Iran or the Black Panther movement and a "white supremacists" movement in the United States. The basic characteristic of movements of this sort lies in their attempt to change the fundamental value structure of a society. However, before attempting to explain the Smelserian theory of collective movement, it is important to note that Smelser developed his theory without any attempt to quantify his hypotheses or empirically operationalize his concepts. Instead, they were elucidated with the help of a large number of appropriate examples, a methodology, in sociological literature known as *systematic comparative illustrations*.

Owing to the centrality of the six conditions - structural conduciveness, structural strain, growth and spread of generalized beliefs, precipitating factors, mobilization of participants for action, and the ineffective operation of social control (Smelser, 1963: pp. 12-21, 270-312, 313-81) in Smelser's analysis of social movements, we should begin our discussion by defining these factors.

The condition *structural conduciveness* refers to the extent of permissiveness of social institutions to generate or to tolerate social movements. This permissiveness should not be taken to imply that the structural arrangements of a society are solely responsible for the occurrences of the movements. It simply implies that under certain societal structures these expressions of dissent are treated more or less harshly than in others. For example, in the democratic and highly structurally differentiated societies the political system allows for certain kinds of protests to take place. For, in a highly structurally differentiated society[12] (such as in United States) the various institutions - political, religious, economic, judicial - are not directly connected with the state. That is, one can protest against the action of a particular institution without such a protest being taken as an affront to the statehood itself. This is because, as Smelser argues, the concept of structural differentiation is closely associated with the concept of legitimacy.[13]   In a democratic society, for instance, often protesters of a certain action of state officials do indeed protest the legitimacy of the particular action, rather than the legitimacy of the office itself taking the action. So one may disagree with and protest the actions taken by the head of state (nuclear arms policy, environmental policy, employment, or antipoverty policy) without questioning the legitimacy of the office itself. In contrast, in a less differentiated society where the social and political institutions are interconnected with the legitimacy of the system itself, no such distinction is possible. In such a case, any protest movement is seen as a threat to the system as a whole and is treated accordingly.

Structural strain refers to the generation of social strain and tension from "ambiguities, deprivation, conflict, and discrepancies."

Structural strain is promoted by economic factors, such as unemployment, poverty, redistribution of income, status or power among groups, or even external threats and war.

Growth and spread of generalized beliefs refers to ideas or beliefs that identify the source of societal strain and suggest solutions to these problems. Smelser, in his exposition, emphasized the importance of not the mere existence but the growth of such a belief system as cause for social movements. These generalized belief structures would include the major ideologies, such as capitalism, communism, democracy, religion, or some other reform ideology (emancipation of blacks or women or even prejudices such as anti-Semitism, etc.). As these belief structures get stronger, the momentum for mass movement increases. As a recent example of this we may mention the rapid spread of Islamic fundamentalism in Iran with the circulation of books, pamphlets and taped messages from then-exiled leader Ayatollah Khomeini, which helped bring about the overthrow of the Shah (Keddie, 1981). Growth of generalized beliefs can also result from the spread of rumors, adding impetus to a mass movement. For example, the role of rumors in precipitating a mutiny by the Indian Sepoys against the British rule in 1857 is well documented.[14] Similarly, in recent years the popular movement to oust "Baby Doc" Duvalier of Haiti received a significant amount of encouragement from rumers spreading of his fleeing the country (*London Times*, February 6, 1986).

Precipitating factors in Smelser's scheme refer to the specific incidents that help crystalize a social movement. These events, large or small, often take on images and significance much larger than life. Quite frequently these events may be carefully planned and orchestrated by the leadership as strategic moves to help sharpen the focus on a certain strain or imbalance within the society. The celebrated incident of breaking the Salt-Law in India by Mohandas Gandhi and the attempt by the American Nazi party to demonstrate in Skokie, Illinois, home of a significant number of Jewish victims of concentration camps, are examples of such deliberate action designed to precipitate a crisis by the opposition leaders. Also, events unplanned by the opposition can serve as precipitating factors, an example of which may be found in the refusal of a black woman Rosa Parks to ride in the back of a public bus (reserved for the blacks) in Montgomery, Alabama, her act of defiance served as a turning point for the civil rights movement in the United States. In fact, every uprising or mass movement will contain a series of such unique events shaping the destiny of the movement. Needless to say, this aspect of collective movement is amenable only to expost analysis by the historians and can no way be predicted.

Mobilization of participants for action refers to the leadership and organizational efficacy for the success of a movement. As mentioned in the previous section, Marx and his followers placed a great deal of emphasis on the leadership and mobilization aspects of a revolutionary movement. Similarly, Smelser asserted that the leadership factor was essential for any kind of movement - norm or value oriented.

The final Smelserian condition for the generation of a social movement is what he calls the *ineffective operation of social control*. These factors refer to the power of the social and political system to control and suppress the antisystemic movements generated by the previous five factors. The effectiveness of social control has two essential forms: cooption and coercion.

The structural functionalist in Smelser saw the society not only in terms of reducing conflict through the imposition of physical constraints in the form of law enforcement and military intervention but also in terms of its capacity to ameliorate conflict and adapt itself to the changed situation, thereby coopting within its fold the forces of opposition. This would take place when the administration agreed to open up channels of communication, show flexibility, and even share power with the opposition leaders, taking away some of the most glaring reasons for creating strains within the society. Thus, in the case of the United States the enactment of various civil rights laws, social welfare programs, and abolition of the overt expressions of racial segregation have helped ease the race relations since the 1960s. In fact, the success of this effort is evidenced by the fact that despite the continuing deterioration of the economic position of blacks and other minorities (Palmer and Sawhill, 1984; National Research Council report, 1989), no significant political opposition has taken shape. A similar example of a society adapting itself to a changing situation and thereby mollifying conflict can be found in the actions of King Juan Carlos of Spain after the death of General Fransisco Franco. Finally, one may also cite the success of the PRI, the ruling party in Mexico, as a glowing example of providing a long history of coopting the opposition. This process of cooption allowed the party to rule Mexico without much significant opposition.

Needless to say, cooption is a very effective method of conflict management within a macrosocietal setup. However, its ultimate effectiveness depends on factors such as the flexibility of the system, proper understanding of the situation by the leadership, elements of trust among the rival groups, and the degree of mutual exclusiveness of the opposing points of view.

System flexibility is often a function of the type of regime. Thus, one can safely assume a democratic society to be far more flexible and accommodating of dissent than the other forms of government.[15] The deliberate policy decision by the administration is an extremely important factor in reducing the level of hostility in the society. Yet like the previous two conditions of leadership and precipitating factors, these policy variables are exogenous to any system of ex-ante explanation of social movement. Finally, the relative position of the opposing groups and the extent of mutual trust are the result of a culmination of historical events, as well as dynamic factors (e.g., response factors) within a movement. The problems of the Arabs and the Israelis in the Middle East and the Catholics and the Protestants in northern Ireland are prime examples of this kind of mutual exclusiveness of positions that precludes possibilities of cooption.[16]

The second type of social control takes place with the administration imposing physical constraints over the growth of a social movement. These constraints are functions of the police and military forces' ability to combat the participants in protest movements. Many insurgency movements around the world have been defeated as a result of successful police and military operation (See Franda, 1971; Gamson, 1974; Ghosh, 1975). However, like the strategies of the extremists on the other side of the fence, excessive (or perceived to be so by a significant portion of the populace, including the moderates) force can sometimes even back fire in provoking more protest movements. Thus, Stark (1972), in a study of the antiwar movement in the United States, demonstrated that while punitive government action can put down an antisystemic movement, it can also add to the confrontative mood by bringing the moderates into the folds of the opposition. In fact, studies at the clinical level as well as the aggregate level (Venieris and Gupta, 1983; Muller, 1985) have lent credence to the hypothesis that the relationship between the government's coercive action and the development of coercive movement is quadratic in nature. This is because, as Gurr (1970) pointed out, the initial reaction to the application of force is counterforce. However, after a point of high turmoil and high coercion, if the system is still able to apply more the protest movements are crushed with the application of brutal force by the government. We will discuss in greater detail the implications of these factors to the dynamics of a political movement in Chapter 5.

Finally, with respect to the negative sanctions by the administration, Smelser (1963, pp. 367-79) also maintained that the presence of harsh measures, followed by a weakness to maintain the level of coercion by the authorities, can push a value oriented movement toward a full-fledged revolution. Giving examples from the Russian Revolution, Smelser argued that at the beginning of the revolution, the Czarist authorities treated the revolutionaries extremely harshly, yet later on they failed to maintain the same level of coercion as the grip of the Romanov regime started to slip, exposing their basic weakness (see Trotsky, 1932). In recent history, similar arguments can also be made with respect to the actions of the Shah of Iran and Ferdinand Marcos of the Philippines toward the end of their respective regimes (Green, 1986; B. Johnson, 1987).

Smelser and the Two Kinds of Social Movements

As noted above, Smelser distinguishes between two types of social movements: norm and value oriented. He related this classification to the six conditions of collective movement. However, from his list of six conditions only three (structural conduciveness, growth of generalized beliefs, and ineffective operation of social control) can clearly determine the character of a movement. The outcomes of the other three conditions, in contrast, would fail to do so.

The structural conduciveness factor is closely connected with the sociological notion of structural differentiation and legitimacy. Structural differentiation refers to the extent to which the major social and political institutions are linked to each other and the value system of the society. Thus, in a communist, a theocratic, or even a secular authoritarian nation the social and political institutions are extremely closely interconnected with the value system of the society in the sense that any criticism or protest against any aspect of the government can be interpreted as an attack on the basic value structure of the society as well. However, in a typical democratic nation with a high degree of structural differentiation (e.g., the United States, argued Smelser), the institutions are perceived to be separate from each other as well as from the basic value structure of the society. Thus, it is possible to protest the action of a particular official, law, or institution without risking the protest being interpreted as an attack on the statehood itself.

The basic implication of structural conduciveness in the Smelserian scheme is the system's ability to provide means of legitimate protest to air grievances and vent frustrations. Owing to their ability to separate the actions of the state from the basic value structure, Smelser argues that the majority of the protest movements in the structurally differentiated societies will take on the character of being norm oriented. However, without such avenues the strains within a society are more likely to generate value-oriented movements. As an example, Smelser (1963: pp. 325-26) pointed out that facing social discrimination, which closed many legitimate channels for venting frustrations, the blacks in the United States developed serious value-oriented movements during the 1960s, whereas the nineteenth-century labor movement in the United States - unlike in many parts of the world - remained confined within norm-based economic struggles. By drawing a similar line of argument, one can add a subscript to the black movement by noting that the passage of the civil rights laws and the consequent opening of legal methods of redressing discrimination have helped a great deal in diffusing value oriented black protest in recent years.[17]

Based on extensive content analysis of the statements published in books and pamphlets by the leaders of the movement, Smelser argued that the growth of generalized belief structure help characterize the nature of a movement. Thus, depending on the leadership, the movement will take on the characteristic of being either norm or value oriented. However, later studies have seriously questioned this assertion that the leadership is clear enough in its direction or in distinction between norm, and value-oriented movements (Stallings, 1973; G.T. Marx and Wood, 1975).

Finally, according to Smelser, the social control factor determines the norm, or value-oriented characteristic of a movement. By being flexible and often permissive, societies can keep movements norm oriented. The alternative to this is of course to push many basically norm-oriented movements toward the path of value orientation. The other three factors, argues Smelser, were not useful in predicting the characteristic of a movement, since the existence of strains, precipitating factors and the mobilization factors, are present in every kind of social movement.

Marx and Smelser

Before concluding the discussion of the two comprehensive theories of collective violence, it is necessary to say a few words comparing the two. Since the difference between the two theories are at the fundamental level of analysis, we will discuss the dissimilarities first, then look into the areas of parallel development, and finally, justify our own position on the subject.

Despite some superficial similarities, the fundamental characteristic that distinguishes the Marxian theory from that of Smelser's - and for that matter all other nonMarxian writers - is Marx's adherence to the labor theory of value. As noted above, all his analyses stem from his theory of exploitation and therefore differs fundamentally in spirit from the nonMarxist writers. Further, unlike Smelser, who is primarily concerned with investigating the causes of collective movements, Marx viewed political violence as an inevitable byproduct of the overall scheme of things and a necessary catalyst to the societal evolutionary process. Marx took a comprehensive approach that is rooted in the philosophical approach of historical materialism. In contrast, Smelser's analysis is not derived from any particular philosophical concern. Smelser recognizes conflict among various groups - religious, ethnic, linguistic, racial - of which economic class is but one. Marx, on the other hand, while acknowledging the tension-producing capacity of other group differences within a society, maintained that they were all basically rooted in the omnipresent economic cleavage that characterizes a capitalist system. Finally, while Smelser distinguishes between the types of movements, Marx did not consider such distinction useful since in his paradigm any act of revolt to bring about socialism would ultimately have to be value oriented. Keeping this in mind, we may proceed to compare the two theories in more detail;

specifically we will evaluate Smelser's six conditions in light of Marxian theory.

Of the six Smelserian conditions for social movement, probably the condition of structural conduciveness offers the sharpest contrast between the two men, reflecting their relative ideological perspectives. For Marx the concept of structural differentiation would have meant an ever increasing level of division of labor and specialization (K. Marx, 1906: pp. 368-404; 1961, pp. 55-162), which to Marx was the very engine that drives the capitalist mode of production to mature, thereby heightening the possibility for revolution resulting from an increased level of exploitation by the bourgeoisie and alienation by the proletariat. Hence, as capitalism progresses, Marx argued, the class distinction gets stronger, and so does class enmity:

Our epoch, the epoch of the bourgeoisie, possesses, however, the distinctive feature: it has simplified class antagonisms. Society as a whole is more and more splitting up into two hostile camps, into two great classes directly facing each other: bourgeoisie and proletariat [Fernbach, 1974, p. 68].

Smelser, on the other hand, saw in the development of capitalism, increased social mobility, distribution of income, power, and prestige based on achievements of individuals, away from ascription. With structural differentiation he saw a greater capability on the part of the society to adapt itself to changing circumstances and to ameliorate conflict.[18]

With regard to the condition of the growth of generalized beliefs, drawing on historical materialism, Marx would have argued that beliefs are really "epiphenomena" - that is, not independent phenomena in their own right, but are the results of the prevailing economic structure in the society.[19] He would probably have argued that only the revolutionary beliefs would generate conditions for social conflict. Religious beliefs and similar ideologies are nothing but "opium" that keeps the potential class hostilities suppressed. However, in this respect, there would be less of a disagreement between the two theories, since Smelser does not question the origins of beliefs and would readily agree that it is the belief structure hostile to the present social system that would generate conflict.

The social strain factors are equally important for both theories. For Marx, with the rise of capitalism the misery of the working class would be exacerbated, which would be one of the prime movers for revolution. Similarly, both Marx and Smelser analyzed (although Smelser, in greater detail) the role of the precipitating factors in providing the "spark" that ignites a potentially explosive situation. For example, Marx viewed the Prussian defeat of the French militia in 1871 as a precipitant for the revolutionary Paris commune (Marx, in Feuer, 1959, pp. 362-69). He also saw the introduction of machinery as the cause of the Luddite movement in England, and the introduction of foreign merchandise as a precipitating cause of the mutiny and turmoil in India in 1857 (Avinery, 1969). The later Marxists, such as Trotsky (1932) saw in the defeat of the Russian army in the Russo - Japanese war as a blow to the peoples' perception of the Czarist regime's legitimacy, which ultimately caused its downfall.

Like Smelser, Marx was concerned about the mobilization factor for the potential participants in a collective social action. As Bendix and Lipset (1966) point out, Marx identified factors such as physical concentration and the ease of communication as important factors for the mobilization of the working class.

With regard to the forces of social control, Marx acknowledged the counter-revolutionary aspects of state coercion. He, however, argued that ultimately the working class army would overwhelm the military might of the capitalist system, as in the final stages of revolution the ranks and file of the police and military force would realize their true class identify and join the forces of revolution (Smelser, 1973, pp. xx - xxi; Marx, in Smelser, 1973, pp. 171-72).

However, Smelser also included in his analysis the power of cooption to bring down a rebellion. Similarly, Marx, in his analysis of the petty-bourgeoisie demonstrated the importance of coopting the middle class by the upper class to prolong the capitalist system of society.

Needless to say, the ideological positions of the two men are different and so are their conclusions. Unlike Marx, Smelser does not predict the inevitability of the demise of the capitalist system. In fact, with increased levels of structural differentiation accompanying economic development, he sees the future of capitalism much more harmonious than their counterparts in the Third World.

However, without going into the direction of societal evolution, our most important criticism of Marx revolves around class affiliation. Do people actually identify with their class affiliation? It is a questeion which can only be settled through empirical verification. However, this certainly does not deny the importance of class. As we will be discussing in the next chapter, if people are in fact swayed by class ideology, there is nothing in our behavioral formulation that is directly in contradiction with a class conflict.

THE MIDDLE-RANGE OR PARTIAL THEORIES

In contrast to the general or comprehensive theories, the middle-range theories concentrate on a limited number of explanatory variables to explain participation in collective social movements. These theories, unlike the ones mentioned above, devote a great deal of effort toward statistical verification of their hypotheses.

Social Psychological Theories: The Case for Relative Deprivation

Social psychological theories of collective movements causally link social conditions, psychological disposition (anger), and aggressive behavior. These theories (also often called the frustration-aggression theories) see peoples' aggressive behavior as a direct result of their frustrations, resulting from their inability to attain goals to which they believe they are entitled.[20]   In the psychological literature, *frustration* is defined as an interference with a subject's goal-directed behavior; *aggression* is behavior designed to injure, physically or otherwise, those who are linked to the origination of frustration.

Figure   3.4

The Frustration-Aggression Hypothesis

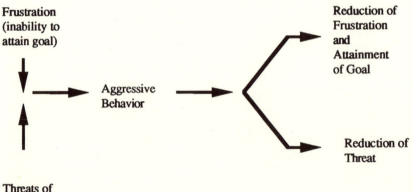

The systematic analysis of collective movements based on social psychological theories have a long heritage, going back over a hundred years to Marx and de Tocqueville.[21] The rigorous treatment of frustration aggression hypothesis began with the work of John Dollard et al. in 1939. At the base of their theory is the hypothesis "that the occurrence of aggressive behavior always presupposes the existence of frustration and, contrariwise, that the existence of frustration always leads to some form of aggression." (p. 1). The fundamental notion of frustration aggression hypothesis can be shown as a causal chain depicted in diagram 3.4.

Note that in this Figure we have introduced another variable psychologically quite closely related to frustration: threats of retribution (Meier, Mennenga, and Stolz, 1941; J. Frank, 1968; T. Gurr, 1970). Together frustration and threat create conditions for anger, which manifests itself through aggressive behavior to reduce the level of frustration, attain goals, or to reduce threats.

The concept of relative deprivation, a derivative of the frustration-aggression theory, has played an extremely important role in the development of a theoretical analysis of the causes of participation in rebellious actions. In Western social science literature, it was first identified by Stouffer and his colleagues (1949).[22] Since their first exposition, various authors have used the term "relative deprivation" with a great deal of differences in their connotation, and even more have used diverse and often conflicting methods for its empirical operationalization. In this section, we will attempt to cast a systematic look at this branch of important literature.

Sociologist J. A. Davis (1959) was probably the first to attempt to model relative deprivation. He did so with reference to two groups: in-group (viewed from the standpoint of the group in question - the rebel group) and out-group. When the members of the in-group, which he also called the have-nots, compare their relative position with those of the out-groups, or the haves, and come short, deprivation is experienced. Unlike Marx, however, these two groups are not distinguished by their ownership of the means of production; rather, they can be based upon any identifiable quality, such as race, religion, ethnicity, or economic capabilities. Davis argues that the comparison with the better-off out-group creates or reinforces social beliefs. He further hypothesized that comparisons are made at random within the in-group. The probability of in-group members experiencing deprivation is the joint probability of each member being deprived himself and of each member comparing himself to another better-off individual. Davis concluded that being a function of the proportion of haves and have-nots, the probability distribution of relative deprivation in the society is a quadratic one (an inverted U shape).[23] That is, the level of relative deprivation is highest when the membership between the two groups is evenly split.

The concept of relative deprivation was further developed by the work of Runciman (1966). Runciman distinguished three types of relative deprivation, which he called *egotistical, fraternal,* and *double deprivation.* Egotistical deprivation occurs when individuals feel personally deprived relative to others in their comparison group. Fraternal deprivation, on the other hand, is a collective concept and takes place when individuals feel that their own group is deprived relative to the other group, although they themselves are personally satisfied. Thus, as a member of a have-not group, I may feel deprived even though I am gratified by my own personal position. Double deprivation results when an individual feels both egotistically and fraternally deprived. Runciman further posits that individuals can experience status and power deprivation as well as economic grievances. He specifies that deprivation will be experienced when one desires something, compares himself with those who actually do have them, and then feels that he deserves the attainment of that object.[24]

Probably the most influential work on the development of the theory of collective rebellion is by Ted R. Gurr (1970). Gurr develops his theory upon the foundation of relative deprivation as an explanatory variable for collective violence. Gurr's hypothesis may be expressed as:

$$CV = f\ (RD) = f\ (\frac{Ve - Vc}{Ve})$$
(3.5)

where,

CV = Collective violence
RD = Relative deprivation
Ve = Value expectations
Vc = Value capabilities

Gurr explained relative deprivation with reference to value positions of expectations and capabilities of a collectivity, defined as any subset of a society. The values are "the desired events, objects, and conditions for which men strive" (p. 25), and value position is the "amount or level of a value actually attained." Value expectations are defined as "the average value positions to which its members believe they are justifiably entitled." He further explains that "value expectations refer to both present and future conditions [of value positions]. Men ordinarily expect to keep what they have; they also generally have a set of expectations and demands about what they should have in the future, which is usually as much or more than what they have at present." (1970; p. 27). These expectations do not refer to idle dreams or wishful thinking, as he makes the distinction between expectations and aspirations. This distinction, Gurr emphasizes, emanates from the fact that expectations are defined with reference to *justifiable* value positions. On the other hand, an aspiration is that which a man hopes to attain but does not necessarily consider to be *rightfully* his. The value capabilities, in contrast, "are the average value positions its members perceive themselves capable of attaining or maintaining" (p. 27).

Gurr then hypothesizes that collective violence is functionally related to relative deprivation. Based on the definition of RD, he further distinguishes among three types of deprivation situations, which he calls decremental, aspirational, and progressive.

Decremental deprivation is characterized by a situation where the group consensus on the justifiable value position (value expectations) has remained stable, but the attainable value position for the members of the group has declined significantly over time. As a result, frustration will be generated in the society as men find out that they can no longer achieve the goals they once could justifiably expect to achieve. In this case the increasing level of relative deprivation in the society will cause political violence.

Gurr provides several examples of political violence resulting from decremental deprivation. For example, he argues that the causes of revolution postulated by Karl Marx, where the level of misery of the working class would deepen as a result of increased levels of exploitation by the capitalist class, essentially characterize a situation of decremental deprivation. Going back to history, Gurr found this model to be useful in explaining political violence in Europe where social strife was caused by the occurrence of natural disasters such as the "Black Death," which essentially lowered people's value capabilities without diminishing their expectations.

The second type of discrepancy between value expectations and value capabilities generates what Gurr calls *aspirational* deprivation. In this case the level of relative deprivation felt within a society increases as the level of capabilities remains the same, but the level of expectations regarding what one can justifiably hope to gain heightens. Gurr posits further that there can be three sources of aspirational deprivation. First, Gurr argues that relative deprivation is generated when the demand for the material goods and services already owned in the community increases due to the demonstration effects. For example, the inhabitants in relatively backward nations may experience aspirational deprivation resulting from an exposure to a more advanced and a materially better-off world. This can also take place as a result of an increase in the value capabilities of the reference group(s).

Second, aspirational deprivation can also take place owing to a new demand for values heretofore not held by the people. This is typically the situation in a postcolonial world, where the capabilities of the inhabitants remain essentially the same, but their demand for new values outstrip the capabilities of social and political system to provide them.

The third kind of aspirational deprivation identified by Gurr takes place when the demand for value positions weakly held before gets solidified. As an example, he mentions the black community in the United States, which used to hold values of aspiration faintly, which became robust with time as the changed social situation prompted them to expect more out of the system than the system was ready for, which caused tension in the race relations in the country.

Finally, *progressive* deprivation, as Gurr claims, explains a longstanding paradox in the study of collective violent behavior. Political historian Alexis de Tocqueville, in analyzing the causes of the French Revolution, noted with some bewilderment that revolt took place not during periods of high oppression and abject poverty but when such a situation was followed by a brief period of relaxation of oppression and relative prosperity. The theoretical explanation of such a situation, as well as its contrary where prolonged periods of relative prosperity are followed by a sharp reversal, was offered in the work of James Davies (1969). He explained such a situation with the help of what he calls the "J -curve." Gurr (1970) argued that the Davies hypothesis can be accommodated within his generalized version of progressive deprivation.

Another development in the concept of relative deprivation was introduced by psychologist Fay Crosby (1976). Crosby specifies egotistical deprivation as a part of a chain of variables including (1) environmental antecedents, (2) preconditions, (3) felt deprivation, (4) mediators, and (5) behavior. Building on the work of Runciman (1966) and Pettigrew (1967), Crosby hypothesized that an individual will experience deprivation when and only when the four preconditions specified by Runciman are joined by a fifth: lack of personal responsibility for failure to obtain something that an individual feels is rightfully his. In contrast, when an individual blames himself for his inability to attain his cherished goal, he will not experience deprivation.

Largely owing to the work of Gurr, of all the theories of collective violence, the frustration aggression theory has gained the widest recognition among later researchers. Several studies attempted to operationalize the concept of relative deprivation either by direct or by indirect methods. The direct method of estimating the extent of relative deprivation is by conducting a survey, asking the respondents how they felt about their reference group. By using this direct method, Patchen (1961) found significant evidence for the existence of a correlation between relative deprivation and collective action. In contrast, researchers such as Nagel (1974) and Lieberson and Silverman (1965) attempted to estimate a quadratic relationship by looking at the economic differences between the distinct social groups. Nagel (1974), for example, in an interesting study of a number of hamlets in Vietnam, found some statistical evidence supporting the existence of such a relationship.

The criticisms of relative deprivation and frustration-aggression theory have, however, been many. For example, several researchers have questioned the importance of *relative* deprivation as opposed to the *absolute* level of deprivation as a cause for sociopolitical unrest. Most of these studies demonstrate that extreme cases of oppression and social injustice can cause political unrest among the most deprived of the society, without any regard to their experiencing a heightening of expectations. Thus, Rude (1960, 1964) in his analysis of the "cargo cult," has demonstrated the importance of rising food prices as an explanatory variable for riots among the poor in France during the French Revolution and in Great Britain. Similar arguments may be found in the analysis of peasant uprisings in Bihar, one of the poorest states in India (see Mukherjee and Yadav, 1980). Fanon (1968), for example, in his shockingly revealing book on the extreme poor, *The Wretched of the Earth*, has drawn similar conclusions.[25]

However, despite the criticism of the concept of relative deprivation by the studies, offering instead absolute deprivation as a cause of political tension,[26] we believe that they are raising a point that can be integrated within the relative deprivation framework. Since in all these cases the research shows a decline in the economic position of those already at the bottom of the economic rung, as a result of rising food prices or the society's inability to provide the basic necessities for even a subsistence living, it can be treated as a case of what Gurr calls decremental deprivation. The peasant uprisings in Bihar, India, for example, can be traced to extreme social injustice and to crimes committed by the rapacious landlords; one can similarly argue that even though for these people their expectations did not go up (a debatable point at best!), the acts of these landlords severely reduced the present level of achievement for these poor people below the point where their survival was being threatened. Thus, in Gurr's formulation if there is a decline in Vc, the actor's propensity to participate in anti-systemic acts will go up unless it is accompanied by a similar decline in value expectations. We can argue that this kind of reduction in people's expectations may happen due to the presence of ideological fervor, such has been experienced in postrevolutionary Soviet Union, Iran, or Libya, or owing to an external threat, such as in Great Britain during the war. During these times people endure hardship quite willingly, and since they reduce their expectations, a decline in their achievements seems all the more tolerable.

However, there is another line of argument, that a straight analysis of relative deprivation cannot take into account. These studies offer criticisms of the theory of relative deprivation which may be classified into two broad categories: those who argue that the inadequacy of relative deprivation is sufficient cause for political unrest and those who argue that violence can occur even without the existence of a sense of deprivation, relative or otherwise, on the part of the participants (neither a necessary nor a sufficient cause).

In the first category, the students of mass violence have argued that along with relative deprivation, one may also include factors such as the perceived legitimacy of the regime by the people (Blumer, 1951; Goffman, 1963; Garfinkel, 1967; Brown and Goldin, 1973; Moore,

1978). These studies have convincingly argued that in the case of a perceived illegitimacy of a regime the factors of deprivation would indeed seem more onerous.

On the other hand, the studies that question the importance of relative deprivation as an explanatory variable, usually point to the right-wing movements, resulting from what is known as *status strain*. It has been pointed out in the literature that while factors such as economic injustice give rise to left-wing movement, any threat to the established order - economic, social, or political - generate right-wing movements. These movements, argue the proponents of this line of reasoning, can take place even without the existence of any deprivation on the part of the participants.

In an important study published in 1964, Daniel Bell, while studying the radical right-wing movements gave birth to the concept of status strain. Status strain may be defined as a situation when one feels dissatisfaction with his own social status. It was further pointed out that status strain has two important components, the fear of a status decline and the fear of status inconsistency.

The fear of status decline is caused when those who are socially well-established feel threatened that their absolute position is to go down. The reactions of the Afrikaners in South Africa facing the prospect of a greater opportunity for nonwhites, or the wealthy landowners in El Salvador anticipating a land redistribution may be explained with reference to status strain.

On the other hand, violence can also be generated because of status inconsistency, the prospect that while the present status of the actor may not go down in absolute terms, his relative standing in the society is being threatened as the hitherto deprived classes of the society start changing the relative distribution of wealth and power. "White power," the Ku Klux Klan, the emergence of Nazi parties in several parts of the Western world, and several riots by the caste Hindus in India against the untouchables may be explained with the help of the concept of status inconsistency .[27]

Both of these hypotheses relating to status strain come to the conclusion that the participants oftentimes do not feel any sense of relative deprivation in the sense that they do not feel that their own level of value capability has gone down with respect to their value expectations (Gurr, 1970). Upon reflection, we can see that the difference between the theory of relative deprivation and status strain lies in the implicit assumption by the former that the individual utility functions are independent of each other, whereas the latter, quite correctly, point to the existence of externalities.[28]

In order to accommodate the question of the interdependence of the utility functions, we may expand our definition of expected achievement (Ve) by arguing that a person's expectations of achievements resulting from a change in the status quo may depend not only upon his own achievements but also on the achievements of other people in the economy as well, whom we can call the reference group. In other words, we are defining these terms in the broadest possible way by assuming that the utility function of the individual (i) is in effect interdependent. That is,

$$U^i = U (Vc^i, Vc^j) \qquad\qquad (3.6)$$

where Vc^j is the level of achievement of the reference group. The existence of interdependent utility functions, or the existence of externalities is crucial for understanding the dynamics of collective movements. For it has been argued time and again that the satisfaction that a person derives within the socioeconomic framework depends not only on his own income but also on that of his reference groups. For example, Kuznets (1965) has argued that it is not only the absolute level of income that is important but also the share in relation to the others. He gave an analogy that a person sitting in an impossible traffic jam, would all of a sudden feel frustrated by the movement in the other lines. Similarly, Runciman (1966), in his early contribution to the formation of the theory of relative deprivation, noted:

The frame of reference [with respect to relative deprivation] can work in either of two ways. On the one hand, a man who has been led to expect, shall we say, promotion in his job, will be more aggrieved if he fails to achieve it than a man whose ambitions have not been similarly heightened. On the other hand, a man taken to a hospital after some minor mishap will feel a good deal less sorry for himself if he is put in a bed next to the victim of a serious accident who has been more severely injured. The same psychological rules apply to groups or classes in a society, or even to nations [p. 9].

Several empirical studies have hypothesized that the causes of political strife are rooted in the feeling of relative deprivation. However, few have attempted to test the hypothesis directly by estimating relative deprivation. At the microlevel, Gurr (1970) attempted to measure the extent of relative deprivation by surveying French and Italian workers.

At the aggregate level the problem of estimating the level of relative deprivation lies in the approximation of the value expectations function. In the literature this problem has been solved by using some form of expectation function based on the realized income. Snyder (1978), for example, used moving average of past income as an approximation. Hibbs (1976), Gupta and Venieris (1981), and Venieris and Gupta (1985) used a more complicated measure by borrowing from the research on the permanent income hypothesis. All these found fairly significant correlation between political violence and relative deprivation within the context of a single country. However, such experiments on cross-national setup yielded statistically insignificant coefficients (Venieris and Gupta, 1983).

Over the years studies based on controlled clinical tests as well as uncontrolled observations have cast doubts on the categorical statement of Dollard linking frustration to aggression. Also, questions have been raised with regard to the link between aggressive behavior and the participant's desire to attain his goals. On the second half of the statement by Dollard et al. (1939) (our first causal leap linking aggression with frustration in Figure 3.4) it has been pointed out that aggressive behavior is but one outcome of frustration. Studies (N. E. Miller et al., 1941; Himmelweit, 1950) have found that there can be five different behavioral responses to a situation of frustration, especially a deep and prolonged period of frustration: submission, dependence, avoidance, apathy, and aggression.[29]

With regard to the second hypothesis regarding the relationship between aggressive behavior and the goal directed behavior, it has been argued that aggressive behavior is instinctive (Freud, 1930; Lorenz, 1966; Holloway, 1968), or even irrational, emotional reaction, not properly linked with frustrations relating to goal-directed behavior (Nieburg, 1962). However, we can argue that many of these studies qualify the essence of the frustration aggression hypothesis rather than contradicting it. In any case if one assumes that aggressive behavior is positively related with the experience of frustration, with the response being modified by the existence of threat, one can establish the theoretical link among the three.[30]

The more important criticism of relative deprivation stems, however, from the fact that while it explains why a man should rebel, it pays inadequate attention to the reasons why even in the face of some extremely serious frustration men choose not to rebel. Further, the theory of relative deprivation has absolutely nothing to say as to the kind of aggressive behavior an individual is likely to be engaged in. We will discuss these two shortcomings in detail in formulating our own behavioral model in the following chapter.

Middle-Range Structural Imbalance Theories

The middle-range social structural theories hypothesize that conflict is generated within a society owing to various structural imbalances. Considering the numerous studies postulating imbalances of the various aspects of the society as an explanation of political violence, we can classify them into four broad categories - economic, social, political, and urban.

Among the studies postulating economic imbalances, one can find the use of unemployment (Snyder, 1975; Gupta, 1977; Gupta and

Venieris, 1981; Venieris and Gupta, 1985), inflation (Gupta and Venieris, 1981; Venieris and Gupta, 1985), income distribution, poverty and social welfare (Russet, 1964; Hibbs, 1973; Nagel, 1974; Gupta, 1977; Muller, 1985), measures of relative deprivation (Snyder, 1975, 1978; Hibbs, 1977; Siegelman and Simpson, 1977; Gupta and Venieris, 1981; Venieris and Gupta, 1983, 1985) and educational imbalance (Lerner, 1963; Galtung, 1964; Geshewender, 1964; Gurr and Ruttenburg, 1967; Coleman, 1968a, 1968b; Gurr, 1968; Hoselitz, 1968; Scott and El-Assal, 1969; Schwab, 1969; Gintis, 1970; Hibbs, 1973; Smelser, 1974; Bowels and Gintis, 1976) as explanatory variables.

Strains can generate within a social structure because of imbalances from discriminations based on ethnic, linguistic, facial, or religious factors (Pye, 1966; Geertz, 1967). Also, sociological literature has identified social structural strains resulting from status strain and status inconsistency (Lipset and Raab, 1970), norm or value inconsistency (Turner and Killian, 1957, 1972), or the perception of illegitimacy of the social order (Blumer, 1951, 1978; Goffman, 1963; Garfinkel, 1967; M. Brown and Goldin, 1973).

Political strains can cause political violence when demands on the political system exceeds the system's capacity to supply (Huntington, 191965, 1968; Almond and Verba 1965; Duff and McCamant, 1968; Hibbs, 1973; Huntington and Nelson, 1978).

Demographic strain causes political violence because it is argued that due to the high concentration of people in urban areas, coupled with a too-rapid a rate of population growth causes the demand for public services and other social needs exceeds the capabilities of the nation and therefore, breeds discontent (Kornhauser, 1959; Hauser, 1963; Tilly, 1964, Rogin, 1967; Cornelius, 1969, Hibbs, 1973, Tilly, 1974; Schwartz, 1976).

Economic Structural Strain

Among the factors that cause strains in the economy, unemployment, inflation, and income inequality readily come to mind. Yet the relationship between political violence and these factors, especially unemployment and inflation, has remained largely unexplored in the literature. One may conjecture that this omission has been caused partly by the fact that so far few economists have shown interest in analyzing the causes of political violence, and hence, sociologists and political scientists have conducted research by using variables most closely related to their sphere of interest. Also, it is interesting to note that so far most of the efforts at building statistical models to explain political violence have concentrated on the inquiries into the structural causes, rather than exploring the dynamic ones. Therefore, most of the available studies are based on cross-section studies using national data.

Given the paucity of comparable data on unemployment, it is hardly surprising that most of the studies did not consider unemployment one of the explanatory variables.

In contrast to these studies, the present author has been involved in research efforts that include both unemployment and inflation as explanatory variables (Gupta, 1977; Gupta and Venieris, 1981; Venieris and Gupta, 1985) and that use time series data (Gupta and Venieris, 1981; Venieris and Gupta, 1985). In these time series analyses of political protest in Great Britain during the period from 1948 to 1967, unemployment was found to be positively correlated with a high degree of statistical significance. When unemployment was introduced as an explanatory variable in a crossnational study (Gupta, 1977), it was observed that the correlation between unemployment and political violence became increasingly stronger with the groups of developed nations. The influence of economic development on the correlation between the two may have a twofold explanation. First, there is always the doubt about the accuracy of the data, especially for the developing nations. Since information on the developed countries can safely be assumed to be a closer approximation to reality, the correlation between the two was observed to be strong and statistically significant. Second, one may also argue that the concept of unemployment is less traumatic in the traditional Third World countries because of the cultural difference in the public attitude toward gainful employment and the existence of extended family structure and other social support systems, which in the long run are probably stronger than the social welfare programs to reduce the level of systemic frustration. However, since there is no direct evidence to support the second proposition, we cannot reject the possibility that this impact of development on the correlation between unemployment and political violence is in fact spurious, resulting from errors in variables.

With regard to inflation, the situation was found to be complicated by the existence of money illusion. So much so, that owing to the relatively small rate of inflation in Great Britain during the period from 1948 to 1967, it was found to have a negative overall impact on political violence as measured by the relevant dynamic multiplier in the simultaneous equation system (Gupta and Venieris, 1981; Venieris and Gupta, 1985).[31] However, one may safely assume that if the inflation rate had been sufficiently high, its disruptive effect would have been felt through an increase in political tension resulting from the arbitrary redistribution of income caused by inflation. Thus, the role of hyperinflation in destroying the basic social fabric and contributing to the establishment of radical governments in several European countries in the post-World War I era and China after the World War II is well documented.

The treatment of education in the context of political unrest has indeed been interesting. Generally, the discussion has taken two different directions. The sociological studies, the majority of which were prompted by the campus unrest in the 1960s in the United States, placed the blame for such activities on the environment of campus life. The studies on political development, on the other hand, essentially concentrated on the role of education in boosting the expectations of people in general and the students in particular, thereby creating a situation of aspirational deprivation, in Gurr's terminology.

The first group of studies (frequently conducted or commissioned by university administrators) often hypothesized quite simply that since political unrest generally concentrated in the large "multiversity" institutions, as opposed to small colleges, there must be something sinister or alienating about the environment of such campuses (Kerr, 1964; Goodman, 1965; Savio, 1965; Schwab, 1969; Scott and El-Assar, 1969; Gintis, 1970; Astin and Bayer, 1971; Smelser, 1974; Smith, 1974; Bowels and Gintis, 1976; Lipset, 1976). Fingers were pointed at various aspects of student life, from impersonal bureaucracy to inattentive professors to the difference in class structure between the liberal students and the conservative trustees and regents of the universities. A few studies even sought reasons for student agitation in their value structures of the families, either trying to establish a correlation between the students' political activities and their liberal upbringing (Wood, 1974; Wood and Ng, 1980), or the students' attempt to discard deliberately the values of their conservative parents (Block, Haan, and Smith, 1969). We believe that many of these studies exemplify the superficiality of understanding of the basic issues of student protest in the 1960s. In fact, it has been repeatedly pointed out that there was no significant disaffection on the part of the students with regard to either the administration (Somers, 1965) or the quality of education provided by the large universities (Somers, 1969; Dunlap, 1970; Wood, 1974). On the other hand, several other empirical studies pointed out the existence of conscription and the university's ready compliance with the draft board to be a significant part of the student protest (Flacks, 1967; Skolnick, 1969). Despite the often-heard assertions of the students discarding the values of their parents, the campus protests died down with the ebbing of the Vietnam War and almost totally disappeared with the end of the draft. If anything, the emergence of the so called "yuppies" should dispel any lingering doubts about a generational shift in value patterns (or atleast in the permamanence there of). In fact, it may be argued that the Vietnam War exposed the urban middle- and upper-middle-class students to the risk of facing a faraway war without any immediate threat to life in the United States, thereby significantly reducing the value capabilities of the members of the affected age group. In other words, it may be convincingly argued that the situation depicted a classic case of decremental deprivation, in Gurr's formulation.

    In contrast, a much more serious effort was mounted by the
scholars of political development in establishing the link between
education and participation in the acts of political violence. These
studies emphasize the fact that education tends to inflate the level of
expectations on the part of its recipients (Lerner, 1963; Galtung, 1964;
Gurr and Ruttenburg, 1967; Coleman, 1968; Gurr, 1968, 1970;
Hoselitz, 1968). In all these studies it has been argued that despite the
positive impact of education in creating human capital stock in a nation,
the disbursement of education in excess of employment opportunity
creates an ideal breeding ground for the discontents and therefore the
future recruits of antisystemic political movements. However, despite
the apparent reasonableness of this hypothesis, Hibbs (1973) found
little statistical evidence in support of this theory of imbalance between
economic development and the spread of education. On the other
hand, he found a statistically significant negative correlation between
political violence and the extent of literacy.
    From the time of earliest recorded scholarship the inequality in
the distribution of income has been regarded as the prime suspect for
generating political ill will and violence. This relationship has been
taken so much for granted that de Tocqueville (1955), for example,
went as far as to assert that whatever the form of revolution, the
principle of inequality would lie at the bottom as the primary cause (p.
302).[32]
    On the other side of the coin, from the standpoint of economic
growth, it has been assumed that inequality of income is not only the
natural outcome of development but also a quite desirable one. This is
because in the dominant Keynesian theory it has been assumed that
savings is a monotonically rising function of income, and thus the
wealthy have a higher average propensity to save, the prime mover of
economic growth.[33] In the planning process several countries in
economic transition, notably Brazil, either have turned a blind eye to
the problem of concentration of income in the hands of a few or have
even encouraged the accumulation of income through favorable fiscal
policies.
    Therefore, it is of no surprise that the relationship between
income and political violence has come under intense scrutiny. Yet
despite the effort the results of these studies correlating poverty with
political violence have been at best mixed. A couple of studies
(Hardy, 1979; Weede, 1981) reported no significant relationship
between the two. Similarly, other studies using land distribution data
(Russett, 1964) and Gini coefficients on household income (Gupta,
1977) found evidence of a weak correlation. In contrast to these studies that used measures of poverty, or a general measure of inequality
(i.e., the Gini index), efforts to correlate political violence with
measures of concentration of income in the hands of the upper class,

have been comparatively more successful. Thus, Nagel (1974), by using data concerning the economic well-being of a number of hamlets in Southeast Asia, found a somewhat stronger correlation with revolutionary political activities. Finally, by using another measure of concentration of income, the income share of the top 20 per cent of the population, Muller (1985) demonstrated a statistically significant positive relationship. Therefore, from the results of these studies we may conclude that the measures of overall distribution and poverty are weaker predictors of political violence than the measures of prosperity or concentration of income.

Students of development have long noted the impact of economic development on the level of political violence. In contrast to the Marxian theory, which would have postulated ceteris paribus of the counteracting forces, the nations would experience political violence at an increasing rate with the maturity of capitalist system, which presumably translates into economic development in our terminology. Researchers such as Kerr et al. (1960), Lipset (1959, 1963), and Dahrendorf (1959) have theorized that political violence is essentially a phenomenon of societies in transition, which is to dissipate with their attainment of economic affluence. However, since the publication of these works in the early to mid-1960s, events in the so-called postindustrial societies have hardly convinced many of the promise of political tranquility with economic development.

Empirical research along this line again points to a mixed bag, a result that can be attributed more to the lack of standardization of the definitions of political violence, as well as economic development, than to the nature of their actual relationship. Feierabend, Feierabend, and Nesvold (1969) reported a mild quadratic relationship between their composite measure of political instability and economic development, measured in terms of per capita gross national product (GNP). Flanigan and Fogelman (1970), by using an additive rating score for political instability, found a negative relationship with development measured in terms of the percentage of the labor force in agriculture and GNP per capita.

In contrast to the researchers who used composite measures of political violence, there are those who used data on an internal war dimension only or who used indicators of both the dimensions individually.[34] Among those who used measures of internal war as the dependent variable, several reported a negative relationship (Rubin and Scheinblatt, 1969, Gupta, 1977); in contrast, Hibbs (1973) reported a quadratic relationship. Cross-national studies using the dimension of anomic violence as the dependent variable, however, generally cite the existence of a quadratic relationship with measures of economic development (Hibbs, 1973; Gupta, 1977; Venieris and Gupta, 1983).

Social Structural Strain

The social structural strain theories postulate that political violence results from imbalances and conflicts within the social class (in a non-Marxian sense) structure. Thus, researchers such as Pye (1966) and Geertz (1967) have attempted to demonstrate the ways discrimination based on race, religion, color, or language generates conditions for collective violence.

Similarly, Lipset and Raab (1970) in their analysis of rightwing movements argued that rather than the absolute level of economic well-being, those who are dropping in their relative standing within the social order are likely to feel what they call "status strain." The ranks of the ultra-right-wing parties, from Hitler's Brown Shirts to the Ku Klux Klan or the Nazi or racist parties in several European and north American countries in the postwar era, are filled with people who feel threatened by the loss of their social status to the Jews, blacks, or other minority or immigrant population. These movements aim at restoring the old "values" by reinstating the old social ordering.

By taking another line of reasoning, Turner and Killian (1957), in their *emergent norm* theory, have argued that conflict situations are created when the emerging social norms clash with the old established norms or values. A similar line of reasoning was adopted by economist Mancur Olson (1968). He argued that for the traditional developing countries too-rapid economic growth, rather than being a blessing, can be a potentially destabilizing factor. This is because as people with traditional values come in contact with new sets of values transplanted from alien lands, along with imported technology and social relationships, tension mounts.

Political Structural Strain

The studies of political structural strain emphasize the role of the legitimacy of the ruling elites in preserving a nation's political stability. Within the domain of the political structural theory of political violence, we may include the *symbolic interactionist* theory of social movements, offered mainly by Herbert Blumer (1978). Blumer argues that contrary to the proponents of the theory of relative deprivation, the presence of social injustice and relative deprivation only provides the necessary condition for social strife. The sufficient condition is provided by the perception of the legitimacy of the regime and the social order. If the social order is perceived by the actors to be illegitimate, then the factors of social injustice will appear to be even more unbearable and hence will create friction.

The work of Seymour Lipset (1959) is often quoted as the authoritative study on political legitimacy. Lipset defined legitimacy by noting that it involved the capacity to engender and maintain the belief that the existing political institutions were the most appropriate or proper ones for the society. Lipset found the concept of legitimacy to be closely related to democracy.[35] The Marxist strategists have always been keenly aware of the need for an erosion of the legitimacy of the political institutions as a prerequisite for a successful revolution.

One can find numerous examples of the importance of legitimacy as a determinant of political violence within a society. The work of Trotsky (1932) described vividly the role of the erosion of the legitimacy of the Romanov regime in the face of military defeats at the various battlefronts in bringing about the Russian Revolution. Trotsky observed that if the existence of privation was enough to cause an insurrection, the masses would always be in revolt. For a revolution to take place, it is necessary that the masses, conclusively convinced of the political bankruptcy of the regime, perceive a revolutionary way out. Thus, there is enough evidence to suggest that during the earlier period of the British raj, the vast majority of the Hindu population in India (and especially in Bengal), who were already accustomed to being ruled by "foreign" Moghul rulers, did not perceive the change in the ruling class as "illegitimate." However, with time, national aspirations developed, which caused a change in perception of the legitimacy of the British rule in India. Also, it has been argued (Huntington, 1961, 1965, 1968) that with development and exposure to the outside world, the citizens of developing nations start demanding political freedom, rights to participate in the political process, or political equality (by minority). These aspirations, over time, tend to outstrip the capacity of the nation to deliver. This growing disparity - which we may call relative deprivation, with respect to political rights - causes political violence.

Strains from Demographic Structure

Among the demographic factors, urban structure has always been viewed in its duality - its enticements and its repulsion, its beauty and its horror, its opportunities and its squalid hopelessness, living side by side, all at the same time. French poet Baudelaire described the city most aptly:

Swarming city, city of dreams
Where ghosts grab strollers in broad daylight.
And so you go your way, stoic, uncomplaining
Through the chaos of the living city.[36]

Hence, the city has long been suspect of providing the ideal breeding ground for the misfits, the mischievous, the alienated, and of course, the revolutionaries. It has been argued (Wirth, 1957) that the very structural conditions of urban life create alienation and revolutionary zeal, as these conditions tend to destroy the old values derived from the roots of cohesive rural life without providing stable substitutes. Urban life also subjects the multitude to appalling living conditions.

Urban living may contribute to the generation of political strife in three major ways. First, the concentration of people, especially the poor, the elderly, and the jobless, increases more than proportionately the demands for public goods. This increased demand soon exceeds the capacity of the society and, as a result, creates conditions for frustration, anger, and revolt (Tilly, 1964, 1974; Snyder and Tilly, 1972, 1974; Shorter and Tilly, 1974).

The second line of reasoning argues that urban living contributes to the heightening of expectations without any regard to people's capabilities (Hauser, 1963; Cornelius, 1969). This is because within the urban structure the rural migrants are exposed to living styles, conditions, and values that tend to inflate their notion of what they can legitimately expect. Yet given the realities, their achievements often fall far short of their expectations. A curious and somewhat serendipitous finding was obtained through the work of Tilly (1974). Tilly found that while the absolute levels of urban concentration provide a good explanation of the level of political violence, the relationship between political violence and the rate of growth of urbanization (net migration) produces a surprising negative correlation. Tilly also showed that historically the periods of rapid urbanization in France in the 1850s, 1920s and 1950s did not produce high levels of political tension. Further empirical corroboration of urban concentration causing conditions for political turmoil was offered by Hibbs (1973). This paradox has been explained by the fact that the new immigrants do not necessarily feel relative deprivation with the same intensity as their neighbors, the long-term residents of the city. First, it takes time for the newcomers to articulate their grievances and effectively organize to challenge the existing system. Hence, Tilly has in fact argued for (without any statistical verification) a lagged relationship between net urban migration and political violence. Second, based on some secondary empirical evidence (McCone, 1969), it has been argued that the new immigrants, despite their very low levels of achievement, usually feel less deprived because of their low levels of expectations, which are still rooted in the old rural values and meager achievements. Hence, for example, it was found that the participants in the Watts riot in Los Angeles came disproportionately from the groups of blacks who had been living in the area for a relatively long period of time (Kerner, 1968).

In line with Smelser's (1963) argument about structural conduciveness, the third line of inquiry speculates that urban societies provide organizational structure conducive to protest movements. Kornhauser (1959) argued that cities provide a ready army of recruits from those who do not belong to any "secondary organizations," (the "primary organization" being the individual's network of family and friends), for example, trade unions, sports or business associations, or ethnic organizations. Kornhauser argued that these rootless people, whom he called the "mass society," fall prey to the organizers of radical movements. He further reasoned that without any formal organizational ties these people, living at the fringes of organized society, become susceptible to the radical ideas of both the left and the right.

In direct contrast, Marx and Lenin argued that the very fact that the workers are concentrated within the relatively small confines of a city creates conditions favorable to organization and mobilization into the revolutionary force. They found no contradiction between the workers' affiliation to the trade unions and their recruitment into the army of the revolutionaries. Criticism of the mass society theory has also been leveled by nonMarxist researchers conducting empirical investigations. Thus several studies (Pinard, 1971; G. T. Marx and Wood, 1975; Halebsky, 1976) found membership in the secondary organizations to be positively correlated with the progress of a movement.

RATIONAL REVOLUTIONARY: THE RATIONAL CHOICE APPROACH

The alternative to formulating broad-based structural theories is to look into the causes of individual motivations. This can be accomplished by formulating a behavioral hypothesis using an *expected utility model*, a part of what is known as the *rational choice theory*. The expected utility model claims its heritage in the work of mathematicians von Neumann and Morgenstern. In their theory of mathematical expectations, von Neumann and Morgenstern wanted to define the logical process that will allow one to choose among uncertain alternatives. Suppose I have two choices: I can either buy a ticket for $3 for the chance of winning $10 in a toss of a coin or pay $4 for the chance of winning $30 in a roll of a dice. Now, since there are only two outcomes in a toss of a coin, my chance of choosing the right outcome is 50 percent. On the other hand, in the roll of a dice, my chances of being correct are one in six, or close to 17 percent. Following their methodology, we can express the problem as one of maximizing my expected net gains, defined as follows:

Expected net gains = (Probability of winning) x   (Reward) - (Probability of loosing)
    x   (Cost)

Thus, in the case of a coin toss, my probability of winning is .5, my reward is $10, the probability of incurring the cost (since there is no chance of a refund in case of a loss) is 1.0, and finally, the cost in this case is the price of the ticket. Therefore, by plugging those bits of information into the above formula, we find the following:

Option A. The coin toss: .5 x $10.00 - 1.00 x $3.00 = $ 2.00

Option B. The roll of a dice: .17 x $30.00 - 1.00 x $4.00 = $ 1.00

By the above calculation, my expected gain from a coin toss is $2.00, which is higher than that from the roll of a dice, $1.00. Therefore, if I am a rational individual, I will choose option A.

　　　The criticisms of the broad-based structural and sociopsychological theories have in recent years generated interest in the development of a theoretical microfoundation for understanding individual motivation to participate in acts of collective rebellion. The rational choice theory has found its application in the analysis of the motivations of individual participants as well as the actions of the leadership of a movement.

　　　In its simplest form the expected utility model states that an individual maximizes his utilities subject to his costs. Therefore, facing an uncertain outcome, an individual evaluates:

$$E(U) = p (R) - (1 - p) (C) \tag{3.1}$$

where

E(U)	= measure of expected utility
p	= probability of success
R	= reward of winning
C	= cost of loosing

　　　The early use of this model (especially empirically) in the explanation of political violence was generally confined to the analysis of action by the leadership. By using this microlevel expected net reward model, several scholars attributed the origin of aggregate conflict behavior to tactical maneuvers by the movement's leadership to force their opponents into a more acceptable position on a particular issue.[37] The distinctive underlying features of this approach are the existence of an issue on which the leadership wishes the opponents to yield position and, second, a "reasonable expectation" of winning the confrontation. This kind of game theoretic[38] "strategic" action has been widely used in the explanation of American race riots and protest movements.[39] Powell and Steifbold (1977), for example, found the tactical theory more useful is explaining hostile political behavior in a small Austrian community.

　　　Economist Gary Becker (1974) has used the rational choice method of calculation of net expected benefit [such as the one explained in equation (3.1)] to explain participation in criminal activities. However, the problem of trying to explain political activities by using the calculation of individual profit and loss stems from the fundamental difference between a political and a criminal activity: criminal activities are undertaken to enrich the individual perpetrator, whereas the participants in political activities aim at achieving rewards for the entire group.

The introduction of the notion of public good, however, generates a different set of problems when explanation for participation is sought based on the principle of individual profit maximization. The notion of economic rationality seems incompatible with the effort to provide public goods, as three logical inconsistencies arise: (1) there is no rational reason for anyone to join the rebellion; (2) there is no rational reason for anyone to initiate a collective action; and (3) once started, a rational individual's contribution should drop off as the goal of the collective action comes close to achievement.

Mancur Olson (1971) in his well-known work *The Logic of Collective Action* demonstrated that by using the calculation of purely individual profits and gains, one runs into the problem of a "free-rider." That is, rational individuals will not take part in a collective action, having realized that even if they do not participate, if and when the nonexcludable public good is obtained for the entire group, they will not be cut off from their share since the distribution of it is not contingent on participation. An excellent example of the dilemma of a free-rider can be found in the question as to whether to subscribe to the public broadcasting system (PBS). Since the survival of the station does not depend on my individual contribution, and at the same time, my receiving the programs is also not contingent on my subscription to PBS, the question is: Why should I ever contribute? Indeed, as Olson pointed out, if one follows the strict precepts of the economic rationality of individual profit maximization, there is no logical reason for anybody to contribute.[40]

Some economists have suggested that one way out of this problem is to assume a reciprocating individual, who somehow matches the actions of his fellow men according to some rule of contribution. However, the assumption of reciprocity, by taking us out of one conceptual problem, leads us into another one. Sen (1967) points out another logical problem associated with the attempt to explain collective actions based on some rule of reciprocity. Simply put, the problem arises because every rational individual, being ready to contribute to the common cause, waits for everybody else to contribute first, so that he can then match his neighbor's contribution. In such a case, therefore, despite an all-around willingness to obtain a public good, it will not be produced. Sen calls this the *assurance problem.*

The third logical problem of explaining collective action based on the principle of individual profit maximization arises from the fact that once started the rational calculation will dictate individuals *not* to contribute as the desired goal of providing the public good approaches fulfillment. This is because with everybody else contributing the rational *homoeconomicus* will realize the decreasing need for contribution. Thus, as a battle nears the end, each soldier must evaluate his own effort, since being too aggressive can mean being counted as the last casualy. Therefore, following this logic, no battle will ever be won, and all the public goods will remain underfunded (Samuelson, 1954, 1955).

The literature on the individual motivations for joining collective political actions has taken two distinct paths. The "private interest" or the "by-product" theories contend that in the final analysis the incentive to participate must come from the possibility of individual gains from such actions. The "public goods" approach, in contrast, posits that the participants are also motivated by the possibility of the provision of public goods.

The origin of the private interest or the by-product theory of collective political action originates with the work of Gordon Tullock. Simply put, Tullock (1971) in his study "The Paradox of Revolution," argues that if a public good, resulting from a successful revolution, is distributed equally to everybody in the group regardless of the level of participation, then the possibility of a reward from the public good cannot be considered to be an incentive to participate. Hence, Silver (1974) elaborates Tullock's position by stating:

Since the benefit to an individual from the consumption of an extra unit of a collective (or public) good is small relative to his cost of producing it [through revolution, for example], "selective incentives" are required to explain participation in production. A "selective incentive" is a non-collective benefit contingent upon the individual's participation in the production of a collective good [p. 63].

Instead, the deciding factor must be the private goods, such as loots of riots or high position in the revolutionary government. Therefore, to Tullock, the paradox of revolution is that contrary to popular myth revolutionary activities are not undertaken for the lofty goals of achieving for the collectivity - rather for the narrow cause of self-enrichment. A similar line of argument has been offered by Silver (1974), Ireland (1976), Roeder (1982).

More formally, their arguments can be explained as follows: Facing a potential revolutionary situation, an individual can either join the rebel forces or remain neutral. Their respective utility functions can be written as:

$$EU(R) = (p_n + p_r) U(Pg) + U(Re) - EU(C_r) \qquad (3.7)$$

$$EU(N) = (p_n) U(Pg) - EU(Cn) \qquad (3.8)$$

where:

EU(R)	= Expected utility from participating in rebellious collective action
EU(N)	= Expected utility from remaining neutral
p_n	= Probability of success of rebellion if the individual is neutral
p_r	= Probability of success of rebellion if the individual is active
U(Pg)	= Utility derived from public goods generated by the success of rebellion
U(Re)	= Utility from the entertainment value of participation in rebellion
U(Cr)	= Utility of cost of participation in the rebellion
U(Cn)	= Utility of cost of remaining neutral

Tullock and his followers hypothesize that an individual joins a rebel group because he derives utility both from the public goods resulting from the success of the rebellion and the entertainment value (the "fun") of participating in an act of rebellion. The individual is also concerned about the cost of participation, which may follow as a result of government crackdown. From the above formulations [equations (3.7) and (3.8)], it is further hypothesized that if an individual is not a leader (and is not suffering from delusion), his perception p_r is likely to be approximately zero, since the participation of an additional individual is going to have a marginal effect on a political movement. Also, Tullock argues that the term C_n, measuring peer pressure or sanction by the dissident group, is going to be minimal as the groups are not likely to have enough resources to force the fence sitters into becoming active participants. Finally, assuming the entertainment value to be minimal, the above set of equations is reduced to:

$$EU(R) = (p_n) \, U(Pg) \, - EU(Cr) \qquad (3.7a)$$

$$EU(N) = (p_n) \, U(Pg) \qquad (3.8a)$$

From the above specifications, it is obvious that if an average individual places any amount of negative utility on government sanctions or the possibility of bodily injury, loss of income, freedom of movement, and even life itself, his calculus will always point toward neutrality as the better course of action. Hence, given only public good as an incentive, a rational individual is going to opt to be a free-rider. The situation can change, argue the proponents of private interest theory, if and only if the potential revolutionaries are swayed by the possibility of private income. Therefore, Tullock (1971) asserts that the so-called pure-hearted revolutionaries are after all just as much motivated by self-interest as those they want to depose from power.

Although private interest theorists minimize their importance in the final decision-making calculus, Silver (1974, pp. 64-65) expanded Tullock's (1971) entertainment motive into a broader framework, that he calls the "psychic income." Silver includes in psychic income factors such as an "individual's sense of duty to class, country, demo-cratic institutions, the law, race, humanity, the rulers, God, or a revo-lutionary brotherhood as well as his taste for conspiracy, violence, and adventure." Therefore, following the Silver modification, we can see from equations (3.8) and (3.8a) that a person can logically join the cause of rebellion if $U(R_e) - EU(C_r) > 0$. That is, if the expected psychic income is greater than the expected punishment, an individual will join the dissident group.

The major problem with Tullock's (1971) explanation is that he fails to distinguish between a revolution, a term that is used to mean a radical change in the sociopolitical structure, and a coup d'état, which is often initiated with the narrow goals of self-interest of a small but powerful group. Thus, it is no wonder that he confuses the motives of the two groups of individuals. Tullock (1971) starts "The Paradox of Revolution" (p. 89) with the example of a "group of pure hearted revo-lutionaries" attempting to overthrow a vicious, corrupt, and inefficient government to replace it with one that is a "good, clean, beneficial, and efficient government."[41] To be certain, in the middle of the article, he gives examples of French and Russian revolutions and then concludes:

In most cases, after all, the new government is very much like the one before. Most overthrows are South American or African and simply change the higher level personnel. It is true that the new senior officials will tell everyone - and very likely believe it themselves - that they are giving better government than their predeces-sors. It is hard, however, to take these protestations very seriously.

One of the reasons it is hard to take these protestations seriously is that in most revolutions, the people who overthrow the existing government were high officials in that government before the revolution [p. 98].

From this quotation the confusion is pretty apparent. In fact, despite Tullock's assertion to the contrary, most of the revolutions that brought about a fundamental change in the sociopolitical system - such as the ones that took place in France, Russia, China, Cuba, and Iran - the new leadership did not come from the ranks of the old rulers. Thus, Dennis Mueller (1979) is absolutely correct in pointing out:

The economic theory of revolution based on the individual maximizing calculus seems much better suited to explaining coup d'état, where the number of actors is small, the odds calculable, and the stakes seemingly large, than it is at explaining "grass roots" revolution [p. 146].

In contrast to the private interest branch of theory of rational choice are those who emphasize the importance of public goods as a motivating force for participation in a collective action. Thus, Norman Frohlich and his associates (Frohlich and Oppenheimer, 1970, 1974; Frohlich, Hunt, and Oppenheimer, 1975), explicitly introduced the concept of public goods in the participation in collective political action as opposed to Becker's (1974) approach of individual gains and losses or Tullock and his followers' theory of the private goods of collective rebellion. These efforts correctly point out that the public goods aspect of participation distinguishes political activity from regular criminal actions for private gains. However, the inclusion of public goods in the individual decision-making calculus requires going beyond the assumption of individual profit maximization, and the direct or indirect recognition of ideology. A number of theoretical studies (Lupsha; 1969; Caplan, 1970; Feagin and Hahn, 1973; Sears and McConahey, 1973; Chamberlin, 1974; Mason, 1984) argued for the recognition of a public goods component as a way out of the logical problems posed by Olson (1971) and Sen (1967). Several empirical studies (Miller, Bole, and Haligan, 1976; Mason and Murtagh, 1985) attempted to show the role of the expectation of collective goods in riot participation in the United States. Subsequently, with the help of a sample survey of actual and potential participants in antisystemic protest activities, Muller and Opp (1986) have provided some direct empirical measurements of the ideological factor in the individual expected utility function.[42] Based on these advancements in knowledge, we may proceed to construct our own behavioral hypothesis for participation in the acts of collective violence.

NOTES

1. Dual economies are characterized by the side-by-side existence of a modern industrial sector with a preindustrial agricultural sector. For a detailed discussion, see Lewis (1968).

2. If despite the optimistic predictions the Western world did not become free of political violence, Hibbs (1976) offered convincing empirical proof that contrary to the expectations of Kerr et al. (1960) neither did industrial strike activities show any tendency to go down.
3. For examples of earlier attempts, see Reitzler (1943), Hoffer (1951), Turner and Killian (1957), and Goodspeed (1962).

4. For a similar kind of classification of theories, see Wood and Jackson (1982).

5. Ivo Feierabend, Rosalind Feirabend, and Betty Nesvold . (1969) define *systemic frustration* as follows:

Systemic frustration ... is defined ... in reference to three criteria: (1) as frustration interfering with the attainment and maintenance of social goals, aspirations and values: (2) as frustration simultaneously experienced by members of social aggregates and, hence, also social systems; and (3) as frustration of strain that is produced within the structures and processes of social systems. Systemic frustration is thus frustration that is experienced simultaneously and collectively within societies [p. 157].

6. Unlike Marx, Ricardo did not give credit to labor as the sole factor of production and argued for the contribution of land as well. Later on, this discrepancy generated an interesting debate by Joseph Stiegler ("Ricardo and the 93% Labor Theory of Value, 1958). For a comparison of the two theories of value, see Tucker, (1961).

7. Marx's views on the role of money have prompted a tongue in cheek analysis of him as a quantity theorist.

8. For an interesting attempt to test empirically the hypothesis of falling rate of profits, see Gilman (1958). For a theoretical defense, see Sweezy (1981); and for criticism, see Steedman (1977).

9. We should note here that, on the one hand, Marx suspected that foreign trade and colonization would postpone the final revolution in the capitalist economies; however, he welcomed the colonization of the feudal nations of Asia and Africa by the Western nations, as this was to introduce the dialectical force of societal evolution in these otherwise stagnant societies. See Avinery (1969).

10. It is indeed interesting to note the conceptual similarities between the Keynesian theory of growth and the ones derived from Marxian writings. See Mattick (1969).

11. Lenin praised this passage as "profoundly true" and "important utterances" however, he later took Kautsky to task for being a revisionist himself by assuming that the revolution would come about through spontaneous outbursts of rebellion by the working class without the leadership of the Communist party.
12. *Structural differentiation* is defined as where the social and political institutions are not tightly interconnected with each other and,

in turn, are not assumed to be inseparable from the basic value structure of a society. Thus, in a democratic society it is possible to criticize a political leader for his personal views or official policies without running the risk of offending the basic value structure of the society. So one may criticize or protest the actions of the president of the United States, as his person is not perceived to be inseparable from the statehood itself. However, a similar action in a less differentiated society, such as the Soviet Union or Iran, may be interpreted as an attack on the basic value structure of the society itself. Smelser and Lipset (1966) distinguish between a structurally differentiated and undifferentiated society with an example as follows:

One point of contrast between simple and complex societies is the degree of differentiation of social structures. In an ideal type simple society, little differentiation exists between a position in a kinship group (e.g., elderly men in a certain class), political authority (since elderly men in this clan hold power as a matter of custom), religious authority (since political and religious authorities are undifferentiated), and wealth (since tribute flow to this position). The social structures are undifferentiated, and an individual occupies a high or low position in all roles simultaneously. A differentiated social structure does not entitle a person membership in specific roles in the occupational structure; a position of importance in the religious hierarchy does not necessarily give an individual access to control of wealth. Thus, though some individuals may simultaneously receive great amounts of different rewards - wealth, power, prestige - these rewards are often segregated in a highly differentiated structure [p. 10].

13. For a definition of *legitimacy* see Lipset (1959). For an excellent discussion of legitimacy as a determinant of social movements, see Moore (1968); and for an empirical correlation between democracy and legitimacy, see Cutright (1968).

14. The "mutiny" was fueled by the widespread fear of forcible conversion into Christianity by the ruling British authorities. This fear was reinforced when the military issued a new kind of bullet whose cartridges had to be torn open by teeth before firing. Rumor spread that the cartridges were greased with fat from cows (sacred to the Hindus) and pigs (considered to be a forbidden food by Islamic law). This provided the immediate cause of the revolt (see Hibbert, 1978).

15. It should be noted, however, that democracy or a majority rule is no guarantee against tyranny by the majority. For example, in a three-person group composed of individuals A, B, and C, it can easily be seen that a distribution advantageous to both A and B but patently unfair to C can be forced upon C based on majority rule. See Arrow, (1951),Blair and Pollack (1979), and Sen (1984). However, in a society characterized by less differentiated groups and a highly

differentiated social structure, such a situation will be less likely to take place.

16. The possibility of a cooption and compromise can be as threatening to people with extreme positions as is the threat of physical violence. Recalling the voting paradox of Professor Arrow, one can understand the reasons behind the high frequency of attacks on the moderates by the extremists.

17. It may be noted here that although value-oriented movements draw more violent reaction from the authorities and consequently, have the potential of being bloody, the concept of value-oriented per se does not imply physical violence. For example, there can be religious movements or reform movements that pertain to the basic value structure of the society without there being much physical confrontation with the authorities. Smelser further argued that even value-oriented movements in structurally differentiated societies will be treated with more tolerance, as they will be seen as no threat to the system as such. However, keeping in mind that Smelser wrote his book before the confrontational days of the Vietnam War, later studies have shown that even the most structurally differentiated societies possess the power to interpret value-oriented movements seriously enough to consider them to be a threat to their own value system. See, Bacciocco (1974), Wood (1975).

18. On this point, we may note that we disagree with Wood and Jackson's (1982) argument that this division into two classes was tantamount to less differentiation in Smelser's terminology.

19. Plekhanov (1929), the "father of the Russian Revolution," explained Marx and Engel's position on the relationship between the "foundation" and the "superstructure" as follows:
   1. The state of the forces of production
   2. Economic relations conditioned by these forces
   3. The sociopolitical regime erected on a given economic foundation
   4. The psychology of man in society, determined in part directly by the whole sociopolitical regime erected upon the economic foundation
   5. Various ideologies reflecting this ideology

20. It may be argued that we have defined *social psychological theories* quite narrowly by making the term virtually synonymous with *frustration-aggression* hypotheses (for a broader definition of social psychological theories, see Wood and Jackson (1982). However, this categorization on our part can be justified by arguing that the other sets

of theories (such as, status inconsistency or emergent norm theory) are better classified under theories relating collective violence with social strain factors.

21. The linking of frustration resulting from the existing social conditions with mass revolts is of course nothing new and was emphasized by ancient Greek scholars such as Aristotle and Indian political philosophers such as Kautilya. See Welldon (1905) and R. Sama Shastri (1967).

22. For an extensive discussion, see Crosby (1976).

23. Note, however, that this is true *given* the level of distribution of wealth.

24. Runciman's formulation of relative "double deprivation" takes into account the individual's identity, both as his own self as well as a member of a group. We develop our model in the next chapter following similar reasoning.

25 For a classic discussion of social injustice and rebellion, see Moore (1966).

26. See Oberschall (1973); G. T. Marx and Wood (1974); and Wood and Gay (1978).

27. For an excellent discussion of different radical right movements, see Lipset and Raab (1970), also see Johnson (1966), and Lupsha (1971).

28. It may be worthwhile to note at this point that there is a significant body of literature where it has been argued that for some kinds of violence the existence of economic strain factors is not necessary and that violent collective action by the masses can take place owing to the influence of external factors. For example, MacCarthy and Zald (1971, 1973) and G. T. Marx (1974, 1982) discussed the role of "agents provocateurs" in generating conflict. Others have implied that power struggle and the strategic maneuvering by the leadership of the opposing parties are better predictors of many incidents of political violence than the existence of factors of deprivation (Schelling, 1960; Boulding, 1962; Ransford, 1968; Tilley, 1969; Axelrod, 1970; Muller, 1972; Riker and Ordeshook, 1972; Snyder and Tilly, 1972, 1974; Almond, Flanigan, and Mundt, 1973; Oberschall, 1973; J. Wilson, 1973; Shorter and Tilly, 1974; Blumer, 1978; Almond and Powell, 1977; Miller, Bolce, and Halligan, 1977; and Crosby, 1979). However, this line of argument does not explain how a significant

conflict situation can develop, where a large number of people are exposing themselves to various kinds of personal and economic risks, without taking resort to their basic calculation of relative advantage of so doing. While their points are well taken in the context of leadership of a movement, it is inconceivable that a significant conflict situation can exist without a widespread feeling of frustration among the participants.

29. Studies based on observation of behavior in situations of extreme and prolonged frustration, such as prisoners of war, inmates of prisons, and occupants of the German concentration camps, do indeed suggest that during such an abnormally high possibility of retribution and a low probability of success, aggression becomes almost the last behavioral response (see Wolfe, 1939; Kogan, 1950; Crawley, 1956; Steiner, 1969).

30. On this also see Gurr (1970, pp. 30-37).

31. In this context it may be interesting to note that in contrast to political violence, the industrial actions were found to be largely free of money illusion. This is because the unions, being more systematic in their leadership, while pressing for their wage demands, take the inflation rate into account (see Gupta and Venieris, 1981; Venieris and Gupta, 1985).

32.   Although this categorical assertion raised few eyebrows in the academic circle, several Marxist writers, such as Plekhanov (1950, p. 29), hailed de Tocqueville's work as "brilliant."

33. For empirical evidence disputing this hypothesis and an argument that the middle class has a higher average propensity to save, see Venieris and Gupta (1986).

34. Based on the work of Rummel (1963), H. Eckstein (1970), and Hibbs (1973), it is generally accepted that the incidents of mass political violence should be analyzed in terms of two dimensions. The first dimension is composed of more nonviolent political acts (such as, protest demonstrations), whereas second dimension consists of more violent acts, such as deaths from political violence. The first dimension of political violence has been called "anomic violence," or "collective protest" demonstrations, and the second dimension is usually called the "internal war." For a more detailed discussion, see chapter 7.

35. As a point of further qualification, we should point out that if, following Lipset, we define legitimacy as the acceptance of the justifi-

cation of the right to rule as morally right and binding on both the masses and the elites, then a society may be partially democratic but illegitimate (Weimar Republic after 1928, see Eyck, 1963) or legitimate but nondemocratic (perhaps Ethiopia during the 1940s and 50s, the present monarchy of Nepal, or even Franco's Spain, Tito's Yugoslavia, and many of the communist nations). The conception of legitimacy involves the knowledge of mass attitudes on the acceptance of the rule and the ruler as morally proper. Hence, for a true operationalization of the concept of legitimacy, we would require information about individual attitude derived through interviews or surveys. However, no such information is currently available, and therefore we will have to measure legitimacy based on surrogate variables. Since democracy is closely linked with the perception of regime legitimacy, we will accept democracy as a surrogate measure for legitimacy.

36. Quoted in Tilly (1974, p. 87). From this passage he took the name for his article, "The Chaos of the Living City." It may, however, be noted in this context that this notion of the very condition of urban life creating levels of poverty and confusion generating urban violence has come under attack. See Blauner (1972).

37. See, for example, Schelling (1960), Boulding (1962, 1966), Axelrod (1970), Riker and Ordeshook, (1972), Almond, Flanigan, and Mundt (1973), and Almond and Powell (1977).

38. Game theory, an offshoot of the mathematical expectaion theory, was developed to analyze strategies under uncertainty. The most commonly used game is called *prisoners dilemma.*

39. See, for example, J. Q. Wison (1961), Eisinger (1973), and Oberschall (1973).

40. For a criticism of the narrow definition of Olson's rationality, see Barry (1978).

41. Tullock (1971) also draws an inaccurate conclusion from Lenin's work on leadership.

42. We have discussed Muller and Opp's (1986) study in detail in the Appendix to Chapter 5.

Part Two:

The Individual: The Logic of Participatory Decision

4

The Behavioral Foundations of a Rational Participant in Collective Rebellion

As to the proposition that passion does not calculate, this, like most of these very general and oracular propositions is not true. ... I would not say that even a madman does not calculate. Passion calculates, more or less, in every man. ... [However] of all passions, the most given to calculation ... [is] the motive of pecuniary interest.

Jeremy Bentham[1]

Universal selfishness as *actuality* may well be false, but universal selfishness as a requirement of *rationality* is patently absurd.

Amartya K. Sen[2]

INTRODUCTION

Our perception of the world is molded through our identity. In traditional economics we have assumed that a man is perennially motivated by his own selfish interest. The criticism of this assumption has come from many quarters. Philosophers such as Herbert Marcuse (1969) and Jurgen Habermas (1970, 1988) have offered strident criticisms of this one dimensional brute of a man. However, the work of sociopsychologists like Erik Erikson (1968) points toward the hypothesis that a man's identity is composed of two different perceptions - the individual and the collective.

Through our activities we want to serve our individual identity, maximize economic goals, and endeavor to achieve social recognition. However, our total perception of ourselves is not composed entirely of this "me centric" individual orientation. We are also social animals, and an important part of our identity consists of who we are in relation to the collectivity. Therefore, besides considering ourselves as individuals and as members of our immediate families, we also seek our identity on the basis of nationality, race, religion, language, and ethnic and cultural heritage. We are happy to work not only for our own interest but also for the welfare of our collective identity.[3] The cognitive process that assigns value to the relative importance between the two identities is governed by acculturation (how different we feel from the rest of society), education, religion, family upbringing, other individual personality traits, and so on, which, in a catchall term, can be called *ideology*. The importance of this collective goal or ideology in inspiring people is indisputable. Throughout history men have achieved amazing feats in the name of ideology. Wars have been fought, physical barriers have been scaled, and no amount of sacrifice has been deemed excessive - all in the name of ideology and our collective identity.

Therefore, if we want to understand the motivations behind participation in the acts of political violence, we must take into account both self-interest and group interest. In so doing, we recognize the existence of dual motivations, where the participant is not only a self-seeker but also one who wants to strive for the common good. In this chapter we will attempt to formulate a descriptive behavioral model for participating that considers the presence of this dual motivations.

WHY MEN REBEL AND WHY THEY DO NOT: AN EXPECTED UTILITY APPROACH

Gurr (1970) called his seminal book *Why Men Rebel*. Gurr offers relative deprivation resulting from frustration as the answer to the rhetorical question he sets forth. However, as we have argued in the previous chapter, the problem of using frustration alone in explaining participation in collective rebellion arises from the fact that (1) the existence of frustration or relative deprivation does not always imply aggression, and (2) the broad definition of *frustration* fails to specify the kind of aggressive act in which an individual is likely to engage. This chapter is going to deal with the first aspect of the problem. The second question will be addressed in the following chapter.

Frustration does not always lead to aggressive behavior. If I am agitated by another person in a supermarket or at a ballpark, I will not automatically attempt to strike him. I may not hit him because:

- I am not sufficiently angry to warrant such reaction, and I may get by with a weaker response such as verbal expressions of disapproval
- It is against the law to assault somebody, and I may face legal action as a consequence
- The offending person is likely to retaliate, and he does seem a good deal bigger than me
- It is against my social norm, and I may invite social sanction by my act
- I am, on moral grounds, opposed to physical violence.

It is therefore clear that the step between frustration and aggression is not direct and is complicated by choice of action (with varying degrees of satisfaction or benefit), fear of retribution, and ideology. As a matter of fact, a rational actor will weigh his choice of action against its possible consequences in light of all these factors. So a model explaining participatory behavior in political actions must include some of these important factors.

Another problem with the frustration-aggression hypothesis in the explanation of political violence is that the frustration that one feels as an individual may not always translate to political violence. Instead it may lead to criminal activities, or an individual may engage in psychotic behavior ranging from homicidal to suicidal. But when will frustration lead to political violence? We argue that for the feeling of frustration to translate into a collective action, it must relate to the collective identity. Thus, if I am poor, or if I am unable to find suitable employment, I will be frustrated. However, in order for my frustration to prod me into participating in an act of political violence, I must feel that my poverty or unemployment is the result of my membership in a group. This group identity forms naturally if I become aware that my economic state is directly linked to my membership in a minority ethnic, religious, or linguistic group. Otherwise, the sense of belonging to a group can be formed by the deliberate actions of a political party or an opposition leader that, for example, demonstrate that my economic achievement is dependent on my membership in the deprived or have-not group. Thus, Marx and Lenin emphasized the need for the "correct leadership" by the Communist party to galvanize the group feelings of the proletariat. Without this leadership, Lenin insisted that the deprived masses will express their frustration either by taking part in spontaneous acts of anger or by engaging in "fruitless economism" (or job actions). In light of this discussion, let us proceed with the task of formulating a model for participating in an act of political violence.

THE MODEL

During the course of a day, an individual (we will call him "i") divides the available hours into work and leisure. In standard economic arguments, we treat an individual's preference for leisure as a residual left over from his option to work, dictated by the marginal productivity of his labor. Therefore, if the marginal productivity of labor goes up or down, marked by his ability to make more or less money per hour, he will adjust his work schedule. The number of hours an individual will opt to work depends on the relative strength of what are known as *income effect*, and *substitution effect*. If an individual is faced with the prospect of a pay cut, by income effect, he will try to maintain his old level of income by offering more hours of work. On the other hand, since the lowering of his income means a simultaneous lowering of his opportunity cost of leisure,[4] he will choose to withhold work and enjoy more leisure time.

During the working hours, an individual gets involved in various kinds of activities, the results of which generate utility to him. Since we have argued that through our actions we strive to satisfy the needs of our individual entity as well as the collective entity, these diverse activities can be broadly divided in two groups: one that aims at enhancing his own utility, and one that promotes the welfare of the group. We will call the first kind of activity (Yi) *economic* or *self-serving* (without any pejorative connotation), and the second one (Pg), we will call *political* or *group-serving*.   Therefore, the economic activities will produce goods and services for individual consumption. We can measure economic income broadly both in absolute as well as in relative terms. In absolute terms personal economic income will include wealth, well-being, enlightenment, skill, power, affection, rectitude, and deference.[5] This individual income can also be measured in relative terms, evaluated in relation to the actor's reference group.

Income generated from political activities, on the other hand, consists of goods and services for collective consumption such as an end to discrimination, a successful revolution that transforms an entire social and economic structure, the toppling of the present regime (perceived as a desirable good), and so on. These are goods of collective consumption. However, they do contain a strong component of expected personal economic wellbeing. Thus, if discrimination ends, it will be a public good for those who are presently being discriminated against in the sense that the changed condition will benefit everybody who is suffering from discrimination. At the same time, it will create individual opportunities for these people to better their own economic lots. Thus, the end of apartheid in South Africa may mean that blacks in general can look forward to a better economic condition. The expectations of private goods resulting from a collective group can of course be different, based on the diverse abilities of an individual. Thus, the end of overt discrimination in the United States effectively divided the black community into two groups: those who could take advantage of the changed situation because of their education, talent, or other factors of opportunity, and those who were less ready and hence were left behind. Also, the attainment of a political good can bring good fortune to the individuals directly associated with the effort to bring it about .

Therefore, let us assume that an individual maximizes his utilities generated from the fruits of these two activities, which can be written as:

Maximize $U_i = U (Y_i, P_g)$ (4.1)

An individual spends his total time (T) by being engaged in either economic activity (Te) or political activity (Tp). We will further assume that for the purposes of conceptual clarity, the economic goods are created exclusively by being engaged in economic activities; the political activities, on the other hand, are solely responsible for the generation of political goods.[6] Also, for the sake of simplicity, we may for the moment assume that the decision to participate in the two activities is undertaken ceteris paribus of the decision to consume leisure. On the face of it, it seems like a drastic assumption. But under the assumption of ceteris paribus, one is expected to divide up his time between economic and political activities, precluding the possibilities that one may decide (1) to consume more of both the activities by reducing leisure, (2) to consume less leisure but work at the two activities at a varying rate, or (3) to reduce total working hours and have more leisure. Even though these are interesting possibilities to ponder, for our analysis the relaxation of assumption of constant leisure will not add anything to the analytical power of the model, since by our marginalist hypothesis an individual will equate each activity (and inactivity) with its price ratio.[7]

The individual economic income (Yi) is easily defined to include factors of personal gain. The political income (Pg), on the other hand, has five specific components: Nonexcludable and excludable goods resulting from the attainment of collective goods, net reward for nonparticipation; loots, or personal income from taking part in political actions; the cost of participation; and an intangible, idiosyncratic, personal "fun factor of rebellion."[8]

We will argue that the actor perceives certain collective political goods to flow out of political activities. He will receive his share of the collective good either as a result of the success of the movement regardless of his effort or as a result of his own individual effort. Thus, for example, as a member of the victorious group in a political struggle, one becomes entitled to the new privileges as new opportunities open up owing to an end to discrimination or the gaining of political independence. This benefit is shared by all the members of the group equally. This is the non-excludable aspect of collective good, which we will call Yg^m, or nonexcludable public goods generated by a political movement. However, collective goods can also generate excludable benefits, the right to be "first among equals." That is, we may also expect to receive special positions, power, or privilege in the new political order. However, this aspect of collective good must be generated by the individual's own effort, which we will call active participation, or participation in a particular act of collective rebellion, i.e., a riot, political demonstration, and the like. This component will be expressed as Yg^a.[9]   This division between excludable and nonexcludable public goods implicitly assumes that the participants of political action are motivated by the prospect of achieving excludable collective goods. This distinction is made to accommodate the Olson -Tullock factor of irrationality of collective action. Indeed, if the equal shares of the spoils of a political movement are assured, then logically it cannot be the motivating factor for participation. For the logic of participation, we must look elsewhere.

The individual decision to join the forces of rebellion for the provision of public goods also depends on what we may call the *net reward of nonparticipation.* We may hypothesize this component to be the reward for sitting on the fence - e.g., government cash reward, special privileges, or position in the present administration - as a part of a pacification program, *minus* the cost of non-participation - e.g., peer pressure or threats from the rebel group. This net reward component will be written as Rn.

We should recognize that often an individual takes part in an act of political defiance with an eye on the expected material benefit, which can vary from a position of power in the next administration to the spoils of "anomie" such as the loot from a riot (L). However, along with the reward, taking part in a rebellion against an established political order also promises some kind of cost to the individual if he is apprehended. This cost factor may include the loss of freedom (prison terms) or income, bodily injury, or even death. These costs factors are included in the term C.

Finally, we come to the intangible benefit of taking part in a political action, what Banfield (1968) and Tullock (1971) called the "fun factor." In economic literature, this is also defined as Joseph Stigler's (1971) "consumption motive" or the "entertainment" aspect of participation. Although empirical evidence (Muller and Opp, 1986) suggests that the contribution of this fun factor to the overall level of participation is trivial, we have introduced this argument to cover the random taste factor for individual participants. The term (ζ) will depict this personal factor of political participation.

The participatory decisions in political actions are complicated by the existence of two external (determined by actions of person[s] other than the individual himself) factors. These are factors of ideology (Φ) and the probability of getting away with the acts of political defiance (p). The presence of ideology acts as a shift factor, which helps magnify the extent of benefits resulting from a political movement (Yg^m and Yg^a). Also, as Silver (1974) has argued, on an apriori basis we may assume that ideology accentuates the personal factor of participation (ζ). People also often participate because of some ideological factor that makes the very act of participation a utility-producing good. Thus, ideology heightens the feeling that belonging to the select group of protesters can itself produce satisfaction and pride in the participant.[10]

The second exogenous factor is the actor's subjective estimation of his probability of *not* being apprehended while taking part in the acts of violence against the established regime. This factor is highly dependent on the capability and willingness of the regime to apprehend the offenders. This factor introduces the element of uncertainty into the decision-making calculus. Notice that this element of chance will affect an individual's expected utility of the attainment of excludable benefits from public goods, loots of riot, and the cost of participation (punishment). It will not affect the other two arguments, the nonexcludable benefits and the personal factors.

Therefore, in sum, an individual maximizes his total utility derived from the two kinds of goods by allocating his time between them. His allocation of time is of course constrained by the total available time. We will call the total time T, and the time spent on economic and political activity, Te and Tp. Since Te and Tp exhaust the total time available, we can write the basic behavior as:

Max. $U(Y_i, P_g)$ subject to $T = T_e + T_p$

By combining the above arguments, the expected utility function is specified as follows:

$$E(U) = U(-Y_i) + U[\Phi \cdot (Y_g^m + p \cdot Y_g^a)] - U(R_n) + p \cdot U(L)$$
$$- (1 - p) \cdot U(C) + U(\Phi \cdot \zeta) \tag{4.2}$$

where:

$U(Y_i)$	= utility of economic goods from nonpolitical activities
Φ	= exogenously determined ideological shift factor
$U(R_n)$	= perceived lumpsum net reward of nonparticipation
$U(Y_g^m)$	= perceived benefit to an individual from the creation of excludable and nonexcludable public goods for his group, by the success of the movement
$U(Y_g^a)$	= utility obtained from taking part in a particular antisystemic act with the primary motivation of producing public goods for the group
$U(L)$	= perceived benefit of obtaining specific private goods (loot) during participation in an act of rebellion
$U(C)$	= perceived cost of participation in an act of collective rebellion, once apprehended
p	= the perceived subjective probability of not getting apprehended in an act of violence
ζ	= idiosyncratic personal traits or the "fun factor"

Before we get involved in a detailed explanation of our behavioral formulation, we should note that the probability of not getting caught (p) is attached only in front of the factors of excludable public goods (Y_g^a), loot (L), and the cost of taking part in a political action (C). The factor of economic income is a legal activity, and therefore (p) is irrelevant toward its consideration. The nonexcludable public good (Y_g^m) and the ideologically affected fun factor $(\Phi \cdot \zeta)$ are not dependent on the probability factor since a fence sitter can also receive a nonexcludable public good if and when it is available. The net reward factor is assumed to be a matter of certainty. The fun factor is based on exogenously determined personal traits and therefore is independent of the probability of being apprehended. On the other hand, an individual is more apt to evaluate his probability of getting caught before taking part in a political action to achieve excludable public goods as well as loots from the spoils.

Let us now investigate the implication of this function on the allocation of time between efforts to achieve economic good and political good. The factors that encourage an individual to take part in a political action are hypothesized to have a positive effect on the expected utility function. On the other hand, the ones generating negative impact will tend to dissuade people from being active participants in a rebellion. The expected utility function presents the sum total of factors producing positive and negative utility to an individual. If this sum is positive (> 0), the individual will participate in an act of rebellion. If, on the other hand, it is negative (< 0), we can expect him to remain passive. Let us now discuss the impact of individual terms on an individual's participatory decision-making process.

The first term in equation (4.2) is Y_i, or the economic or individual income that a person is expected to receive under the present sociopolitical condition. Since an individual allocates his time between producing economic and political income, the inclusion of this term implies several important factors. Thus, if the marginal utility that one derives from economic goods is greater than that from political goods, the actor will be less inclined to join a rebellion. This is because the opportunity cost of lost economic income will be greater than the utility that the acquiring of the additional utility of political good will provide. The concept of opportunity cost of income has always been an important determining factor in the analysis of participation in the acts of political violence. Marx, for example, exhorted the proletariat to recognize that they had nothing more to lose than their chains.

Therefore, if Y_i increases, it will have a dampening effect on the level of political participation. However, one should also be quick to recognize that the lowering of the opportunity cost of economic income does not necessarily point to an increased participation in political activities. This is because an actor may experience conflicting psychological forces, analogous to an income and substitution effect. The income effect implies that when income goes down, people tend to maintain their old level of income, and as a result, they will tend to work harder than before. On the other hand, a reduction in income causes the opportunity cost of income to go down, which can tempt one to reduce his work effort. Similarly, in the case of participation in political violence, it has been found that contrary to the Marxian notion of "class hatred" the existence of poverty does not necessarily imply the possibility of a revolution. In fact, studies have noted that the poor peasants and even the urban poor, for example, are the most difficult recruits for the cause of a revolution.[11] This is because with poverty comes the need to devote most of the day's time to earn a living for survival. Therefore, the relative opportunity cost of lost income is extremely high for these groups of people. On the basis of the above discussion, we will be safe to hypothesize that in the aggregate the impact of an increase in economic well-being will have a dampening effect on the level of participation. On the other hand, at the individual level, the outcome of a decrease in income on the participatory decision will be ambiguous, as it will depend on the relative strengths of income and substitution effect.

Before getting into an explanation of the political goods in our expected utility function, we should note that in contrast with past literature, we have distinguished the perceived benefits of participation in an *act* of collective rebellion from those emanating from a *movement*. We define a movement as a sum total of all the similarly motivated individual acts of rebellion. This conceptual distinction is important because although an individual may feel that the possible success of a movement may change his personal or group well-being, his own participation may have little bearing on the movement, except in the case of a well-recognized leader. Consequently, his decision to join a particular act of rebellion may not be contingent on the success of the movement.

The perception of an increase in the excludable collective good will provide an incentive for people to take part in political actions. Therefore, we sum up our hypothesis that an increase or decrease in nonexcludable collective goods (Yg^m) will have no effect on the level of participation, whereas the relationship between the perception of excludable public good (Yg^a) and the propensity to participate in political action is likely to be positive.

Turning to the other variables in our expected utility model, it is fairly obvious that there are costs and benefits attached not only to the act of participation but also to nonparticipation. The net benefit of nonparticipation in an act of collective rebellion is expressed by the term Rn, which has two components: $Rn = Rp - Cn$. The benefits of nonparticipation can include rewards from a government pacification program or even a position of power in the present administration. We will denote this aspect by the term Rp. The costs of nonparticipation, on the other hand, are different kinds of "peer pressure," ranging from social ostracism to outright threats from the rebel group. Therefore, we may note that participation in political activities is inversely related to the value of Rn. That is, if the benefit of nonparticipation (Rn) is positive, the actor will be inclined not to participate. The importance of a norm such as peer pressure has been highlighted by Axelrod (1986). It has similarly been demonstrated to have significant explanatory power in the recruitment process of the peasants in the rebel forces in Vietnam (Popkin, 1979).

The material or purely private costs and benefits of participating in an act of rebellion are similar to a crime model such as the one developed by economist, Gary Becker (1974). The reward in this case is the perceived gains from expected loot $[p \cdot (L)]$. The cost is the dissatisfaction of being punished if apprehended $[(1 - p) \cdot C]$. The impact of an increase in the possibility of apprehension $(1 - p)$ will add to the risk factor and as such will diminish an individual's utility of political goods.

Finally, we hypothesize that the effect of an increase in ideology (the desire for political goods) and the personal factor ($\Phi \cdot \zeta$), by definition, will increase an individual's desire to participate in acts of political dissidence. There may be somewhat of a difference of opinion in the relative strength of this fun factor in motivating an individual to take part in a political action. Thus, contrary to the assertions of Banfield (1968) and Tullock (1971), in their sample survey of antinuclear power protesters in West Germany, Muller and Opp (1986) found it to be insignificant. One way of resolving this contradiction is to note that there is a qualitative difference between the participants in a protest demonstration, which is an expression of pure political view, and the rioters, many of whom take part because of the prevailing condition of anomie. The corroboration of this view may be found in some of the most interesting riot studies conducted by Manus Midlarsky (1972). Midlarsky found statistically significant results demonstrating the "contagion" effect of riot participation, or the fact that riot behavior is actually imitated as the smaller cities tend to duplicate the riot conditions of the larger cities.

We have mentioned before that our formulation avoids the problem of free ridership. Let us present our arguments more formally. Our behavioral formulation is free of the free-ridership problem because of two factors. First, the presence of strong ideology can inflate one's expectation of excludable public goods. Also, to those who are more susceptible, ideology can heighten their fun factor, regardless of the calculation of costs and benefits.

Second, Mason (1984) has argued that the omnipresence of free ridership may not be assumed, for the following reasons. He argues that some form of discrimination (such as in law enforcement and in judicial decision making) can be viewed as a normal nonexcludable public good that can rationally motivate individuals to participate in a riot. This occurs because an increase in group size will not reduce the amount of public goods available for each individual member. Therefore, despite the fact that the relative contribution of each individual will continue to decline as the group gets larger, the motivation for joining the group and contributing to it will come from the fact that the perceived benefit for the individual will not go down with the increase in the size of the group.[12] So contrary to the proposition of free ridership, contributions to the collective cause can come from the ideologically motivated, the less-than "pure hearted" revolutionaries (to borrow Tullock's [1971] term) who expect excludable public goods, and from those who contribute because the marginal utility of the nonexcludable collective good does not diminish with the increase in the group size.

In summary, our generalized expected utility framework has five distinct conceptual components: (1) the opportunity of income under the present sociopolitical order, (2) the utility (based upon ideological perception [Φ]) from excludable and nonexcludable public goods produced by a movement (Yg^m) as well as by an act (Yg^a), (3) the net reward of nonparticipation (Rn), and (4) the expected material costs and benefits of participating in an act of collective violence [$p \cdot (L)$ - $(1 - p) \cdot (C)$] and (v) the ideologically influenced personal trait, or the fun factor ($\Phi \cdot \zeta$). Having specified the relative impact of the five factors on the participatory decision, we can hypothesize that a potential participant maximizes his expected utility, subject to his time constraint, as shown in equation (4.2).

From the above behavioral function, we can hypothesize that an individual maximizes his total utility by engaging in activities producing private and public goods. However, in the process he faces the time constraint imposed by its finite availability. We can analyze the choices open to an individual by using the standard tools of microeconomics. This has been depicted in Figure 4.1 (also, for a mathematical explanation, see the Appendix to Chapter 4). In this Figure, the vertical axis measures utility producing political goods, and the horizontal axis measures economic goods. Let us assume that an individual "i" can produce C_0 amount of political goods if he were to devote his entire working time to it. On the other hand, he can produce E_0 amount of economic goods by pursuing his private economic goals. The line C_0E_0 can be called the *budget line*, as the individual is confronted with his finite time period. Any point along this line will measure the effort that he will be willing to devote to the production of the two goods.[13]

How an individual will choose the proper mix of the two goods will depend on two factors: (1) his perception of the relative utility of the two goods, dictated by the extent of ideological orientation, and (2) his ability to convert time in producing either of the two goods by devoting an additional unit of time. In other words, the indifference curves depict the individual preference, whereas the budget constraint demonstrates the impact of the physical environment on his choice of mix for the two goods. Let us analyze the impact of these two factors on an individual's allocative decision.

In Figure 4.1, the curve IC is the standard indifference curve, indicating the various combinations of the two among which the individual is indifferent. As can be seen from the Figure equilibrium will be reached at the point where the indifference curve IC is tangential to the budget curve, C_0E_0. At that point, P_0 amount of time will be devoted to the production of political goods, and Y_0 amount of time will be spent on the achievement of economic goods.

However, this point of equilibrium will change if there is a change in the actor's ideological position. Since we have defined ideology as the preference for public goods, if - owing to the effect of a successful leader - an individual becomes ideologically inclined, he will tend to prefer public goods over private goods. History is replete with examples of leaders like Lenin, Gandhi, Mao, or the Ayatollah Khomeini, who have ideologically inspired people to join political

Figure   4.1

Optimal Allocation of Time and the Impact of Ideological Shift

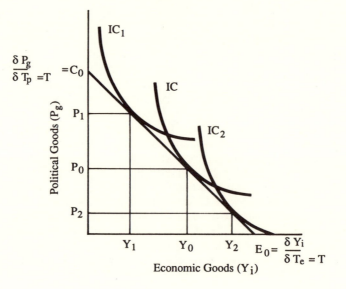

movements, often ignoring their own individual economic welfare. Therefore, the followers of these leaders have shown a strong preference for public goods. The impact of an increase in the ideological fervor can be shown by a shift in the indifference curve to the left (from IC to IC_1), whereby an individual will be inclined to spend more time in producing political goods. In contrast, a decline in political ideology will cause a rightward shift in the indifference map (from IC to IC_2), and this shift will be translated in terms of a lowering of demand for political goods.

Figure   4.2

Impact of a Change in the Relative Cost of Goods

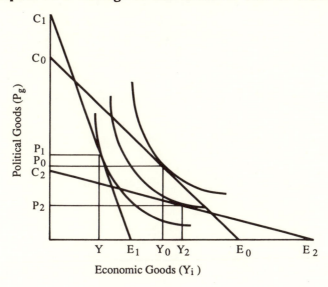

The ability of an individual to produce either of the two goods by devoting an additional unit of time involves several economic and political factors. Thus, in a society that offers a great deal of social and economic mobility, the capability of an individual to produce private economic goods is considerable. Therefore, an individual living in such a society will find it more profitable to spend his time in the pursuit of economic goods. If, on the other hand, his ability to produce economic goods is restricted by the sociopolitical system, by imposing discrimination based on factors beyond the control of the individual, such as ascriptive factors like race, religion, language, or ethnicity, his capability to produce economic goods will be severely diminished. In such a case, he will be tempted to maximize his utility by attempting to produce political goods.

The perceived capacity to produce political goods will of course depend upon a combination of Neil Smelser's (1963) conditions: structural conduciveness, or the ability of an individual to engage in acts of political dissent without evoking actions by the authorities; effectiveness of social control, the capacity of the authority to impose negative sanctions on the participants of rebellion; and mobilization. Within a political system offering a high degree of structural conduciveness, an individual is likely to engage in political activities more readily than in an authoritarian one. Similarly, if an authoritarian regime possesses a great deal of capacity to inflict cost on the dissidents, then there will be less of an opportunity to produce political goods. Therefore, the democratic forms of government will be characterized by a higher level of dissident activities than an authoritarian one.

We may attempt to demonstrate the impact of a change in the environmental conduciveness in producing either of the two goods. This situation has been demonstrated with the aid of Figure 4.2. In this Figure, we have shown two scenarios, one in which political goods become cheaper to produce in relation to the economic goods, and the other where economic goods are produced more easily than political goods.

Let us start with the initial position of equilibrium between the two goods in Figure 4.1, where our subject was engaged in producing P_0 amount of political goods and Y_0 amount of economic goods. Let us assume that in this case the level of ideological orientation remains unchanged.

A change in the perception of an individual regarding his ability to convert an additional unit of time into economic or political goods can take place if his economic opportunities become limited or his political opportunities becomes enhanced. The existence of unemployment or discrimination in the workplace can impose severe restrictions on an individual's economic capabilities. Facing this constraint on his economic ability, the actor may find in relative terms a lowering of opportunity cost for engaging in political activities. This change in the relative cost of the two goods can also take place if the costs of engaging in political activities go down, which can happen if the capacity to deliver retribution by the authorities weakens or is perceived by the actors to be so. Then the expected capacity to produce public goods will go up, and so will political participation. This is typical of a situation when the authorities lose control owing to the gathering momentum of a revolutionary movement. Reasoning that they can be more effective in producing political goods, the potential participants show enhanced eagerness to engage in acts of collective rebellion. In Smelser's (1963) analysis, this has been shown under the conditions of mobilization of opposition and ineffective social control. There can be other situations where suddenly an individual may find his political opportunities enlarged. This can take place after the end of a colonial rule or following the introduction of democracy after a long period of military or other kinds of despotic rules. This sudden change in structural conduciveness causes people to reevaluate the marginal productivity of time in producing the two goods. With political reform and freedom, economic opportunity for the general masses seldom changes over night. What does change is the cost of engaging in political activities and the expectation that their involvement in political activities will be able to provide the participants with rewards. Therefore, it is small wonder that de Tocqueville noted that the introduction of freedom almost always seems like an introduction to chaos and political anomie. Many countries coming out of colonial rule faced a prolonged period of explosion of political activism. Countries under long spells of dictatorial rule, such as Spain, Portugal, and Bangladesh, to name but a few, faced similar condition. Even the Soviet Union is facing a welling of political emotions in the wake of *glasnost*.[14]

Going back to the Figure 4.2, the relative lowering of the price of political goods is shown as a leftward shift in the budget line to the new position, P_1E_1. As a result of this shift, an individual is apt to alter his allocation of time to produce less economic goods (Y_1) and more political goods (P_1).

The reverse is of course expected when economic opportunities enlarge relative to political opportunity. If economic opportunities increase steadily, an average individual develops a greater stake in the economic system, as he tends to share in the all-around prosperity. Therefore, with the rising opportunity costs of participating in political activities, the potential participants will be largely discouraged. Even those disenchanted ones at the fringes of the economy will find it impossible to develop a large enough support base to mount an effective opposition, that has a reasonable chance of success. Thus, it is no surprise that despite the ample existence of social injustices during the rule of President Park Chung Hee - or Chile, during the early years of Augusto Pinochet's reign - South Korea, having enjoyed a significant level of steadily rising economic prosperity, showed little appetite for political radicalism. However, with the rate of economic growth slowing down, the nation has increasingly started showing signs of stress and tension (Chalmers Johnson, 1988).

The relative opportunity cost of political participation can increase as a part of a different scenario. Suppose the cost of procuring public goods has suddenly gone up. This increase in price can be the result of a government's get-tough policy, such as the enactment of a new law or the declaration of national emergency or the suspension of fundamental rights - ones that have been undertaken by many governments under political siege - or the deployment of the military to combat growing political unrest. Facing this increased level of cost, ceteris paribus, an individual will restrict his consumption of public goods, as the budget constraint will move clockwise to the right of the original line. This will induce the individual to consume Y_2 amount of economic goods and P_2 amount of political goods. For a more formal presentation of these points, see Appendix to Chapter 4.

EXPECTED UTILITY MODEL AND INDIVIDUAL
BEHAVIORAL PROFILES

The sight of looting, burning, and violent chanting by black rioters during the 1960s shook up the American psyche in a way it had not been done before. As a result a great deal of research effort was directed at uncovering the "profile of a typical rioter." In the midst of all the confusion, it was as if the nation were trying to meet its challenger. The early efforts at discerning the typical rioter essentially took two distinct paths. One conveniently coincided with the popular impression, which is reflected in what is known as the *social marginality hypothesis*, and the other with the less pathological image of the "new urban black."

The social marginality hypothesis contends that the typical rioter belongs to the fringes of the society. The typical group of these atypical individuals consists of the criminal elements, the chronically unemployed, and otherwise the dredges of the ghetto society, for whom rioting was no more than the anomic expression of the frustration inherent in their alienated life situation resulting from individual shortcomings or circumstances. This view was squarely reflected in the 1965 McCone Commission. Similarly, Edwin Banfield (1968) in his controversial study portrayed the rioters as an anarchic group of alienated black youths who took part for "fun and profit."

Without taking the obvious moral and political overtone of this social marginality hypothesis, several other empirical studies attempted to draw a correlation between participation in riots and the level of frustration, measured in terms of actual achievements in income, education, housing, and job status.   Thus, Downes (1968, 1970) argued that riot participation should have a positive correlation with unemployment, and a negative correlation with income. Ford and Moore (1970) explained the motivation to participate as resulting from lower-quality housing and frustration felt as a result of a white/black income differential, which was considered as a measure of actual discrimination in the job market. In a separate study, similar results were obtained by Morgan and Clarke (1970), where their hypothesis with regard to the extent of deprivation felt by an individual, measured in terms of consumption of housing quality, job status, and education, correlated positively with the actual level of participation.

However, confusion reigned as studies came up with conflicting findings. Sometimes different researchers provided different empirical evidences. Other times, within the same study contradictory results appeared, with some variables pointing toward corroborating the frustration-aggression hypothesis, and other variables providing inconclusive or even contrary results. For instance, A. Miller, Bole, and Halligan (1977) questioned the validity of the relative deprivation theory by showing little empirical evidence of a growing level of systemic frustration (again measured in terms of white/black income differential) among the blacks prior to the riots. In fact, Lieske (1978,

1979) found a *negative* relationship between income differential and riot participation. Similarly, Morgan and Clarke (1970) demonstrated that while, as expected, housing inequality was positively correlated with riot participation, increasing job equality had a negative statistical association with severity of rioting. Caplan and Paige (1968), in a study of riot participation in Newark and Detroit, failed to find statistically significant difference in the economic characteristics between the participants and the nonparticipants. Similarly, when Spilerman (1970, 1971) controlled for black population size and region (South and nonSouth), he found that none of the community characteristic variables, such as income, unemployment, education, or housing, were significantly associated with riot frequency. Therefore, he concluded that the riots took place because of a prevailing feeling of frustration among the black population that can not be accounted for by the aggregate characteristic variables.

Much of the diversity of these above mentioned studies results from a ubiquitous problem in social science: namely, researchers using widely varying measures of relevant variables and employing different methodologies. However, the problem still remains as the overall tenor of these studies points to a less than stable profile of a riot participant. Even the Kerner (1968) report provided us with the profile of an average rioter with some characteristics falling in the category of the social marginality hypothesis and others clearly not. Thus, they reported:

The typical rioter in the summer of 1967 was a Negro, unmarried male between the ages of 15 to 24. He was not a migrant. He was in many ways very different from the stereotype. He was born in the state and was a lifelong resident of the city in which the riot took place. Economically his position was about the same as his Negro neighbors who did not actively participate in the riot.

Although he had not, usually, graduated from high school, he was somewhat better educated than the average inner-city Negro, having at least attended high school for a time.

Nevertheless, he was more likely to be working in a menial or low status job as an unskilled laborer. If he was employed, he was not working full time and his employment was frequently interrupted by periods of unemployment.

He feels strongly that he deserves a better job and that he is barred from achieving it, not because of lack of training, ability, but because of discrimination by employers.

He rejects the white bigot's stereotype of the Negro as ignorant and shiftless. He takes great pride in his race and believes that in some respects Negroes are superior to whites. He is extremely hostile to whites, but his hostility is more apt to be a product of social and economic class than of race; he is almost equally hostile toward middle class Negroes.
He is substantially better informed about politics than Negroes who were not involved in riots. He is more likely to be actively engaged in civil rights efforts,

but is extremely distrustful of the political system and of political leaders [p. 73 - 4].

The ambiguity and confusion regarding the "typical" profile of a rioter caused a new group of studies to crop up. Thus, studies like Caplan (1970), Feagin and Hahn (1973), Fogelson (1971), Geshwender (1968), Lupsha (1969), and Sears and McConahey (1973) provided an alternate image of a more ideologically inclined participant who saw his participation as more of a political act than as one of anomic expressions of frustration and anger. Their description of the "new urban black" (Sear and McConahey), or the new "ghetto man" (Caplan) reflected more accurately the profile provided by the Kerner Commission.

However, we would argue on the basis of deductive reasoning that it may be less than useful to try to look for a one typical participant in the causes of rebellion and more fruitful to recognize that these collective actions are carried out by various people with diverse motivations. We can classify people's participatory behavior on the basis of their dominant motivation.

The expected utility model, as explained by equation (4.2), can be used to develop representative behavioral profiles. We may point out here that it is indeed difficult to measure empirically individual expected utility functions, and we will postpone our discussion on the problems of measurements and estimation until the next chapter. However, it may suffice to note here that we can obtain corroborating evidence of behavior corresponding to the postulated utility functions from several secondary sources, such as the Kerner Commission report (see Kerner, 1968). Also, the Rand Corporation has undertaken several indepth studies of the individual participants in antisystemic political violence around the world (see for example, Kellen, 1979; Cordes, Jenkins, Kellen, 1985). We have summarized the individual profiles in the following Figure 4.3.

In the most obvious case, the benefits of taking part in an act of rebellion is greater than the cost of such an action, the individual will be a *participant*. That is, if

$$U[\Phi \cdot (Yg^m + Yg^a) + p \cdot L + \Phi \cdot \zeta] > U[(Yi) + Rn + (1-p) \cdot C] \qquad (4.3)$$

then the person is likely to take part in the act of rebellion since he obtains a net gain in his expected utility. Notice that the left-hand side of the equation (4.3) is composed of ideologically filtered perceptions of utilities resulting from a social change, the lure of private pecuniary benefit (loot), and the fun factor. We may call these the *pull factors* of participation. The right-hand side, on the other hand, consists of the prospects of loss of personal income and the factors of coercion (C) and cooption (Rn). These are the *push factors* of participation.

Figure   4.3

Classification of Individual Behavioral Profile

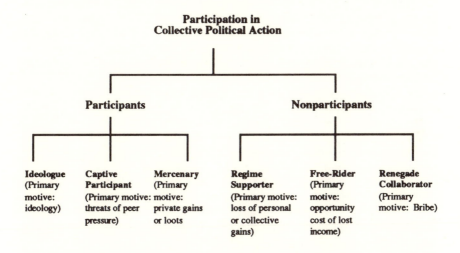

Within the group of participants, if the ideological component (Φ) is predominant, he is likely to be an *initiator* or an *instigator*. This is because this individual will mainly respond to the expected utility derived from unobservable, intangible benefits, with less regard for the low initial probability of success of the movement.   The logical problem of initiation of a collective action has always behooved the economists since in the beginning the probability of success of a movement is more in question. Therefore, to a rational individual the question of participation should always remain paramount. Sen (1967) called this the "assurance" problem, where all the participants, despite being convinced of the necessity of the provision of a particular public good, wait for the others to initiate, so that they can then reciprocate. Therefore, with everyone waiting for everyone else to initiate, a movement, despite widespread support, may not to start at all. In fact, the way out of this prisoner's dilemma lies in finding the mouse who is willing to volunteer to tie a bell around the neck of the cat; this mouse is likely to be the most ideologically inclined one.[15]   In fact, studies on actual riot behavior, such as the Kerner report (Kerner, 1968), shows that the beginning of a riot is typically characterized by the participation of individuals with a relatively high degree of ideological commitment. It is particularly exemplified by the fact that the beginning of the riots are often characterized by destruction of properties with high symbolic value, such as the "symbols of the white establishment." It is not until such actions have proceeded to the point that looting becomes potentially profitable that symbolic property destruction begins to be replaced with outright looting.

Among the group of participants whose primary motivation for participation is not based on an ideological perception can be either the *captive collaborators*, or the *mercenaries* (or the *criminal elements*) . If we find some participants who are not convinced that the movement is going to benefit them individually or their group, yet, who still take part because of the threat from the rebel force, we will call them the *captive collaborators*.[16] In terms of our expected utility equation, for these individuals the term Rn is positive and is greater than all the other cost factors taken together.

Within the group of participants, especially in the riots, we always find people who are in the act in the expectation of material gains for themselves alone, with no ideological inclination (Φ=0), and extremely low opportunity cost of lost income ($Yi \simeq 0$). This group of people's expected utility function is really the truncated version of our equation (4.2), and consists solely of the material cost benefit part of participation in a political action. That is, this group of individuals will participate if and only if $[p \cdot (L) > (1-p) \cdot C]$. The behavioral pattern of these people will be approximated by the criminal models developed by scholars such as Gary Becker (1974). We will call these people mercenaries or the criminal elements.[17]

If, on the other hand, the expected utility for staying with the system is less than the cost of opposing it, then we will have a nonparticipant :

$$U[\Phi \cdot (Yg^m + Yg^a) + p \cdot L] < U[Yi + Rn + (1 - p) \cdot C]$$

Within the group of non-participants, there can be three more subgroups: the supporters of the regime, the free riders and the renegade collaborators. If the sum of expected utility of $[\Phi \cdot (Yg^m + Yg^a)]$ is zero - that is, the individual finds no ideological reasons for believing that the collective good generated by the success of the movement will be beneficial to his group (Yg^m) or to himself - the income potential within the present political system is significant; and if the possibility of material gains that the actor can hope to get away with is less than its potential risk $\{[p \cdot (L) - (1 - p) \cdot (C)] > 0\}$, we can expect to find a regime supporter.

However, if from the group of nonparticipants, we find a group with the above expectations pattern except for the fact that the ideological factor is positive $\{[\Phi \cdot (Yg^m + Yg^a)] > 0\}$, we will call them the free-riders or the sympathizers. In other words, these are people for whom the perception of group or individual benefit from the success of the movement is clear; however, they are unwilling to participate in the acts of rebellion because they find the cost in relation to the benefit to be unacceptably high.

Finally, among the nonparticipants, we have those individuals who, despite their ideological convictions to the contrary, choose not to take part in the action because the government is able to bribe them successfully to work against their true group interest. Thus, in contrast to the freeriders, their inaction is not motivated by the potential loss of income or the threat of retribution from the government but from the material benefits that the authorities offer for their collaboration. We can call them the renegade collaborators. History always treats these individuals harshly, as history is often written by the victorious side. We have summarized our individual profiles in the following Figure 4.3.

INDIVIDUALS, THEIR MOTIVATIONS, AND COUNTRY PROFILES

The individual profiles developed above can also help us understand and classify the countries according to the predominance of the types of individuals in various countries. By using the profiles of the majority of the people, we can classify a country as *stable*, *disenchanted*, and *unstable*. Countries with a vast majority of the people falling in the category of regime supporters will be considered *stable*. This category will include, in various degrees, countries of North America, western Europe, Japan, Oceania, and the wealthy Arab countries such as Kuwait and Saudi Arabia.

A disenchanted country profile may be one in which, around a bedrock of nonparticipants, we have a significant group of free-riders or sympathizers.[18] These countries may exhibit absence of radical political activities and remain dormant indefinitely, until such time when the right precipitating and other structural factors convert more people into the ranks of participants and provide the opposition with an appropriate leadership.[19] In a rather interesting study, Timur Kuran (1988) attempted to explain why certain nations (such as, Iran) enjoying an outward calm, suddenly develop revolutionary fervor with an unexpected speed. This, he hypothesizes is caused by individuals possessing two sets of expected utility functions, one publicly stated and the other, privately held. However, we can argue that one does not need to assume the existence of two sets of expected utility functions. In fact, one can argue that as the prospect of converting time into political goods improves with changing new environmental factors (such as mobilization, emergence of new leadership, or the right antecedent events), the fence-sitters begin to jump into the bandwagon. This sudden change in behavior quickly plunges a deceptively calm, disenchanted nation into the depth of a revolutionary movement.

The next stage from these disenchanted nations is that of an unstable nation, characterized by widespread violence threatening its political structure. In these countries, for a significant number of people the potential net benefit of staying within the system has finally fallen short of the net benefit of joining the rebel forces. The recent events in the Philippines, Haiti, Iran, El Salvador, and Nicaragua, among others, may provide examples of such a situation.

TYPES OF REBELLIOUS ACTS AND THEIR PARTICIPANTS

In the previous section we have argued that people join rebellion for various reasons, and therefore it will be futile to look for just one single profile of "the revolutionary." Similarly, the acts of rebellion themselves vary a great deal. Taylor and Hudson (1972) in their *World Handbook of Political and Social Indicators* report data on five acts of collective rebellion: political demonstration, riot, political strikes, armed or guerrilla attacks (symbolic acts of terrorism or a bank raid), and assassinations. Let us first look at the definitions of these acts.

The handbook defines [20] *protest demonstration* as "a nonviolent gathering of people organized for the announced purpose of protesting against a regime, government, or one or more of its leaders; or against its ideology, policy, or lack of policy; or against its previous action or intended action" (p. 66). Therefore, people taking part in political demonstrations will be those whose motivations are going to be other than economic. Without the possibility of looting (which will transform a protest demonstration into a riot), and the likelihood of easy detection by the authorities, the participants in protest demonstrations are likely to find their impetus in the ideological content of their action. Also mixed with the ideological factor, in every action, we are to find individuals taking part because of their "consumption motive" or the fun factor. However, protest demonstrations being the weakest form of political defiance, with the correspondingly low level of payoff, we can expect the ideological factor among its participants to vary in inverse proportion to its size. That is, the smaller the size of a protest demonstration, the more ideologically (and noneconomically) oriented are the participants likely to be (recall the march of the mothers of lost children in Argentina). With the increase in the size of the protesting crowd, we can expect to find that the possibility of detection by the authority will diminish. This will encourage those with less ideological conviction and the "fun seekers."

A *riot* is defined as "a violent demonstration or disturbance involving a large number of people. The term "violent" implies the use of force, which is usually evinced by the destruction of property, the wounding or killing of people by the authorities, the use of riot control equipment such as clubs, gas, guns, or water cannons, and by the rioters' use of various weapons" (p. 67). Since a riot, by definition, involves a large number of people and destruction and looting of property, we can find in such incidents the greatest concentration of motivations: ideology, criminal intents, as well as fun and adventure seekers.

A *political strike* is defined as "any strike by industrial or service workers, or students, for the purpose of protesting against a government, its leaders, or a government policy or action".[21] Again, this political action, at the outset, carries little possibility of economic gains. In fact, in their attempt to close down a part of the economy, we can frequently expect to find in political strikes a large number of participants who are likely to fall under the category of captive collaborators. These are the people, usually small shopkeepers and day laborers, who will participate in a boycott because of threats of retribution from the organizers of the riot.

The definition of *armed attack* is "an act of violent political conflict carried out by (or on behalf of) an organized group with the object of weakening or destroying the power exercised by another organized group. It is characterized by bloodshed, physical struggle, or destruction of property" (p. 67). The immediate purpose of a terrorist attack is to gain political clout and possibly an increase in recruitment by the success of their campaign. There are numerous examples where the political aims of a nationalistic group have been served well through this policy of intimidation through terroristic activities, such as the Irgun and the Stern Gang in Palestine, or the EOKA in Cyprus. These acts of bombing of government properties and personnel aim at making the holding of power too expensive.

Therefore, the guerrilla attacks are under taken as military actions against the established political regime, to create "propaganda by deed" or to obtain money or (such as from bank holdups) ostensibly to promote the cause of the revolution. In the case of a military action, or propaganda by deed, the participants' primary motivations are ideological, or the possibility of excludable public goods. However, when actions are taken with some monetary objective (for example, through state-sponsored terrorism or bank looting ostensibly for the cause of the revolution), one can safely assume that along with the ideologues we can find some who would be categorized as the criminal elements (Laquer, 1977).

The handbook includes in an *assassination* "any politically motivated murder or attempted murder of a high government official or politicians. Included in addition to national leaders, are mayors of large cities, members of the cabinet and national legislature, members of the inner core of the ruling party or group, leaders of the opposition, and newspaper editors." [22] Again, if the assassination is carried out for no monetary gain, the acts can be motivated by reasons of ideology (such as the assassination of Archduke Ferdinand by Gavrilo Princep) or coercion (the assassination of Leon Trotsky). Needless to say, political assassinations for money can also be carried out by paid assassins (the criminal element). These are often the results of state-sponsored terrorism where a state government keeps on its covert payroll people who carry out acts of political murder.

Therefore, on the basis of the above discussion, we can conclude that the acts of protest demonstration, destruction of property of symbolic value during a riot, political strikes, assassinations, and armed attack events without any economic gains will be carried out by individuals for whom the ideological factor (Φ) is predominant. Those with mixed motives will join actions where there is more of a possibility of economic gain. Similarly, coup d'états will attract people with mixed motives as the smallness of the rebel group will make the possibility of excludable public goods a primary motivating factor.

Finally, it is possible that within a political movement we are likely to come across individuals whose primary motivation is the fun or entertainment aspect of taking part in an act of collective violence. However, empirical evidence gathered by Muller and Opp (1986) point to the relative insignificance of the fun factor in determining political participation. For a detailed discussion of their work, see the Appendix to Chapter 5.

THE USES OF A DESCRIPTIVE BEHAVIORAL MODEL

Having labored through our formulation of the behavioral model for participation in the acts of political violence, one can legitimately ask the necessity for such an endeavor. Questions can be raised with regard to the use of an expected utility model in general, or the choice of our specific model in particular. Among the general questions that can be asked, the most fundamental question regarding the use of the rational choice approach is, How much of one's decision to join an act of political violence is a rational one? Even by accepting the rationality of the participatory decision, one can raise the question of efficacy of an exercise based on an expected utility model, which, after all, is not amenable to direct testing with observable data. If the proposed behavioral hypothesis can not be falsified, does it not fail the Popperian criterion for tautological reasoning? With regard to the specific model, which explicitly uses ideology as a part of the objective function, questions about its superiority over the other available hypotheses can be raised. And finally, within the model the measurability of the ideological factor becomes an important question.

Each of these questions is important enough to be discussed at length. Therefore, in the following section we will attempt to defend our definition of rationality as it relates to human choice. The second question, the Popperian objection, is probably the most difficult to deal with. However, with regard to the problem of the inability to test an expected utility model directly, we can simply point out that models based on the expected utility hypothesis have played an extremely important role in explaining human behavior in the fields of economics and political science. Also, a great deal of effort is currently being directed in the field of experimental economics to ascertain empirically the various components of utility functions. In any case the importance of the use of a rational choice model lies in its ability to provide insights into the dynamics of the individual decision-making process, which can be an invaluable tool for the analysis of public policies. Analysis of participatory behavior, which is based on the hypothesis that an individual is attempting to maximize his individual as well as group utility, can pave the way for understanding the potential participants. The vast historical literature on the actual occurrence of political movements pays but scant attention to the participants, their motivations, the sources of their group identity, and the ideological inspirations. Our model emphasizes the need for extended studies on the sociocultural and economic profiles of the participants of political movements. Thus, for the appropriate public policy to counter political violence, one must understand the recruitment grounds of the potential participants and the appropriate policies to reduce tension and achieve peace and stability. We will reserve further comments on the public policy issues for the concluding chapter. As for the question of relative superiority of our model over the others, we will devote the rest of this section to the discussion. Finally, the question of empirical estimation of ideological factor will be relegated to the Appendix to Chapter 5, where we will discuss how two recent studies - one in political science and one in economics - have attempted to estimate the ideological factor in individual decion-making calculus.

In order to answer the question of the advantage of our formulation over the previous efforts, let us recapitulate briefly. The decision to participate in acts of collective rebellion against an established political order has come under scrutiny from the various branches of social sciences. The economists, particularly those operating within the public choice framework (Tullock, 1971, 1974; Gunning, 1972; Silver, 1974; Roeder, 1982), have attempted to show that the participatory decision originates within the confines of individual profit maximization. This has come to be known as the byproduct theory of revolution. Recent efforts in political science and sociology (Smelser, 1963; Gurr, 1970), in contrast, have correlated structural imbalance or the existence of relative deprivation with the occurrence of rebellious acts.

However, the problem with the economic approach is that while focusing on the logical inconsistencies resulting from free ridership, it explains why people *should not* take part in an act of collective rebellion but fails to explain why they actually *do*. But since Tullock (1971) finds the "paradox" since collective goods benefit everyone regardless of the degree of participation, the lure of common goods cannot be the motivating factor to a rational economic man.[23] Therefore, Tullock contends that there must be an ulterior motive, such as the spoils of victory.

On the other hand, sociologists and sociopsychologists while explaining why men *should* rebel in the face of systemic frustration, fail to explain why frequently they *choose not to*. This is because the relation between frustration and aggression is not isomorphic and is complicated by the existence of other factors such as taste, fear of retaliation and ideology. Therefore, in our formulation, we attempt to provide a comprehensive framework for analyzing various motivations in the participatory decision-making process of collective rebellion by explicitly recognizing collective utility within the objective function of a potential participant.

A decision to participate in the acts of political dissidence is not a binary one but rather a complex continuum involving various dimensions. The motivation for participating in an *act* of rebellion may be different from that of sympathizing or benefiting from a *movement*. In our proposed model, we attempt to distinguish between those two motivations. There are also various levels of involvement: A person could be a participant, an instigator, a mercenary, or a free-rider.[24] Therefore, we argue that it may be an oversimplification to search for a typical, unchanging profile of a potential participant. As relative opportunity costs, probabilities of apprehension, and perceived value of public goods and so on alter over time, individuals with different characteristics are drawn into the movement. We provide a generalized model of participation from which different behavioral profiles can be derived.

Another significant departure in our analysis is the explicit incorporation of time as a basic constraint in the behavioral model. Time, the ultimate scarce resource, has to be allocated to alternative competing activities. In our expected utility model the heart of the maximization postulate is the optimal allocation of time for the production of either economic or political goods. With the inclusion of the opportunity cost of time in the behavioral decision-making process, structural variables such as unemployment, demographic profiles, and labor mobility become directly relevant.

"RATIONAL REVOLUTIONARY": SOME CONCLUDING REMARKS

The application of the expected utility model in the analysis of collective rebellious behavior begs the question of rationality on the part of the participants in the acts of collective violence. The image of a violent, wild-eyed revolutionary, with his guns blazing, or blowing himself up in a suicidal attempt to accomplish his impossible political goals, provides us with a typical example of an emotive, if not an irrational, act. Therefore, it is hardly surprising that the pervasive view among the experts and the casual observers of collective violent behavior, alike is the notion that a large part of these decisions are not rational - at least not in the way one's decision to engage in normal economic activities - is determined.[25] However, any such assertion would call for the definition of rational behavior. The point is sufficiently important to warrant a brief look at this age-old question of human rationality. This is because in the case of total "irrationality" there can be no behavioral explanation of individual action as there is no way to model or predict random behavior. Therefore, some researchers have deduced a strong corollary to this hypothesis: that the capability to explain behavior implies the understanding of the basic rationale of the decision process of the subject.[26] However, in contrast, recent experimental evidence suggests (Machina,1983; Allais, 1952; Slovic, 1966; Kahneman and Tversky, 1972, 1973, 1979; etc.) that the concept of rationality can not ignore the simultaneous existence of systematic biases.

The broad definition of rationality, as it has been accepted in economics, implies (1) internal consistency of choice, and (2) maximization of self-interest (Sen, 1987, pp. 10-28). Despite some important variations, the consistency criteria states that it is possible to explain the set of actual choices as resulting from maximization of some binary relations (Debreu, 1959; Richter, 1971). However, as Sen (1987) points out, "However, no matter what these conditions are, it is hard to believe that internal consistency of choice can itself be an adequate condition of rationality" (p. 17) Indeed, dogged consistency can raise admiration, but rationality of choice, in the least, must establish a correspondence between what one wants and how one goes about trying to achieve it. Therefore, the second criterion of rationality, the maximization of individual utility, is included as the criterion to judge the rationality of action. Our present discussion of the question of rationality of the participants in collective political action will take two separate paths. First, we will examine the validity of the above-stated criteria of economic rationality; and second, we will look into the question of whether rationality demands maximization of self-interest to the exclusion of all else.

Economic Rationality

By following the logic of economic rationality, we arrive at the seemingly obvious example of a rational choice of action: In the case of certain outcomes an individual would choose the one providing the highest level of utility; in the case of uncertainty, he would prefer the option with the highest expected utility. To most of the economists this assumption has been taken as beyond reproach and has been accepted as self-evident. Thus, Paul Samuelson in his seminal work, *Foundations of Economic Analysis* (1948) stated that many economists would "separate economics from sociology upon the basis of rational or irrational behavior, where these terms are used in the penumbra of utility theory " (p. iv). This statement is particularly important as it posits two separate hypotheses, both of which have raised doubts in recent years. First, the rational *homoeconomicus* is assumed to be a consistent utility maximizer, and second, it conjectures that this rationality is confined only to the aspects of economic transaction. The rest, falling in the realms of sociology, political science, or psychology, will presumably fall in the area of emotion or otherwise non-utility-maximizing behavior.

With regard to the economic actor, the ubiquitous utility maximizer, the experimental economists are being hard-pressed to find empirical evidence of his existence even in controlled laboratory situations. As for the rest of the social sciences, on the other hand, forceful arguments are being offered toward the hypothesis that a similar kind of explicit or implicit utility maximization remains at the heart of most of political and sociological decision-making processes (Buchanan and Tullock, 1962; Simon, 1979). In order to have a proper understanding of the issues involved, we need to put our discussion in historical perspective.

The question of rationality of human choice has confounded anybody who has dared to look closely at the process. Plato spoke of the "rubble of senses" experienced through the sensory organs. Left to themselves, they remain chaotic and pitifully impotent, until they are ordered into meaning, purpose, and power, and understood and appreciated according to Justice, Beauty, and Truth. However, despite attempts to provide a structure of human reasoning, Plato acknowledged the lack of definition and universality of the concepts of Justice, Beauty, and Truth, especially of the last two.

The Age of Reason emerging from the Dark Ages put human rationality in sharp focus. The decline of blind faith and the consequent universality of normative standards begged the question of the appropriate definition of rationality of choice. From Bacon to Spinoza to Voltaire, the unquestioned faith received a crude jolt, thereby paving the way for the acceptance, in its place, of structured, "scientific" reasoning. The detachment of faith from reason was finally accomplished by Kant with his transcendental philosophy. Despite this important separation, the word *rationality* failed to achieve an acceptable objective definition. Therefore, the seemingly innocuous, self-evident truth of rationality came under vehement attack from philosophers such as Herbert Marcuse (1969) and Jurgen Habermas (1970), who found in its very concept the societal desire for domination and exploitation.

If the concept of rationality contains dubious implications from the philosophical standpoint, the examination of human rationality at the individual level has so confounded the researchers that they have warned us about the "bleak implications of human rationality" (Nisbet and Borgida, 1975). Similarly, Kahneman and Tversky (1972) and Slovic and Lichtenstein (1968) after extended studies were hard-pressed to characterize man as "a reasonably intuitive statistician" and noted systematic biases in human reasoning that violate some of the fundamental principles of rational decision making under uncertainty.[27] This confusion in defining rationality for economics led Sen (1977) to conclude :

There have been, in fact, been very few systematic attempts at testing the consistency of people's day-to-day behavior, even though there have been interesting and contrived experiments on people's reaction to uncertainty under laboratory conditions. What counts as admissible evidence remains unsettled. If today you were to poll economists of different schools, you would certainly find the coexistence of beliefs (i) that the rational behavior theory is unfalsifiable, (ii) that it is falsifiable and so far unfalsified, and (iii) that it is falsifiable and indeed patently false [p. 325].

At any rate, however, most students of human behavior would at least agree that the process of human choice can be distinguished between competence and performance (Chomsky, 1968). The competence aspect of human rationality refers to the subject's reasoning capability, or his capacity of intuitive deduction according to the rules laid down in formal logic. This intuitive capability for deductive reasoning refers to the interplay of the logical participles: not, and, if, some, and every. Despite the inevitable controversy regarding any statement on the definition of human reasoning competence, this part of the question - that is the subject's reasoning competence - is relatively simpler to understand and somewhat easier to establish than analyzing the link between competence and performance. Thus, a "reasonable" man, having made a "reasonable" analysis, may take a position significantly different from that derived from the analysis (Davidson, 1982, pp. 3-20). This deviation cannot be explained without taking resort to the subject's taste, value, ideology, faith, fear, and myth.

Therefore, the process of human reasoning can be seen not as one single sweeping chasing of maximization of utility, but as an end product of two successive filtering mechanisms (Elster, 1978a, 1979b). The first filter is defined by the set of structural constraints that identifies the set of feasible actions from a larger set of abstractly possible courses of action. The second filter - assuming there is no discrepancy between his action and his analysis, conversely, a somewhat tautological position that a person's final action is truly the outcome of his cognitive evaluation - refers to the process that enables the actor to choose the best course of action from within his feasibility set.

The distinction of this two-filter process is extremely useful in viewing the seemingly endless, and often confusing, literature on rational behavior. To begin with, we may start out with the traditional economic view, typically and most forcefully expounded by Becker (1976b), who extends it to all aspects of human choice. Thus, in response to the critics who cast doubt on the rationality of choice, Becker emphatically states :

Human behavior is not compartmentalized, sometimes based on maximizing, sometimes not, sometimes motivated by stable preferences, sometimes volatile, sometimes resulting in optimal accumulation of information, sometimes not. Rather, all human behavior can be viewed as involving participants who maximize their utility from a stable set of preferences and accumulate an optimal amount of information and other inputs in a variety of ways.

If this argument is correct, the economic approach provides a unified framework for understanding behavior that has long been sought by and eluded Bentham, Comte, Marx and others [p. 20].

In other words, in the economic view of choice, once the dimensions of the feasibility set are determined, we will be able to ascertain the rational choice of the actor, given the stability of his preference function. Therefore, Becker defines rationality with a somewhat weaker set of conditions. Becker (1976) explains all facets of human behavior from the basic calculation of a net expected benefit function with the ubiquitous assumption that an increase in the cost of a single input relative to others will reduce its use. That is, he defines rationality as the subject's cognitive capability of recognizing the relative marginal cost of his options and acting to minimize cost subject to a given gain.[28] In the vast area of definition of human rationality, Becker seems to define it with the least common denominator and therefore probably has found the widest acceptance in economic literature.

In contrast, we find the structuralists who, in their extreme form, deny the very existence of choice, as the first filter becomes so dominant that in the end the actor does not find more than one feasible choice of action. For example, McFarland (1969) states: [29]

The structuralist would emphasize the bounding of political activity by social structure (including class) and values (including ideology). The behaviorists would emphasize political decision making within these bounds. The structuralist would study the fence around the cattle; the behaviorists would study the activity of the cattle within the bounds of the fence [p. 135].

Therefore, a strict structuralist would view choice as no choice at all, predetermined by class, culture, and religious and social values. This argument of no-choice is particularly prevalent in some quarters of sociological reasoning, where the outcomes of individual actions such as involvement in crime, drug use, or certain other kinds of pathological behavior such as incest, wife battering, or alcoholism are seen as determined by the individual's environmental factors. Thus, for example, the economist would argue that for a person growing up in an urban slum any behavior other than dropping out of school and taking up a criminal way of life will be irrational, given the fact that the returns to investment for going to school will be significantly below the forgone income from illegal activity. Therefore, one policy prescription of this view will be to reduce the attractiveness of illegal activities by imposing harsh penalties (cost factor) for engaging in such activities or alternatively, if possible, to increase the payoff for staying in school. Sociologists, in contrast, may argue that even the demonstration of increasing the cost of illegal activities relative to the socially desirable activities may not be enough to convince the hapless person, who will find justification for participating in illegal activities from such factors as sociocultural values, peer pressure, and family background. Therefore, according to this point of view, a successful program of rehabilitation must start with a change in the sociocultural and family environment.

The middle ground between the "unbounded" and completely structure-bound definition of rationality is given by Herbert Simon. Through his numerous works over the years, Simon has argued in effect, that man is not smart enough to be "rational" in the strict economic sense of the term. This inability to reach the "optimal" choice among an infinite set of options is largely the result of man's cognitive limitations. Therefore, the missing link between analysis and actual performance lies in the labyrinthine organization of a set of conceptual vignettes rather than a single, coherent structure. The contribution of Simon to the analysis of human choice has been the understanding of not only the external constraints but also the internal, cognitive constraints that inexorably shape our reasoning process. Therefore, according to this theory, which Simon alternately calls "bounded," "procedural," or "calculated" rationality, a human being is no longer viewed as an optimizer but rather as a "satisficer." That is one who, being confronted with an incredible variety of alternatives and payoffs, and even being somewhat uncertain and "fuzzy" about his own goals, arrives at a decision which will satisfy the unclear goals with sufficient payoffs.

We certainly do not hope to resolve the age-old question in this study. However, the difference among these competing theories of rationality of human choice may not be as irreconcilable as they appear to be at first glance. Thus, philosopher Donald Davidson (1976) quite convincingly argues that there is a general presumption of rationality in the study of human affairs; if we are to attribute intelligibly attitudes and beliefs, "we are committed to finding, in the pattern of behavior, belief and desire, a large degree of consistency" (p. 108).

Rationality and Self-Interest

If we cannot question the consistency aspect of the question of rationality in the study of social sciences in general and economics in particular, we may take issue with the question of the ubiquity of the assumption of maximization of self-interest. Indeed, we may legitimately raise the question: What is so sacrosanct about self-interest? Human beings being social animals, why should a decision to act in the interest of the group be necessarily considered irrational or based on emotion rather than logic? Sen (1987) expresses this argument the best:

Why should it be uniquely rational to pursue one's own self-interest to the exclusion of everything else? It may not, of course, be all that absurd to claim that maximization of self interest is not irrational, at least not necessarily so, but to argue that anything other than maximizing self-interest must be irrational seems altogether extraordinary [p. 15].

The obvious pitfall of the assumption of a perfect correspondence between selfishness and rationality is the basic inability to explain a large chunk of human interaction. As we have noted, by following the Olsonian (1971) logic of the free-rider, no public work in democracy will ever be funded, no call for a social change will ever be followed by action, no battle will ever be won. Therefore, in our analysis of participation in the acts of political violence, we have explicitly introduced ideology or group welfare as another aspect of the maximand. Unfortunately, in economic literature any kind of altruistic or ideological behavior has been traditionally termed as "noneconomic" (Peltzman, 1982) or even simply "irrational" (Bartzel and Silberberg, 1973). However, recent trend in economics is slowly recognizing the need to accept ideological factors within the framework of economic rationality (Arrow, 1972, Stigler, 1981), or at least it has been recognized that the existence of such factors is not inconsistent with the economic view of human behavior (Becker, 1974, 1976; Hirshleifer, 1977, 1985). Also, empirical evidence is fairly consistent in its finding that in certain areas of political decision making economic interest variables play a surprisingly weak role, whereas the hypothesis that pure ideological factors play no part in the decision-making process is quickly rejected (Kau and Rubin, 1979; Kalt, 1981; Kalt and Zupan, 1984).[30]

If we accept the proposition that rational behavior *can* include factors of ideology, are there reasons to believe that such contamination is likely to be more prevalent in the political sector than in choosing instruments of private pecuniary gains? Kalt and Zupan (1984) argue that there are three reasons to believe that the answer may be affirmative.[31]

First, altruistic behavior contains a clear component of improving the conditions of the members of a group. This collective good attribute makes the demand for collective goods susceptible to the free-rider problem within the market system. As Samuelson (1954) pointed out, the actions taken by the government (through its coercive capabilities) offer a solution to the free rider problem in the marketplace.

Second, in much of political activities, an individual has little control over the outcomes and to promote his own investment effectively. Therefore, an individual is more apt to choose on the basis of tastes, preference, or ideology (Brennan and Buchanan, 1982).

Third, pecuniary political gains or losses have to be shared, and specific costs and benefits remain unknown. Therefore, an individual may feel the warm glow of moral rectitude by doing the "right thing" having chosen according to his ideological calling. Also, since the exact costs and benefits of public goods often remain undetermined in the minds of the ordinary citizens, the opportunity costs of ideology (in terms of forgone pecuniary returns) may appear to be lower in the political arena than what they may be in the marketplace.

Therefore, in summary, we have argued that the decision to participate in acts of political violence by no means can be rejected as irrational or purely emotive acts. We have also noted that the rational choice approach to human behavior is, without a doubt, the best available behavioral hypothesis. However, at the same time, we must be prepared to recognize the absurdity of the viewpoint that any goal other than the one of selfishness constitutes irrationality. Hence, we should broaden the definition of human rationality to include the desire to maximize group interest .

APPENDIX TO CHAPTER 4:
THE EFFECTS OF A CHANGE IN THE RELATIVE COST OF PARTICIPATION

Our behavioral model starts with the assumption that an individual maximizes his utility derived from the two products, private and public, subject to his time constraint. That is:

Max. U (Y_i, P_g)
subject to: $T = T_e + T_p$ (A4.1)

By combining the above arguments, the expected utility function for participating in political activities is specified as follows:

$$E(U) = U[-Y_i + \Phi \cdot (Y_g^m + p \cdot Y_g^a) - R_n + p \cdot L - (1-p) \cdot C + \Phi \cdot \zeta]$$
                                                                  (A4.2)

Following arguments in chapter IV, the following relationships may be hypothesized:

$$\frac{\delta E(U)}{\delta Y_i} \gtrless 0; \quad \frac{\delta E(U)}{\delta Y_{gm}} = 0; \quad \frac{\delta E(U)}{\delta Y_{ga}} > 0; \quad \frac{\delta E(U)}{\delta \Phi} > 0;$$

$$\frac{\delta E(U)}{\delta R_n} < 0; \quad \frac{\delta E(U)}{\delta p}) > 0; \quad \frac{\delta E(U)}{\delta L}) > 0; \quad \frac{\delta E(U)}{\delta C} < 0; \quad \frac{\delta E(U)}{\delta \zeta} > 0.$$

The directional change of expected utility from a change in income, δY_i, (especially a negative change or a reduction in income) is indeterminate due to the presence of income and substitution effects. If income effect is stronger, the individual will be less apt to participate. On the other hand, if the substitution effect is stronger, then we will see an increased level of participation. However, we may safely hypothesize that for most instances, the substitution effect of political participationj is likely to be stronger than the income effect.

The expected utility from a political movement (δYg^m) has been assumed to be equal to zero. This is because, following Tullock (1972), we have argued that since a political movement creates nonexcludable public goods, the utility derived from the success of a movement will have no impact on an individual's decision to allocate time between public and private goods.

The utility derived from participating in an act of political dissidence (δYg^a), in contrast, is positive, and an increase in the perception of the relative utility of participating in a political action will cause an individual to increase his time spent on political activism. If an individual believes that he can produce more political goods by engaging in dissident activities, then his participation will no doubt increase.

The impact of an increase in the ideological fervor ($\delta\Phi$) is likely to be positive on the expected utility function. Therefore, the result of an increase in an individual's ideological position will be his greater willingness to participate in acts of political defiance.

An increase in the net cost of nonparticipation (δRn) will cause an individual to withdraw from political activism, as he will be either bribed or threatened to do so.

The decision to participate in an act of collective rebellion depends on the subjective probability that an actor assigns on his chances of getting away with his activity without being apprehended (δp). Therefore, any change in this perception in favor of the probability of not being caught will tend to increase an individual's appetite for political participation.

Finally, we can safely assume that an increase in the perception of obtaining private goods from participation in political action (δL) will augment an individual's desire to participate, whereas the extent of his personal loss will dampen his enthusiasm for participation (δC).

From our hypothesis that a potential participant maximizes his expected utility, subject to his time constraint, as shown in equation (A4.2), the resulting Lagrangian function takes the form of:

$$L^* = U\left[Yi\,(Te) + Pg\,(Tp)\right] + \lambda\,(T - Te - Tp) \tag{A4.3}$$

by differentiating with respect to Te and Tp, we get,

$$\frac{\delta L^*}{\delta Te} = \frac{\delta Ui}{\delta Yi} \cdot \frac{\delta Yi}{\delta Te} + \lambda \tag{A4.4}$$

$$\frac{\delta L^*}{\delta Tp} = \frac{\delta Up}{\delta Pg} \cdot \frac{\delta Pg}{\delta Tp} + \lambda \tag{A4.5}$$

Setting equation (A4.4) against (A4.5), and rearranging the terms, we obtain the necessary condition for expected utility maximizer's efficient allocation of time between economic (or political) and political activity:

$$\frac{\delta U_i/\delta Y_i}{\delta U_p/\delta P_g} = \frac{\delta P_g/\delta T_p}{\delta Y_i/\delta T_n} \tag{A4.6}$$

This maximizing condition implies that the ratio of marginal utilities from the consumption of economic and political goods has to be equal to the rate at which both goods can be created by expending an additional unit of time. The lefthand side of equation (A4.6) depicts the subjective individual valuation of utilities derived from the two competing activities. This rate determines the slope of the indifference curves in Figure 4.1. The righthand side of the equation captures the environ-mental conditions under which both goods can be obtained by the allocation of an additional unit of time. If these ratios are not equal, it implies that an individual obtains more satisfaction out of consuming one good or the other. For instance, ceteris paribus, the politicization of an individual may increase his ideological commitment and raise the amount of time spent on political activity. This increase in the consumption of political goods will diminish then marginal utility from an additional dose of political activity, and raise the marginal utility from economic activity, due to the law of diminishing utility. Consequently, both ratios on the lefthand side of equation (A4.6) will equalize at a higher level and attain the point of equilibrium. In terms of Figure 4.1, the slope of his indifference curve will be steeper as in IC_1 (rather than IC). The point of equilibrium is likely to be such that he spends relatively more time in political activity.

The straight line in Figure 4.1 depicts the budget constraint and shows the rate at which an individual will convert an additional unit of time into either political or economic good. Thus, the extreme points of the budget line measure the quantity of either good that the individual can have if he spends all his time on procuring just one good. Therefore, by spending all his time on procuring economic goods under the present sociopolitical system, an individual can earn E_0 amount of economic goods, or P_0 amount of political goods. At these extreme points, the rate at which an additional unit of time will create an additional dose of income of either goods will be equal to the total allocation of time.

In Figure 4.1, we have assumed that the cost of procuring the two goods will remain constant (as shown by a straight-line budget curve). However, there is no reason to believe that the marginal rate of transformation is likely to remain constant. There is no conceptual reason why the law of diminishing returns will not be operative in this case also. Further, it is entirely possible that the cost of one good may change with relation to the other. Thus, with an increasing level of economic development, it may be easier to produce more economic goods per unit of time. Therefore, an individual will be tempted to consume more economic goods than political goods. Similarly, it is conceivable that during the period of political turmoil the opponents of the present political system may find it easier to press for and obtain political goods. During those times, we can expect a wider participation in political activities.

NOTES

1. From Bentham, (1963, p. 37).

2. From Sen, (1987, p. 16). Emphasis Sen's.

3. The importance of group psychology in shaping individual behavioral is well accepted in various branches of behavioral sciences. For example, the human relations school of management was born in 1932 when Elton Mayo and F. J. Roethlisberger reported the results of an experiment they had been conducting for the past five years at the Hawthorne plant of the Western Electric Company. They found that people generally seem to work better and are more productive when their performance on the job is made the object of flattering attention by a group of researchers. Similarly, the later development of this humanistic school, boosted further by the work of psychologists such as Maslow (1962), has bolstered the case for group identity in individual performance.

4. We may explain the opportunity cost of leisure by using the following example. Suppose Mr. A were earning $10 an hour. Therefore, if he did not work one hour, he stands to loose $10, which is therefore his opportunity cost of leisure. However, if he starts making less than his former wages, the opportunity cost of leisure will also register a corresponding decline. This lowering of opportunity cost may result in a decision to consume more leisure. Thus, as a result of a stiffening of a progressive income tax, a spouse may decide not to go out and work owing to the lowering of the opportunity cost of leisure.

5. For a discussion of broadly defined income in political analysis, see Lasswell and Kaplan (1950).

6. It is entirely conceivable that economic activities can create political goods or, conversely, that political activities can produce economic goods. Thus, an economically successful man may find it easier to make an impact in the political arena. Similarly, a highly visible politician may find economic success. A case in point (without trying to trace the direction of the causal link) is the fact that the average

incomes of the members of the U. S. Senate, as well as the House of Represen-tatives, are substantially higher than the national average. Therefore, this assumption is one of convenience rather than substance.

7. For a model which includes leisure as a third alternative, see Gupta and Singh (1988).

8. It may be noted here that for conceptual reasons we have to assume that all these incomes are tangible or measurable in monetary terms. The factors of personal gains are relatively easily understood to have measurable economic components. The case for political income is less clearcut.   From equation (4.2), the measures for Rn, L, and C are clear.   For Yg^m and Yg^a, it is the dollar value attached to the attainment of a specific public good. For example, the end of racial discrimination (the goal of a political movement) can increase the expected earnings of the members of a hitherto discriminated group and reduce the income differential due to job discrimination. However, we must admit that the fun factor does not seem to have much tangible property.

9. For the sake of simplicity, we are assuming that Yg^m and Yg^a are independent of each other; however, it is quite conceivable that there exists a strong degree of inter-dependence between the two. That is, a strong belief in the prospect of the generation of nonexcludable (Yg^m) public goods can create further impetus for taking part and actually contributing to the process of achieving it (Yg^a).

10. See, for example, Wolf (1986).

11. The importance of the desirability of public goods as an important factor in individual decision-making process was empirically demon-strated by Muller and Opp (1986).

12. It should be noted that even though we have drawn the budget constraint as a straight line, implying a constant rate of transformation, it is likely to be influenced by the law of diminishing marginal rate of transformation. In such a case, the budget line will be convex to the origin.

13. It is ironic to note that the anomic condition following the end of a repressive era offers the military or some other despot the opportunity to seize control of the political system under the pretext of bringing stability and order.

14.   The problem of free rider-ship for a collective project was beautifully explained in an mythological story from India. A king wanted to dig a large reservoir for drinking water for his subjects. When after months of digging no water was found, the king asked his loyal (but rational) subjects to contribute a bucket of milk one evening so that it would turns instead into a lake of milk. However, each subject reasoned that nobody would be able to detect his bucket of water in the milk, so the following morning the lake was found to be full of beautiful clear water with no trace of milk. (I am grateful to Professor Bimal K. Motilal, Spaulding Professor of Philosophy, All Souls College, Oxford University, for the illustration).

15.   The case of Patty Hearst working for the Simbionese Liberation Army provides us with a clear example of such an individual. Popkin (1979) provides examples of the rebel threat in recruiting peasant revolutionaries in Vietnam.   Similar incidences have been widely reported in other revolutionary situations of both right - and leftwing inspiration.

16.   It is interesting to note that almost all political systems attempt to brand the opposition activists, especially those who are engaged in violent acts of protest, as the criminal elements of the society and refuse to consider them separately from the other criminals. However, quite frequently those lines are taken for the purpose of political propaganda and their own public consumption.

17.   Countries such as Mexico, where several recent polls have revealed a deep-seated pessimism about the capability of the present sociopolitical system to provide justice or generate economic growth (*Wall Street Journal*, December 29, 1986), may be considered to be examples of disenchanted nations.

18.   It may be noted that while a charismatic leader can convert free-riders into active participants, similarly, frequently the events of smoldering discontent produce their own leadership. The case of Cory Acquino in the Philippines is a case in point. See Bryan Johnson (1987).

19.   The definitions of protest demonstration, riot, and armed attack events were taken from the *World Handbook* (pp. 66-67). The definitions of political strikes and assassinations were taken from the computer data sheet available from the Inter University Consortium data.

20. See footnote 19.

21. See footnote 19.

22. We have mentioned in the previous chapter that Tullock's (1971) "paradox" arises because he does not distinguish between the motivation to join a revolution - defined as an effort by a large segment of a society to bring about a fundamental change in the existing sociopolitical structure, and a coup d état by a small group of individuals with a limited goal of removing the present ruler.

23. There can be variations in the extent and nature of participation as well. For example, an individual may choose to participate in a non-violent demonstration but not in an assassination attempt.

24. Surprisingly, the basic irrationality viewpoint of the participants in political violence is held by some of the most prominent scholars whose names are associated with the early development of the structural theories of collective rebellious behavior. Therefore, we felt obliged to examine the question of rationality of action within the present context.

25. Muth (1961), for example, has defined rationality as the ability to explain actual behavior with a set of independent variables. His concept of rationality requires that the the psychological expectations of economic actors are on the average equal to the true expected values. Thus, within the framework of regression analysis, if one expresses P_t as the vector of price realizations at time t, X_{t-1} as as a set of predetermined variables, and ε_t as the vector of error term, which picks up all the unexplained variations in P_t, then we express the regression equation as: $P_t = \alpha + \beta \cdot X_{t-1} + \varepsilon_t$. If the error term is normally distributed and is free from systematic biases, then in the Muthian sense the ability of the model to explain the central tendency of the distribution is rationality. For a discussion of rational expectation and economic rationality, see H. Singh (1986).

26. For a series of extremely interesting articles, see the volume 4 of the *Journal of Behavioral and Brain Sciences*, (1981). In this issue, especially see L. Jonathan Cohen, (1981, pp. 317-70).

27. The fundamental behavioral precept inherent in Becker's formulation is that an individual maximizes his utility function Zi subject to the budget constraint Ci, where Zi's are the utility yielding commodities and Ci's are the individual's investments to the production of the Zi's. This formulation yields the first-order equilibrium condition of

$$\frac{\delta U_i}{\delta Z_i} = \lambda \frac{\delta C_i}{\delta Z_i} = \frac{\lambda}{\delta Z_i / \delta C_i} = \frac{\lambda}{MPC_i}$$

where λ is the actor's marginal utility of investment and MPC_i is the marginal price of commodity i. Since in equilibrium the ratio of these prices must equal the ratio of their marginal ability, it implies an inverse relationship between the relative level of consumption of a commodity i and its marginal cost of production (investment). This behavioral precept, insists Becker, is fundamental to any rational choice.

28. Jon Elster (1979 a), however, takes issue with McFarland and holds that values essentially fall in the second filter, excepting for when values determine the visibility of alternatives or the ones that are considered to be lexicographically superior to others.

29. For a rejection of the ideological factor on empirical grounds, see Peltzman (1982), and for a reply, see Kalt and Zupan (1984). It may be interesting for the noneconomists to note the hesitancy with which economists are willing to accept the possibility of the existence of ideology in one's decision process. Thus, while providing empirical proof of "pure ideology" influencing the voting behavior of the law-makers in the United States Congress, Kalt and Zupan accept ideology only in the penumbra of taste by almost apologetically adding : "Do individuals really get utility from these sources? It is not our intention here to dispute tastes. We take the presence of ideological tastes as given by introspection and observation" (p. 281).

30. Even though the choice of political goods may have a greater component of ideological factors, the purely economic choices can scarcely be considered to be completely free of ideological contamination.   Thus, the campaign by the U. S. garment manufacturers to promote the purchase of goods with the "Made in U.S.A" label was a clear case of appealing to the patriotic sentiments of the American consumers. Indeed, there are plenty of examples where people may choose "pure private" goods based on some sort of ideological preference. Therefore, we may conclude that the separation of economic and political goods on the basis of the ideological component in the decision-making process is only relative, rather than an absolute, consideration.

5

The Individual and His Environment

Revolutions in democracies are mainly the work of demagogues. Partly by persecuting men of property and partly by arousing the masses against them, they induce them to unite, for a common fear brings even enemies together.

Aristotle[1]

INTRODUCTION

Having discussed in the previous chapter an individual's motivations for joining collective rebellion, in this chapter we would like to explore the individual's relationship with his environment. We will also take this opportunity to establish linkage between our individual behavioral hypothesis and the structural theories of participation in the acts of collective rebellion.

We posit that a person's decision to participate in a collective rebellious action is shaped by his internal evaluation of expected utility, which in turn is influenced by the external environmental factors, defined as factors exogenous to the expected utility model. We classify the external factors into three broad groups: those generated from the opposition, those arising from the authorities, and those resulting from unpredictable, uncontrollable events that shape the course of our history. Thus, the process can be described with the help of Figure 5.1.

To the left of the Figure, we have placed the deliberate actions of the forces of opposition; to the right, we have shown the influence of the authorities. Through their actions, the opposition attempts to

influence the potential participants. They attempt to accomplish their
goal by the use of what we may broadly term as factors of leadership
and coercion. The leadership factor, in turn, can be seperated into the
capacity to spread ideology and the capacity to administer and mobilize
the forces of opposition. The other aspect of their arsenal consists of
their coercive capabilities, by which they can compel a potential fence
sitter to become an active participant. The environmental forces on the
side of the government also consist of its perceived legitimacy and the
capacity to impose negative sanctions on the dissidents. As can be
seen from the Figure, the impact of environmental factors, under the
control of the opposition, will naturally add to the causes of
insurrection, whereas the factors influenced by governmental action are
designed to reduce the level of conflict and to maintain the status quo.

Figure   5.1

Factors of Individual Motivation and
the External Environment

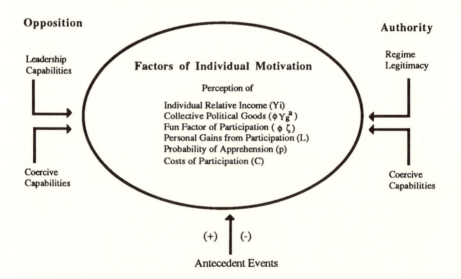

At the bottom center of the Figure we have placed the
antecedent events. The antecedent events are the generalized versions
of Smelser's (1963) "precipitating events." We do not call it
"precipitating" because the results of these unpredictable events can go
in either direction: either to ameliorate or to exacerbate a conflict
situation. Thus, a particular incidence, such as Rosa Parks's refusal
to sit at the back of the bus, can be the crystallizing factor, *the* battle
cry for a movement. Similarly, an event where the government makes

certain conciliatory gestures that help ease a tense situation, can lower the level of conflict in a society.

Leadership tends to affect people's participatory behavior in two ways. First, it heightens the emotional appeal of the expected public goods. Or in our equation (4.2), the factors of leadership impact peoples' perception of utility from a public good, what we call the ideological factor (Φ). The impact of this deepening of ideology on participatory decision has been demonstrated in Figure (4.1) in the previous chapter. The other aspect of leadership lies in its capability to mobilize the forces of opposition. With a higher level of participation all around, it creates an atmosphere where the previous fence sitters are able to downgrade their probability of getting apprehended and are therefore tempted to participate in the acts of rebellion. Also, with a higher level of mobilization, an individual may perceive the fact that there is a greater chance of his political demands being fulfilled. Therefore, in his estimation the marginal productivity of his time in producing political goods will increase.

On the other hand, the balancing factor in the equation of participation is played by the authorities by their capacity to squelch the rebellion by apprehending and punishing the perpetrators. We will discuss the factors of leadership and coercion at length in a later section.

LINKING THE EXPECTED UTILITY MODEL WITH THE STRUCTURAL THEORIES OF COLLECTIVE REBELLIOUS BEHAVIOR

First, let us examine the link between our proposed expected utility model and Smelser's (1963) theory of collective behavior. A behavioral approximation of an aggregate utility function may be achieved through Smelser's notion of "value added." Borrowing the term from economics, Smelser saw the process of societal movement toward a greater discontent and consequent violence as essentially a change in the overall value position of society. To put it differently, the change in the aggregate belief structure (i.e., the conviction of the people in general that the society in its present form is incapable of providing the maximum possible level of utility to each individual) is behaviorally linked to a fundamental change in pertinent environmental variables. Similarly, we can argue that while it is almost impossible to verify empirically individual behavior on the basis of maximizing expected utility function, it is possible to determine the functional relationship to a change in the expected utility function [$\Delta E (U)$]. We posit that the conceptual similarity between the Smelserian concept of value added and our change in the expected utility position would allow us to build the necessary linkage, both theoretically as well as empirically between the two theories.[2]

In order to establish the linkage between the two theories, let us recapitulate Smelser's theory of collective behavior. Smelser (1963) explains a change in the value position of society in terms of six factors: structural conduciveness, growth of generalized beliefs, structural strains, mobilization of participants, precipitating events, and ineffective social control.

Structural conduciveness determines the capacity of the structure of society to tolerate dissent. Democratic nations accept the right of peaceful protest as a fundamental right of their citizenry. As a result individuals can demonstrate their dissatisfaction with the policies of the government publicly without fear of severe punishment (C). In the previous section, we have argued that the demand for public goods depends on their relative costs. Thus, it is obvious that as the cost of procuring public goods goes up relative to the private good, the demand for the former will diminish. Smelser argued that the democratic nations will experience higher frequencies of incidents of political dissidence than the authoritarian and other nondemocratic nations. In these nations, owing to the lack of structural conduciveness, when violence does erupts, it takes on the most serious value-oriented form.

Figure 5.2

The Commitment Curve for Public Goods

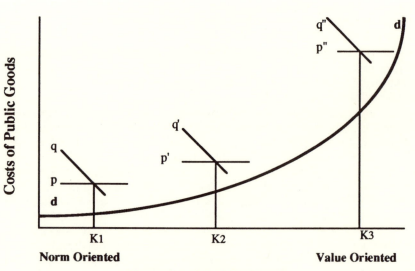

The Smelserian arguments can be explained within our theoretical structure with the help of Figure 5.2. In this Figure, the horizontal axis shows the continuum of public goods. At this point let us assume that the greater the quantity of public goods, the greater is the resulting change in the existing sociopolitical system. The demand for public goods close to the origin signifies low-level demand for marginal changes within the political structure. The quantity of change demanded increases as we move away from the origin, and at the extreme, it translates into a demand for a total change in the social, political, and economic structure of a nation. In other words, the call for a total revolution.

We will further assume: (1) that with the increase in the quantity, the quality of public goods changes from norm oriented to value oriented and (2) that the quantity of public goods is a function of time spent in producing public goods. In Figure 5.2, the vertical axis measures the price of procuring public goods. We hypothesize that, given a set of environmental factors and an expected level of retribution, each potential participant evaluates his demand for public goods with respect to his willingness to pay for them. Thus, we can assume that for an individual the downward-sloping curve q measures his demand for public goods. For these public goods, he figures that he would be willing to pay p amount of price.[3] This simultaneous assessment yields a potential demand for K_1 amount of public goods for individual i. For individual j and m, this equilibrium is reached at points K_2 and K_3. We may call the point of equilibrium between an individual's demand for public goods and the price that he is willing to pay for it - an individual's point of commitment. This point of commitment is the psychological contract that one makes with one's own self to achieve a collective good, given a perceived set of costs and benefits. As we have argued above [shown in Figure 5.1], the environmental factors affect an actor's level of commitment, and any change in the environmental condition causes him to reevaluate his commitment.

By summing the individual commitment functions, we can obtain the aggregate level of collective commitment for public goods within a society (shown as the curve, dd in Figure 5.2). The elongated shape of the collective commitment curve points to the fact that there will be more people willing to contribute smaller portions than those who are willing to pay the ultimate price, which, in this case, can mean even life itself. From Figure 5.2, we can see that a change in the environmental condition leading to an overall increase in the level of commitment on the parts of the potential participants (for example, resulting from the emergence of an inspiring leadership) will cause a rightward shift in the curve (not shown in Figure 5.2). Similarly, a lowering of the aggregate commitment level (caused by factors such as an increase in economic prosperity) will make a left ward drift in the curve.

Figure   5.3

The Relationship between Aggregate Commitment for and
the Cost of Public Goods

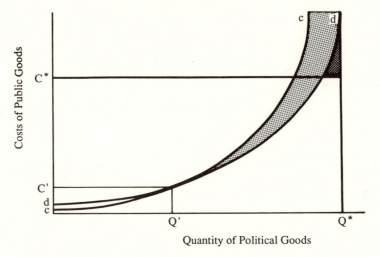

Quantity of Political Goods

On the other side of this aggregate commitment curve for public
goods is the *actual* cost of obtaining it. The actual cost of procuring
public goods is a function of the regime policy. Thus, if the authorities
take a liberal policy toward the acts of dissidence, then they will
impose relatively little costs on those who would want to disagree
openly with the government's policies.[4] On the other hand, the
government's decision to get tough with the political activists will be
tantamount to an imposition of a higher level of cost. Within a
democratic system both the demand curve for sociopolitical change and
the costs curve will typically demonstrate an exponential shape. That
is, the cost of an antisystemic act will be low with a low ambition for a
social change. Examples of such low-level norm oriented activities
include writing critical evaluations of government policies for the news

papers, petitioning local congressmen and senators and lobbying for a particular action, or joining nonviolent protest demonstrations aiming at changing a particular law. In these cases the goal of a political action is limited, and so will be the cost. The cost, however, will rise precipitously with a greater demand for public good, calling for a more fundamental change in the sociopolitical and economic order. For example, the political authorities will react with the full force of repression if one actively attempts to overthrow the government forcibly or otherwise try to bring about a value-oriented change. In which case, the potential cost will match the impact of such an action.

In Figure 5.3, the curve dd traces the group's commitment curve for public goods at each price level, that is, the price the individual members in the aggregate will be willing to pay for a particular level of public good. The curve cc, on the other hand, measures the cost that the government will be willing to inflict at each level of demand. From the Figure, it is clear that the two parties (the government and its opponents) will arrive at the point of equilibrium, at which the opposition will enjoy Q' amount of political goods at a cost of C'. The movement will not stop before this point, as the marginal productivity of time in producing political goods will exceed the marginal cost of taking part in the acts of dissidence. At points beyond Q', in the shaded area, the government's imposition of cost for attempting to obtain political goods will exceed people's desire to pay for it. Therefore, political good beyond this point will not be worth its cost, and the society will settle for a situation where the authorities will be willing to compromise with the dissident group to provide them with Q' amount of public goods in return for domestic national tranquility.

In this context, we may note that a shift in the aggregate demand can take place as a result of a change in the leadership capabilities. The arrival of a new leader capable of inspiring the masses will result in a greater willingness on the part of the individuals to commit themselves to pay more for political goods, and hence the demand for political goods will go up. This kind of shift in the aggregate demand curve is also possible in response to a provocative "antecedent incident."

The situation is radically different in an authoritarian nation. A dictatorial political system is not able to cope with dissent. Owing to the plurality of the political structure, a democratic government can dissociate its legitimacy from most of its policies. Therefore, it is possible to disagree with policies of the administration.without calling into question its legitimacy. In contrast the nondemocratic nations are not accorded such convenience, and opposition to any of its policy is viewed as a direct assault on its political legitimacy. In such nations any conflict can take on the character of value orientation, which the regime wants to suppress with the utmost show of force. The possibility of an extremely high cost factor for any form of dissent translates into a horizontal actual cost line, C*, drawn at the top of

Figure 5.3. Therefore, from the Figure, it is clear that within such a system political activism with limited goals is not cost-effective. Hence, despite high levels of disaffection within the general public, the system experiences an outward calm for a long time until the dissidents feel ready - both in number and in commitment - to take on the political system head-on at a considerable amount of potential cost to the participants. At such a point, as a result of a widespread desire to have a value oriented change, the country experiences violent revolutionary movements. Another way of looking at it is to argue that if the cost of political dissention is horizontal and is almost invariant with the seriousness of the act, then it is only logical for the rebel members to demand the maximum quantity of public goods.

Growth of generalized belief refers to ideologies or group perceptions that develop through the process of historical evolution and grip a nation. These ideological components determine a person's commitment to the causes of revolution (Φ). In equation (4.2) the ideological components impact the perception of the future rewards resulting from the success of the movement (Yg^m) as well as a particular action of collective violence (Yg^a). This situation has been demonstrated in Figure 4.1. In terms of our aggregate commitment curve, a growth in generalized belief in a society will magnify people's demand for public goods, and increase their willingness to bear the costs of dissident activities. Therefore, in such a case, our aggregate commitment curve in Figure 5.3 will register a vertical shift (not shown in the diagram), and the authorities will have to compromise to a greater degree to achieve political stability.

Economic hardships caused by factors such as unemployment, inflation, unequal distribution of income, or discrimination based on racial, religious, linguistic, or ethnic background add to the causes of structural strain. In our model, these factors will impact a person's perception of his utility of staying within the system. An individual's capacity to achieve nonpolitical private goods has been represented by (Yi). Beyond the point of the income effect overwhelming the substitution effect,[5] the lowering of benefits of staying within the system will enhance the temptation to join the forces of rebellion, which, in terms of our Figure 5.3, will be expressed as a vertical shift in the demand curve of political goods. At this point, we may also note that in the case of discrimination or deep unemployment, the income effect may be insignificant, as no attempts to augment economic capability (in the case of discrimination) or to maintain the old standard of living (in the case of unemployment) will be successful.

Precipitating factors are the unique events of history around which a political movement is crystallized. These events may alter the perception of participants about the relative merits of staying within the present political system and may add to their conviction for the need to join a movement. In our framework, it may add to a person's ideological stance (Φ). These events may also force the authorities to a confrontation and impose further restrictions on the activities of the members of the aggrieved group, thereby reducing yet more (or adding the perception thereof) the members' potential economic income (Y_i) and, consequently their stake in the present system. The importance of forcing a situation of confrontation has been well accepted as a part of the extremists' strategic planning.[6] The rationality of the strategy for eliminating the moderates has been theoretically demonstrated by Kenneth Arrow (1951) in his discussion of the "paradox of voting."[7]

Mobilization of participants acts as a cumulative factor in a collective movement, as potential participants (sympathizers) downgrade the perception of the probability of their getting apprehended (1 - p), with increased mobilization finding comfort in numbers. This "band-wagon effect" may help explain the unruly, emotional crowd behavior reported with horror by Le Bon (1895), where the participants in a riot could act on their emotions without any inhibition within the anonymity of a large crowd. Also, an increase in the mobilization of the opposition can cause a potential participant to reevaluate his political opportunity. With the prospect of a successful movement, a sympathizer may turn into an active participant. The effect of this changed perception of prospects of producing political goods has been shown in the previous chapter (Figure 4.2).

The role of the effectiveness of social control in the Smelserian paradigm refers to the capacity of the established system to apprehend and punish the participants of collective rebellion. This relates to the cost factor (C) in our expected utility model. In terms of Figure 5.3, an increase in the government's willingness (if within the capacity) to coerce will cause a downward shift in the cost curve, which will bring down the need for the ruling elite to compromise with the dissidents.

The theory of relative deprivation can also be accommodated within this expected utility model. In fact, the work of Runciman (1966) is directly complementary to our behavioral model.[8] Runciman explained participation in terms of what he called "egotistical" (a feeling of personal deprivation resulting from the failure to reach one's own goals), "fraternal" (the failure of the group to achieve its goals), and, "double deprivation" (a feeling of deprivation both personally and as a member of a deprived group). As Crosby (1979) pointed out, egotistical deprivation alone would lead to criminal or sociopathic behavior. We would argue that if there is only fraternal deprivation, it is most likely to lead to "sympathizer" behavior. However, double deprivation may cause an individual to take an active role in a political movement.

If we broaden the definition of Gurr's (1970) value expectation to include goods and services that an individual expects to get from a change in the present political system, we can see that it also relates clearly to a visionary or ideological position and, as such, can be included in the term Y_g. Therefore, if people are convinced of the inability of the present system to provide them with what they perceive to be "rightfully theirs," the gap between Y_i (defined as value capability by Gurr) and $[\Phi \cdot (Yg)]$ (defined as value expectations), can approximate relative deprivation. Hence, an increase in $[\Phi \cdot (Yg)]$, ceteris paribus, causes what Gurr calls aspirational deprivation. A decrease in $[\Phi \cdot (Yg)]$, ceteris paribus, causes decremental deprivation, and a simultaneous increase in $[\Phi . (Yg)]$ and a decrease in Yi, is termed progressive deprivation by Ted Gurr.[9]

The theory of status inconsistency developed by Daniel Bell (1964) explains right wing radicalism. According to Bell, an individual not only is concerned about his own absolute level of well-being but also evaluates it with respect to the achievements of others in the society. Therefore, even if one group's (usually the dominant one) level of achievement remains the same in absolute terms, it can feel aggrieved if it finds its relative standing in the society in jeopardy as a result of rapid achievements by some other group. This points to the existence of an interdependent utility function and as such is easily accommodated within our broad definition of economic achievement (Yi). Also, as has been forcefully pointed out by Crosby (1979), the theory of status inconsistency is perfectly compatible with Gurr's explanation of decremental deprivation.

Tilly (1974) pointed out that the absolute level of urban concentration acts as a major correlate with incidents of collective rebellion. In the expected utility framework, it can be contended that urban living exposes an individual to various ideologies consolidating his perceived need for a social change $[\Phi \cdot (Yg^m + Yg^a)]$, and lowers (owing to population concentration) his subjective estimation of being apprehended $(1 - p)$. In contrast the new immigrants to the city, with less knowledge of the terrain and the urban environment, assess upward their costs of joining a riot. This difference in the rate of participation between the recent urban immigrants and the natives was noted in the Kerner report (Kerner, 1968), where the rioters were found to be coming at a disproportionately higher rate than those who were born in the city.

Through empirical work over the last two decades a host of aggregate variables have been found to have strong correlation with the occurrence of political violence.[10] We may close this section by briefly pointing out how these variables can influence an individual's participatory decision. This list of aggregate variables would include unemployment, inflation, education, income distribution, percentage of youth in the national population, and level of economic development.

From our behavioral formulation, it is obvious that the impact of unemployment on the participatory decision is likely to be considerable. This is because with unemployment an individual's private income (Yi) dwindles. Along with it goes down the opportunity cost of political participation. Therefore, people will naturally be tempted to attempt to produce political goods instead of making futile attempts at producing economic goods. Their participation will of course depend on the relative responsiveness of the system to deliver political goods. Thus, in a politically volatile situation an individual who is already without gainful employment may reason that his opportunity to create political goods is significant. This feeling is likely to intensify if the cause of his unemployment can be tied to a specific cause such as racial, linguistic, religious, or ethnic discrimination. The more obvious the characteristics of these roots of discrimination are, the deeper will be the group sentiment. Thus, discrimination based on apparent racial differences is likely to produce stronger identity with the group cause. When the difference is not based on race but religion, this group feeling can be similarly intensified if the members of the victim group can be identified by their names or by required identification papers specifying religious affiliation. In this context, we may point out that based on our model we can safely say that if a group cannot be identified, there can be little impetus for collective goods. Thus, in a democratic society, that is religio-ethno-linguistically homogeneous - or alternately, provides a great deal of economic mobility - large degrees of economic inequality will be tolerated.

Passage of civil rights legislations and prosecutions of overt expressions of racial discrimination have brought about a greater degree of political and racial harmony in the United States. As a result the minorities, despite questionable economic gains and mounting evidence of a widening economic gap during the years of the Reagan administration, have shown little desire for violent political activism; even some of the minority groups (for example, the Hispanics) have voted for the Reagan administration and the Republican ticket in large numbers. Viewed in this light, we can conclude that the Marxian "class" distinction can hardly be a unifying force in such countries or any other, for that matter, where (unlike the midnineteenth century) economic and social mobility has been less of a factor of ascription and more of individual achievement. Therefore, it is no surprise that few political struggles around the world are truly based on class distinction. Rather, conflicts, at the base, are rooted in other divisive factors such as race, religion, language, or ethnicity, mixed in with resulting class differences. This assertion, however, is not a categorical denial of the Marxian hypothesis of class struggle in the true sense of the term. In feudal societies, where economic opportunities are defined by the parentage of an individual, given a large degree of income inequality, class can indeed be a unifying cause. The French, Russian, Chinese, Cuban, and possibly Nicaraguan revolutions are examples of class struggle. However, contrary to the Marxian assertion, it is doubtful that in the matured industrial societies with a certain amount of socioeconomic mobility political struggle can be based on class distinction alone.

Unlike unemployment, inflation is likely to be less than a significant contributory factor to political violence, unless of course the country is in the grips of a persistent hyperinflationary situation, casting doubt on the very foundation of the nation's economic system or on the present administration's capability to reduce the ill effects of a raging inflation. In fact, our previous empirical finding confirms the hypothesis that owing to the presence of "money illusion," where a certain amount of inflation gives a false sense of economic betterment, a small amount of inflation can even be a factor reducing the level of political participation (Gupta and Venieris, 1981).

Despite the age-old fear of income inequality fomenting political discontent, empirical results have been anything but decisive. This lack of hard empirical proof of correlation is partially caused by our inability to measure income inequality (Sen, 1973). Also, by looking at our model, we can see that the relationship between income inequality and political participation is likely to be complicated by a host of other factors, such as the relative opportunity to produce political goods, the relative strength of income and substitution effect among the poor, the perception of socioeconomic mobility, and the presence of an identifiable group ideology.

Foreign trade, and exposure to the outside world, was hailed by Karl Marx as an instrument for introducing the dialectical force and conflict in the stagnant, backward societies he called the "Asiatic." In his colorful language, he described the situation:

[The bourgeoisie] ... draws all, even the most barbarian, nations into civilisation. The cheap prices of its commodities are the heavy artillery with which it batters down all Chinese walls, with which it forces the barbarian's intensely obstinate hatred of foreigners to capitulate. It compels all nations , on pain of extinction, to adopt the bourgeois mode of production .. to become bourgeois themselves. In one word, it creates a world after its own image [Avinery, 1969, p. 3].

The introduction of foreign influence, therefore, erodes the legitimacy of the traditional political order. As a significant number of people become convinced of the group welfare of an alternate political system, and a new ideology takes root, the nation is besieged with incidents of political violence.

Another important contributory factor in the determination of the level of political violence is the size of youth population. In any incidence of mass insurgency, the disproportionate presence of youthful participants is almost impossible to ignore. Why are the young drawn to political violence? By resorting to our behavioral hypothesis, we may begin to provide some answers. Since most of these young participants do not work for a living and stay with their family, their economic well-being is not dependent on the time they spend in pursuing political activities. That is, when they come home after battling the authorities, their room and board are still assured. There is certainly an opportunity cost aspect of not spending time in school and getting an education. However, if their future economic well-being is independent of their educational achievement, owing to the presence of a high rate of unemployment or discrimination or both, their perception of the opportunity cost of time spent on political activity is likely to be meager. Therefore, the pictures of stone throwers in the occupied territories of Israel or the riot participants in Watts show a preponderance of youthful participants.

Also, at this point we may conjecture as to the reasons behind the lure of left-leaning ideologies to the young. Winston Churchill once commented that if one is not a socialist when he is young, he does not have a heart, but if he remains a socialist past his youth, he does not have brains. On an a priori basis this statement, made in jest, makes perverse economic sense. Recalling the assertion of philosopher John Rawls (1971), if I do not know how the pie is going to be divided, by following the rational strategy of *maximin,*[11] I should ask for an equal share. By the same logic, a young person who has not yet entered the working world faces uncertainty regarding his future share of the economic pie. Therefore, a young individual (unless he is assured of his disproportionately large share already) can be a maximizer of future utility by demanding an equal share. This is likely to be particularly true of middle-class youth. The children of the wealthy segment of the populace (the bourgeoisie, if you will) who are sure of their economic future (because of their land-holding or business ownership, which is expected to produce the current income stream, as enjoyed by their fathers) are less likely to be drawn by the philosophy of equality.[12] On the other hand, the children of the middle class, whose parents' economic prosperity is dependent on jobs they cannot bequeath, will feel less certain of their future and hence will find such philosophy more appealing. Therefore, from this perspective, Marx's prediction of revolutionary leadership coming from the well-educated middle class stands to reason.

THE OPPOSITION:
THE ROLE OF LEADERSHIP

Having explored the linkage between our behavioral hypothesis and the structural theories of collective rebellious behavior, we may devote the following few pages to the explanation of the two external influences on the individual decision-making process: the opposition and the authority. The opposition impacts the individual decision-making calculus through its influence on ideology and its administrative capacity to channelize systemic frustrations into actions of viable political opposition.

Therefore, leadership impacts an individual's decision to participate in two ways. The leaders can successfully imbue ideological fervor among the potential participants, the result of which will be an increased level of participation, often without any regard to monetary compensation for their effort. Second, leadership can develop administrative capability to reach a large number of potential participants and mobilize a sizable force of opposition. Marxist strategists such as Lenin, Mao, Trotsky, and to some extent Castro and Guevara were acutely aware of the need of leadership in focusing people's frustrations and alienation toward a goal-directed revolutionary effort. Therefore, in order to analyze the role of leadership, let us first look into ideology. In the following section, we will define ideology, analyze its determinants, discuss the problems of its inclusion in a behavioral model, and offer some suggestions about its econometric estimation.

Leadership and the Ideology of Collective Action

Ideology is one of the most troublesome terms in social sciences. The *New Webster's Dictionary* defines *ideology* as " a system of philosophy which derives ideas *exclusively* from sensation" (emphasis mine). It goes on to define it as an "abstract speculation, especially of a visionary or impractical nature." It is therefore no surprise that the term ideology should be a pariah in the realm of social sciences. If something is exclusively derived from sensation, as opposed to reason, and is assumed to be devoid of practicality, as social scientists we have very little to go by since by making it an exclusive territory of "sensation," we essentially take it out of the realm of explanation. Therefore, the ideological factor has evaded serious analytical probing by social scientists until recently.

The inclusion of the "ideological" factor in our model also needs explanation since it can make the explanation tautological or trivial. This is because whenever we cannot explain some behavior, we can easily point to the ideological factor as an answer to all the residual nonexplainable factors. Therefore, the conceptual problem of including ideology in a model is the fact that it may be contended that the inclusion of ideological orientation as a separate argument in the utility function may close the model and result in a tautology. This is particularly true as one can use ideology as a "grab bag" for anything unexplainable and place all unexplained or inexplicable phenomena phenomena squarely on the unobservable variable "ideology." However, we would like to note that, as Becker (1976b, P. 7) has argued, it is not the closure of the model that should be the issue but whether it is closed in an analytically useful way. That is, the question should be asked whether its inclusion yields a "bundle of empty tautologies" or provides the basis for predicting behavioral responses to various changes. Hence, by including ideology as a separate argument in our expected utility function, we cannot keep it as a residual factor and must provide some behavioral explanation for it as well. In other words, by including ideology in our argument, we oblige ourselves to explain it.

Ideology: A Definition

The term *ideology* can be defined in various ways. However, within our expected utility framework, we will define ideology simply as the perceived utility from collective goods. Thus, we have assumed that an individual maximizes his utility derived from two kinds of goods: private and public. For the sake of the present discussion, we will define ideology as *preference for collective goods*. In symbolic terms, we have assumed that an individual derives his utility from economic goods (Yi) and political goods (Pg). Thus, may rewrite our utility function (equation 4.1):

Max Ui = Ui (Yi, Φ· Pg)

The factor Φ measures the proportion in which an individual prefers to consume public goods in relation to private goods. It is therefore an individual's revealed preference for public goods. This Φ factor may be called preference for collective goods, altruism, or ideology. For our present discussion, we prefer to call it ideology.

The Determinants of Ideology

In our behavioral formulation the ideological component Φ determines the optimal mix between the two goods. The importance of ideological preference has been widely recognized in every walk of life; the explanation of group ideology has attracted attention from scholars of different fields. For example, a serendipitous discovery in the 1930s during a routine examination of the relationship between industrial production and working conditions revolutionized the theory of administration and started the behavioral branch of administrative science. The results of this experiment conclusively proved that individuals were motivated by factors other than their own material gains. They were also inspired to work for the group. This finding eventually launched the psychology-oriented branch of management theory, known as the behavioral or humanistic school of management. Similarly, recent works of social psychologists have lent credence to the hypothesis that human beings do not consider themselves in isolation from the rest of the society, and in fact this tendency to associate themselves with a larger self, the collective identity, is an extremely important factor in human motivation (Volkan, 1988).

We can classify the voluminous literature on the determinants of ideology into two groups: (1) ones that assume that ideological orientations are determined endogenously within the same structure of the individual rationality of attempting to maximize individual welfare, and (2) ones that somehow assume that the roots of ideological preference are external to the individual rationality structure such as, culture, heredity, class membership or group affiliation, and peer pressure. Figure 5.4 depicts the overall classification.

Economists, by and large, form the first group, which tends to believe that ideology is but a reflection of man's basic selfish instincts. Economists have tried to grapple with the determinants of ideology that cause altruistic behavior among rational economic actors who, by definition, are motivated by nothing other than their self-interest. Thus, in his biography of Thomas Hobbes, John Aubrey (1898) mentioned a conversation between Hobbes and a clergyman. Seeing Hobbes giving alms to a beggar, the clergyman inquired if Hobbes's action was not inspired by Christ's exhortion to be generous to fellow men. To this Hobbes replied that his benevolence was independent of Christ's admonition, since even an act of altruism reflects man's base instinct of self-interest. He reasoned that one engages in seemingly selfless activities such as giving alms to a panhandler because the very act gives him selfish pleasure by relieving him of the onerous task of having to set his eyes upon the unsightly misery of this wretched individual. The later development of utilitarianism by Jeremy Bentham and his followers bolstered the conviction of altruism being based on individual cost-benefit analysis. Needless to say, this kind of reasoning gives rise to tautology and completely fails to explain the differences among the individuals, or among the members of various groups, and the intensity of fervor to engage in acts that are going to benefit somebody else at the expense of the donor.

Figure 5.4

Origins of Ideology

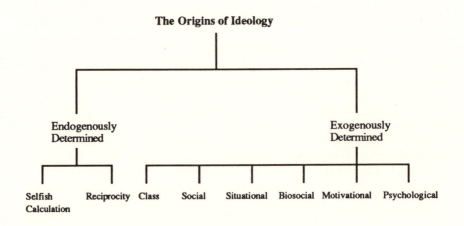

In recent literature, some economists have taken a somewhat different approach. They maintain that our altruistic tendencies are reflective of our effort to maintain some kind of parity or reciprocity with the fellow members of the group. For example, Hatfield, Walster, and Piliavin (1978) have argued that individuals will attempt to maintain equity in their social relationships with the other members over time, where "equity" is defined as a situation in which outcomes equal net reward (rewards minus costs). This model of matching donations to collective causes and receiving benefits from them is determined by the perception of equality by each contributing and recipient member of the community, where equilibrium is reached when everybody's revealed preference (preferences manifested by actions of the individuals) matches everybody else's expectations. Let us explain this point. According to this line of reasoning, we contribute to collective causes with the expectation of reciprocity of action. Thus, I contribute to my church (a collective cause) with the expectation that others will too. We all match contributions and receive benefits from the common cause. A point of equilibrium is reached when everybody's expectations about themselves and everybody else are matched. If, however, they do not, we reevaluate out commitment to the cause. Thus, we all seem to have a vague notion of "fair share." If, for example, we find out that others are contributing more or less than what we expect them to, we change our level of contribution accordingly. Thus, upon hearing that our neighbors are contributing more, we may want to increase our own share, and vice versa. Similarly, we are incensed by stories of welfare fraud and as a result, tend to withdraw our support for our contribution.   Other writers (Guttman, 1978; Sugden, 1984) have devised more complex rules of reciprocity.[13]

If attempts to explain the logic of collective action run into logical difficulty while assuming selfish motivations, the introduction of externally imposed preference functions for collective goods produces different kinds of problems. Karl Marx, for example, assumed almost a deterministic model when he argued that an individual is likely to act according to his own class interest, which is determined external to his rational thinking process, his class association.[14]

The fundamental inability of the rule of individual profit maximization to explain such behavior as the effort to provide collective goods or altruism (or, by our definition, preference for public goods) has prodded economists and political scientists engaged in developing behavioral models to introduce ideological factors through the back door without calling them so.[15]   Thus, several authors have accepted the external origin of individual preference for collective goods. For instance, Laffont (1975), Collard, (1978, 1983), and Harsanyi (1980) have argued that as a member of a group an individual makes a commitment by choosing the level of effort that he would most prefer every member of the group make, and then, having made this determination, obliges himself to make at least that much effort. This rule has been widely called *Kantian* or as Harsanyi (1980) calls it, a principle of "rational commitment." Hardin (1978) has used this notion of a "calculating Kantian" who, instead of looking at his personal costs and benefits, makes the calculation of net gains from the standpoint of his group.[16]

We find the similar embracing of the notion of an externally generated ideological preference in the work of Howard Margolis (1982). Margolis comes very close to our formulation when he argues that an individual has two utility functions - what he calls the S- utility, and the G-utility. The S-utility measures the utility of the self (in our formulation, Y_i), and the G-utility measures group utility (in our formulation, P_g). To Margolis, we make decisions about the relative shares of the two utility functions based on some notion of "fair share."

In contrast to the economists the social psychologists have offered the situational theories of the origin of ideology. This group of theories (Aronfreed and Paskal, 1968; Hornstein, Fisch, and Holms, 1968; Rosenhan, 1969) emphasizes the role of external environmental variables in shaping one's ideological orientation. The empirical models based on these theories, for instance, have found altruistic ideology as dependent on the pressure to conform to group norms (Blake, Rosenbaum, and Duryea, 1955; Bryan and Test, 1967), or the desire to imitate other altruistic models (Bandura and Walters, 1963; Bandura, 1973).[17] The desire to join a collective movement was also found to be positively correlated with the actor's experience of success or failure in similar previous endeavors (Berkowitz and Connor, 1966). On the other side of the coin, Darley and Latane (1969) provided evidence that where group norm is not well defined (and consequently, the external pressure to confirm to the group norm is minimal), the member's desire to contribute to the cause of the collectivity is diminished. Latane and Rodin (1969) arrived at the same conclusion to find that the effort for collective goods is inversely related to the group definition of altruism. Wallace and Sadalla (1966) argued that where transgressions from the group norm, which might ordinarily lead to reparative altruism, are private as opposed to public, help is less likely for the effort to procure nonexcludable public goods.

The criticism of the situational theory of the origin of group ideology can take three different forms: limited relevance, the problem of individual variation over time, and lack of necessary reinforcement. However, we will argue that all these criticisms have somewhat diminished validity, given the purpose of our study.

First, researchers such as Saranson, Smith, and Diener, (1975), based on individual psychological study estimated that the environmental factors account for only about ten percent of the total variance, whereas the personality factors account for another nine percent, indicating a rather complex explanation of altruism. However, for us, interested primarily in the behavior of the aggregate, the individual variation may not be of much significance, unless of course the situational factors fail to explain the variations of behavior in the aggregate.

Another group of studies (Krebs, 1975, 1978) have attacked the underlying assumption of the situational theory - that the theory assumes that every individual is going to react similarly given a similar

set of environmental factors. Krebs (1975) argued that it not only fails
to account for individual variations but also is unable to provide a
rationale for a dissimilar behavioral response to the same set of stimuli
by the same individual over time. Also, Krebs rightfully points out
that the interpretation of many of the studies exploring the situational
correlates of altruism is open to the ubiquitous problem of
interpretation of the definitions of relevant variables and their
measurement (Krebs, 1975, 78). However, many of these criticisms
arising mostly from psychologists and other non-social scientists,
however cogent, go to the heart of empirical research in the realm of
social science. In social science, when exploring aggregate
relationships, we cannot but ignore individual variation under the
assumption of random variation and "white noise" and concentrate
instead on explaining the central tendency of the distribution.

The third problem of the behaviorally oriented situational theory
lies in the fact that its advocates, at least implicitly, rely on motivational
principles derived from behavioral psychology to supply an
explanatory base. Thus, reinforcement of some kind is assumed in the
behavioral response. However, much of altruistic behavior, especially
when done anonymously, cannot be accounted for by the situational
theory, as by definition of anonymity, there can be no reinforcement of
behavior (Losco, 1986). However, again, when considering overt
behavior such as participation in the acts of political violence, this
criticism finds less relevance.

The main proponents of the evolutionary approach to altruism
are the sociobiologists or anthropologists. The evolutionary theories of
altruism center around the notion of "inclusive fitness" (Hamilton,
1964; Mayr, 1965; E. O.Wilson, 1975). The concept of inclusive
fitness refers to the notion that "individual organisms act in such a
manner as to maximize the preservation of genes they share with
related others" (Losco, 1986, p. 329). Thus, any act of selflessness
for the benefit of the group is ultimately related to primal desire to
increase the number of related genes (D. S. Wilson, 1980). The
development of the evolutionary theory can also be traced to the widely
known work of Konrad Lorenz (1966), who has argued over the years
for the biological origins of violence and warfare.

However, we have experienced numerous examples of
altruistic behavior across the group or related gene pool that cannot be
explained by the instinct for inclusive fitness. Trivers (1971) has
attempted to solve the paradox by assuming a desire for reciprocity.
That is, when I do something nice for an unrelated person, by my act I
express the desire that a similar act of kindness be shown to me under a
reverse situation. Trivers argues that this kind of reciprocal altruism is
particularly prominent in species with a relative long life span. It is
also a function of advanced intelligence, mutual dependence, low
dispersal rate, and absence of a strong linear dominance hierarchy.
This line of analysis has been extended to the study of social, political,
and economic interaction by researchers such as Willhoite (1980) and

Masters (1983). The shortcoming of this instinctive biological theory is that it produces a narrow and rigid explanation of human behavior and takes the acts of altruism outside the realm of behavioral explanation.

There is no way to resolve this longstanding controversy over the determinants of ideology. However, for our purpose it will suffice (or at least satisfice) to note that although the value of ideology in the explanation of human social, political, and economic behavior is coming under sharp focus in the recent literature, a lot more effort should be devoted to the systematic exploration of its determinants. Therefore, for our study we will point out the importance of ideology as an explanatory variable for collective political behavior and assume it to be externally determined by a set of environmental variables that reinforces one's group identity.

Groups and Group Ideology

We defined ideology as the preference for collective goods for the group in which the potential participant belongs. From this premise, we can deduce that the intensity of ideological fervor is likely to deepen with the recognition of one's group identity. Looking at the formation of group identity, we can divide it into two categories, which we can call *ascriptive* and *adoptive*. An ascriptive group is based on birth. Thus, divisions along the lines of ethnicity, language, or even religion can be classified as ascriptive groups. Membership in these groups is involuntary and is impossible to renounce.

In contrast, groups can also be formed according to tastes, preference, or economic achievement. Thus, one may want to join a radical environmental group such as Green Peace, an antiabortion group, or an animal rights activist group. These groups can be called adoptive group.   Marx placed membership in economic classes squarely on birth. Within the context of the late-nineteenth century, the categorization of economic class in otherwise homogeneous societies of Europe as ascriptive made sense. In today's heterogeneous world - even in the developed democratic world - despite advances made in the provision of equality of opportunity and social mobility, it seems that a vast majority of the so-called economic classes also follow along the lines of some other kinds of ascriptive group membership. Therefore, one may look at conflict in United States, northern Ireland, or South Africa either as expressions of class conflict or as manifestations of racism.

Looking at the formation of groups we may ask, What causes the deepening of ideology or group identity? On an apriori ground, we may argue that the strength of a group identity will be the function of how separate a group feels from the rest of the society. If the group is based on obvious ascriptive features based upon race, ethnicity, or language, the group identity is likely to be stronger than when they are not so readily apparent. Thus, the Afro Americans in the United States or the blacks in South Africa, the Sikhs in India, or the north Africans in France, for example, may fall in this category. Also, within the same race, religious affiliation may be distinguished by names. In such cases, the feeling of alienation from the larger society may be just as strong. Second, this feeling of alienation is likely to be reinforced by the degree of discriminatory practices. Thus, a Polish American in the United States may be distinguished by his last name, and if he is a Catholic, he may also feel alienation from the larger Protestant culture; however, the fervor of his antisystemic political activity as a part of his ethnic group will depend on the extent of discrimination he faces outside his community as a member of his group. As the level of discrimination increases, his group identity will deepen, thereby sharpening his perception of the utility of the collective good - the elimination of discrimination.

Groups based on adoptive membership, such as antiabortion groups, may also feel alienation from the rest of the society that condones abortion. In such a case, a member of such a group has the advantage of not being recognized as a member of a minority group. For him, his sense of group identity will be reinforced by factors of provocation, such as the passage of laws liberalizing abortion. Also, these groups are likely to be of a temporary nature, as membership, unlike in the case of ascriptive groups, cannot be readily bequeathed.

Specifically, research in sociopsychology (Deaux and Wrightsman, 1984) distinguishes several inter-dependent factors that determine the internal dynamics of group behavior to solidify group allegiance. These are size, communication, cohesiveness, and leadership. From the antiquity of the Aristotelian inquiry into the optimum size of a city-nation, scholars have attempted to determine the relationship between size and group effectiveness. However, controlled experiments on the question are feasible only in very small groups (i.e., see Davis, et al. 1976), therefore, is seems that for generation of political violence the other three aspects are more important than the absolute size of an opposition group.[18] The group size is meaningless when effective communication within the group is limited or there is a lack of cohesion or leadership.

The capacity of a group to reinforce the group feeling depends to a large extent upon the nature of communication. Analysis of past rebellions shows the importance of communication in forging a group identity. For example, during the Sepoy mutiny in India during 1857, the dissident soldiers had started to distribute symbolic loaves of bread as a symbol of solidarity.[19] Similarly, taped messages from the exiled Ayatollah, distributed through the vast networks of mosques, formed the basis of revolution in Iran (Abrahamian, 1986). Recent research in sociopsychology has also stressed the structure of the communications network (Shaw, 1978).

The term cohesiveness implies the closeness of purpose and feeling that is prevalent within a group (Vraa, 1974, Davis et al. 1976). This emotional attachment is dependent on the nature of the goal, as well as the possibility of external threats and the feeling of "separateness" from the larger group. Thus, a small group, or minority, may depict extreme closeness of views and purpose when the members feel isolated from the rest of the society and are threatened. In such a situation, it will be quite likely for members to subvert their individual preferences for group welfare. This sense of cohesion can also be based on cultural heritage or religious beliefs.[20]

Finally, the extent of group allegiance can be a function of the charismatic nature of leadership. We may combine the factors of communication, cohesion, and leadership into what we may broadly call factors of administrative capability.

Leadership and the Administrative Capability of the Opposition

If the existence of systemic frustration provides the necessary condition for political violence, the level of leadership and the administrative capability of the opposition deliver the sufficient condition for an uprising. In the communist literature, we can see two distinct strategies being advocated for ushering in a successful proletarian revolution. Marx's ambiguous position in his simultaneous assertion of the inevitability of the collapse of the capitalist system and introduction of socialism, on the one hand, and the need for the leadership role of the Communist party, on the other hand, created a schism in the later communist literature and produced two distinct lines of political strategy. Thus, Kautsky contended that the spontaneous sparks of revolt were sufficient in bringing down the present system, whereas Lenin forcefully asserted the need for correct leadership in a successful revolution.

This latter line of reasoning was further bolstered by Lenin and Mao, and to some extent by Leon Trotsky.[21] Mao (1972a and 1972b) essentially held that revolutions may be historically inevitable, but the timing of their deliverance must be done through skillful political maneuvering by the "professional revolutionaries." Mao emphasized the role of leadership and the necessity to develop a strong administrative network of the party faithfuls based upon "politicization" of the proletariat. Mao repeatedly pointed out in his writings that the politicized peasantry (meaning, peasantry convinced of the futility of staying within the present political economic system and the efficacy of the future socialistic society) must provide the cover for the guerrillas and carry on their administrative network.

In contrast to Mao, many communist activists in Latin America, following Che Guevara, have assumed a stockpile of "class hatred" that is ready to explode from the first revolutionary spark. Therefore, they downplayed the need to establish an elaborate party network or to spend time on the "politicization" (political education) of the masses. Instead, they attempted to provide this revolutionary "spark" by taking up armed actions against the government and the establishment. This similar line of revolutionary strategy was taken up by the Naxalite guerrillas in the eastern part of India during the late 1960s under the leadership of Charu Mazumder, where they attempted to "ignite" the assumed omnipresent "class hatred" by the so-called "revolutionary acts" of armed attacks on the oppressive village landlords and the notorious money lenders (Ghosh,1975; Banerjee, 1980).[22]

However, the problem of assuming a wide-scale ideologically based revolutionary or counterrevolutionary sentiment among the populace is that frequently these assumptions are made by the ideologues for whom these may be the reflections of wishful thinking. The failures of Che Guevara, as well as the humiliating defeat for the U. S. backed troops in the Bay of Pigs, offer ample examples of the follies of such drastic assumptions. Second, by looking at our expected utility model, it is obvious that for a person to change from a sympathizer to an active participant, they would require a lot of convincing. For the extremely poor, the "lumpen proletariat," who are existing at the subsistence level, the income effect of a reduction in income is likely to be stronger than the substitution effect. That is, facing the prospect of losing even a subsistence wage can be substantial, as these people would be reluctant to divert time from the production of economic goods to political goods even in the face of extreme sociopolitical privation. Hence, it is hardly surprising that manifest reaction among the South African blacks, even in the face of extreme social injustice, is not uniformly against the white regime. As for the relatively affluent, living above the minimum subsistence, the opportunity costs of income can be significant, especially when the alternative is not very obvious and the ideological position is not very well formed. Therefore, for any movement to be successful one would need to convince the potential participants that his own needs and his group's need would be best served by his joining the forces of the opposition for which one needs the administrative capability of the opposing party.

By using three variables, ideology, mobilization, and administrative capabilities of the opposition, we may develop a useful descriptive scheme for classifying rebellions. This has been depicted in Figure 5.5.

In this Figure, let us start from the lower-left-hand corner of the box. If we have low ideological fervor, low mobilization, and low administrative capability, we are going to find a "sleeper" situation even in a nation with a high degree of systemic frustration. Naturally, with the presence of high levels of these three factors we are going to find successful revolutions (the upper-right-hand corner of the box). Thus, in Iran, we find a strong opposition to the Shah emanating from the religious fundamentalists who not only provided the ideological justification but also, through the network of mosques, offered an effective administrative structure. In contrast, the Shah's administrative apparatus increasingly became isolated from the masses (Abrahamian, 1986).

A revolutionary movement is likely to fail, however, if it has ideology and mobilization but little administrative capability with the opposition leadership. A situation of a high degree of mobilization and organization capability with little ideology will deliver an organized riot (sometimes even by the forces sympathetic to the government, such as the one that took place in the aftermath of the assassination of Indira Gandhi in India). A large number of disorganized bands of aggrieved people will create conditions of mob violence similar to the recent riots in several U.S. cities.

Figure 5.5

Factors of Opposition Leadership and the Outcomes of Political Movements

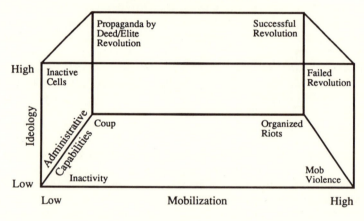

The left-hand side of the box is characterized by a low level of mobilization. A political action, failing to get much popular support, will get into symbolic acts of "propaganda by deed' if there is enough ideological fervor among the participants. This is the typical situation for a terrorist campaign. These acts do not carry any particular political motive or strive to achieve any specific political goods. Instead, they expect propaganda for their cause and assertion of their frustration to the rest of the world. Typical acts terrorism fall in this category.

When a small, cohesive group is formed with a high degree of administrative capability, a conspiracy is hatched for a coup d'état.

Without indoctrination and with an effective organization, one can expect the rebellion to remain contained within a small group and to cause coups d'état or elite revolutions such as the ones that occurred in Turkey (1919), Japan (1868), Egypt (1952), and Peru (1968) (see Trimberger, 1986). Thus, in many Latin American countries, where the forces of opposition among the masses are almost nonexistent in ideological indoctrination and administrative capability is confined within the military, the only logical outcome of systemic frustration is coup d'état.

THE RULING AUTHORITY

Regime Legitimacy

The role of the ruling authority, in contrast to the opposition, rests with its two capacities. They are the capacity (1) to gain legitimacy among the people and (2) to inflict punishment on the unconvinced defiants.

The importance of legitimacy as a precondition for political stability has been well recognized in the literature. As we have noted above, communist writers such as Trotsky were keenly aware of the role of political legitimacy in creating a revolutionary condition and maintained that for a revolution to take place the shroud of legitimacy of the political authorities must be blown away. Lipset (1959), in his widely cited work, defines legitimacy by noting that it involved the capacity of a political system to engender and maintain the belief that the existing political institutions are the most appropriate or proper ones for the society. The varied literature seems to point to two sources of political legitimacy: the democratic form of government, and the maintenance of economic prosperity.

As is evident from the title of Lipset's article (1959), "Some Social Requisites of Democracy: Economic Development and Political Legitimacy," the concept of legitimacy is almost intertwined with democracy. This is because it has been emphasized that since democracy is dependent on the will of the majority, which is exercised through the widely acceptable rule of the national constitution, a government based on democratic principles enjoys legitimacy in the eyes of its citizens. However, we should remember that political legitimacy is essentially a subjective assessment by the citizens of a country. Therefore, if, following Lipset, legitimacy is conceived as the acceptance of the justification of the right to rule as morally right and binding on both the masses and the elites, then it is possible that a society may be partially democratic but illegitimate, such as the Weimar Republic after 1928, or legitimate but nondemocratic, such as the present one-party rule in Japan, Ethiopia during the 1940s, and the present-day monarchy of Nepal or even Thailand. The conception of legitimacy involves knowledge of mass attitudes on the acceptance of the rule and the ruler as morally proper.   Hence, for a true operationalization of the concept of legitimacy, we would require information about individual attitude derived through interviews or surveys.   However, no such information is currently available, and such counterexamples are relatively rare.   Therefore, in the political science literature, especially in the empirical studies, democracy has been conveniently used as a surrogate for the concept of perceived legitimacy of a regime.   Thus, Bwy (1968b), in his attempt to explain political instability in Latin America, defined legitimacy by the degree of democratization by using a composite scale devised by Fitzgibbon (1967).   Therefore, we can deduce that a constitutional democracy, by its very nature, generates legitimacy.   The nondemocratic forms of government, on the other hand, may lack wide-scale legitimacy as they are ruled by a very small number of people in the country.   This can change, however, if the dictator is able to inculcate in his people a strong sense of ideology, which appeals to their collective identity. Thus, many communist rulers, as well as charismatic autocrats, such as Qaddafi of Libya, Straussner of Uruguay, Nasser of Egypt, and Khomeini of Iran, to name a few, have been able to hold on to power through their appeal to the national ideology.

Another powerful source of regime legitimacy is its promise of economic prosperity.   Recalling Lipset's (1959) definition, it is obvious that if the regime can generate the belief that it is the most appropriate for the society through its past economic performance, then the public becomes convinced of its legitimacy, despite its shortcomings in many other areas.   Thus, it is no surprise that the incumbent president, or the ruling party, has an excellent chance of returning to power in a democratic election.   Therefore, a powerful opposition movement is unlikely to take place in the midst of continuous economic prosperity.   A long economic prosperity will mask all social injustices as long as there is a reasonable hope that the enlargement of the economic pie will increase at least the absolute size of the share.   There are numerous examples of nations that despite a strong authoritarian rule, appalling human rights violations, glaring corruption, or other social and economic injustices tolerate the rule of a government that can provide them with a sustained level of economic prosperity.

Therefore, the feeling of regime legitimacy is reinforced by ideology and economic prosperity.   South Korea, during the presidency of Park Chung Hee, and Taiwan have been able to provide both of these two factors to their people, in terms of a strong xenophobic, anticommunist ideology, as well as a prolonged period of economic prosperity (C. Johnson, 1988). However, as the fear of a North Korean invasion waned and the nation experienced certain economic slowdowns, the South Korean government of Chun Doo-Hwan lost its legitimacy with a large segment of the population, especially the young South Koreans. This ultimately forced a change in its political system.

Government Coercion

The other important factor in determining an individual's response to a potential conflict situation is the expected loss from a government retribution. As we have argued above, this expected loss is determined by the probability of getting apprehended $(1 - p)$ and the severity of punishment (C).   We can, therefore, divide the government's action to subjugate political opposition into two aspects: *extensiveness* and *intensity* of coercion. The extensiveness factor impacts individual actor's perception of the subjective probability of his getting apprehended, and the intensity of coercion formulates the perception of the magnitude of his loss, once apprehended.

The probability of getting apprehended depends on the capability of the nation's security system, as well as the nature of participation in the acts of violence against the political system. Thus, in a country with a highly sophisticated police network, aided by advanced technology in communication, the political system's capability of detection and apprehension is likely to be substantial. However, even in nations without a technologically advanced communication system, this capability can be significant by the wide participation of the general population in securing the nation against those who intend to undermine the present political order. Thus, in China the use of the "Granny patrol," or the use of elderly women and men as neighborhood informers, enhances greatly the capability of detection of any political dissension.   The second part of the cost function relates to the severity of punishment once apprehended. In the strict authoritarian as well as in the communist nations, such as in the Stalinist Soviet Union, the severity of punishment has been notorious. When confronting an uncertain cost, a rational individual evaluates the expected value, that is, the probability of being apprehended, multiplied by the severity of punishment. Therefore, in the following discussion, we will refer to this composite factor as the "extent of coercion" or simply "coercion."

The relationship between the extent of coercion and dissident participation has received extensive attention by psychologists and social psychologists and - based on the accumulated empirical evidence collected both at the clinical experimental level and by using aggregate national data - points to a quadratic relationship. That is, contrary to popular supposition, the introduction of coercive force will not have an automatic negative impact on the frequency and intensity of participation in the forbidden activity. This is because, as Gurr (1970) argued, that to counter force with force is part of man's biological makeup. Therefore, in the beginning of the coercive process, or when the authorities begin to apply negative sanctions, the participants react predictably by mounting even more counterforce.[23] This process of matching force with force continues up to the point where what Gurr calls the "equilibrium of high coercion and high violence" is reached.[24] Beyond this point the complexion of confrontation changes as the participants become convinced of the resolve of the authorities and their willingness to use brutal force to bring down the expressions of defiance. The existence of this quadratic relationship, depicted in Figure 5.6, has been confirmed in laboratory experiments, as well as in studies using aggregate national data (Hibbs, 1973; Venieris and Gupta, 1983; Muller, 1985; Ziegenhagen, 1986).[25] Also, in an interesting study of riot behavior in a number of cities in the United States, Chalmers and Shelton (1975) found evidence that while the deployment of the local police force only added to the intensity of the riots, the introduction of the National Guard (demonstrably a stronger response) brought down the participatory enthusiasm.

Figure 5.6

The Relationship between Coercion and Participation in Collective Violence

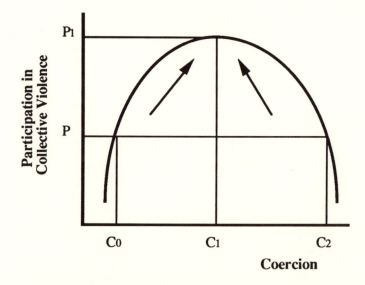

This aspect of the individual response to the prospect of repression has been particularly puzzling as the rational reaction of an increase in cost is likely to be a diminished level of participation in political activities. Thus, in discerning the impact of the perception of expected cost of participation in collective political action, Muller and Opp, (1986), in their social experiment, report similar findings that go against the grains of rational choice theory: That is, respondents who believe that rebellious behavior is likely to be costly show a somewhat greater tendency to participate than those who believe otherwise. The authors speculate that this "anomaly " may reflect a "martyr" syndrome or, alternatively, that higher expected costs may be closely intertwined with the perception of a higher desirability of public goods.

Apart from the assumption of the biological makeup of the human animal, another explanation of the quadratic relationship between coercion and defiance, based on an observed bias in the perception of probability, can be posited. The expected utility theory postulates the hypothesis that individuals assess the prospective outcome of uncertain alternatives by multiplying the probability of success by the reward. However, French mathematical economist Allais (1952) noted a paradoxical behavioral trait, that in the field of behavioral economics has come to be known as the *Allais paradox*. Controlled laboratory experiments within the expected utility framework indicate that participants facing a high probability level tend to overcompensate systematically for changes in probabilities. Conversely, individuals demonstrate a lack of sensitivity to small probability changes at low probability level. An example may clarify this interesting case of behavioral anomaly. Consider the following two cases. Suppose we are faced with two uncertain outcomes; the first alternative promises to pay $1 million with a probability of wining one in ten (p = 0.1), whereas the second alternative gives $50,000 with a certain chance (p = 1.0) of wining. Under the precept of objective rationality, the actor is expected to choose the first alternative, as its expected value of $100,000 ($1,000,000 x 0.1) is greater than that of the second alternative, $50,000 ($50,000 x 1.0). However, repeated experiments with subjects reveal a preponderant preference for the certain outcome with a smaller reward factor. Similarly, in the second case, suppose we have two alternatives: The first alternative carries the reward of $1 million, and the second alternative promises $5 million, with the corresponding probabilities of winning being one in 10,000 (p=0.0001) and one in 100,000 (p = 0.00001). Again, despite the fact that the first alternative carries a higher expected benefit ($1,000,000 x 0.0001 = $100 > $5,000,000 x .00001= $50), the players seem to get more attracted by the size of the reward and tend to choose the second alternative. Therefore, the literature on the Allais paradox concludes that when the probability is extremely high, people's decisions tend to be more influenced by the probability, whereas when the probability factor is extremely low, the decisions are governed by the size of the reward.[26] Although the evidence is still inconclusive as to the general nature of probability transformations, (particularly with respect to its stability over individuals and its dependence on outcomes), most behavioral studies find that the subjective probabilities tend to be higher than objective ones as outcome becomes more desirable, reflecting some kind of "wishful thinking" (Slovic, 1966; Rosett, 1971; Kahneman and Tversky, 1979). In view of these fairly robust experimental results, we may expect the perceived probabilities in our expected utility model to be subject to the same kinds of biases and distortions. Therefore, facing a relatively low probability of being apprehended (low extensiveness of government coercion), a potential participant is likely to respond relatively more to a change in the perception of ideological [$\Phi \cdot Y_g)$] as well as material payoffs (L) in the initial stages of the movement. However, as the extent of coercion begins to increase, and the probability of apprehension gets larger and larger, the potential participants tend to focus more on the near certainty of the loss factor, rather than the prospect of gains. This, along with Gurr's (1970) "biological makeup," and Muller's (Muller, 1985; Muller and Opp, 1986) "martyr syndrome" can offer justification for the seemingly irrational response at the early stages of coercion.

THE DYNAMICS OF POLITICAL ACTION

So far we have attempted to analyze the motivations behind participation in actions of collective violence for the achievement of public goods. However, by combining the various arguments, we can construct a theoretical model describing the development of a political movement.   The dynamic system outlined below is based on the interaction of two parties, the government and the opposition. For the sake of simplicity and the convenience of using geometric tools, we confine our analyses to the interaction of only two groups.   The analysis can, however, be extended to sectarian and more complex kinds of social movements involving multiple parties.

In the discussion above, we have developed several behavioral relationships. Thus, in Figure 5.7 we trace the level of political violence as a function of the factors of systemic frustration. In Figure 5.7 the curves measure people's propensity to take on an active role against an established political system. In line with our previous reasoning, we have assumed the relationship to be positive. That is, the higher the level of systemic frustration, ceteris paribus, the higher the propensity to participate in antisystemic activities. We may note that in this Figure the role of leadership is subsumed. Based on the action and the ability of the leadership to influence the ideological perception and interpretation of events - with the other environmental factors influencing the overall level of frustration remaining the same - the reaction curve (a) can shift upward (a') or downward (a''). It may also be noted that this shift represents activities similar to a "political entrepreneur" performing the role of a catalyst (Frohlich et al., 1971). For instance, it can be seen that a certain level of systemic frustration, f_0, can be translated into different levels of political reaction based on the capability of the opposition leadership to inspire and mobilize people.   Therefore, depending on the leadership, f_0 amount of systemicfrustration can generate p_0 (moderate), p_1 (low) or p_2 (high) levels of political violence.

Figure 5.7

The Relationship between the Factors of Systemic Frustration and Collective Violence

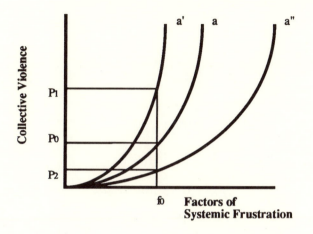

Figure 5.8

The Coercive Reaction of Government to Collective Violence

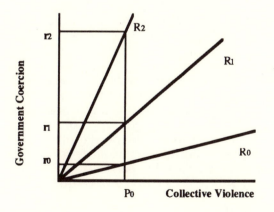

The Figure 5.8 illustrates government's reaction to a situation of political violence. Thus, facing a certain level of opposition (say, P_0), the government may elect to react mildly along the line R_0, moderately along R_1, or with a high degree of ferocity, R_2, producing r_0, r_1, and r_2 levels of coercion.

Figure   5.9

Government Policy, Systemic Frustration, and Collective Rebellion

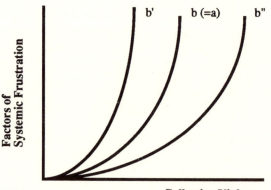

Figure 5.9 depicts the response of the authorities toward the factors of systemic frustration in the face of collective rebellion.   In this Figure, the lines b, b', and b" plot the impact of government action in mitigating or instigating the causes of political violence. If the government, facing mounting opposition, does nothing to reduce the actual causes of systemic frustration, according to this diagram, we will get line (b), a mirror image of line (a) in Figure 5.7. In this case the government does nothing to reduce tension, but neither does it exacerbate the situation by taking punitive economic or political measures. However, if a government takes on a provocative posture (e.i, increases the price of food stuff during a period of food riot), the curve may shift upward from b to b'. If, on the other hand, the government takes a conciliatory position and reduces political tension by granting concessions to the opposition demands, the reduction in resulting political activity will be shown by a downward shift in curve b to b".

An interaction of the factors represented in the above four diagrams (Figures 5.6 through 5.9) demonstrates the simultaneity in the relationship and has been combined in Figure 5.10. In this Figure, we develop a theoretical model of dynamic interaction between the

Figure 5.10

The Dynamic Interaction between Government and the Opposition

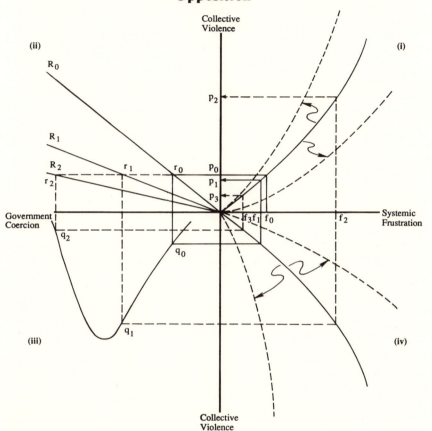

government and the forces of opposition and depict the interaction by combining the four diagrams within a four-quadrant diagram.

We start from the north eastern quadrant of the diagram, which we call quadrant **i**. In this quadrant the horizontal axis measures the factors of systemic frustration, and the vertical axis measures the extent of collective violence. Let us assume that the society is experiencing a frustration level represented by the point f_0. This level of systemic frustration can be caused by environmental factors such as unemployment, income inequality, discrimination, and high inflation.

This level of systemic frustration from the structural strain factors generates, say, p_0 level of collective violence. Facing p_0 level of political violence, the authorities in the government have three options: to respond mildly along the reaction function R_0, moderately along R_1, or severely along R_2. If the authorities decide to react in a mild fashion, say, according to the reaction function R_0 in quadrant **ii**, a government response of r_0 level of coercion will result.

This government reaction of r_0 level of coercion prompts a further round of political protest, which is shown as the point q_0 in the southwestern quadrant **iii**. Facing this new level of violence, a government, apart from the coercive measures, may try to take positions (1) to mollify the situation by taking steps along the reaction line b", (2) to aggravate the situation by taking further divisive action along b', or (3) to maintain the the current situation (along the mirror image of line $b = a$). Supposing the government does not try to change the overall environment, then it is apparent from the diagram that the level of political violence in the society will reduce to f_1 in the next period.

It is also obvious from the diagram that the situation can alter by a unilateral action by the government, by the opposition, or as a result of inflammatory action by both the parties. In a situation where both the parties attempt to overmatch the action of the other, the situation will escalate toward an explosive cycle. If they just match each other's action, we will have a situation of a perpetual cycle of violence, with neither party "upping the ante" nor taking any measures to reduce tension. If, on the other hand, one party remains conciliatory, there is a chance of overall tension subsiding, providing of course the peaceful stance is not interpreted as a sign of weakness, in which case the pressure for the final victory can intensify (in our Figure, a leftward shift in the response curve in quadrant **i**).

Figure 5.10 also points out that if the government applies coercion but acts less than decisively, along the reaction line R_1 in the second quadrant (**ii**), facing a p_1 level of violence, this reaction function will produce a coercion level of q_1. This action, being seen as an act of provocation, can heighten the level of violence to the point p_2 even when the authorities maintain the same level of environmental condition (by remaining along the line b in the fourth quadrant).

The government may also decide to react with the utmost show of force. If the government is able to deliver a swift and decisive blow to the opposition movement, it can bring about tranquility at a huge cost of human rights abuse and the sacrifice of other fundamental rights guaranteed by the democratic constitutions. This result is depicted by following the government reaction function R_2.[27]

However, we may note that a government's ability to deliver a coercive measure in a, sudden, and decisive manner and to sustain it, if necessary, for a long period of time is limited by several factors, such as the legal and political structure of the country, the level of domestic and international support for the opposition movement, the level of technology, and the administrative efficiency of the regime. In a country with a tradition of strict adherence to law and procedural justice (typically a Western democratic nation), this show of force may be extremely difficult to achieve; or if achieved, it will be almost impossible to sustain. In such a case the power of persuasion will have to be taken resort to, which will call for the alteration of the lines on the Fourth quadrant, meaning a significant reconciliation and redressing of the grievances of the opposition. We will have a chance to elaborate on the policy prescriptions in our concluding chapter.

THE DYNAMICS OF SECTARIAN VIOLENCE

In the above discussion, we have assumed the interaction between the government and the opposition. Before concluding this chapter, let us examine the dynamics of another another type of violence: sectarian violence. A sectarian violences can often take on a life of its own. Frequently the main driving force in a sectarian violence is the need to react to the other party, rather than any immediate economic or political issue. For this type of violence, these issues might be at the bottom of the initial conflict. However, with the passage of time the members of the two opposing groups engage in a feud where, despite well-defined economic or political goals, it becomes more important to react to the other group's acts of aggression than to resolve any immediate issue. In such situations, debates between the groups end up being exchanges of charges of "atrocious acts" perpetrated by the other. The violence in northern Ireland, Lebanon, or Sri Lanka may have taken on this characteristic of sectarian violence. We may express the dynamics of sectarian violence with two simple equations. Suppose, the two feuding groups are A and B. For simplicity, let us assume that how A is going to react this time depends on the acts of B in the previous time period, and vice versa. That is, we can write:

$$Ra = a_0 + a_1 Rb_{(-1)} \qquad\qquad (5.1)$$
and
$$Rb = b_0 + b_1 Ra_{(-1)} \qquad\qquad (5.2)$$

where:

Ra and Rb	= reactions of group A and B, respectively
	Subscript (-1) denotes the previous time period
a_1	= reaction coefficient of group A
b_1	= reaction coefficient of group B

Notice that if the size of the reaction coefficient is equal to one, then it means that the group is electing to react in a way that is of equal proportion to the act of its rival. That is, both parties are operating under the principle of "a tooth for a tooth, an eye for an eye." If the coefficient is greater than one (two teeth for one), then the group is "upping the ante," and has decided to respond more than proportionately. A conciliatory gesture by a group, however, will be signified by a less-than-one size of the reaction coefficient (a tooth for two teeth). Now, by substituting (5.1) into (5.2), we get the following second order difference equation:

$$Ra = a^*_0 + a_1(b_0 + b_1) Ra_{(-2)}$$

which yields:

$$Ra = a^*_0 + a_1 b_1 Ra_{(-2)} \tag{5.3}$$

where, a^*_0 is equal to $(a_0 + a_1 b_0)$.

Therefore, from equation (5.3) it is clear that by taking a reactionary mode, whatever group A chooses to do today - after being modified by the actions of the other group - comes back to determine its decision two time periods later. Now, from this equation we can deduce three possible scenarios: First, if the parties engaged in a sectarian violence choose to retaliate in the same measure, the conflict can go on indefinitely. In many cases around the world, we see that both parties seem to have a pretty good idea of what is a measured response, and until the point that one of the parties becomes convinced that the other one is opting for an escalation, the level of violence may go on at a steady rate. The conflict in northern Ireland, to a large extent, can be taken as an example of this kind of perpetual violence. Second, in contrast, if both the parties want to react more than proportionately (or if the product of the of their two reaction coefficients is greater than one) conflict will soon escalate beyond control until at least one of them ceases hostility either by strategic choice or out of sheer exhaustion. The Iran-Iraq war, which slowly escalated over an eight-year span, may be a case in point of such a situation. And third, if at least one of the parties decides to retaliate less than proportionately, then there exists a strong possibility that in time the level of violence will tend to subside. As an example of this, we may cite the case of the Hindu-Sikh conflict in India. After the assassination of Indira Gandhi, some Hindu thugs and the criminal element in several cities went on a rampage of looting Sikh properties, raping and killing indiscriminately (Akbar, 1985; Tully and Jacob, 1985). But, after the situation was brought under control, the Sikh extremists started to retaliate. However, the reaction of the Hindu community in the face of extreme provocations were relatively muted. At least as a partial result of this policy, at the time of this writing the Sikh extremist movement seems to be on the wane.

The three scenarios have been shown with the help of the following three cobweb-type Figures. Figure 5.11 depicts the cycle of perpetual violence. In this diagram we have combined the reaction curves of the two rival groups. The northeastern segment of the diagram traces the reaction of group B, given the action of group A. The mirror image of this segment is located in the north western quadrant, where B's reaction is shown, given A's action. The southern quadrants are 45^0 lines reflecting back A's reaction onto the first quadrant. Now, from this Figure it is clear that if both A and B decides to follow the strategy of quid pro quo, then their reactions are also along 45^0 lines. In such a case, once started, violent actions will continue to follow one another in an endless series, with neither party wanting to escalate or mitigate the conflict.

Figure 5.11

Cycle of Perpetual Violence

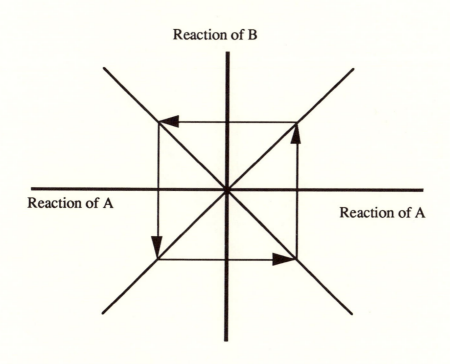

Reaction of B

Reaction of A

Reaction of A

The most unfortunate scenario of an explosive cycle of violence has been drawn in Figure 5.12. In this case, both parties are willing to over match the opponent's action. This is a situation that we can call the strategy of extracting "two teeth of one tooth." By following this strategy, group B will react more than proportionately to A's initial act of provocation. This is shown in the northeastern quadrant of Figure 5.10, where the reaction of B is traced along a line that has a slope steeper than the 45^0 line. Similarly, in turn, A chooses to react more than proportionately to the reactions of B. It is obvious that in such a situation the level of violence will continue to escalate, following a cobweb pattern, until the point of complete exhaustion of one or both parties is reached. Therefore, unless one of the parties has the capability to sustain loss to a very high degree, any victory by either party will be hollow, and a stalemate will find them both at the point of complete devastation. The situation in Lebanon, at the time of writing, seems to resemble this scenario of explosive violence.

Figure 5.12

Cycle of Explosive Violence

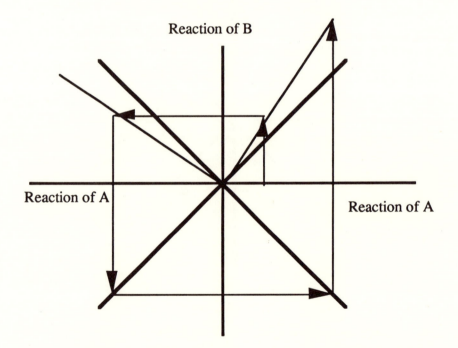

Finally, we can consider the most hopeful scenario of a gradually diminishing level of violence. This situation has been depicted with the aid of Figure 5.13. It is clear from this diagram that if both parties try to deescalate the level of conflict, the movement along the two reaction curves will ultimately lead to a peaceful resolution of conflict.

These three scenarios explain the dynamics of sectarian violence. Even though these Figures depict a consistent strategy of repeating the same line of tactics, in reality a conflict may take on a more complex pattern of discontinuous or on-again--off-again policies of escalation and mitigation. We may note at this point that this scenario can also be used to explain conflict between nations. For a recent example of a similar (but more complicated) exposition see Bruno de Mesquito and Lalman (1987).

Figure 5.13

Dampening Cycle of Violence

Reaction of B

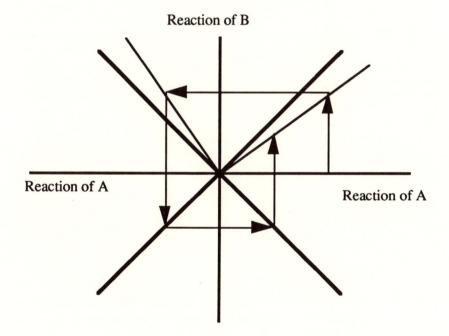
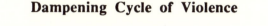

Reaction of A

Reaction of A

POLITICAL STRATEGY AND THE DYNAMICS OF POLITICAL STRUGGLE

V. I. Lenin was emphatic in his advocacy for revolutionary leadership and political strategy. To Lenin, revolutions are not born in a vacuum, either as a result of a historical accident or as an inevitable outcome of an inherently flawed economic system, but are consciously shaped by the use of shrewed strategies. Owing to the development of analytical tools such as game theory, in recent years an increased level of research effort has been devoted to the study of political strategies; the study of political strategy has become an area of scholarly research in its own merit. However, we do not have the space or the purpose to develop a fullblown theory of revolutionary strategy. Instead, we would like to demonstrate some of the strategic reasons why opposition movements can get more entrenched, causing a deep hemorrhage in the body politic as well as the aggregate economy.

To begin with, let us briefly analyze a scenario from the stand point of the two parties involved - the opposition and the authority. Through the work of Professor Kenneth Arrow (1951) and Duncan Black (1958), we know that a society characterized by single-peaked preference functions will always find a compromised solution. Let us explain. Suppose, in a democratic society, we have three groups of individuals (A, B, and C), each of which has a single vote to express their preference for one of three options (1, 2, and 3). Option 1 is the most favorable to the opposition, where they win everything; 3 is where the authorities win an unconditional surrender of the opposition; and 2 is a compromise solution. Let us suppose that the group preference patterns are as follows: Group A prefers 1 to 2, and 2 to 3. Group B prefers 2 to 1, and 1 to 3. Group C, however, would like to have 3; if not 3, then 2; otherwise, 1. We can write their preferences as:

A	$1 > 2 > 3$
B	$2 > 1 > 3$
C	$3 > 2 > 1$

In the above example, it is clear that the forces of moderation will win over the two extreme preferences because for the choice between 1 and 2, 2 will be the winner as the majority (in this case, two groups) will prefer it to 1. Similarly, while choosing between 2 and 3, the majority preference will be in favor of 2. Therefore, through the democratic process of majority voting, the society will choose the second option. We arrive at this equilibrium because in this case every individual has a single-peaked preference function. Arrow, in his famous "paradox of voting" pointed out that if for strategic reasons, one group decides to have a double peaked preference function, whereby they would advocate an all-or-nothing preference, the situation will change such that the society will have no compromise solution. Thus, let us assume that group C changed its preference as follows:

A	$1 > 2 > 3$
B	$2 > 1 > 3$
C	$3 > 1 > 2$

In this case the society will be unable to choose the compromise solution since now between 1 and 2, 1 will be chosen, and between 2 and 3, 3 will get the nod from the majority of the voters. Hence, we will and instead, will settle for an extreme position.

Figure 5.14

Single-Peaked Social Preference

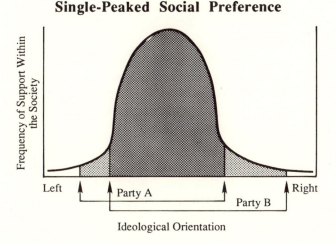

Ideological Orientation

Arrow's findings have some profound implications for us. For our analysis, his findings imply that a society may not always reach consensus and harmony and may often be besieged by extreme points of view. For example, consider the following situation. In Figure 5.14 we are measuring the extent of public support along the ideological spectrum from extreme left to extreme right. Now, if the society has a single-peaked preference function, such as the one drawn in the above Figure, we are likely to get a typical bell-shaped curve, with the maximum public support going toward the policies in the center. This strong central tendency of frequency of political support will cause the candidates of opposing parties, in their effort to capture the maximum amount of votes, to get closer and closer to the center in such a way that there may remain little substantive differences in their respective proposed policies.   The results of the recent U.S. presidential election have typically demonstrated this tendency, as both George Bush and Michael Dukakis, in their effort to be the candidate of the "mainstream," were drawn closer to each other.   Therefore, the opposition party may start out from the left of the center, whereas the authorities may start from the right.   However, as campaign progresses, sensing the strength of public opinion, both will be drawn toward the center, thereby creating a large set of indistinguishable policy advocacy.   In contrast, in a society characterized by a bi-polar preference function, such as the one depicted in Figure 5.15, the danger of taking a centrist position is obvious.   In such a situation the only way to maximize the chances of getting the most public support is to embrace either of the extreme positions.   Clearly, for this reason it is difficult to develop the voice of moderation and compromise in a place like northern Ireland, South Africa, or the Middle East.

Figure 5.15

Double-Peaked Social Preference

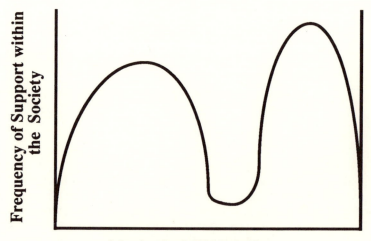

Ideological Orientation

Let us now discuss how the presence of a small extremist group can stand in the way of building a natural coalition and arriving at a compromise solution. Suppose in a society there are four groups: A, B, C, and D. A and B are leftists whereas C and D are rightists. Let us assume that A and D are ideologically extreme groups, on the other hand, the other two are moderate pragmatists, with B at center left, and C, at center right . We will define extremism by two

left, and C, at center right . We will define extremism by two characteristics: ideological position and ideological purity.[28]

Figure   5.16

Cumulative Support for Ideological Position

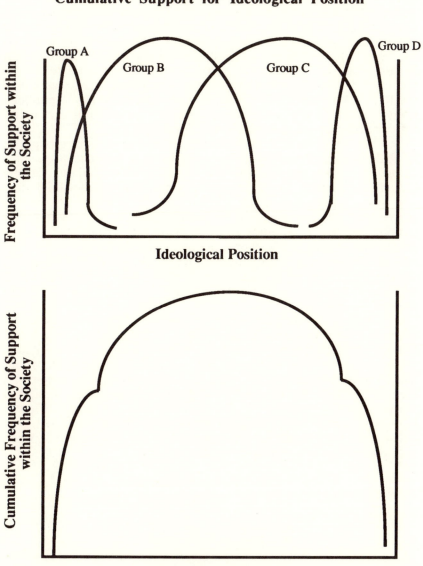

Assuming that the ideological spectrum is measurable in a meaningful way, in statistical terms the ideological position of a group may be measured by the deviation of the group mean (m) from the population mean (μ), whereas their ideological purity is measured by the standard deviation (σ) of the members' ideological belief structure. Thus, a group i will be called more extremist than group j if $|(\mu-m_i)| > |(\mu-m_j)|$; and ideologically "pure" if $|\sigma_i| < |\sigma_j|$. We have shown the difference among the various groups diagrammatically in Figure 5.16. Although it is generally expected that an extremist group will be characterized by both extremism of ideological viewpoint, and their ideological purity, there may be exceptions. Thus, one may argue, on the basis of the presidential elections in the postwar era in the United States, that the Democratic party has demonstrated itsel to be ideologically further removed from the mainstream U. S. voters than the Republican party. However, it is also true that the Republican party has shown a much stronger tendency for coherence in belief structure (ideological purity) than the Democratic party.

Before analyzing the social choice among the four groups, let us abide by two rules of the game. First, let us define *strict preference* as one where an individual is decisive over his preference for one option over another. Thus, in symbolic terms, if an individual i prefers a to b, we write this as a > b. On the other hand, if an individual is indifferent between a and b, we write this as a ~ b. We further hypothesize that if within a group of two an individual has a strict preference of a over b, whereas the other is indifferent between the two, the society will prefer a over b. By the second rule of the game, we assume transitivity of choice; that is, if a is strictly preferred over b, whereas the chooser is indifferent between b and c, a will be strictly preferred over c.

Having defined our terms, let us elaborate on our example. Suppose in our hypothetical society of four groups that group A is a left-wing extremist party with a high degree of ideological purity such that facing the choice among options 1, 2, and 3, its members would like to have only option 1. Their disdain for compromise compels them to be indifferent between 2 and 3, as they reject both. Similarly, the right-wing extremist group D prefers only 3 and is indifferent between 1 and 2. In contrast, the centerleft group prefers 2 to 1 to 3, whereas the center-right group prefers 2 to 3 to 1. Thus, we can write their preferences in symbolic terms as:

A	1 > 2 ~ 3	Extreme left
B	2 > 1 > 3	Center left
C	2 > 3 > 1	Center right
D	3 > 2 ~ 1	Extreme right

From this scheme it is clear that if social preference is based on majority vote, 2 will be the choice. This is because, based on our rule, between 1 and 2, 2 will be strictly preferred over 1 twice, whereas 1 will be preferred over 2 only once. Similarly, between 2 and 3, 2 will be the social choice (see Figure 5.16).

However, since the extremists in group A do not find the compromise acceptable, they may stage an incidence of political violence, similar to the burning of a bus, killing a woman with two children, by the Arab protesters on the eve of an Israeli election in 1988, or the assassination of Indira Gandhi, the prime minister of India by the members of a dissident Sikh separatist movement. Facing such an attack, the moderate groups can either recognize that the attack was the work of a minority (with the moderate groups keeping their preferences in tact), in which case option 2 will remain the choice of the majority of the population, or one or both the moderate groups can take on extreme positions. It is interesting to note that under this condition the change of preference of any one of the two moderate groups will deprive the society of a clear preference, and the society will drift toward a bipolar situation will little chance for a peaceful compromise.

Let us elaborate. The deliberate act of provocation by minority group A can alienate the moderates in the moderates of group C. If the members of group C decide to retaliate, one of three outcomes is possible.

Situation One. In retaliation, punishment is meted out without any regard to the group membership of the members of the opposition (groups A and B). Facing indiscriminate recrimination, group B may be radicalized in their ideological position and mirror the preference pattern of group A. As a result the moderates in the right-wing group will lose support for the compromise solution of option 2, as both groups A and B become indifferent between options 2 and 3. Thus, with both groups A and B preferring $1 > 2 \sim 3$, between 1 and 2, 1 will be the majority choice. Similarly, between 2 and 3, 3 will be strictly preferred by the majority. However, between the two extreme positions 1 and 3, there will be no social preference, with both receiving two votes each.

Situation Two. The action of the members of group A may turn off the moderates of the center-right party, and they may change their preference to mimic the extreme rightwing preference pattern (group C preferring $3 > 2 \sim 1$). Again, the victim of such a change will be the force of moderation and compromise, as option 2 will lose support against option 3. This will once again rob the society of its compromise position, as in the case of situation 1.

Situation Three. Finally, the cycle of violence resulting from the terroristic actions by a faction of the opposition group and the consequent retaliatory actions by the government may succeed in radicalizing both moderate groups, in which case the social preference function will take on the bipolar characteristic depicted in Figure 5.15.

This example shows the precariousness of the balance of power within a society besieged with groups of people holding extreme points of view. Looking around the world today, we find all-too-frequent examples of deepening of political crisis engineered by the extremists of both sides of the political spectrum. Since any compromise of position is deemed abhorrent to the radicals, the most rational of political strategies for the extremists is to attempt to eliminate the middle ground and squelch the voice of moderation. Therefore, it comes as no surprise to learn from various news accounts that almost two thirds of all the victims of Sikh extremists in India are members of the moderate faction of the movement. Similarly, a disproportionate number of victims of the Palestinian movement have been those Palestinians who had dared to advocate some kind of compromise with Israel. This is a necessary feature of any violent movement.

On the other side of the coin, being prodded by the extremists on either side, if the authorities react as if the entire dissident group belongs in the extremist camp, the stage is set for deepening conflict. For example, in the aftermath of *intefada*, the Israeli policy was guided by those who believed that indiscriminate use of force was the best policy to bring down the movement. As a result, a *Wall Street Journal* story headlines: " A Year of Violence Divides, Yet Unites West Bank Family. After 4 Months in Desert Jail, 'Good Arab' Father Now Sides with a Radical Son" (1988, p. 1). Actions such as this, in effect, assume that the entire West Bank population belongs to the extremist group and therefore is a fair target for retaliation. Such indiscriminate violence plays directly into the hands of the perpetrators, as their ranks swell with new recruits, the former fence-sitting sympathizers and even the regime supporters, who lose their stake in the present political system. Also, the burning and looting of business by the opposition and the imposition of discriminatory rules by the authorities lower the opportunity costs for political activities. Further, indignation, threats of coercion from the extreme dissident groups, and other primordial motives such as revenge add fuel to the revolutionary zeal of those who had so far been happy to be mere sympathizers. Therefore, to achieve the bipolarity of social choice, the terrorist group attempts to engineer what we call the antecedent events with the goal of maximum propaganda effects.

The strategy of terror has been used by both the Right and the Left as a defensive as well as offensive weapon. Thus, as a defensive weapon, terrorist activities have been used to preserve the status quo. Examples include the Ku Klux Klan after the Civil War, the Organization del'Armie Secrete (OAS) in Algeria, the esqudrao da Morte in Brazil, or the so called "death squad" in El Salvador, to name a few (Moss, 1971). Also, terrorism as an offensive weapon has been widely used to force a confrontation with the authorities. The activities of the Weathermen in the United States, the Tupamaros of Uruguay, the IRA, the Red Army of Germany, the Basque Separatists, and the PLO are included in the long list of groups ready to use terroristic acts as an offensive tool. In conducting a campaign of terrorism, the choice of target is of utmost importance. While an action against a well-chosen, universally hated symbol of repression can inspire and mobilize support for a movement, a poor choice of target can give a dissident terrorist organization a political setback. Also as an example of a successful terrorist attack, we can cite the bombing of King David Hotel in Jerusalem.[29]

Therefore, from the point of view of the extreme dissident group, it can indeed be a valuable strategy to try to eliminate the cause of compromise. Similarly, from the point of view of the political moderates it is equally important to recognize the true nature of the opposition, their motivations as well as potential strength. For if the extreme dissident activities are confined within a small group of individuals, then it stands to reason not to equate the rest of the group as having the same motivation. In such a case a crisis can be averted by isolating the extremist group politically and promoting the voice of moderation and cooperation.

Throughout the history of revolutionary movements we find two common mistakes that contribute to the cause of escalation of violence and deepening of political crisis. They are the assumption of universality of revolutionary profile and the assumption of cost-effectiveness of coercion. We will discuss the impacts of such assumptions in the concluding chapter.

APPENDIX TO CHAPTER 5:

MEASUREMENT OF IDEOLOGY AND OTHER FACTORS OF INDIVIDUAL DECISION MAKING

Several studies have attempted to measure the factors of individual decision making empirically. Since we do not plan to do so ourselves, it is worthwhile to look at two such efforts. The first study aims at directly measuring the individual utility function by conducting an attitude survey, whereas the second attempts to estimate indirectly the effects of ideology upon the decision making calculus by using a suitable surrogate variable.

Participation in Political Action

Muller and Opp (1986), set about empirically testing the rational choice model of rebellious collective action (RCA). The rational choice approach to RCA as developed by Olson (1971) emphasized the "free-rider" problem (see Chapter 3). Therefore, the only conclusion that can be reached from his analysis is that people take part in rebellious collective action because of the expectations of personal gains of power, status, or some other material benefits (such as loot). To this, Tullock (1971) added the "fun factor" or the "entertainment factor" of participation. The inevitable outcome of their analysis is that to reduce political violence the national authorities must increase the cost of participation. In contrast to the crowd of largely economists who were pursuing the byproduct theory of rebellious collective action, a number of political scientists (Frohlich and Oppenheimer, 1970, 1974; Frohlich, Hunt, and Oppenheimer, 1975) were emphasizing the importance of the perception of the desirability of public goods in the individual decision-making process.

By combining the two approaches, Muller and Opp specified their behavioral model as:

$$E(R) = (\, p_i + p_g \,) \cdot V + E(F) + E(A) + E(O) - E(C_r)$$

where:

$E(R)$ = Expected utility of the participants in rebellious collective action

p_i = Probability of success of the movement, given the participation of the individual

p_g = Perceived influence of the group in the provision of public goods

V = Value of rebellious collective action in terms of public goods

$E(F)$ = Fun factor of participation

$E(A)$ = Expected social affiliation value

$E(O)$ = Expected value of conforming to behavioral norms to the "important others."

$E(Cr)$ = Expected costs of rebellious collective action

The behavioral function was estimated by surveying the general public in New York city and students and faculty of Columbia University and New York University during the Spring/Summer of 1978.   Data were also collected, with a somewhat different questionnaire, from the general public in Eimsbuttel and Geesthact, a district of and a small town near Hamburg,West Germany, respectively. The two locations in West Germany were chosen for their activism in the anti-nuclear power plant protests. The survey was conducted in 1982. Although both data sets point to similar results, the New York City survey, unlike the West German Survey did not include measures of selective incentives and costs. Therefore, in this brief description we will concentrate on the results of the German survey.

Dependent Variables

Muller and Opp collected data on two sets of dependent variables measuring the propensity to take part in rebellious collective action. The first one is the potential for participation, based on the expressed intention of the respondents, and the second one is the actual participation based on past performance in seven categories of rebellious behavior. The seven acts of rebellious behavior are (1) participation in a forbidden demonstration, (2) engaging in resisting arrest, (3) breaking through barricades and the like during demonstrations, (4) painting slogans against nuclear power plants, (5) participation in an occupation of a construction site for a nuclear power plant, (6) attacks and sabotage against nuclear power plants, and (7) attacks on individuals responsible for the construction of nuclear power plants.

A composite Aggregate Participation Potential scale (R_p) was constructed by summing participation weighted by intention across the seven categories of behavior. An Aggressive Behavior index (R_b) was created by adding the frequencies of aggressive behaviors performed in the past by the respondent.

Independent Variables

Five sets of independent variables were estimated from the survey results:

1)   *The public goods value of rebellious collective action*

V_s =   A composite measure of public good value of rebellious collective action, based on the respondents' support for the present political system

V_n =   A binary measure of the perception of desirability of public goods (= 1 if the respondent feels discontent with nuclear power plants; =0 otherwise)

2)   *Perceived influence on the provision of public goods* (p_i)

This index was created to ascertain whether a non-elite, ordinary participant felt that his own participation had any influence over the success of the movement.[30]

3)   *The entertainment motive* (E(F))

This index was created to the basis of responses on the following three statements:

(a) If I protest against the construction of an atomic power station, this activity is fun for me.
(b) Although I am an opponent of nuclear energy, I somehow find it unpleasant being active against atomic power Station.
(c) I feel inhibited to show that I am against atomic power Station.

(4)   *Behavioral norms of important others* (E(O))

        In order to ascertain the importance of peer pressure and the impact of the approval of the reference group, a complex method of rating was used to first identify the "important people" and then to appraise the respondents' perception of their (the members of the reference group) approval of participation in rebellious collective action.

(5)   *Social affiliation rewards and costs of rebellious collective action* (E(Cr))

        On a seven-point scale, social affiliation rewards (such as power and prestige) and costs (such as being labeled "leftist" or "crazy," being injured by police, or being identified for *Berufsverboten* - prohibition from work in the public sector) of participation were measured.
        Having operationalized the dependent and independent variables, Muller and Opp performed ordinary least squares on the data. The results countered the general free rider propositions of Olson. Based on the regression results, no statistical relevancy for the fun factor could be established. The variable measuring the perceived importance of the desirability of public goods (in our terminology, the ideological factor) was found to be highly statistically significant. Muller and Opp concluded that " in regard to an average citizen's choice of whether to rebel, consideration of what is collectively rational can override the individually rational logic of private interest theory" (p. 485). However, paradoxically, they found a positive correlation between the expected costs of participation and the levels of actual or intended participation. This, they theorized, is possibly linked to the attachment of higher value to a public good when the cost factor is higher, or to some kind of a martyr syndrome.

Congressional Voting Behavior

        The economics of regulation concerns itself with the study of the formulation of legislation affecting the economy. The notion of ideology being an anathema, economic theory of regulation has long suffered the inability to explain a great deal of public policy with the tools of self-interest alone. Thus, it has been argued that in the formulation of a public policy, four groups of individuals get involved, the voting public, the lawmakers, the bureaucrats, and the interest groups. The proponents of the self-interest theory maintain that each of these groups works exclusively in their own selfish interest. In an extremely interesting effort, Joseph Kalt and Mark Zupan (1984) looked at the formulation of a specific legislation. They evaluated the voting records of U.S. legislators on the Surface Mining Control and Reclamation Act (SMCRA), which came about as a result of a protracted political struggle. Congress passed two versions of the legislation in 1974 and in 1975. On both occasions, they were vetoed by President Gerald Ford. The SMCRA was finally signed into legislation by President Jimmy Carter in 1977. The act requires the restoration of stripmined land to its premining state. Also, the act established an Abandoned Mine Reclamation Fund and clarified previously indefinite property rights to water and land in areas underlain by strippable coal.

The self-interest theory would dictate that congressional votes would follow the economic interests of the constituents: In a democratic society the representatives are likely to vote with an eye toward their reelection, so their voting pattern should reflect the economic interests and demographic patterns of their constituents. However, this study and others (Mitchel, 1979; Kau and Rubin, 1979; Kalt, 1981) that attempted to correlate economic interest variables with voting patterns showed a surprisingly weak correlation.   The econometric results for Kalt and Zupan (1984) improved significantly when a variable measuring the senators' ideology (measured in terms of ratings given by an ideological watchdog, the League of Conservative Voters) was introduced. Even when controlled for all the other variables, the factor of pure ideology was found to possess a significant explanatory power, surpassing those of economic interest.

NOTES

1. *Politics*. V. c. 322 B.C.

2. Let us elaborate the point. Although we cannot aggregate the expected utility function of each individual explicitly, we can, however, hypothesize that a change in the aggregate expected utility function is influenced by systemic conditions that determine the expectations of each participant. This problem is analogous to the economic problem of a direct estimation of the aggregate production function. Gross national product (Y) is commonly assumed to be produced by an aggregate level of capital stock (K), labor (L), and technology (τ): $Y= f(K,L,\tau)$.   However, since it is extremely difficult to quantify capital and technology to estimate the aggregate production function directly, economists have found it easier to explain the rate of growth of income ($\Delta Y/Y$) with the help of aggregate behavioral variables. Similarly, we can hypothesize that $\Delta E(U) = f(X_i)$, where the X_i's are the external stimuli variables that determine the marginal productivity of time devoted to political and economic activity in the aggregate. We can therefore hypothesize that these stimuli factors are related to the factors influencing the value added in Smelser's analysis.

3. This price is measured both in terms of each individual's assessment of his opportunity cost of participation (forgone personal income) and in terms of the risk of being apprehended and punished for taking part in anti-government protest activities.

4. A case in point is the Jewish protests in Israel, for which the authorities show an extraordinary extenet of tolerance. See Sam Lehman-Wilzig (1990).

5. The reader may be reminded that income effect in this case refers to the individual's desire to maintain his old standard of living, which will allow him even less time to devote to revolutionary activities even in the face of a lowering of income capabilities. The substitution effect, on the other hand, will prompt him to seek more of the political goods, as they are relatively more easily obtained (cheaper in terms of marginal effort) than the economic goods.

6.   The importance of precipitating events in the process of a movement is undeniable. Following this logic, extremists often strategize to eliminate the moderates by provoking extremism on the opposite side. This issue has been theoretically expounded by Kenneth Arrow (1951) in his "paradox of voting." The point was not lost on the practicing revolutionaries such as Che Guevara (1985). As he pointed out: "The [Latin American] dictatorship tries to function without resorting to force. Thus, we must try to oblige the dictatorship to resort to violence, thereby unmasking its true nature as that of the reactionary social classes. This event will deepen the struggle to such an extent that there will be no retreat from it" (p. 13).

7.   The paradox of voting can be briefly described as follows: suppose in a community we have three voting groups (A, B, and C) of equal numerical strength, facing choices among three alternatives: 1, 2, and 3. Group A prefers 1 to 2, and 2 to 3; B prefers 2 to 1, and 1 to 3; and group C prefers 3 to 2, and 2 to 1. We can organize their preferences as follows:

Group A   1 > 2 > 3
Group B   2 > 1 > 3
Group C   3 > 2 > 1

In the above preference schedule it is obvious that in a pairwise choice the moderate second alternative (2) will be the winner, since it wins by a majority vote against both 1 and 3. However, the social preference can indeed be confused if an extremist group, say C, wishes to vote in a seemingly contradictory fashion by declaring its preference as 3 > 1 > 2. This kind of all-or-nothing choice results in a situation where there is no clear winner. In the political arena, similarly, often the extremist groups attempt to force a conflict situation to eliminate the middle-of-the-roaders. For example, it was widely reported that in El Salvador the left-wing radicals, who did not participate in the national election, were in fact asking their supporters to vote for the right-wing extremist candidate, as his win would eliminate the chances of a compromise and a democratic solution.

8. See Chapter 3 above for a more detailed discussion of Runciman's (1966) work and the development of the concept of relative deprivation.

9. We may point out here that unlike Gurr, who maintains an explicit specification of relative deprivation function [Relative deprivation = (Value Expectations - Value Capabilities)/ Value expectations], we do not make our specification of deprivation exact. Instead, we express it simply in terms of realized income (in Gurr's terminology, "value capabilities") and the income that we can expect to have in case of a successful political movement (translates into "value expectations"). Therefore, we argue that Ted Gurr's hypothesis, expressed in implicit functional form, yields a similar formulation as ours.

10. For a detailed discussion of these factors, see Chapter 3, on factors of economic strain.

11. In the nomenclature of "Game Theory," the term maximin implies the dictum of maximizing one's minimum gain. That is, facing a situation of chosing among a number of alternatives with uncertain payoffs, a rational strategy would be to pick the one that carries the prospect of minimum loss.

12. Based on this line of argument, we may throw in an as yet untested hypothesis, that the average age of the participants of a leftwing movement is likely to be lower than their rightwing counterpart.

13. In this context, it is interesting to note that despite the fact that micro-economic literature on altruism is generally based on rules of selfish reciprocity, in the area of macroeconomics scholars have noted (without explanation, of course) an increasing level of preference for public goods with an increase in the affluence of aggregate economy. In the economic literature, this phenomenon is known as *income elasticity of demand for public goods*. That is, as income increases, the societal demand for public goods becomes less elastic. In other words, with affluence, public goods, that were deemed only luxury items before tend to be viewed as necessity. For instance, in the United States, public facilities such as buildings, curbs, car parking, and even buses are designed to facilitate access to handicapped people

in wheelchairs. Within the present social context, these are considered to be essential items. However, spending money on such items in developing countries will only be considered as frivolous.

14. However, it should be noted that he also suggested that in the revolutionary process, the leadership will come from the members of the petite bourgeoisie who, being armed with the "correct ideology," betray their own class interest. Thus, while analyzing the French Revolution, Marx observed that by 1845 "a large part of the English and French proletariat had already become *aware* of its historic mission, and worked incessantly to clarify this awareness" (in Bottomore and Rubel, 1964, p. 233). However, besides these proletariat leaders who were working in the interest of their class, Marx predicted the contradictory behavior of some of the bourgeois ideologues by stating:

Just as... at an earlier period, a section of the nobility went over to the bourgeoisie, so now a portion of the bourgeoisie goes over to the proletariat, and in particular, a portion of the bourgeoisie ideologists, who have raised themselves to the level of comprehending theoretically the historical movement as a whole. [Bottomore and Rubel 1964, p. 186].

15. Kenneth Arrow (1951, 1979) has demonstrated that given the most innocuous set of constraints, in a nondictatorial society, social preferences can not be constructed on the basis of individual preferences alone. This is known as the "the impossibility theorem."

16. Hardin (1978) argues, "The issue will not be whether he himself benefits more from his contributions than the...[action]...costs him [as in Olson's logic], but whether he and the group of like-minded activists benefit more from their group actions than those actions costs" (p .5).

17. Bandura (1973) calls this the "social learning theory" and explains it as follows:

Vicarious reinforcement - perception of positive outcomes accruing to others is a powerful source of motivation, and that observational incentive plays an especially important role in social activism, for here the chances of quick success are poor, but protest behavior is partly sustained by the long-range attainments of groups that have persevered in their effort [p. 206].

18. The problem with research on group behavior in the area of social psychology is that frequently it is conducted on small-groups. Therefore, the results obtained in controlled small group situations may not be applicable to large, uncontrolled social groups.

19. For a vivid description of this unique method of communication, see Christopher Hibbert (1978), especially, chapter 3, "Chupatties and Lotus Flower," pp. 59 -74.

20. For a discussion of cultural factors of political participation, see Lehman-Wilzig (1990).

21. While Lenin was unequivocal in his assessment of the need for revolu-tionary party organization, Leon Trotsky (ironically, a great organizer himself) maintained that for the revolutionary participation by the masses the loss of political legitimacy of the regime must be demonstratively evident.   Thus, he observed (1932) that if the existence of privation was sufficient to cause an insurrection, the masses would always be in revolt. For revolution to take place, it is necessary that the masses, convinced conclusively of the political bankruptcy of the regime, perceive a revolutionary way out.   In contrast, Mao, while assessing the revolutionary conditions in China in his early essay entitled "A Single Spark Can Start a Prairie Fire" (1972b), asserted that it would be task of the party to bring about the revolutionary condition. Thus, he writes:

Some comrades in our party still do not know how to appraise the current situation correctly ... Though they believe that a revolutionary high tide is inevitable, they do not believe it to be imminent.... They seem to think that, since the revolutionary high tide is still remote, it will be labour lost to attempt to establish political power by hard work... They do not have a deep understanding of the idea of accelerating the nation-wide revolutionary high tide through the consolidation and expansion of Red political power [pp. 65 -66].

22. It is ironic that like Guevara, Marighela, Mazumder, and many other leaders of communist insurgency, a similar line of strategy was taken by the Central Intelligence Agency (CIA) in planning the Bay of Pigs invasion, where they assumed the existence of widespread counterrevolutionary sentiments among the Cubans, who they expected to come out in droves in support of the invasion as soon as the news got out (Wyden, 1979).

23. Gurr (1970) explains: " The most fundamental human response to the use of force is counter force. Force threatens and angers men, especially if they believe it to be illicit or unjust. Threatened, they try to defend themselves; angered, they want to retaliate" (p. 232).

24. It is not very clear why it should be a point of "equilibrium." If at all, in all likelihood this point is an unstable point.

25. For an empirical criticism of this quadratic specification, in general, and Muller's (1985) estimation of the relationship between government repression and political violence, in particular,see Hertman and Hsiao (1988). Also see, Muller's (1988) reply.

26. For an excellent discussion of the "Allais Paradox," and its subsequent development, see Machina (1983).

27. An example of this kind of swift and decisive action may be found in the actions taken by the Mexican government in response to a student riot in 1968, where on October 2, the military opened fire on a peaceful student demonstration killing, according to one estimate, at least 50 and wounding (many critically) another 500 (Heller, 1983). As Heller noted:

Where more subtle techniques of co-option and selective repression had failed, the indiscriminate use of brute force worked. The level of violence used by the government at Tleteloco terrorized the general public and staggered the student movement. [p. 183]

A similar kind of action was taken by the Chinese authorities to put down the so called "pro democracy" movement in Beijing in 1989.

28. For an excellent discussion on the strategies of collective violence along this line, see De Nardo (1986).

29. On the other hand, Robert Moss (1971) provides us with an example of a failed terrorist action. In June 1971, in Istanbul, a 14-year-old schoolgirl was held hostage by some members of the Turkish People's Liberation Army. After a gun battle and a successful rescue of the hostage, the indignant crowd broke through the police line to lynch the lone surviving guerrilla as he shouted, "We are doing this for you."

30. Contrary to the free-rider assumption, participants in both countries felt that their own participation had made a difference in the ultimate outcome of the movement.

Part Three:

The Aggregate: The Impact of Political Instability on the Economy

6

Impact of Political Instability:
The Anatomy of an Economic Crisis

POLITICAL INSTABILITY AND THE ECONOMY: A
DESCRIPTIVE OVERVIEW

It is a well-accepted fact that a sustained level of serious political disturbance can have disastrous consequences for an economy. Looking around the world today, we find frequent examples of countries - such as, Lebanon, Nicaragua, El Salvador, Iran, Ethiopia, Bangladesh, Sudan, Mozambique, Chad, Angola, South Vietnam, Laos, Cambodia, and northern Ireland, to name a few - where prolonged political turmoil has caused serious damage to the economy. Yet of all the topics related to political violence and collective rebellion, the least researched is their impact on the aggregate economy. This omission, as we have argued above, has resulted from the refusal of neoclassical economics to deal with factors of political instability. Looking at the aggregate economy, it is obvious that such assumption of sterility of economics from the sociopolitical environment is not backed up by reality. As a matter of fact, it would hardly cause a debate to assert that for the economy to function properly it must have political stability. If there is no stability of the political institutions, or the actors do not have faith in the fairness of the political system, free flow of economic transaction cannot take place because of two fundamental factors. First, a transaction implies a contract. And a contract cannot easily be made without an implicit trust between the parties, with somebody acting as an impartial referee to settle disputes. The classical writers recognized this. The social contract theorists recommended that the authorities live up to their share of responsibility by providing a fair, stable government. The nineteenth century liberal thinkers did not see much economic role for the government but insisted on its judicial and military responsibilities for the provision of internal stability and external security. The organization theorists like Max Weber saw an impartial, incorruptible, invariant bureaucracy, based on an accepted legal foundation, to be the prerequisite for economic prosperity. The second reason that political instability imposes cost on the economy is that it introduces an additional dose of uncertainty in an already jittery market clamoring for predictability of the future.

However, neoclassical economists - and curiously enough, even the post-war writers - were guilty of assuming away political environment from their analyses. The compartmentalization of social science led each discipline to develop its own methodology and nomenclature, independent of each other. This academic equivalence of the destruction of the Tower of Babel resulted in the study of the causes and effects of political instability falling through the cracks. Therefore, in this chapter we will attempt to come out of the neoclassical economic paradigm and trace the impact of political instability on the aggregate economy.

Before we look into the impact of political instability on the economy, let us examine the process of equilibrium analysis in macroeconomics. In macroeconomics the economy is divided into three markets: the commodity market, the money market, and the labor market. In the commodity market the individual economic actors decide how much to consume, save, and invest with respect to a certain interest rate. In the money market they decide how much liquid asset to hold with respect to a certain level of real interest rate. And in the labor market they attempt to come to a point of equilibrium for their labor supply with respect to the price level. The commodity and money market comprise the demand side of the economy, whereas the points of equilibrium in the labor market determine the level of aggregate supply. The point of equilibrium between the demand and the supply sides is called the *point of general equilibrium* in the market.

In order to trace the impact of political instability, let us imagine the following scenario: A typical Third World nation is experiencing a prolonged period of severe political instability resulting from a guerrilla war or a civil war is being waged by a determined group of dissidents. For the sake of simplicity, let us assume a number of restrictions, which we can relax later on in the analysis.   To begin with, let us assume that the nation does not enjoy a prominent position in the strategic geopolitical game, so that no external force is ready to bankroll the economy.

Within the above scenario it is fairly obvious that owing to a sustained level of insurgency by the opposition the citizens will start losing their faith in the capacity of the economy to provide them with the necessary opportunity for a sustained economic future. Therefore, they start looking around for investments to hedge against this additional source of uncertainty (Sandmo, 1969). Facing uncertainty, they increasingly demonstrate their lack of faith in the economic condition and economic institutions by resorting to "hoarding." While hoarding, the individuals basically have two options: They can either store their money under the proverbial mattress (thereby withdraw money from the natural flow of economic activity), or they can send their money illegally (as few countries allow a free remittance of money abroad) to a safer haven, such as a Swiss bank, or to a politically stable nation.[1] The weary investor may have another option, which is different from pure hoarding or syphoning of money to other countries where money is physically withdrawn from the economic cycle; they can buy gold, silver, or other precious metals.[2] The reason for the purchase of these items is of course the fact that they are perceived to be free of political risks. However, insofar as they are seen as assets chosen as a part of an investment portfolio, they will take away money that otherwise would have been consumed, or saved in the regular financial institutions. In the aggregate, this tendency will result in a higher price of gold, silver and other precious metals, and a possible drop in the consumption and savings.[3]

Assuming that the money an individual decides to hide under the mattress, comes from the amount he would have otherwise consumed or saved implies a reduction in the aggregate level of consumption and savings in the nation.[4] The syphoning off of money to another country works like a leak in the flow of economic activities, and acts as a net loss to the economy. The resulting reduction in consumption will create a downward multiplier, which will cause the economy to settle for a lower level of equilibrium of income and employment. Notice that without the hoarding factor a reduction in consumption would have increased savings, thereby increasing the level of loanable funds, which in turn would have lowered the rate of interest in the market, paving the way for an economic recovery. Similarly, owing to hoarding, a reduction in savings will not boost consumption to allow for an upward multiplier to take the economy to a higher level of prosperity. As we will note throughout this discussion, the introduction of uncertainty from political instability can rob the market of many of the automatic, self-correcting equilibrating mechanisms.

Let us now look at the money market. In the money market, equilibrium is reached between money demand and money supply. Money is demanded by the individuals within the economy, and money is supplied by the government. Keynes in his *General Theory* (1936) divided money demand into two categories. In the first category, money was held to satisfy the "transaction motive," which he described as the need to hold cash to "bridge the interval between the receipt of income and its disbursement" (p. 195). The portion of this cash holding is of course much less in the credit card-using developed nations. However, in a Third World nation, this propensity to hold cash for transaction may be substantial. The second reason for holding cash, according to Keynes, is to satisfy people's "speculative motive." This motive is based on the assumption of people as speculators who are perennially in search of economic betterment by switching their asset holdings between money and bonds.

Therefore, in effect, we are modifying the Keynesian hypothesis to include in the money demand a third kind of motive: hoarding. In economics the demand for this cash holding is called the *real balance* demand. The real balance demand is assumed to be dependent on the market interest rate. That is, when the market interest rate goes up, an individual would reevaluate his opportunity cost of holding non-interest-bearing cash and will be tempted to keep a higher portion in the interest baring assets. There has been no systematic effort at discerning the impact of political instability on the real balance demand. However, since the occurrence of political violence may imply various kinds of risks and uncertainties, we may hypothesize, on apriori grounds, that in such a situation an individual's real balance requirement is likely to go up.

By combining the above scenarios in the commodity market and in the money market, we can see that in such a case government's monetary policy will become largely ineffective. No matter how much the government may try to induce consumers to increase their consumption demand, and the investors to increase their investment, by increasing the money supply, the existence of a high level of uncertainty will fail to induce them to get involved in a higher level of economic activity. This situation is analogous to the much-feared *liquidity trap* experienced during the great depression. Owing to the impotence of monetary policy resulting from the liquidity trap, the multiplier process could not work fully in the U.S economy during the period from 1934 to 1940, where, despite a hefty 70 percent increase in real money supply, real gross national product could not grow at a sufficient rate to make a sizable dent in the unemployment rate.[5]

The labor market will also be affected by political instability, as the occurrence of violence will impose a physical constraint on the nation's capacity to produce. This hindrance will be physical, as opposed to the economic ones discussed above. This physical hindrance to production will show up wherever there is widespread violence. The rising tide of violence will affect the labor market by directly interfering with the nation's production process. The rebel forces may sabotage or otherwise impede the smooth functioning of the manufacturing sector. Politically motivated strikes may cripple the economy. Factories may close due to lack of security or sabotage by the guerrilla forces. The movements of troops from the opposing parties will disrupt agriculture. In the fields, farmers may be displaced and prevented from engaging in agricultural activities by the direct threats from the rebel force. Or the farmers may even be relocated (as they were in South Vietnam) by the government to keep them outside the sphere of influence of the opposition. Conscription and a rising death toll will drain the economy of able-bodied workers. Also, apart from the factory workers and farmers, political instability takes its toll on the nation's precious supply of trained manpower. For example, the war-torn Nicaraguan economy has experienced the severe migration problem of highly trained professionals.[6] A similar loss of trained manpower has been experienced in Cuba, South Africa, Labanon, Israel, and Iran. In fact, every war-torn nation experiences mass migrations of this sort. These migrations and other obstacles to production can and do have deleterious effects on the economy.

Figure 6.1

Impact of Political Instability on Market Equilibrium

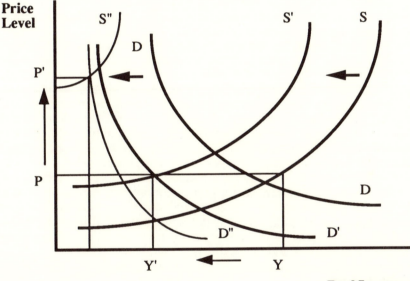

The total economic impact of political instability, therefore, can be traced by combining the results of the three markets. By tracing the points of equilibrium between the commodity and money markets, we can derive the aggregate demand curve of the economy, whereas the points of equilibrium in the labor market provide us with the aggregate supply curve. We can demonstrate the point of general equilibrium by equating the demand side (the points of equilibrium between the commodity and the money market) and the supply side (the points of equilibrium between labor demand and labor supply). This is done with the help of what is known as the aggregate demand and aggregate supply curves, as has been depicted in diagram (6.1).

In Figure 6.1, the curve DD represents the aggregate demand and the curve SS the aggregate supply in the economy. Let us assume that with political stability, the economy has settled for the general equilibrium point, with price level P and a real gross national income of Y.   As a result of political instability the aggregate demand and supply curves shift to the left.   These shifts cause the point of equilibrium to move to the point Y', showing decline in gross national income.   However, the result of political instability on the economy many not manifest itself through an economic depression,in fact, in most cases politically unstable countries also tend to experience a severe kind of inflation.   We may explain such a scenario by extending our analysis a bit further.

In the above discussion, we had assumed that the market rate of interest will be unaffected by the level of political instability. However, on reflection, it seems safe to assume that in the financial market the net effect of political instability is likely to be translated as an increase in the rate of interest.   This increase in the rate of interest will be caused by two factors.   First, the presence of hoarding will lower the amount of money available for lending to prospective borrowers.   Second, the market interest rate is influenced by the level of uncertainty.   The rising level of uncertainty will be reflected in the financial market in terms of a higher rate of interest.   Again, without political uncertainty an increase in the rate of interest would have increased people's desire to save, and reduced their inclinations to hold liquid, non-interest-bearing assets.   These two forces would have helped to increase the supply of loanable funds, which would have brought down the rising trend of interest rate.   However, none of these fortuitous events take place in a politically unstable economy.

At this point we may relax another one of our assumptions and introduce the government sector to the economy.   It seems reasonable to believe that during the period of civil war the government will be hard-pressed to maintain a balanced budget and will incur a sizable deficit.   This deficit will be caused by the dual effect of lowering government revenue and increasing its expenditure.

Government finances its expenditures from the revenues that it collects from taxes, which are dependent on the level of economic activities in the economy.   A vibrant economy will produce a bountiful harvest of tax revenue.   In a sluggish economy, on the other hand, tax revenue is likely to dwindle.   However, in spite of the lowering of tax revenue, owing to the presence of insurgency, the authorities may be compelled to spend more and more on the military, internal security, and other pacification programs.   This increased level of government spending and a low level of tax revenue will cause a budget deficit.

The government deficit may be financed either by borrowing or by simply printing more money.   If the government attempts to finance the deficit by borrowing, it will produce a "crowding-out" effect in the already-squeezed capital market, the effect of which will manifest itself in terms of yet-higher interest rates.   If, on the other hand, the government attempts to finance the deficit by increasing the money supply, given the environmental constraints on the level of aggregate production and investors' reluctance to increase their investment, this will only produce high levels of inflation. The results of these factors have been shown as shifts in the aggregate demand and supply cuves to the positions DD" and SS". This outcome of such a shift is a lower level of economic activity coupled with an increase in the price level.

The foreign sector of the economy, likewise, will not be untouched by the effects of political instability. The level of uncertainty will drive away foreign investors who would have supplied the nation with much-needed capital. Also, as the normal production process gets impeded, manufactured items for sale abroad may not be produced, cash crops may not be planted, and mines and other sources of natural resources may remain inactive. On the other hand, despite the reduction of exportables the nation's need for imports may not decrease, as the government may feel the increasing need to import, especially military hardware to fight back the opposition challenge.

Therefore, in sum, a strife-torn economy will be characterized by high unemployment, low income, and inflation. However, the extent to which this extremely gloomy prognosis will materialize will depend on the magnitude of external assistance, especially by a superpower, or the nation's capacity to finance its debts through the sale of its natural resources, for example, oil, as in the case of Iran. With foreign money cushioning the shock, the economy may limp along for some time without showing the overt signs of a crisis.

There may, however, be one slight silver lining in this scenario: After the revolution, or the attainment of political stability, business and consumer confidence may return. The accumulated saving and hoarding, finding a higher assured rate of return, may find their way back to the nation's income stream. This phenomenon is similar to what is known as the *real balance effect*, or *Pigou effect*, named after its discoverer A. C. Pigou (1943, pp. 343-351). The Western world experienced this kind of surge in economic activities immediately after World War II.

In the beginning of this scenario, we had assumed that the affected economy does not draw any superpower attention, which allows them to receive a huge amount of money in economic assistance. We can easily relax this assumption now and see that in such a situation the full impact of economic crisis on the strife-torn economy will not be felt. The debilitating, negative impact of budget deficit and lack of savings will be masked by the inflow of foreign money. However, in the long run this will only create an artificial situation of economic normalcy.   Since money from foreign government assistance can only substitute for domestic saving but not for investment, it seems like a safe conjecture to state that in such a situation the economy will rapidly become equivalent to a "welfare junky," totally dependent on foreign assistance. This will be particularly true for the client states of the United States, where the government will have to depend upon the private market to provide investment. With a high degree of political instability, private initiative for domestic capital formation may be quite difficult.   On the other hand, for the Soviet client states like Cuba, where foreign assistance helps government run investment projects, the situation may be somewhat different.   However, in any case the artificiality of the situation may weaken the basic structure of the economic system of a politically unstable nation in the long run.

We will present our arguments more formally in the following section.

POLITICAL INSTABILITY AND THE ECONOMY: THE DERIVATION OF A MULTIPLIER

In this section, we will show the impact of an exogenously determined political instability on the general equilibrium of a typical Keynesian macro-economic system. The derivation here follows the standard methodology found in any intermediate text book (see for example, Branson,1979).

The equilibrium in the commodity market is depicted by the so-called IS curve, and is defined as:

$$y = f(c, i, g) \qquad\qquad (6.1)$$

that is, disposable income (y) is determined by the level of consumption (c), investment (i), and government spending (g). As we have mentioned above, we may assume that contrary to the simplifying assumption that an individual can either save or invest his additional income (Δy), we add a third category, hoarding. Hoarding, in this case, is being defined as withdrawal of money from the income stream of the economy, which can take the form of either hiding money under the "mattress" or sending it outside the country to a safer haven. Based on previous empirical findings (Venieris and Gupta, 1986), we note that hoarding is positively correlated with the level of political instability in the nation.

However, the portion of this hoarding coming out of the propensity to save and consume is an empirical question of which we have no a priori knowledge. Hence, we will make a simplifying, but not entirely unreasonable, assumption that the hoarded money is distributed between the propensity to save and consume by some fraction q, where $1 > q > 0$. In other words, facing the prospect of political turmoil, an economic actor will lower both his consumption as well as his savings. Hence, we may rewrite equation (6.1), as:

$$y = c(y, \rho) + i(r, \rho) + g \qquad\qquad (6.1a)$$

where, ρ is the level of political instability, and r is the rate of interest. Thus, we have added ρ to the standard economic specification, which assumes that aggregate consumption is determined by the level of disposable income alone. We have similarly modified the standard neoclassical hypothesis to assume that the level of aggregate investment is a function of the market rate of interest as well as the uncertainty generated by the level of political instability in the nation. Thus, from accumulated empirical evidence, we may safely hypothesize that:

$$\frac{\delta c}{\delta \rho} = c^{*\prime} < 0; \quad \frac{\delta i}{\delta \rho} = i^{*\prime} < 0$$

while the standard economic hypothesis assumes:

$$\frac{\delta c}{\delta y} = c' > 0; \quad \frac{\delta c}{\delta r} = i' > 0$$

Hence, we hypothesize that during periods of political uncertainty the economic actor will increase the portion of unrecorded forgone consumption (hoarding) and will also reduce his level of investment. This change in economic behavior is translated as a shift in the IS curve to the left.

Drawing from our observations in the commodity market, we may further hypothesize that the money market will not be unaffected during periods of instability in the polity. In the money market the equilibrium function for the demand and supply of money is given by the so-called LM curve. On the demand side, money is held for speculative purposes (expressed as l) - that is, to invest in stocks and bonds - as well as for transactional purposes (expressed as k) - that is, to meet day-to-day need for transaction of money. Since the speculative demand for money is highly susceptible to uncertainty, we may hypothesize that the demand is determined not only by the market rate of interest - as has been traditionally conjectured - but also by the level of political instability (ρ). Thus, the modified LM function can be written as:

$$\frac{M}{P} = l\,(r, \rho) + k\,(y) \tag{6.2}$$

where, M is the *given* money supply, and P is the price level. Note that we hypothesize:

$$\frac{\delta l}{\delta r} = l' < 0$$

$$\frac{\delta l}{\delta \rho} = l^{*\prime} < 0$$

$$\frac{\delta l}{\delta y} = k' > 0$$

Hence, from our formulation, as a result of the introduction of political instability, the real balance demand for money will increase, thereby shifting the LM curve to the left.

On the supply, or the production side of the economy, we may assume that the supply of labor will be unaffected by the level of political instability, since there is no a-priori reason to believe that peoples' preference for work changes significantly in response to a situation of political uncertainty. However, we posit that a much stronger case may be made in relation to the demand side of labor; where the level of political instability may show up as an additional bottleneck in the production process due to the increasing number of political strikes, work stoppages, and other acts of sabotage.

Thus, we may express the demand and supply of labor, respectively, as:

$$y = y (N, \ K, \rho) \tag{6.3}$$

$$P. \ F \ (N) = p.(P).q(N), \ \rho \tag{6.4}$$

where
  N = Labor input
  K = Existing capital stock

Equation (C.3) is the aggregate production function, where goods and services are determined by the labor input, the capital stock and a bottleneck constraint imposed by the level of political instability. Recalling the four equations, we may specify our general equilibrium model:

IS curve: $\qquad\qquad y \ = c \ (y, r) + i \ (r, r) + g \qquad$ (6.1a)

LM Curve: $\qquad\qquad \dfrac{M}{P} \ = \ I \ (r, r) + k \ (y) \qquad$ (6.2)

Production Function $\qquad y = y(N, K, \rho) \qquad$ (6.3)

Supply of Labor: $\qquad\quad P. \ F \ (N) = p.(P).q(N), \ \rho \qquad$ (6.4)

From this above set of equations, we can now derive the total multiplier for political instability factor. We may start by first differentiating (C.1a) totally, which yields:

$$dy = c'.dy + c^{*}.d\rho + i'. \ dr + i^{*}.d\rho + dg \tag{6.1a'}$$

Similar transformation on the money market function (the LM curve) yields:

$$d\left(\frac{M}{P}\right) = l'.dr + l^{*'}.d\rho + k'.dy$$

Solving for dr, we get:

$$dr = \frac{[\left(\frac{-M}{P^2}\right) \cdot dP + l^{*'}.d\rho + k'.dy]}{l'} \tag{6.2a'}$$

The next step is to replace dP with the expression for the slope of the aggregate supply curve, which gives the price change needed to restore equilibrium for a given change in y on the supply side. Given a level of political instability (ρ), an increase in P will be given by:

$$dP = \frac{dP}{dy}|_{s,\rho} \cdot dy \tag{6.5}$$

Now, by substituting (C.5) in (2a') and rearranging, we obtain:

$$dr = \frac{M}{-P^2} \cdot \frac{dP}{dy}|_{s,\rho} \cdot dy + k'.dy - (l^* . d\rho) . l$$

Finally, substituting (6.6) in (6.1a') and rearranging, and then solving for dy, we derive the total multiplier with respect to the two exogenous variables - ρ and g:

$$dy = \frac{1}{1 - c' + i'.\left(\frac{k'}{l'}\right) + \left(\frac{M}{-P^2} \cdot l'\right).\left(\frac{dP}{dy}|_{s,\rho}\right)} \cdot [(c^{*'} + l^{*'} + i^{*'}). \, dr + dg]$$

The implications of this new multiplier are quite interesting when compared with the traditional economic multiplier. We may note that since we have assumed the rate of interest to be free of the effect of political instability, the multiplier itself (the denominator) remains unchanged. What changes in this case, is the numerator, signifying an exogenous shift as a result of political instability. The direction of this shift can be determined by the signs of the coefficients. Hence, in order to recognize the direction of the movement, we need to consider each of the partial derivatives separately.

We have argued above that both c^* and i^* are less than 0. Similarly, we have conjectured that $l^{*'} < 0$. Hence, it is obvious that each segment of the numerator has negative coefficients, implying a strong negative impact of political instability on the economy.

NOTES

1. For example, a recent estimate by Morgan Guarantee Trust Co. (reported in Wall Street Journal, "Crippling Export: Mexico's Capital Flight Still Racks Economy, Despite Brady Plan," September 25, 1989, p. 1) puts assets (in $billion) held abroad by various Latin American countries during the decade 1977 to 1987, as follows: Mexico $84; Venezuela $58; Argentina $46; Brazil $31; Colombia $7; Ecuador $7; Uruguay $4; Bolivia $2; Chile $2; and Peru $2.

2. Melvin and Cherkaouri (1988), for example have empirically demonstrated the positive correlation between gold prices and political instability in the Middle-East.

3. The reason we say "possibly," is because the ultimate effect on the aggregate consumption and savings will depend upon the relative strengths of propensity to save and consume between the buyers and the sellers of gold and other precious metals.

4. Controversial economist Ravi Batra (1988), for example, has recommended "pure hoarding" as a hedge against economic instability resulting from a crash in the U.S monetary system.

5. See R. Gordon (1984: 180-183).

6. *The Wall Street Journal* of September 29, 1988

7

Political Instability:
An Empirical Definition

When you *cannot* express it in numbers, your knowledge is of a meagre and unsatisfactory kind.

Sir William Thompson (Lord Kelvin)

And when you *can* express it in numbers, your knowledge is of a meagre and unsatisfactory kind.

Frank Knight[1]

INTRODUCTION

The riotous 1960s generated a renewed interest in the study of political violence in this country. Through pioneering work in the fields of political science, sociology, and social psychology, considerable insight was gained into the systemic determinants of mass political violence. Recently, economists are showing increasing interest in exploring the simultaneous relationship between sociopolitical instability and economic development (Gupta and Venieris, 1981; Venieris and Gupta, 1983, 1985, 1986; Stewart and Venieris, 1985; Yoo, 1985; Melvin and Cherkouri, 1988). However, despite the fact that the list of publications in this area during the last couple of decades has indeed been impressive, one is struck by the singular lack of commonality in the empirical definition of political instability. In essence the issue at hand translates into the classical problem of representing a multidimensional variable with a univariate one. Yet from the standpoint of an empirical researcher, it may be quite important to construct a composite measure. The construction of such a measure may be important for various kinds of socioeconomic research, public policy analyses, and performance of risk analysis for foreign investment.

In this chapter we suggest a new approach toward solving this vexing problem. Fortunately, one of the most important developments in applied statistics in the past ten years has occurred in the area of qualitative response models, also known as quantal, categorical, or discrete models (Amemiya, 1981). This recent popularity in the use of multivariate qualitative response models in the social science literature can be accounted for by the increasing need to deal with discrete or qualitative variables such as the one at hand. In the era of scientific positivism the social scientists, in general, and economists, in particular, have shown disdain for subjective judgments in empirical research. Yet it is clear that any attempt at defining a variable such as political instability would call for subjective value judgment, a search for which in the quantitative techniques alone is bound to be futile.

Hence, having recognized this, we propose to go in the opposite direction of the previous research that looked into the incidents of political violence to define stability. Rather, in this study, first we would like to define the term *political stability*. Then having defined *stability*, we would treat the question of *instability* as one of conditional probability - that is, given this definition of stability, which incidents of political violence explain the relative instability of a nation? This approach would obviously beg the question of the subjectiveness of the starting definition of political stability. However, in defense, it may be pointed out that there can hardly be any universality in the definition of political instability and, indeed, we may expect the definition to vary with the purpose of inquiry.

The following discussion will be broken down into four main areas: definition of the problem, discussion of methodology and estimation of coefficients for the construction of a composite measure of political instability, the tests of construct validity, and a concluding section pointing out the possibilities and limitations of the present analysis.

THE PROBLEM

The problems of constructing a composite indicator for political instability are as varied as the incidents of violence themselves. However, we may broadly classify them in two groups: (1) definitional or conceptual and (2) empirical.

The first definitional problem that we find in dealing with our undertaking is the fact that all the available data sets contain a number of manifest variables of political violence. Once used for statistical analyses, it may be argued that the researcher is explaining only that particular incident rather than the concept under question, e.g, the political stability of a nation. The argument is analogous to the question of whether the intelligence quotient (IQ) measures intelligence or GNP per capita measures development. For a good measure one needs to establish a direct one-to-one relationship between the concept and the indicator. Otherwise, if we consider the variable assassination of a head of state to be the indicator of political instability, then by using it as a variable in our analysis, we will explain the conditions under which an assassination may take place or may analyze the impact of such an act on the economy or polity at large, but may not explain the intended variable, political instability.

The second definitional problem associated with the construction of a composite indicator of political violence is the fact that there exists qualitative differences among the types of violence. The overall environment of political violence within a nation may be classified into three broad categories: violence against the regime, violence within the regime and violence by the regime. The first category of violence would be exemplified by the incidence of mass or collective movements. The second category would include successful and unsuccessful coup d'états. Violence by the regime may be accounted for by the frequency of political executions.

Even within the category of mass violence, there exist qualitative differences. Fortunately, this area has been quite extensively studied. Through the path-breaking work of researchers such as Rummel (1963), H. Eckstein (1970), and Hibbs (1973), it is generally agreed on that the incidents of mass violence should be classified into two groups. The first group has been alternately called *anomic violence* or *protest demonstration*. The second group has usually been termed *internal war*. We shall call the first group of variables anomic violence since it represents an anomic condition or a state of lawlessness, and hence we believe it is more reflective of the situation. This group is composed of incidents such as riots, political strikes, and anti-government demonstrations. The second dimension, which we will call internal war, would include more violent acts such as guerrilla attack events, deaths from domestic violence, and political assassinations.[2]

However, the political stability of a nation depends not only on the behavior of the masses but also on the elites or small organized groups that usually are part of the regime itself, such as the army, which manifest themselves through coups or attempted coups. Political violence can also be committed by the governing regime. Needless to say, when violence is committed by the government, the line between legitimate attempts to preserve the law and the creation of yet another dimension of political instability is indeed very thin. Thus, Taylor and Jodice (1982) include political execution as a form of government coercion along with the imposition of censorship and political restrictions. However, owing to the obvious qualitative difference between (a) the suspension of some or all personal and civil rights and (b) outright killing, we would consider political executions to be a contributory, rather than a restraining, factor to the overall scene of the political instability of a nation. The dimensions of political instability may be shown as follows:

Figure   7.1

Dimensions of Political Instability

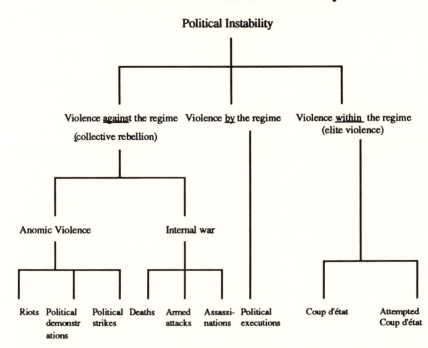

The existence of these qualitative differences compounds our problems of constructing one single vector of continuous variable depicting the overall stability of a nation for comparing cross nationally as well as over time for an individual country. Researchers have dealt with these problems in two ways: either by using more than one measure or by attempting to construct one measure of a composite indicator. The first group obviously circumvents the problems of constructing one single index and hence avoids the question altogether. Among the researchers falling in this category, Hibbs (1973) used the measures of the two dimensions by averaging the log transformed values of the incidences within each dimension and then attempted to look into the causes of their origin independent of each other. Similarly, Bwy (1968b) used factor scores to characterize each dimension. Tanter (1966), in contrast, used "representative" variables, that is, the two variables that loaded the highest in each group representing that dimension. Therefore, for them the number of deaths came to represent the dimension of internal war, whereas anomic violence was represented by the frequency of protest demonstrations. However, despite the differences among these three measures, Hibbs (1973) has shown that empirically they are not very far apart since they are very highly correlated with each other.

Without going into the relative merits of each of these indicators, we may safely point out that they obviously do not yield one single measure to afford comparison across the nations or even for one single nation, over time. The other important problem associated with the two measures of mass political violence is the fact that the relationship between anomic violence and internal war may be influenced by a third factor, namely, development. Thus, while for many individual nations the two dimensions of political violence may covary over time, when comparing the nations across the spectrum of economic development, it has been shown (Gupta, 1977) that they tend to vary inversely. As nations become more developed, there seem to be more incidents of anomic violence and progressively less of internal war. For instance, in the latter part of the 1960s, by the measure of anomic violence, the United States will be considered the most unstable of the nations while countries like Vietnam and Indonesia will top the list by the measure of internal war.[3]

Therefore, owing to the differences among dimensions, it would be impossible to comment on the comparative stability of nations without the help of coefficients reflecting relative weights in determining overall stability. Even over time in any particular nation, one would be hard-pressed to look at data and to determine trends in stability without prior knowledge of the relative importance of various incidents of political violence. However, for an individual nation, if the two dimensions of political violence are highly correlated, then the empirical problem of creating just one vector of indices may be solved by choosing one dimension or the other. Thus, Gupta and Venieris (1981) and Venieris and Gupta (1985), while looking into the case of Great Britain, chose the number of antigovernment political demonstrations as the sole indicator of political violence. Since for Great Britain the frequency of political demonstrations was found to be closely correlated with other indicators of political violence, it may be argued that a choice of any one would be a good representation of political stability.

In contrast, Muller (1985) used the number of deaths as the variable representing the political instability of a nation. This use of a single variable begs the previously posited question of correspondence between a multidimensional phenomenon such as political instability and the measuring variable. The other significant effort at constructing a composite indicator of political instability belongs to I. Feierabend, R. Feierabend, and B. Nesvold (1969). In their widely cited study, they constructed a scale of political instability for 84 communist and noncommunist countries for the period from 1948 to 1967 by assigning subjective weights to the various manifest variables of political violence.[4]   The criticism of their approach lies in the obvious arbitrariness of the assignment of weights.   However, even if one disagrees with the methodology of constructing the weighting scale, their final ranking of the nations would elicit little debate, at least for the countries at the extreme ends of the spectrum.   Thus, while one would consider the Netherlands and Luxembourg to be the epitome of stability, Indonesia and South Vietnam, in contrast, during a period of violent civil war and communist uprising represented true pictures of unstable nations.

        Another attempt to construct a composite measure for political instability was used by Venieris and Gupta (1986).   In their study, they used the classification of Feierabend, Feierabend, and Nesvold to estimate a discriminant function.   Then the resulting factor scores were taken as measures of political instability.   The problem with this method is that while accepting the classification of Feierabend and coauthors, they incorporated their biases and shortcomings, which we have explained above.

THE DATA

        For the present analysis, nine measures of mass, elite, and regime political violence were included (see Figure 7.1).   At this point an important decision regarding the data had to be made in determining the time of the study period.   In the literature, there is a trend toward averaging the incidents over a period of time, as opposed to taking the annual totals for individual countries.   The wider acceptance of the averaged figures stems from the argument that political instability is indeed a long-term concept, the essence of which cannot be captured by the widely varying annual events data in any particular year. However, the choice of an appropriate time period poses some thorny empirical questions.

        The wide variance in the frequencies of the incidents between years poses a significant problem of defining the "true" nature of the political profile of the nation.   For the relatively infrequent, major political events, such as coup d'états, the coefficients derived by averaging the frequencies will contain an upward bias for the individual years, since the frequency of incidents for the individual years will be more dramatic in either direction than the mean. Therefore, since the definition of stability should include a time period longer than a year, several empirical compromises have to be made. One such compromise made for the present study, was to avoid averaging the frequencies of successful and unsuccessful coup d'états. This was done because of the dampening effect of the mean.   For instance, a country experiencing one coup during the five-year period will have a value of 0.17.   However, when calculating the indicator for an individual year in which a single incidence of coup d'état has taken place, the value would be five times more dramatic.   Hence, this will provide an unrealistically high number for the year. As a compromise for these two rather infrequent events, we used dummy variables that assumed the value of 1.0 if the event took place within the study period, and 0, otherwise.

Finally, along with the nine incidences of instability, we included a tenth one, political legitimacy of the government. The use of this variable in the measure of political instability needs explanation, since its use assumes that a democratic country is more politically stable than a nondemocratic one. Empirically, therefore, while comparing two nations with similar frequencies of political violence, we will hypothesize that if one of the countries is a democratic one and the other one is not, then the former is inherently more politically stable than the latter. This is because democracy tolerates more expressions of dissent and enjoys the perception of legitimacy from its people. The importance of perceived legitimacy on the stability of a nation has been widely accepted in the literature. Lipset (1959), in defining legitimacy, noted that it involved the capacity of a political system to engender and maintain the belief that the existing political institutions were the most appropriate or proper ones for the society. The Marxist strategists have always been keenly cognizant of the need for an erosion of the legitimacy of political institutions as a prerequisite for a successful revolution. Thus, Trotsky (1932) observed that if the existence of privation was enough to cause an insurrection, the masses would always be in revolt. For a revolution to take place, it was necessary that the masses, being conclusively convinced of the political bankruptcy of the regime, perceived a revolutionary way out. However, despite the importance of legitimacy as a determinant of political instability, empirical verification of the hypothesis is problematic due to the qualitative nature of the variable. The work of Bwy (1968a) is noteworthy in this area of operationalization of the concept of legitimacy of the government. He defined legitimacy by the degree of democratization by using a rating scale devised by Fitzgibbon (1967) for a number of Latin American countries. The underlying implication is that democracy is synonymous with the perceived legitimacy by the masses, and consequently, the democratic nations have a larger capacity to withstand political turmoil. For instance, despite the high levels of political violence experienced by the United States in the 1960s and Great Britain in the 1970s and 1980s, they would still be considered as stable nations compared with other Third World nondemocratic nations experiencing relatively little political violence.

However, it should be noted that the majority of the countries falling in the category of democracy are from the Western industrial nations. Hence, it is entirely possible that the dummy variable for democracy and legitimacy will pick up effects above and beyond democracy such as economic development. We believe that this contamination does not diminish, and may indeed enhance the qualitative aspect of the variable legitimacy. To be sure, Lipset (1959), confirmed that democracy was positively related to the state of economic development among the 20 republics of Latin America and a number of European and English-speaking nations. "Concretely," he argued, "this means that the more well-to-do a nation, the greater chances that it will sustain democracy." Specifically, Lipset assumed economic development to be a cluster of four variables: wealth, industrialization, urbanization, and education. Similarly, in separate studies Lerner (1958) and Cutright (1963) showed that voting participation (and the extent of democracy) is a function of urbanization, literacy, and media participation, all closely related to the level of national economic affluence.

However, more serious questions, may be raised on the other side of the variable legitimacy, which lumps all nondemocratic nations together. Literature in political theory provides a full list of this intricate taxonomy (Almond and Verba, 1963). The dichotomous distinction of regime type may be defended on the ground that there is no way one can rank order the various political structures in terms of their closeness to democracy or legitimacy. Hence, we felt justified in using the dichotomized variable. See the Appendix to Chapter 7 for a detailed description of the definition of democracy.

METHODOLOGY

Having defined and justified the data, we may proceed toward constructing an index for political instability. The index was created in two steps. In the first step, we classified the countries into groups of relative political stability. The data were pooled for the average of three five-year periods, 1953-57, 1963-67, and 1973-77, giving us a total of 312 observations (3 x 104). In the second step, the index function was created by explaining the classification with the help of the ten manifest variables of political violence.

Step One: With the objective of classifying our sample set of 104 noncommunist countries into groups without any a priori assumption about their relative stability, cluster analysis was used. The use of Cluster Analysis allows one to classify cases into similar groups by measuring distances among them. However, the use of the full analysis was deemed less than useful, since it would have classified the countries into clusters of similar levels of frequencies of the incidents of instability, but these clusterings would not have provided us with a continuum from stable to highly unstable.[5] However, Cluster Analysis does provide us with measures of the Euclidean distances, the square root of the sum of the squared differences between the values of the variables for any two cases. Thus, the Euclidean distance between two cases (j and k) is defined as:

$$d_{jk} = \sum_{i=0}^{n} \sqrt{(x_{ij} - x_{ik})^2} \qquad (7.1)$$

For discerning the level of political stability, our first task was to provide an empirical definition of "political stability." Our definition of a stable nation is simply the one *with zero level of incidents of political instability* and *is a democracy*. Having made this definition of stability, we calculated the standardized distance for each country from this hypothetical country. We posit that the farther a country is from this definition, the more unstable it is. Since the data set contains a tremendous amount of variability, the standardized values of the variables were used instead of the raw data. It is important to point out that by estimating the distance from the hypothetical country by using a normalized data set, we are in effect, measuring the relative position of each country by a global (noncommunist) standard.

However, the problem of using an unqualified distance measure is that it does not distinguish between the various types of political violence and assigns an equal weight. This gives rise to the problem that since the developed countries experience more incidents of anomic violence, they are ranked equally with countries such as South Vietnam and Indonesia, countries experiencing more serious kinds of violence. In fact, by using all the variables in the sample, United States turns out to be the most unstable country in the world during the period from 1963 to 1967. Therefore, to eliminate this problem we recalculated the distances by omitting the three variables of anomic violence (the frequencies of political demonstrations, riots, and political strikes).

Having made these important value judgments, and then by using the resulting standardized distances, the countries were classified into groups. We may note that these classifications were obtained without arbitrarily assigning the relative weights for the ten individual manifest variables of political instability but by assigning equal weight to the standardized values of the measures of internal war and the measures of elite violence, coups d'état, and unsuccessful coups d'état. This, as we will see, yields lower weights for the measures of anomic violence in the functions for creating the index for political instability.

Step two: In the second step, two alternate functions for creating an index of political instability were obtained by use of a discriminant analysis and a multinomial Logit model. These models are used to explain the differences between two groups. Thus, if we have two or more groups of countries classified according to their relative levels of political stability, then these models can help us explain which manifest variables of political instability account for the classification.

The two functions were estimated by pooling the three five-year averages for the countries in the sample set.[6]   At this point we should emphasize that it is considered to be a "cardinal sin" in empirical analysis to try to explain a dependent variable created with the help of the independent variables themselves.   However, the methodological justification of such an act can be found in the fact that by conducting this regression analysis we are not testing any hypothesis per se.   Also, on reflection it seems obvious that no discriminant analyses can be completely free of this "contamination," since any prior classification of cases must be influenced by the manifest or latent variables to be used as independent variables in the subsequent analysis.

The first composite index function for political instability was obtained by using a discriminant analysis of the pooled data of 312 observations (104 x 3), with three groups of countries, classified by the mean $\pm$ .5 standard deviation. We should point out that while standardized values of the independent variables were used for classification of the countries, the unstandardized values were used in the estimation of the index functions. This distinction allows us to use the raw data for each country for calculating the index, which itself is based on the comparative world standard.

The discriminant analysis yields the following equation:

$$PIQ^* = 1.14 + .0007 \ PD + .0049 \ RT + .0086 \ PS + .43*10^{-5} \ D + .13 \ AS +$$

$$.0008 \ AA + .0033 \ PX + 1.38 \ CD + .264 \ UCD + .92 \ GP \qquad (7.2)$$

*   89% of the countries were correctly classified

where:
PD   = Number of political demonstrations
RT   = Number of riots
PS   = Number of political strikes
D   = Number of deaths from political violence
AS   = Number of assassinations
AA   = Number of armed attack events
PX   = Number of political executions
CD   = Dummy variable for the occurrence of coups d'état
UCD   = Dummy variable for the occurrence of unsuccessful coups
            d' état
GP   = Government profile (= 0 if democracy; = 1 otherwise)

While for the discriminant function we used a three-way classification,[7] the number of groups had to be increased for the Logit model in order to prevent it from converging too quickly. The Logit model, which calculates the probability that a country will be classified as unstable by treating the relative cell frequencies as the dependent

variable, was estimated by using 13 groups of countries.[8] The choice
of the number of groups needs some explanation. A larger number of
groups affords us a finer distinction among the nations and thus
prevents us from lumping countries that are several standard deviations
away from our definition of stability.   However, for the estimation of
the Logit function, this advantage had to be weighed against the
problem of consistency. Since the probability of a particular group
membership was approximated by the relative cell frequencies, the
estimators are biased for small samples.   In fact the estimated
parameters are consistent when the sample size in each group gets
arbitrarily large. This additional requirement for consistency is more
stringent than the usual requirement that the total sample size is large,
and is necessary to ensure that the distribution of observations
associated with each group attain normality. Due to this additional
requirement, we made sure that the frequencies within each cell were
not less than ten.[9] The resulting estimated equation is given below:

$$PIQ^* = 1.41 - .00099 \text{ PD} - .015 \text{ RT} - .011 \text{ PS} - .0098 \text{ PX} - .39 * 10^{-4} \text{ D}$$
$$\quad\quad (1.3)\quad\quad (1.8)\quad\quad (1.6)\quad\quad (4.34)\quad\quad (5.42)\quad\quad (6.8)$$

$$\quad - .33 \text{ AS} - .0032 \text{AA} - 3.11 \text{CP} - .502 \text{ UC} - 1.14 \text{ GP}$$
$$\quad (15.4)\quad (7.3)\quad\quad (11.1)\quad\quad (3.5)\quad\quad (11.1) \quad\quad\quad\quad\quad (7.3)$$

ADJUSTED R-SQUARED = .92
F-STATISTIC (10, 305) = 88.7
* t values in parentheses

     The two methods of estimation yield similar results and, as
such, do not provide us with any a priori justification for choosing one
over the other. The estimated functional relationships may be used for
constructing composite indexes for political instability, which can be
used for both cross-national comparison, aand comparison over time
for an individual nation. Figure 7.2 depicts the instability indicators,
calculated by using equation (7.2) for four selected countries between
the years 1948 and 1982.
     From these plotted instability indicators, over time it is evident
that the United States experienced political instability in the 1960s,
whereas Iran became progressively unstable in the Seventies.
However, the levels of political instability in the United States are
dwarfed by countries like Greece and Argentina, as they experienced
more violent forms of violence.

Figure 7.2a

Political Instability Quotient for Selected Countries, 1948-82

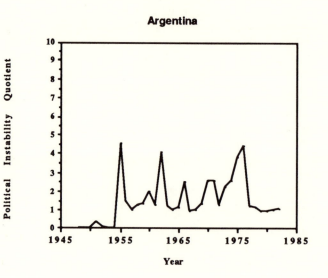

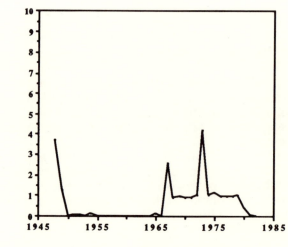

Figure 7.2b

Political Instability Quotient for Selected Countries, 1948-82

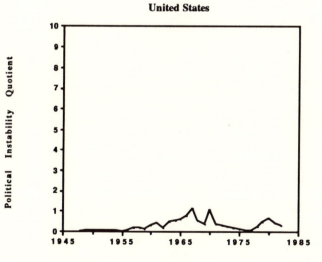

Iran

United States

Political instability may also be viewed in the context of a single country. This was done by holding 1948 (a stable year) as the base for the United States. The results are plotted in Figure 7.3. In this diagram the relative importance of the turmoil of the 1960s may be viewed in its proper perspective.

Figure 7.3

Index of Political Instability for the United States

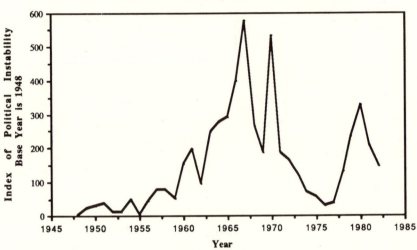

By using the discriminant function [equation (7.2)] we have computed the index of political instability for 104 noncommunist countries in our sample. We provide tables of time series data for the 35 years spanning from 1948 to 1982 in the Appendix at the back of this book for the use of future researchers.

TESTS OF VALIDITY

The central problem associated with the construction of an index such as this is the fact that the concept "instability" is unobservable and hence is not amenable to direct testing of the validity of the measure. Therefore, in order to ascertain the relevance of the measure, it was tested for construct validity.

The test of construct validity involves relating a measuring instrument to an accepted scale or a theoretical framework in order to determine whether the instrument is tied to the concepts it is attempting to measure. In their early work Campbell and Fiske (1959) suggested that similarity in the underlying properties of measurement would yield similar results. Conversely, by using a dissimilar rating scale, one is liable to get a substantially different ranking.

For our index of political instability, we propose to verify construct validity with a two-pronged test by exploring (1) its compatibility with other accepted rankings and (2) the capacity of the existing structural theories to explain political instability among nations measured by our indicator and the capacity, in turn, of our index to duplicate empirical results, showing its impact on the aggregate economy.

As the first step to test the construct validity of our ranking, we calculated Spearman's rank correlation between our rankings against those obtained by Feierabend, Feierabend, and Nesvold (1969). The correlation between the two is 0.72 and is significant at the 0.001 level. The difference that exists may be explained by the fact that (1) the two studies used different data sets with different definitions of the incidents of political instability; (2) we used political legitimacy as an independent variable in our study; and (3) the Feierabend ranking was based on a much longer time period (1948-66) whereas ours is based on three five-year periods. Despite such differences, the high correlation points to a significant degree of conformity between the two rating scales.

As the second step toward the testing of the validity of our index, we offer (1) the ability of the independent variables of an aggregate behavioral model to explain political instability and (2) the index of political instability to explain variances in aggregate investment and the rate of growth of income. Hence, the results of the following two chapters should be regarded as proofs of the construct validity of the index.

CONCLUSION

Despite frequent academic use by social scientists, the term *political instability* in the national context has not been systematically operationalized. Numerous studies have implicitly or explicitly equated national political stability with one or more manifestations of mass violence, which raises question with regard to the correspondence between the concept and the variable(s) used in the analyses. In this chapter we have argued that a definition of political instability must start with a subjective definition of stability to allow a direct correspondence between the concept and the manifest variables.

Since the 1960s, political scientists, sociologists, and sociopsycholo-gists have contributed to the understanding of the systemic causes of political violence. Lately the impact of political instability on national economic growth is being explored. This larger focus on political instability calls for a discussion regarding the construction of a composite measure. Notwithstanding the ubiquitous problems associated with representing any multifaceted social phenomenon with a single unidimensional index, the alternative is the use of arbitrary judgment or the generation of several conceptual problems resulting from the use of erroneous variables in the ever-increasing number of quantitative studies. Therefore, having recognized the remaining conceptual problem with our index of political instability, we will proceed to use it in our empirical analysis.

APPENDIX TO CHAPTER 7:

DEFINITION OF DEMOCRACY

Within the national context, *democracy* is a particularly problematic term to define. Buried under so many layers of philosophy, propaganda, and various descriptions, it is indeed difficult to choose a single criterion by which one can classify the countries in a clear, dichotomous distinction of democratic and nondemocratic nations. Among the various scholars attempting to define democracy, social philosopher Karl Popper, in his characteristic parsimonious style, defines it as a system where transition of power can take place within the rule of law without bloodshed.[10] However, despite the cogency of such a definition, for the operationalization of the notion of democracy, we needed to follow a more structured approach. In this process, we defined a nation as democratic if it had a civilian government, if the effective head of state were elected, and if the effective head of state were operating within some measure of checks and balances. The process has been described with the help of a self-explanatory flowchart (Figure A7.1). The data for the variable Regime Type was collected from Arthur Banks (1971). The data are available for all the countries in the study between the years 1948 and 1966. For the years after 1966, several books including *The Statesman's Yearbook* were consulted to determine the nature of the regime for the countries. During the 1950s and 1960s several of the Third World countries were under colonial rule. During those periods they were assigned the status of a nondemocratic form of government.

It should be note, however, that in our definition of democracy we have been able to specify only the form and not the "spirit" of democracy. Thus, a nation may have a superficial democratic structure without having democracy in the true sense of the term. Japan is an obvious case in point (see Hidaka, 1988). Similar arguments can also be made with regard to Mexico and several other Third World nations.

Figure 7.4

Definition of Democracy

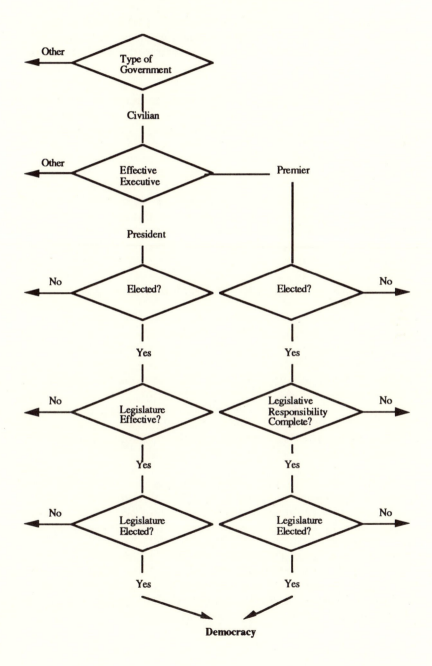

NOTES

1. Sir William Thompson, *Popular Addresses*, edition of 1888-89, and Frank Knight, both quoted in D. McClosky (1983).

2. We should be quick to qualify here that some of these acts may not be considered as acts of "mass" violence, since certain acts of terroristic armed or guerrilla attacks and assassinations may be carried out by a very small number of individuals.

3. This change of composition of the manifestations of the societal frustrations from more violent to less violent with development can be accounted for by resorting to Smelser's (1963) analysis of social movement. Smelser used the nature of the generalized beliefs (of the participants) to classify movements as norm or value oriented. The former is concerned with limited normative changes (e.g., immediate economic issues), whereas the latter attempts to change broad overall social values. Smelser further argued that societies with highly differentiated institutions (the democratic nations) are likely to experience norm-oriented movements (e.g., protest demonstrations) since in such societies there is "the structural possibility of demanding normative change alone" (p. 278). In contrast, without these possibilities in the authoritarian, less differentiated societies, the expressions of mass dissatisfaction will assume a more violent form of revolt.

Oberschall (1973) and Gurr (1970) similarly argued that since the authoritarian regimes do not permit political protests, they are more likely to produce radical movements. Similarly, Coser had earlier (1956) observed that conflict was less likely to occur in authoritarian regimes than in democratic ones but that conflict would be more intense when it did occur. This relationship between conflict and democracy transcends economic affluence, as we will see in subsequent discussion that economic development and democracy are very closely related.

4. For their study the authors collected original data on the following indicators and assigned intensity weights (in parentheses): regularly scheduled elections (0); dismissal or resignation of cabinet officials (1); peaceful demonstrations or arrests (2); assassinations (except of head of state) or sabotage (3); assassination (of head of state) or terrorism (4); coup d'état or guerrilla warfare (5); civil war or mass execution (6). By using this cardinal weighting scheme, Feierabend ranked the countries for the entire 18-year period of their study. However, a better (less skewed) ranking was obtained when the period was broken into three six-year periods and the scores averaged.

5.   For a discussion of cluster analysis, see Jambu and Lebeaux (1983).

6. The pooling of cross-section and time series data pose a number of stochastic problems. First, we would like to know if there is any structural shift in the model within the three time periods. To test the null hypothesis that there have been vertical shifts in the structure, we calculated the standardized values within each time period and then obtained the following equation:

$$\text{PIQ} = 1.74 + .00006\ D - .0025\ PD + .00589\ AA + .611\ AS + 1.73\ CD$$
$$\phantom{\text{PIQ} = } (10.4) \quad (4.5) \quad\quad (.17) \quad\quad (.1) \quad\quad\quad (7.0) \quad\quad (6.5)$$

$$+0414\ PS + 1.388\ UCD + .0189PX + .00475\ RI + 3.50\ IL - .005\ FT$$
$$(3.1) \quad\quad (6.6) \quad\quad\quad (4.4) \quad\quad (.02) \quad\quad\quad (20.3) \quad (.4)$$

$$+ 0.72\ ST$$
$$(.02)$$

R-SQUARED = .77
$F_{(10,351)} = 114.7$

Where: FT = 1 for the period 1953 - 57; 0 otherwise
         ST = 1 for the period 1963 - 67; 0 otherwise

The lack of statistical significance of the intercept dummies fail to convince us of any vertical shift of any kind during the 30 year period under study.

Pooling time series data with cross-section data also causes problems in that there may exist serial correlation across time, across the cases, as well as between the two. However, in this case, since we took three discrete time periods over a span of three decades with a gap of five years between the successive periods, it seems reasonable to assume the nonexistence of serial correlation over time. Hence, the ordinary least squares method was used to estimate the pooled equation. For a similar assumption see Stewart and Venieris (1985).

7.   The ability of the independent variables to explain group membership remains stable regardless of the number of groups; however, a finer classification allows us to distinguish between the countries at a more detailed level.

8.   The logit model is based on the cumulative logistic probability function and is specified as: $P_i = F(Z_i) = F(\alpha + \beta X_i) = 1/(1+e^{-Z_i}) = 1/[1+e^{-(\alpha+\beta X_i)}]$, where, P_i = the probability that a country will be

classified as unstable, given the incidents of political violence X_i, and are approximated by the relative cell frequencies of the individual groups. That is, $P_i = r_i/n$, where r_i are the cell frequencies for group membership, and n is the total number of observations in the sample population. (Pindyck and Rubinfeld, 1981).

9.   See Berkson (1965); also see Cox (1970).

10. Popper (1988) writes:

How is it the state to be constituted so that bad rulers can be got rid of without bloodshed, without violence?...The modern so-called democracies are all good examples of practical solutions to this problem...[they all adopt] the principle that the government can be dismissed by a majority vote...[Democracy thus means] not a theory of the 'rule of the people,' but rather the rule of law that postulates the bloodless dismissal of the government by a majority vote. [pp. 19-22]

8

Political Instability:
A Structural Explanation

INTRODUCTION

In this chapter we will attempt to offer some structural explanations of political instability. In Chapter 4 we developed a behavioral model for the explanation of motives for joining an act of aggression against an established political system. It is fairly obvious that a model based on expected utility theory does not lend itself to direct empirical testing. However, one way of solving this problem, especially in the aggregate, is to hypothesize that a person's actual choice of action (in economic terms, his revealed preference) is the result of a change in his expected utility as a result of the changes in the environmental variables. This change in the aggregate can be accounted for by the structural variables. In symbolic terms, we can express this as:

$$\Delta E(U_i) = PI = f(X_j) \qquad (8.1)$$

The above formulation states that a change in the perception of expected utility is reflected in the expression of political instability (PI), the extent of which is determined by X_j, a vector of structural variables. In Chapter Five we have argued that this concept of a change in expected utility is similar to Smelser's (1963) "value added."

Having made this assumption, which facilitates a quantum jump from the individual to the aggregate, we are able to test our hypotheses. However, before delving into empirical testing, let us establish a connection between the factors in our model and the aggregate variables.

Our behavioral model contains factors of individual income, factors of collective or political income, factors of government retribution, and factors of ideology. In the aggregate the measure of real per capita income can be accepted as an indicator of personal income. Therefore, we hypothesize that the relationship between political participation (in violent action) is likely to diminish with the rising level of affluence. The reason for this inverse relationship rests with the relative opportunity cost of time. With a higher level of income an individual will face the prospect of losing a greater amount of money by taking time off from his normal economic activities.

Other structural factors of economic strain also capture the dwindling strength of the opportunity cost of taking time away from economic activities and devoting it to political actions. Thus, unemployment can be linked to the increased level of political participation, as the costs of such actions are small for the unemployed individuals. Similarly, the presence of a large number of young people may contribute to the cause of an increased level of political activity, as for these youths, who are yet to enter the job market and are assured of their room and board, the opportunity cost of joining is again relatively small.

During our discussion, we had mentioned that it is extremely difficult to quantify political income. However, as we have argued before, peoples' perception of political opportunity changes as a movement gains momentum. Therefore, we can assume that the trend of past levels of political instability can be considered as a good surrogate for this change in perception of political opportunity (or the marginal productivity of political income of time). Also, it should be mentioned that since the ability to impose sanctions for not participating depends on the strength of the opposition movement, the measure of past mobilization can also approximate the aspect of peer pressure in our behavioral formulation.

The cost factor of participation is directly linked to the extent of government's coercive activities. This measure should include both the extent of surveillance (linked to the probability of getting caught) and the degree of punishment (the physical cost of participation).

Finally, we come to the factor, ideology. It is of course quite evident that the factor of ideology is the most difficult variable to measure. However, again we can look for a suitable set of surrogate variables. Recalling that we have defined ideology simply as the preference for collective good for the group to which the potential participant belongs, we can look for factors that reinforce or reduce this group identity. Thus, we can look for variables influencing the perception of social and economic class. In the data set provided by the Inter University Consortium, there is a measure of ethnolinguistic factionalism. We can use measures such as that one to approximate the environmental factors that accentuate the divisions within a society and therefore contribute to the feeling of group identity. On the other hand, we can assume that the permeation of education can broaden people's horizon to diminish the divisive perception of group identity within a society. Indeed, we can point to the studies of the development of groups promoting ethnic violence such as the Nazis and the Brown Shirts in Europe, the Skin Heads in Great Britain, and the Ku Klux Klan in the United States; the participants are overwhelmingly from the less educated working classes of the society. Therefore, we can include education as a factor contributing to the waning of group identities. However, in this context we must mention that this relation between the feeling of segregation and education relates to the entire society. Thus, if the entire society comes to be more educated, individuals may start to look beyond their own group identities; the privileged ones may start to question the legitimacy of their own privileged positions, and the less privileged ones will be offered new economic opportunities. On the other hand, the spread of education within the group suffering from the ill effects of discrimination without any change in the social structure is likely to do just the opposite and foment political discontent. For example, the Kerner Commission (Kerner, 1968) reported that the participants in the black riots were somewhat better educated (especially by the then prevailing community standard) than the rest.

The perception of class division based on economic achievement has been at the heart of most left-wing radical philosophy. An extremely unequal distribution is responsible for creating a chasm between the "haves" and the "have-nots." Hence, the measure of income distribution can be accepted as an indicator of the ideological perception of group identity within a society.

However, at this point we should stop and remind the reader that while discussing the relationship between the behavioral factors and the aggregate variables we must not give the impression that these linkages are precise and without contaminating influence from other factors. For instance, we classified education as a determining factor for ideology. Yet it obviously has a strong correlation with income. Therefore, we continue with our discussion by pointing out the most compelling relationship between two variables, which in most cases are not exclusive.

EMPIRICAL RESULTS

Having established the conceptual linkage between the behavioral factors and the manifest variables, let us attempt to test some of the important hypotheses with empirical data. While deciding to employ the proper methodology for testing our hypotheses, we decided to use a cross-section model of 104 noncommunist countries. The use of the cross-sectional model carries with it some important theoretical implications. It has been pointed out (Coleman, 1968a) that a cross-section model either implicitly or explicitly assumes that the causal process has resulted in a state of equilibrium. In other words, such models assume a stable causal relationship between the dependent and independent variables, which is likely to remain invariant over a considerable period of time. This assumption, needless to say, can prove to be a rather heroic one. On the other hand, the cross-section models enjoy a distinct advantage over those based on time series data. The cross-section models, in contrast to the time series models, measure long-term changes (Kuh and Meyer, 1957; Kuh, 1959). Thus, cross-section models are able to pick up the impacts of variables that change over a long period of time or over the spectrum of development. Therefore, by using a cross-section model, we are able to ascertain the impacts of long-term structural factors, such as income distribution, educational achievement, or the extent of economic development on political instability. Since our purpose in this part of the book is to develop a long term model of economic growth, we decided to use a cross-section model.

The best of both worlds could have been achieved by pooling cross-section with time series data. However, our efforts at building such a model were frustrated as we were constrained by the availability of data. The data reflecting short-term changes such as unemployment are not available across the nation in comparable form.[1]

In this chapter we derive our estimated results by using the ordinary least squares method. The purpose of this exercise is to explore the basic nature of the relationship between the dependent and the independent variables. However, the relationship between the dependent and independent variables is complicated by the fact that they form a part of a simultaneous equation system and so are dependent on each other. This simultaneity results in some inherent flaws in estimation that cannot be corrected by using the ordinary least squares method. Therefore, in Chapter 9, we will specify the entire system of equations and will use the three-stage least squares method to estimate the relevant parameters.

Factors of Personal Income and the Opportunity Cost of Political Activity

Economic Affluence

In our behavioral formulation, we made the hypothesis that the relationship between personal income and participation in acts of political dissent is negative. At the aggregate level we test our hypothesis by regressing political instability quotient for the year 1967 (PIQ67) against gross national product per capita (Y/N) of that year. The best estimate is available by using the (natural) log of gross national product per capita:

$$PIQ67 = 2.455 - .299 \ln\left(\frac{Y}{N}\right) \qquad (8.2)$$

t   (10.2)*   (7.2)*

R-Squared = .33
F (1,102) = 51.2
N   = 104
* Significant at .01 level

The above results show that the relationship between per capita income and political instability is negative and is highly significant.

Youth

Any analysis of the participants in political violence reveals a disproportionate number of youths, with ages varying from the lower teens to the upper twenties. We have argued that their participation can be explained by the fact that these young participants have a very low opportunity cost, since they are not the major breadwinners in the family. Therefore, their level of present economic well-being is largely unaffected by their participation in political activities. However, since it is difficult to set arbitrary limits on the ages of these youthful participants in order to discern their effect on the overall level of political instability, we decided to use a surrogate variable. Since the rate of growth of population is positively correlated with the fraction of youth in the population, we have used the rate of growth of population (dPop) as an independent variable in explaining political instability. Our effort yields the following equation:

$$Q67 = .432 + .147 \, dPop \tag{8.3}$$
$$t \qquad (4.0)^* \quad (3.5)^*$$

R-Squared = .11
F (1,102) = 12.3
N = 104

The above result confirms the hypothesis of a statistically significant relationship between youth and political participation.

Participation in Political Action and Political Opportunity

Mobilization

It stands to reason to argue that an individual's perception of his ability to convert time into collective political goods depends on the state of mobilization of the opposition. Thus, as a movement gains momentum, many potential participants who had previously chosen to sit on the fence, will decide to join the movement. To capture this aspect of the explanation, we decided to use a distributed lag model - that is, explaining the extent of the current years' political instability by resorting to the previous year's level of instability.

However, the problem with the use of such an autoregressive model is that if we use several past years' information, it can cause multicollinearity. Therefore, we decided to use a composite measure of distributed lag.[2] For this, we define our specification as follows:

$$PIQ67 = b_0 + \sum_{j}^{n} b_{(1-j)} \tag{8.4}$$

In estimating the coefficients of the lag structure, we shall use the Lagrangian interpolation method. In particular, we assume $b_{1,(-j)} < b_{1,(-k)}$ for all $|j| < |k|$ and specify:

$$b_{1,-j} = \Pi_0 + \left(\frac{1}{j}\right)\Pi_1 + \left(\frac{1}{j^2}\right)\Pi_2 \qquad\qquad j = 1,2,....,n$$

The above equation is asymptotic toward Π_0. To force the lag structure to approach zero as j increases, we assume that $\Pi_0 = 0$. Since during the collection of data for the political instability indicator we took periods of five years for the sake of consistency, we will assume that an individual's memory for participatory decision making does not extend beyond the fifth year. That is, for us $n = 5$. These assumptions imply that $\Pi_2 = -5\,\Pi_1$. Therefore, equation (8.4) is specified as:

$$PIQ67 = b_0 + P_1\,\omega \qquad\qquad (8.5)$$

$$\omega = \sum_{j=1}^{5} \frac{1}{j}\,PIQ_{-j} - 5\sum_{j=1}^{5}\frac{1}{j^2}\,PIQ_{-j}$$

By using the above specification, we estimated the equation as:

$$PIQ67 = .365 - .0969\,\omega \qquad\qquad (8.6)$$
$$t \qquad\qquad (5.2)* \quad (7.4)*$$

R-Squared = .35
F (1,102) = 54.7*
N   = 104

From the above equation the specification of the distributed lag model provides us with the following coefficients for the lag structure:

$$\beta_{2(-1)} = \Pi_1 - 5\,\Pi_1 = -4\,\Pi_1 = .3876$$
$$\beta_{2(-2)} = \frac{1}{2}\Pi_1 - \frac{5}{4}\Pi_1 = -\frac{3}{4}\,\Pi_1 = .0727$$
$$\beta_{2(-3)} = \frac{1}{3}\Pi_1 - \frac{5}{9}\Pi_1 = -\frac{2}{9}\,\Pi_1 = .0727$$
$$\beta_{2(-4)} = \frac{1}{4}\Pi_1 - \frac{5}{16}\Pi_1 = -\frac{1}{16}\Pi_1 = .0061$$
$$\beta_{2(-5)} = \frac{1}{5}\Pi_1 - \frac{5}{25}\Pi_1 = 0\;\Pi_1 = 0.0$$

which is:

PIQ67 = .365 + .3876 PIQ66 + .0727 PIQ65 + .0215 PIQ64
        + .0061 PIQ63

Therefore, the above results sustain our hypothesis regarding mobilization and participation.

There is another variable measuring the mobilization potential, that has been used extensively in the literature of the structural explanation of political violence, that is, the extent of urbanization. However, our estimations yielded only ambiguous and often statistically insignificant results. Therefore, we decided not to include urbanization in our analysis.

Cost of Participation in Political Action

Government Coercion
The cost of participation depends on the probability of getting caught as well as the severity of punishment. However, in a cross-national setting a full set of variables showing clearly the impacts of these two aspects of the cost factor does not exist. Therefore, we will have to make do with what is presently available. For us the variable of government sanction was obtained from the Inter University Consortium. The very idea of a composite index of government coercion is problematic because of the existence of factors such as the heterogeneity of government measures, the intensity of actionand the difference between the actions of (1) prevention and apprehension and (2) punishment. Therefore, this variable contains some serious shortcomings. Specifically, the data on government coercion suffer from three limitations. First, the measure lumps a whole host of factors without the use of any kind of systematic weightage. Second, for our purpose, it does not distinguish between the factors of surveillance, which impact the perception of the probability of getting apprehended, and the cost of political participation, namely, the severity of punishment. Finally, it is really an incremental measure of government sanction rather than an absolute one. Thus, a government that promulgates actions of repression without any change in the law or action will not show up in this measure. Hence, we consider this to be one of the weakest of the variables included in our analysis, and we will be particularly careful in interpreting the estimated results from our empirical exercise. However, despite the various shortcomings, this is the best available data set. Therefore, we used it to test our hypotheses regarding the linkage between political instability and government sanction.

While attempting to discern the relationship between coercion and political participation, the early experiments showed no systematic trend. This ran contrary to our previous finding of a quadratic relationship. However, on reflection it was clear that our measure of political instability includes within it an important factor that is not a measure of political participation per se. It is the shift factor for dictatorial regimes. Therefore, the reason behind our inability to find the familiar trend is the presence of two qualitatively different relationships depending on the existence of democracy in the nation. Hence, we ran the equation with a pair of dichotomized "slope dummies":

$$Q67 = .587 - .0178 \ (\mu_1 \cdot CRCN) + .00024 \ (\mu_1 \cdot CRCN)^2$$

t   (9.2)*   (2.0)*   (3.1)*

$$+ .036 \ (\mu_2 \cdot CRCN) - .0003 \ (\mu_2 \cdot CRCN)^2 \qquad\qquad (8.7)$$

            (5.1)*   (3.8)*

R-Squared	=	.34
F(4, 99)	=	13.0
N	=	104

where:

CRCN	=	Government coercion for the year 1967
μ_1	=	1 if democracy
	=	0 otherwise
μ_2	=	0 if democracy
	=	1 otherwise

We can derive some extremely interesting observations from the above estimated equation. To begin with, the two forms of government depict two different relationships. With the democratic form of government the immediate effect of the imposition of additional coercion (from the definition of the government coercion variable [Taylor and Hudson, 1972], it is clear that this is really a measure of the imposition of an incremental amount of coercion) is to bring down the level of political instability. However, contrary to the previous hypothesis, the result of an increase in coercion beyond a certain point acts as a provocation. This result may indicate that in a democracy the ultimate resolution of a conflict must come through negotiations and through the workings of the democratic system, rather than by the use of brutal force. Also, in a democracy with a well-defined set of laws and a guarantee of fundamental rights, it may be quite difficult to maintain a high level of repression, which in the end, owing to the freedom of the press and the judicial system, will add to the cause of the rebellion by converting the moderate factions in the society to the plight of the rebel group. In addition, the legal limits, by exposing the impotence of the authorities to deliver coercion, can seriously undermine the government's credibility.

The situation is just the opposite in an authoritarian, nondemocratic nation. In these countries, the hesitant use of government force is interpreted as a sign of weakness and is therefore taken as an act of provocation for further violence. The estimated equation also implies that in such a political system if the authorities possess the power to impose extreme penalties, it would be the safest way to quelch a dissident movement. Hence, recalling our behavioral formulation of Chapter 5, where we argued that in a nondemocratic nation, for a rebel group the only cost-effective demand for public goods is to ask for a revolutionary change in the society, we can see from our empirical results that also for the government the most "profitable" course of action is to impose the maximum amount of coercion. These two hypotheses point to the serious nature of potential conflict in a nondemocratic nation.

Another interesting implication of our findings are obtained by deriving at the points of maxima and minima on the two functional forms. From the above equation, we can see that the point of minimum political instability is caused when a democratic nation applies approximately 37 units of additional coercive measures a year. At that level of coercion a democratic nation, by our measure, experiences .26 units of political instability. It is interesting to note that within our sample of 35 democratic and 69 nondemocratic nations, the two types of political systems represent remarkably similar coercive behavior. In fact with the democratic nations having a mean of 11.6 and a standard deviation of 23.5 units of coercion compared with the nondemocratic nations' mean of 12.4 and 22.2 standard deviation, their difference is statistically insignificant. However, due to the diametrically opposite relationship between coercion and political participation, the impact of coercion in the two types of political systems is remarkably different. The democratic nations reach their minima at 35 units of coercion, which we find to be more than $\pm 1\sigma$ of the sample average. Hence, it seems that most of the democratic nations follow the prudent path of not provoking further acts of political violence by crossing the threshold of tolerance for government coercion. On the other hand, the point of maximum instability is reached when a nondemocratic nation decides to impose 60 units of coercion, which is 2.13σ away from the mean. This result may indicate that the authorities of the non-democratic nations are either unwilling or unable to produce enough coercive measures to have government repression as an effective source of deterrent. However, this apparent hesitancy in imposing coercion may reflect the fact that the indicator represents not the absolute but the additional level of coercion. Therefore, in a naturally tolerant democratic nation an additional measure of coercion acts as a deterrent until it threatens the very rights of the citizens which made the nation a democracy to begin with, at which point it ceases to maintain its efficacy and tends to act more as a provocation for further acts of protest. In contrast, in the nondemocratic nations, already filled with heavy-handed repression, the law of diminishing returns sets in, and it becomes increasingly difficult to be effective with yet another measure of suppression. Hence, if anything, our empirical results point to the limits of power and the need to find a political rather than a military solution for most social conflicts.[3]

Factors of Ideological Perception

Ethnolinguistic Factionalism
        The ideological perception of group identity is based upon the extent of division along factional lines within a society. We decided to use the measure obtained from the Inter University Consortium, published in the *World Handbook of Political and Social Indicators*, (Taylor and Hudson, 1972). Taylor and Hudson provided three different measures of cleavages within a society. They listed measures based on ethnic division, linguistic division, and a combined measure of ethnolinguistic division. Each data set has its own strengths and weaknesses. However, since Taylor and Hudson (pp. 214-18) found a close correlation among the three measures, our choice among them was guided by the completeness of the data set. Since the data compiled by the Department of Geodesy and Cartography of the State Geological Committee of the Soviet Union (Atlas Narodov Mira) contained a complete set for all the countries in our study, we decided to use it. Also, this index provides a composite measure of ethnolinguistic factionalism within nations.
        By regressing ethnolinguistic factionalism (ELF) against the political instability quotient for the year 1967, we received:

$$PIQ67 = .424 + .826\ ELF \qquad\qquad (8.8)$$
$$t \qquad (4.9)* \quad (4.9)*$$

R-SQUARED   = .19
F(1, 102)   = 23.8
N   = 104

Education
        Next, we hypothesize that the spread of education will reduce ideological fervor within the society since education will promote economic mobility. Also, it will help broaden the horizon of the citizens to accept their difference without prejudice. The following regression was estimated by using per capita expenditure per pupil on education (EDUCN), in 1967 U.S dollars, as the independent variable:

$$PIQ67 = .954 - .0074\ EDUCN \qquad\qquad (8.9)$$
$$t \qquad (16.2)* \quad (5.8)*$$

R-SQUARED   = .25
F(1, 102)   = 33.2
N   = 104

Class Distinction
          In our scheme the final variable that captures the extent of
group identity on the part of potential dissidents is the depth of
economic class distinction. The class division within a society is
reflected in the distribution of income. Throughout history, no other
factor has been suspected of causing political turmoil more than the
distribution of income. In his Politics v.c, Aristotle in 322 BC
observed that revolutions are the products of demagogues who incite
the masses against the wealthy. Aristotle also noted that the best
safeguard against a political upheaval is the proliferation of the middle
class. He wrote:

In every state the people are divided into three kinds: the very rich, the very poor,
and thirdly, the those who are between them. Since, then, it is universally
acknowledged that the mean is best, it is evident that .. a middle state is to be
preferred; for that state is most likely to submit to reason.....

But it is clear that the state where middle ranks predominates is the best, for it alone
is free from seditious movements. Where such a state is large, there are fewer
seditions and insurrections to disturb the peace; and for this reason extensive states
are more peaceful internally, as the middle ranks are numerous. In small states it is
easy to pass the two extremes, so as to have scarcely any middle ranks remaining;
but all are either very poor or very rich [Politics, iv. 11].

          However, despite the age-old suspicion of a maldistribution of
income fomenting political strife, most of the previous attempts to
establish a correlation between political violence and distribution
obtained confusing results (see Chapter 3).   Part of this inability to
establish this relationship can be attributed to the data themselves.
Other than the measure of political violence, which has varied from
researcher to researcher, the composite indicator of income distribution
is itself riddled with contradictions and short comings. For example,
Sen (1973) has demonstrated the conceptual problems emanating from
the composite measures of income distribution, such as the Gini index.
Therefore, we decided to abandon the composite measure in favor of
the relative income shares of groups in the economy. We divided the
economy into three income groups: the wealthy, the middle class, and
the poor. The wealthy class is defined by the top 20 percent of the
population; the middle class, the next 40 percent; and poor class, the
bottom 20 percent of the population. As a measure of distribution of
income, we used their share of the total economic pie. In our equations
the variable T20 measures the income share of the wealthy class; M40,
the share of the middle class, and B40, the share of the bottom 40
percent of the population.
          However, while attempting to test our hypothesis with regard
to the distribution of income, we encountered a data problem. The
most widely used data on income distribution were complied in a

World Bank study, published by Shalil Jain (1976). However, this data set presents us with two problems. The first problem with this data set is that the years of collection vary from country to country, with most falling during the mid-1960s. Second, the data set contains information on only 49 countries. Therefore, for us to use this information for our sample of 104 countries for the year 1967, we had to extrapolate the data.[4] This can be done by offering a behavioral explanation for income distribution and by assuming the validity of the trend to obtain estimation for the countries in our sample.

An examination of the voluminous literature on the size distribution of income reveals two distinct strands of thought.[5] The first strand is born out of the analysis of Simon Kuznets (1955), where the size distribution of income is regarded as a result of economic development. The duality theory of economic development holds that the transitional economies are characterized by the simultaneous existence of a traditional (typically agricultural) sector and a modern (typically an industrial) sector, with the traditional sector having a lower but less unequal income than the modern sector. Therefore, it was assumed that as the country traverses through the path of development, there is a transfer of resources from the traditional to the modern sector. As a result the level of per capita income increases, but so does income inequality. The level of income inequality, however, decreases as the nations approach the "developed" status. This is known as Kuznet's inverse U-hypothesis of income inequality and economic development.

The second strand of thought takes more of an "institutionalist" approach, which hypothesizes that the level of income distribution is dependent on factors such as a country's political system, its role in the international trade system, the strength of the labor union, its level of education, and the extent of government involvement in the economy.[6]

The empirical work of Ahluwalia (1976a, 1976b) and Paukert (1973) lent support to the Kuznets hypothesis of an intersectoral shift, whereas Adelman and Morris (1973) and Papanek (1978) support the institutionalist view point. By combining the two approaches, we formulated our behavioral hypothesis:

$$\gamma_i = f (Y, r, N, As, Af, La, Rt) \qquad (8.10)$$

where:

γ_i	= Income share of the ith group
Y	= GNP per capita
r	= Rate of growth of real GNP per capita
N	= Rate of growth of population
As	= Dummy variable for the Asian countries
Af	= Dummy variable for the African countries
La	= Dummy variable for the Latin American countries

Rt   = Dummy variable for regime type, with democracy = 1; = 0 otherwise

The estimation of the relative income shares poses a problem. That is, if each income share is estimated independently, their sum total may not add up to 1. In order to ensure that the total of the income shares is equal to 1 ($\Sigma \gamma_i = 1$), we jointly estimated the coefficients for the three income classes.[7] This is done as follo:s. Suppose we have three relative income shares - the share of the top 20 percent of the population (T20), the share of the middle 40 percent, and the share of the bottom 40 percent. In such a case, we may write:

$$T20 + M40 + B40 = 1 \tag{8.11}$$

By dividing both sides of the equation by B40, we get:

$$\left(\frac{T20}{B40}\right) + \left(\frac{M40}{b40}\right) + 1 = \left(\frac{1}{B40}\right) \tag{8.12}$$

Now we may specify Logit functions to estimate the coefficients for the ratios (T20/B40) and (M40/B40). Then, by using these two equations, we can estimate the relative income share ratios, which - when used in equation (8.12) - yields the estimated values of the share of national income for the three population groups.

The estimated Logit equations for the fraction of the two-income share are:

$$\ln\left(\frac{T20}{B40}\right) = -4.857 + 2.16 \ln\left(\frac{Y}{N}\right) - .178 \left(\ln(\frac{Y}{N})\right)^2 - .02\ R + .096\ As$$
t   (2.3)*   (2.9)*   (2.9)*   (.3)   (.3)

$$+ .436\ Af + .384\ La - .143\ N - .101\ Rt \tag{8.13}$$
    (1.3)   (1.3)   (1.3)   (.6)

R-SQUARED = .42
F (8,40)   = 3.4*
N   = 49

$$\ln\left(\frac{M40}{B40}\right) = -1.16 + .70 \ln(Y) - .052\ [\ln(Y)]^2 - .045\ R + .257\ As$$
t   (.83)   (1.9)*   (1.3)   (1.3)   (1.2)

$$+.179\ Af + .172\ La - .145\ N + .088\ Rt \tag{8.14}$$
    (.8)   (.8)   (1.9)*   (.8)

R-SQUARED = .20

F (8, 40)   = 1.2
N   = 49

From this set of two equations, we estimated the income shares of the three groups, and then tested their closeness of fit. The results are as given in Table 8.1

Table   8.1

Comparison of Actual and Predicted Series of Income Share

	T20	M40	B40
Correlation coefficient	.72	.73	.58
Regression coefficeint of actual on predicted	.98	.97	.96
Theil's inequality coefficeint	.99	.96	.99

By using equations (8.13) and (8.14), we obtained the estimates of the relative shares of the three income groups for our entire sample of countries. These estimated values were used to derive equations for discerning the impact of the relative income share of the three economic classes on political instability:

Q67 = -2.28 - .017 TOP20   (8.15)
 t   (1.1)   (1.5)

R-SQUARED   = .02
F (1, 102) = 1.5
N   = 104

$$Q67 = 2.73 - .065 \text{ MID40} \tag{8.16}$$
$$t \quad\quad (9.6)^* \quad\quad (7.0)^*$$

R-SQUARED   = .32
F (1,102)   = 48.9*
N   = 104

$$Q67 = 4.52 + .034 \text{ BOTTOM40} \tag{8.17}$$
$$t \quad\quad (4.7)^* \quad\quad (3.9)^*$$

R-SQUARED =   .13
F (1,102)   =   15.1*
N   = 104

From the above set of equations, we see that the share of the top 20 percent of the population yields ambiguous and statistically insignificant results. We can also see that the situation changes considerably when we introduce the income share of the middle and poor classes. The concentration of income in the hands of the poor is strongly associated with instability, whereas the share of the middle class shows a highly significant negative correlation with the level of political instability. Therefore, these results point to the verification of Aristotle's 2,000 year-old hypothesis that a strong middle class is an excellent guarantee for political stability.

Next, let us ponder the effect of a redistribution on the political stability of a nation. Since we have assumed that the economy is distinguished into three groups, the upper-income (TOP20), middle-income (MID40), and the poor (BOTTOM40) groups, in a zero-sum game the gain of one group must come at the expense of another group. Thus,

$$\Delta M \equiv \Delta T + \Delta B$$

By dividing through by ΔM, we get:

$$\left(\frac{\Delta T}{\Delta M}\right) + \left(\frac{\Delta B}{\Delta T}\right) = 1$$

$$\text{or, } \left(\frac{\Delta B}{\Delta T}\right) = \left(1 - \frac{\Delta T}{\Delta M}\right)$$

Therefore, following this logic, we can discern the effect of a redistribution on political stability by running a regression as:

$$PIQ67 = a_1 \left(\frac{T20}{M40}\right) + a_2 \left(\frac{B40}{M40}\right) \tag{8.18}$$

where coefficients a_1 and a_2 denote the response of the middle class to a redistribution of its share in favor of the rich and the poor class, respectively. Now, if we include both the redistributive variables in our equation, we run the risk of generating singularity of the matrix. Hence, we rewrite the above equation (8.18) as:

$$PIQ67 = a_0 \left(\frac{T20}{M40}\right) + a_1 \left(1 - \frac{T20}{M40}\right)$$

$$= a_1 + a_2* \left(\frac{T20}{M40}\right) \tag{8.19}$$

where: $a_2* = a_0 - a_1$

Therefore, by running the above (8.19) form, we obtained:

$$PIQ67 = \quad 1.11 + \quad .308 \left(\frac{T20}{M40}\right) \tag{8.20}$$

t   (4.0)*   (6.8)*

R-Squared   = .31
F (1, 102)   = 46.3*
N   = 104

From this equation we can now estimate the relevant coefficients for a redistribution in favor of the wealthy and the poor group from the middle income group:

$$PIQ67 = 1.42 \frac{TOP20}{MID40} + 1.11 \frac{BOTTOM40}{MID40}$$

From the above results it is obvious that the middle class is not only the pillar of stability; it is also extremely guarded about its income share. Any attempt to redistribute income from the middle class, either to the wealthy or to the poor, will raise their ire.

By using the same logic, we estimated the result of a redistribution of income from the wealthy group:

$$PIQ67 = 2.53 - 10.44 \frac{MID40}{TOP20} \tag{8.21}$$

t   (9.5)*   (6.7)*

R-SQUARED   = .30
F (1, 102)   = 44.9
N   = 104

This equation, therefore, implies:

$$PIQ67 = -7.91 \frac{MID40}{TOP20} + 2.54 \frac{BOTTOM40}{TOP20}$$

The above estimated relationships point to the fact that a redistribution from the wealthy to the middle class contributes to the stability of the nation, whereas an attempt to increase the income share of the poor by taking from the rich causes trouble for the political authorities.

CONCLUSION

In this chapter, we tested some of the behavioral hypotheses with aggregate data. However, the occurrence of political instability in a nation cannot be considered in isolation. Rather, it should be considered as a part of a larger simultaneous system where the economic, sociological, and political factors influence the generation of acts of political dissidence, and the level of political instability impacts the economic environment of a nation. In such a situation an estimation of the relationship by using the ordinary least squares method, based on a single equation model, will not provide us with efficient estimators. Therefore, in the following chapter, we propose to estimate the causes of political instability within a simultaneous equation system by using the three-stage least square method.

NOTES

1. For the use of a similar model in explaining political instability with the help of time series data, see Gupta and Venieris (1981) and Venieris and Gupta (1985).

2. I have used this distributed lag model in my previous work with Venieris (see Gupta and Venieris, 1981; and Venieris and Gupta, 1983). Douglas Hibbs has used a similar model in explaining the occurrence of industrial conflict. See Hibbs (1976).

3. To test the hypothesis that the quadratic forms within the two regime types are in fact linear, we estimated a restricted form by suppressing the quadratic terms from equation (8.7). This yielded:

$$PIQ67 = .644 + .0012\mu_1 \cdot CRCN + .0141\mu_2 \cdot CRCN \qquad (8.7a)$$
$$t \qquad (11.25)^* \quad (.33) \qquad\qquad (5.25)^*$$

From this equation (8.7a), we tested the null hypothesis that the coefficients for the quadratic terms are equal to 0. The resulting ratio is distributed as F (3, 99) and was found to have a value of 79.1, which is greater than the critical value of F at 1%, 3.95. Therefore, we rejected the null hypothesis.

4.   Our sample consists of the following countries. We have shown the year for which the data were available in parenthese: Chad (1959), Niger (1960), Nigeria (1959), Sudan (1969), Tanzania (1964), India (1957), Morocco (1965), Senegal (1960), Sierra Leone (1968), Tunisia (1971), Bolivia (1968), Ceylon (1963), Pakistan (1964), South Korea (1966), Malaysia (1958), Ivory Coast (1959), Zambia (1959), Brazil (1960), Ecuador (1968), El Salvador (1965), Peru (1961), Iraq (1956), Philippines (1961), Colombia (1964), Gabon (1960), Costa Rica (1969), Jamaica (1958), Lebanon (1960), Barbados (1951), Chile (1968), Mexico (1963), Panama (1969), South Africa (1965), Argentina ((1961), Trinidad (1958), Venezuela (1962), Greece (1957), Japan (1962), Israel (1957), United Kingdom (1964), The Netherlands (1962), West Germany (1964), France (1962), Finland (1962), Norway (1963), Australia (1967), Denmark (1963), Sweden (1963), and United States (1969).

5. For one of the latest discussions of the literature and the estimation of functional relationship of size distribution of income, see Tsakloglou (1988).

6. It may be noted that Kuznets (1955) was not totally oblivious to the sociopolitical determinants of income distribution and in fact hypothesized that these factors become more important in the later state of economic development.

7. For a discussion of the methodology of joint estimation, see Zellner and Lee (1964). For another example of the use of this technique, see Schmidt and Strauss (1975).

9

Political Instability and Economic Performance: A Political Economic Model of Growth

INTRODUCTION

Having discussed the causes of the origins of political instability, and then having explained its impact on the economy, we are now in a position to develop an expanded model of economic growth. The standard neoclassical model takes only the economic variables into account, holding the sociopolitical environment in abeyance, under the ubiquitous assumption of ceteris paribus. However, in a clear contrast, this model takes a broader view of economic growth. The inclusion of factors of the sociopolitical and institutional environment carries some important theoretical implications.

The inclusion of sociopolitical variables in general and the factors of political violence in particular changes the traditional neoclassical/ Keynesian model of economic growth in three major ways. First, the neoclassical model holds that economic development is a gradual and continuous process, characterized by a monotonic growth path from less development to the cherished state of a developed economy. Under our expanded system of political economy of growth, the process may contain sharp changes and discontinuities resulting from institutional changes, such as the overthrow of a government.

Second, for neoclassical economics the developmental process is harmonious and cumulative, based on automatic equilibrating mechanism. For our system of politicaleconomic growth, a stable equilibrium is not automatically reached and may require some dramatic structural or governmental policy changes. This disequilibrium process is quite different from the rather mechanical knife-edge problem of the Harrod- Domar model and, hence, so are the solutions.

Third, the most glaring contrast that separates the two models lies in their respective outlooks. For the neoclassical model, there is a pervasive optimistic outlook concerning the possibilities for and the benefits of continued economic growth. This results in the acceptance of, without question, the so-called trickle down theory. The belief that with development all the boats will rise, as the tide of economic prosperity comes in justifies a skewed distribution of income in favor of the wealthy at the initial stages of economic development. It has been argued that since the wealthiest group has the highest propensity to save and invest, a redistribution of income in their favor will enhance economic expansion, which, in time, will reach the lowest of the economic classes. In our integrated model, while not explicitly denying the trickle down effect, it is emphasized that even if there is a slow trickle down toward the bottom of the economy, there is no guarantee that those who are left out of prosperity will wait their turn patiently. In fact, it is entirely possible that in a race for economic prosperity people's expectations will outstrip their willingness to accept social injustice. As a result, their ever-increasing demand for economic and political goods will out strip the capacity of the present political system to provide. This structural divergence between demand and supply can cause serious problems for political authorities, with disastrous consequences for the future growth of the economy. Therefore, in contrast to the neoclassical model the prevailing outlook for our model is a good deal less optimistic.

THE MODEL

In Chapter 7, we developed a comparative static analysis of general equilibrium by including political instability as an endogenous model. In this chapter we would like to develop an impressionistic growth model, the parameters of which are to be estimated by data from 104 noncommunist countries. Again, we are excluding the communist countries from our data set because of the possibility of systematic biases in the availability of data, especially in the area of political violence.

Our empirical growth model is based on one of the most simple models developed by Sommers and Suits (1968). Sommers and Suits explained developmental process of nations with the help of three simple equations:

$$\left(\frac{d(Y/N)}{Y/N}\right) = r_0 \, Gcf - r_1 \left(\frac{dN}{N}\right) \tag{9.1}$$

$$Gcf = g_0 + g_1 \left(\frac{y}{N}\right) - g_2 \left(\frac{Y}{N}\right)^2 \tag{9.2}$$

$$\left(\frac{dN}{N}\right) = \frac{n_0}{n_1 + (Y/N)} + n_3 \tag{9.3}$$

where:

Y   =   Gross national product
N   =   Population
Gcf =   Gross capital formation

In this system the first equation is the surrogate for a production function, where the rate of growth of per capita income is a function of gross capital formation and the rate of growth of population. The second equation behaviorally relates gross capital formation to the level of per capita GNP. The quadratic formulation demonstrates the fact that while in the beginning of growth nations tend to invest (and save) a large part of their income, with affluence their rate of investment goes down. This increasingly smaller marginal contribution to capital outlays beyond a certain level of affluence is explained by the fact that at very high levels of income, countries have satisfied most of their capital needs and can devote a larger percentage of any per capita income increase to consumption goods. Finally, the third equation is an asymptotic curve showing the negative relationship between income and the rate of growth of population.

When the parameters of this set of three simultaneous equations were estimated, despite the model's simplicity, they produced surprisingly accurate results. Since our purpose is to develop a descriptive model of growth, we found this model to be of great use. Therefore, we can develop an integrated model of political economic growth by including factors of political instability in this system.

Since we want to explore the simultaneous linkage with political instability, we have included it within the framework of Summers and Suits, (1968) model, which has been drawn at the top of Figure 9.1 within the ellips. The inclusion of political instability changes the system substantially. Now, at the bottom of the diagram (within the rectangular space) are the factors of individual motivation - the factors of individual utility and collective utility. The structural variables, in combination with factors of ideological orientation, affect the process of utility maximization of the individuals, and the sum total of their individual decisions impact the level of political stability in the aggregate. The level of instability in the polity increases the perception of uncertainty, which results in a lowering of capital formation in the economy. The level of political instability also affects the aggregate production function, as it stands in the way of the normal functioning of the economic sector; the physical hindrance to the production process can result (1) from work stoppages and shop closures due to political strikes or (2) the conscription of the farmers either by the government to fight the rebellion, or by the rebel forces to fight the authorities. Therefore, the rate of growth of per capita income is impacted from two different sources. First, the uncertainty resulting from political instability lowers the rate of capital formation in the economy. Second, the rate of growth of income is itself lowered as normal economic activities are hampered physically by the environment of violence.

Figure   9.1

The Structure of a Political Economic Model of Growth

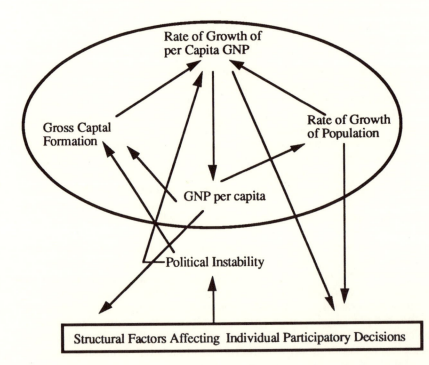

By culling our results of estimation from Chapter 7, then by altering the functional forms of Sommers and Suits (1968) and adding a behavioral equation for per capita expenditure on education, we can specify the simultaneous system as follows:

$$\left(\frac{d(Y/N)}{Y/N}\right) = r_0 \, Gcf - r_1 \left(\frac{dN}{N}\right) - r_2 \, PIQ \tag{9.4}$$

$$Gcf = g_0 + g_1 \left(\frac{Y}{N}\right) - g_2 \left(\frac{Y}{N}\right)^2 - g_3 \, PIQ \tag{9.5}$$

$$\left(\frac{dN}{N}\right) = \frac{n_0}{n_1 + (Y/N)} + n_3 \tag{9.6}$$

$$\begin{aligned}
PIQ = {}& p_0 - p_1 \ln (Y/N) - p_2\, m_1{*}CRCN + p_3\, \mu_1{*}CRCN^2 + \\
& p_4\, \mu_2{*}CRCN - p_5\, \mu_2{*}CRCN^2 - p_6\, \omega + p_7\, ELF + p_8\, EDCN \\
& + p_9\, Top20 + p_{10}\, Mid40 + p_{11}\, Bottom40 \tag{9.7}
\end{aligned}$$

The system is closed by specifying the identity:

$$\left(\frac{Y}{N}\right) \equiv \Delta \left(\frac{Y}{N}\right) \cdot [1 + \left(\frac{Y}{N}\right)_{-1}]$$

where:

CRCN	= Government coercion for the year 1967
μ_1	= 1 if democracy; 0 otherwise
μ_2	= 0 if democracy; 1 otherwise
ω	= Composit variable of distributed lag
ELF	= Factors of ethnolinguistic factionalism
EDCN	= Per capita expenditure on education
Top20	= Income share of the top 20 percent of the population[1]
Mid40	= Income share of the middle 40 percent of the population
Bottom40	= Income share of the bottom 40 percent of the population

THE ESTIMATION RESULTS

The parameters of the above system were estimated by using the three-stage least square method. The results of our estimation are listed below:

$$\left(\frac{d(Y/N)}{Y/N}\right) = .133\ GCF \quad - \quad .551 \left(\frac{dN}{N}\right) - \quad .645\ PIQ67 \tag{9.8}$$

$$t \qquad\qquad (4.93) \qquad\quad (2.73) \qquad\quad (1.91)$$

R-Squired= .14

$$\left(\frac{dN}{N}\right) = \frac{1815}{867.3 + (Y/N)} - .007 \tag{9.9}$$

R-Squired= .54

$$GCF = 2.99 + .00461 \left(\frac{Y}{N}\right) - .00000205 \left(\frac{Y}{N}\right)^2 - .188 \, PIQ67$$

$$t \qquad (7.21) \qquad (5.20) \qquad (4.88) \qquad\qquad (1.24)$$

$$- 3.18 \, B40 + 1.21 \, M40 \qquad\qquad\qquad (9.10)$$
$$(1.85) \qquad\quad (.27)$$

R-Squared = .58

$$PIQ67 = .0098 - .0423 \ln \left(\frac{Y}{N}\right) + .065 \left(\frac{dN}{N}\right) - .0023 \, \mu_1 \cdot CRCN$$

$$t \qquad (3.28) \qquad (2.78) \qquad\qquad\quad (.84) \qquad (1.19)$$

$$+ .000166 \, \mu_1 \cdot CRCN^2 + .0094 \, \mu_2 \cdot CRCN$$
$$(2.04) \qquad\qquad\qquad\quad (.73)$$

$$-.0000315 \, \mu_2 \cdot CRCN^2 + .0311 \, \omega + .0012 \, ELF$$
$$(.91) \qquad\qquad\qquad\quad (2.04) \qquad (.40)$$

$$- .0857 \, EDCN + .0035 \, T20 - .056 \, M40 \qquad (9.11)$$
$$(1.14) \qquad\qquad (.10) \qquad (1.034)$$

R-SQUARED = .65
N   = 104

From the estimated equations, we can see that our hypotheses, derived by using the ordinary least square method, are holding for the three-stage least squares method. Equation (9.9) indicates that a percentage increase in the level of political instability will reduce the rate of growth of per capita income by approximately six tenths of one percent. Of course, the total effect of political instability on the rate of growth of income will be larger as the level of political instability impacts negatively the rate of gross capital formation in the economy. Owing to the nonlinear nature of the system, it is not easy to derive dynamic multipliers for political instability. Therefore, to derive the implications of a change in some of these variables, we will have to resort to the dynamic simulation of the system.

By expanding equations (9.10) and (9.11) by the same logic as has been discussed in Chapter 7, we obtain equations (9.10a) and (9.11a).

$$GCF = .00461 \left(\frac{Y}{N}\right) - .00000205 \left(\frac{Y}{N}\right)^2 - .188 \, PIQ67 +$$
$$2.99 \, T20 + 4.20 \, M40 - .017 \, B40 \qquad\qquad (9.10a)$$

$$PIQ67 = -.0423 \ln\left(\frac{Y}{N}\right) + .065 \left(\frac{dN}{N}\right) - .0062 \, DmG + .000166 \, DmG^2$$
$$+ .0094 \, DcG - .0000315 \, DcG^2 + .0012 \, ELF$$
$$- .0857 \, EDCN + .0133 \, T20 - .0462 \, M40$$
$$+ .0098 \, B40 + .1244 \, PIQ66 + .0233 \, PIQ65$$
$$+ .00684 \, PIQ64 + .00194 \, PIQ63$$

$$(9.11a)$$

Statistical Significance of the Factors of Ideology

Note that under the three-stage least squares method the estimates of the t statistics are only asymptotically efficient. However, the system can, nevertheless, be manipulated to test certain hypotheses. One such hypothesis that we tested was the relevance of the factors of ideological orientation. This was done by using the Wald test procedure. The Wald test allows one to test jointly the significance of a number of estimated coefficients. The results of the test yields a chi-squared distribution with one degree of freedom. The square root of the chi-squared value is the t statistics, the distribution of which is almost the same as a two-tailed t statistic based on more than 50 observations. Since we have 104 observations, the result of the Wald test is efficient. To test the statistical relevance of the factors of ideology, we set the null hypothesis that the coefficients for education and ethnolinguistic factionalism are equal to zero. By running the above set of equations with this restriction, we obtained the chi-squared value 15.1 (t = 3.9). Since this is significant at the .01 level, we reject the null hypothesis and accept the hypothesis that ideological factors contribute significantly to the understanding of political instability.

SIMULATION GAMES

Political Instability and Economic Growth

The results of the estimated system were also used to derive several interesting conclusions based on simulation games. First, we wanted to know the impact of political instability on economic growth. This was done by using a dynamic simulation technique on the estimated system of equations, assuming perfect political stability (by setting PIQ = 0). Then we simulated the model two more times. We set PIQ equal to the mean level of political instability for the underdeveloped nations for the year 1967. We then repeated the exercise by assuming a political instability factor of one standard

Figure   9.2

Political Instability and Economic Growth

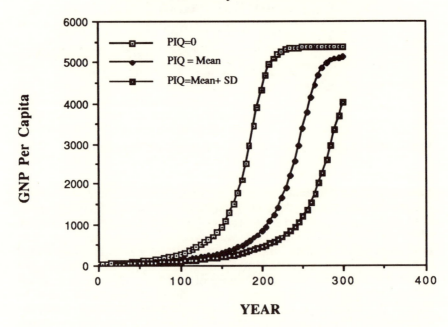

deviation away from the mean. The results of our simulation have been plotted in Figure 9.2.

From the above Figure, the devastating effect of political instability is readily apparent. For example, starting with a per capita gross national product of $40 (the per capita GNP of Upper Volta, the poorest nation in our sample, for the year 1967 at 1963 constant U.S. dollars), we simulated the growth of GNP over a 300-year period. Based on this simulation game, we can see that a nation experiencing no political instability, will grow at a much faster rate and will reach a higher asymptotic level of income than a nation experiencing an average rate of political instability (PIQ = .76) every year. In such a case, for example, starting with $40 of per capita income, a politically stable nation will reach $500 of per capita income in approximately 110 years. However, a country experiencing a mean amount of political instability will be able to reach this income 40 years later. A country experiencing a level of political instability equal to the mean plus one standard deviation will require 70 years to traverse this distance. The predicament of this country becomes even more dire during the transitional period, where it falls further and further behind. We have plotted the loss of income resulting from political instability in the Figure 9.3.[2]

Figure   9.3

Loss of Income Due to Political Instability

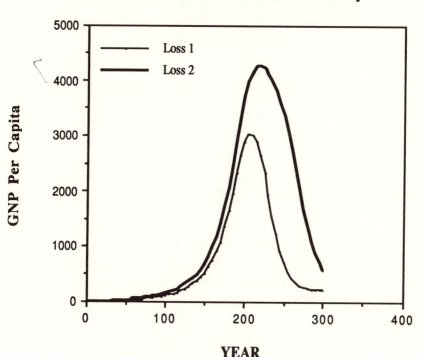

In light of this finding, it is particularly disheartening from the standpoint of the developing nations where the political environment of nondemocratic rule stands in the way of economic growth. It is of course true that we see many examples of countries, such as South Korea and Taiwan, that do not have democratic forms of government and yet are progressing very rapidly. In support of the results of our simulation game, we may simply point out that in this game we take a rather long-term view of development. And so there is every reason to believe that a nondemocratic nation in general is basically unstable, which in the long run can cost it economic prosperity.

Effects of Income Redistribution

Next we wanted to discern the impact of redistribution of income. For that we reformulated our system of equations and observed the result of a redistribution of income in favor of the three economic classes individually. The redistribution of income in favor of the three economic classes was measured by defining:

$$\varphi_i = \frac{\gamma_i}{1-\gamma_i} \quad i=1,3$$

where

φ_i is the income share of an economic class (γ_i) relative to the share of the other two classes

Therefore, the effect of a redistribution of income in favor of the top 20 percent of the population will be measured by:

$$\varphi_1 = \frac{TOP20}{MID40+BOT40}$$

Hence, an effect of an increase in the income share of the members of the top 20 percent of the population (φ_1) relative to the income share of the middle and poor classes, can be measured by regressing φ_i against a dependent variable. Similarly, the variables φ_2 and φ_3 will provide us with the estimate of a redistribution of income in favor of the middle and the poor class, respectively.

The effect of a redistribution of wealth on the performance of the economy (measured by the rate of growth of per capita income) is likely to show up in two different areas of our specified system of equations. First, in the context of discourses with regard to the standard neoclassical/Keynesian economics and so-called supply-side economics, it has been argued that a redistribution of income in favor of the wealthy will increase the level of aggregate investment in the economy. This argument is at the root of the so-called trickle down theory. On the other hand, as we have seen above, the other area of our system, which will be affected by a redistribution of income is the level of political stability. Therefore, the total effect of a redistribution of income will be felt through the simultaneous interaction of the various functional forms, some of which will be favorable to the growth of income and some of which will be unfavorable to it. The final outcome of a redistribution will depend on the relative strength of the income increasing and income decreasing forces. Hence, in order to determine the effect of redistribution of income, we altered the specifications of our equations on gross capital formation and political instability and then reestimated the whole system for the three economic classes. This exercise yielded the following sets of results:

Redistribution in favor of the wealthy class:

$$\frac{\Delta(Y/N)}{Y/N}\Bigg|_t = .095 \text{ GCF} - .477 \text{ N} - .123 \text{ PIQ67} \tag{9.12}$$
$$(3.10)(1.31)(1.13)$$

R-Squared = .16
N = 104

$$\text{GCF} = 16.01 + .015 (Y/N) - .00000361 (Y/N)^2 - .188 \text{ PIQ67}$$
$$(3.31)(5.12)(4.42)(1.10)$$

$$.918 \, \varphi_1 \tag{9.13}$$
$$(1.28)$$

R-Squared = .51
N = 104

$$\text{PIQ67} = -1.80 - .845 \ln(Y/N) + .085 \text{ N} - .019 \, \mu_1 \cdot \text{CRCN}$$
$$(2.01)(2.57)(1.63)(1.82)$$

$$+ .000327 \, \mu_1 \cdot \text{CRCN}^2 + .00153 \, \mu_2 \cdot \text{CRCN} - .000074 \, \mu_2 \cdot \text{CRCN}^2$$
$$(2.64)(1.84)(0.92)$$

$$- .0335 \, \omega + .036 \text{ ELF} - .0334 \text{ EDCN}$$
$$(1.90)(3.0)(1.66)$$

$$+ 1.69 \, \varphi_1 \tag{9.14}$$
$$(2.13)$$

R-Squared = .31
N = 104

Redistribution in favor of the middle class

$$\frac{\Delta(Y/N)}{Y/N} = .094 \text{ GCF} - .436 \text{ N} - .259 \text{ PIQ67} \tag{9.15}$$
$$(3.08)(1.04)(0.28)$$

R-Squared = .16
N = 104

$$GCF = 23.24 + .016\,(Y/N) - .00000369\,(Y/N)^2 - 1.915\,PIQ67$$
$$(4.25) \quad (5.27) \quad\quad (4.55) \quad\quad\quad (1.02)$$

$$-.143\,\varphi_2 \tag{9.16}$$
$$(1.21)$$

R-Squared = .52
N = 104

$$PIQ67 = -4.68 - .495\,\ln(Y/N) + .079\,N - .0158\,\mu_1{*}CRCN$$
$$(1.97) \quad (2.13) \quad\quad\quad (1.52) \quad (1.65)$$

$$+.000279\,\mu_1{\cdot}CRCN^2 + .0136\,\mu_2{\cdot}CRCN - .000051\mu_2{\cdot}CRCN^2$$
$$(2.52) \quad\quad\quad\quad (1.67) \quad\quad\quad (0.66)$$

$$- .0296\,\omega + .029\,ELF - .0192\,EDCN - 6.00\,\varphi_2 \tag{9.17}$$
$$(1.60) \quad\quad (2.66) \quad\quad (1.05) \quad\quad (2.07)$$

R-Squared = .40
N = 104

Redistribution in favor of the poor class:

$$\frac{\Delta(Y/N)}{Y/N} = .147\,GCF - .603\,N - .659\,PIQ67 \tag{9.18}$$
$$(4.90) \quad\quad (1.59) \quad (0.87)$$

R-Squared = .16
N = 104

$$GCF = 16.78 + .017\,(Y/N) - .000004\,(Y/N)^2 - .490\,PIQ67$$
$$(8.08) \quad (7.22) \quad\quad (5.62) \quad\quad\quad (0.4)$$

$$-13.45\,\varphi_3 \tag{9.19}$$
$$(1.11)$$

R-Squared = .52
N = 104

$$PIQ67 = \underset{(1.66)}{.987} - \underset{(1.36)}{.116} \ln(Y/N) + \underset{(1.43)}{.076} N \underset{(1.26)}{-.010} \mu_1 \cdot CRCN$$

$$+ \underset{(2.05)}{.000158} \mu_1 \cdot CRCN^2 + \underset{(0.77)}{.00585} \mu_2 \cdot CRCN - \underset{(0.67)}{.000044} \mu_2 * CRCN^2$$

$$\underset{(2.45)}{-.0403} \omega + \underset{(1.87)}{.0995} ELF - \underset{(0.58)}{.002} EDCN + \underset{(0.35)}{0.42} \varphi_3 \qquad (9.20)$$

R-Squared = .60
N   = 104

By using these three sets of simultaneous equations and reestimating the equations, we simulated the result of a redistribution in favor of one group at the expense of the remaining two. For our simulation, we created a hypothetical country with similar sets of exogenous variables (e.g., the amount of government coercion, the level of ethnolinguistic factionalism, etc.), the values of which reflected the average for all the countries within the sample. We obtained from the sample the minimum, maximum, and mean values of income share for the three economic classes. Then, in order to estimate the effects of an increase in the income share of the three groups, we increased the income share by the annual rate of .01 percent for 20 years. Therefore, the question that our simulation game attempts to answer is, If we increase the income share of a particular group when its share is at the sample minimum, maximum, or average, what is the effect on the rate of growth of the economy? Since the effect of a redistribution is likely to be dependent on the level of economic development, we evaluated the results at per capita incomes of $40, $500, $100, $2,000, and $3,000. Within the context of the sample period, the choice of the per capita GNP covers almost the entire spectrum of national economic development.

The table shows the results of a redistribution of income in favor of the people classified as the bottom 40 percent of the population. As can be seen from the table, at the lowest level of per capita GNP (approximately the per capita GNP of the poorest nation in the sample, Upper Volta), a redistribution in favor of the poorest group of people actually causes a decline in the rate of growth of per capita income. This is because - as can be seen from the specification of the equation system - an additional amount of national resources given to the bottom 40 percent of the economic class at the expense of the other two creates a climate for further political conflict. At the same time, such a redistribution reduces the level of investment at the aggregate level. Hence, the situation of double jeopardy causes an economic reversal for the nations at the lowest level of development.

Table 9.1

Redistribution of Income in Favor of the Poor Class and Economic Growth

Per Capta GNP	Minimum (6.1%)	Mean (14.1%)	Maximum (23%)
	Rate of Growth of Per Capita GNP		
$40	-0.90%	-.0.28%	-0.54%
$500	1.34	1.13	0.85
$1000	2.35	2.13	1.84
$2000	2.70	2.54	2.32
$3000	1.81	1.71	1.56

The situation, however, changes when the nations get a minimum foothold in the path of development. At a higher level of economic prosperity the nations can attempt to improve the lots of the poor and still maintain a positive rate of economic growth. But as can be seen from the table, the rate of growth of income slows down as the income share of the poor is increased at higher levels of economic prosperity for these people. This situation translates into the classical case for a trade-off between efficiency (measured in terms of the rate of growth of per capita GNP) and ethics (measured in terms of a greater share of income for the poor). We have plotted the trade-off in Figure 9.4 (holding per capita income level at $40). It may be noted at this point that several economists, such as Brennan (1973), have argued that this trade off between ethics and efficiency should be evaluated within the prospect of an economic loss to the wealthy as a result of an increased prospect of revolution stemming from an overtly skewed distribution of wealth. We may mention that our above diagram traces the path of the "pure" trade-off, free of the potential costs of political upheaval.

Figure   9.4

**The Effect of Redistribution of Income In Favor of
the Poor Class**

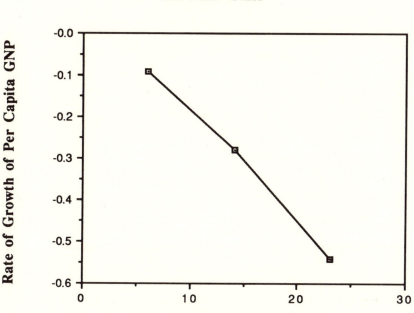

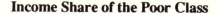

Income Share of the Poor Class

If a redistribution in favor of the poor class provides us with the classic downward-sloping trade-off line between ethics and efficiency, our findings with respect to a redistribution in favor of the wealthy run contrary to the traditionally held position. The traditional Keynesian economics argues that since the marginal propensity to save and invest is positively linked with the level of personal income, an increased share for the rich is going to produce the highest rate of economic growth. Although this position, the basic ingredient of the trickle down theory, is true when we consider only the economic variables to the exclusion of the social and political dimensions, the broadening of the horizon of the traditional economic model demonstrates the problems of such a position. Since an increase share for the wealthy can provoke the wrath of the poor, and especially the middle class, the resulting political instability can wipe out the advantages of the incremental amounts of savings and investment resulting from such a redistribution. Therefore, our simulation game found that an increased share of the pie for the wealthy does not produce an ever-increasing rate of economic growth (Table 9.2).

Table 9.2

Redistribution of Income In Favor of the Wealthy Class and Economic Growth

Per Capta GNP	Minimum (36%)	Mean (53%)	Maximum (71%)
	Rate of Growth of Per Capita GNP		
$40	1.98%	1.83%	1.50%
$500	2.98	2.83	2.49
$1000	3.51	3.36	3.02
$2000	3.44	3.32	3.05
$3000	2.57	2.48	2.28

Therefore, according to the table, a redistribution in favor of the top earners in the nation creates a situation of a loss of economic efficiency and basically depicts a similar pattern of relationship between income share and economic growth as similar to the poorest segment of the population. The result of a redistribution of income in favor of the wealthy group at the lowest level of economic development ($40 of per capita GNP) has been plotted in Figure 9.5.

Figure 9.5

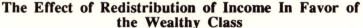

The Effect of Redistribution of Income In Favor of
the Wealthy Class

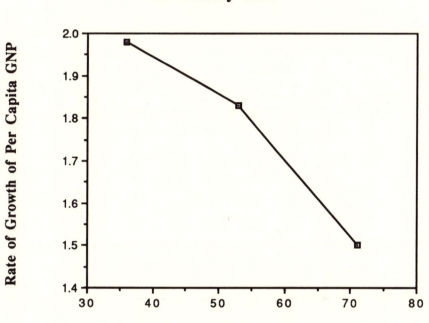

Income Share of the Wealthy Class

Finally, we can look at the impact of a redistribution in favor of
the middle class. Although the marginal propensity to invest of the
persons of the middle class is lower than that of the wealthy, and an
increased share of national income even causes a slight drop in the
aggregate level of gross capital formation [see equation (9.16) above],
this negative effect on the rate of growth of income is more than offset
by the tremendous decline in the propensity to produce political
violence.

Table 9.3

Redistribution of Income In Favor of the Middle Class and Economic Growth

Per Capta GNP	Minimum (20%)	Mean (33%)	Maximum (43%)
	Rate of Growth of Per Capita GNP		
$40	3.52%	3.84%	4.20%
$500	4.99	5.35	5.73
$1000	5.59	5.92	6.26
$2000	3.83	5.29	5.49
$3000	2.97	3.98	4.12

The effect of an increased level of political stability is felt throughout the economy, as a stable polity provides the economy with the necessary condition for expansion. Therefore, a redistribution of income to the middle class generates the highest level of economic growth. This empirical reaffirmation of the ancient Aristotelian position has been depicted in the Figure 9.6 where we have plotted the relationship between the rate of growth of per capita GNP and the income share of the middle class, evaluated again at $40 of per capita GNP.

The effect of an increased level of political stability is felt throughout the economy, as a stable polity provides the economy with the necessary condition for expansion. Therefore, a redistribution of income to the middle class generates the highest level of economic growth. This empirical reaffirmation of the ancient Aristotelian position has been depicted in the Figure 9.6 where we have plotted the relationship between the rate of growth of per capita GNP and the income share of the middle class, evaluated again at $40 of per capita GNP.

Figure   9.6

The Effect of Redistribution of Income In Favor of the Middle Class

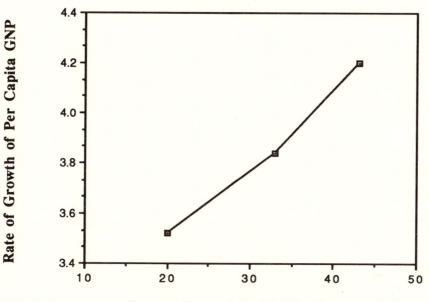

Income Share of the Middle Class

A POLITICAL ECONOMIC MODEL OF GROWTH

In the standard economic theories of growth the projected path of national income is the result of purely economic relationships. The inclusion of the causes and effects of political instability, in clear contrast, allows one to analyze the path of growth of national income in the broader context, where the growth of income is the outcome of the dialectical process between two forces, which can be called income increasing and income decreasing.   The standard economic relationships, such as savings, investments, export earnings, and foreign assistance, as well as investment in human capital (such as expenditure on health, education, and nutrition) will form the income-increasing force. The factors causing political instability, on the other hand, will be part of the income-retarding force.   The resulting developmental path is depicted in Figure 9.7.

Figure   9.7

A   Political   Economic   Model   of   Growth

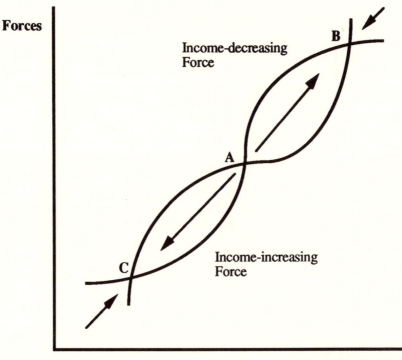

In the vertical axis of our diagram, we are measuring the relative strength of the two forces, whereas the horizontal axis measures the level of per capita income. As can be seen from the figure, the economy will grow if the income-generating force outweighs the income-retarding force. In contrast, if the income-increasing force falls short of the income-decreasing force, the level of the economy will experience a reversal, and as a result, the level of per capita income is going to come down, and the economy will drift downward to settle at a lower level of equilibrium. Thus, in our diagram, the point A is an unstable equilibrium. If moved to the right of point A, the positive force will carry the economy to a higher level of income and economic development to point B. At point B the nation will be at a stable equilibrium, which can also be a point of economic stagnation. At this point, strides have been made to achieve the higher level of income; however, to move further would be to invite political turmoil, as that may call for a truly radical change in the political and economic structure, which may upset the existing power system.

To the left of point A the negative forces overwhelm the positive ones, and the economy, through a process of prolonged political instability, will settle for a lower level of income and economic development at point C. One can think of several examples (e.g., Iran, Lebanon, Nicaragua) of political instability leading to a loss of a significant amount of national progress.[3] We would argue that the strength of the above exposition over the traditional model of economic growth lies in the fact that while a purely economic model fails to explain economic stagnation and reversals, our model will be able to explain change in the direction of economic growth resulting from the failure of the nation to reach political stability and thereby to provide the necessary condition for economic progress.

NOTES

1. Notice that the variables of income share are estimated.

2. It is interesting to note that in the Centennial Edition of the *Wall Street Journal* (July, 1989), developing countries were ranked for their development potential in the next millenium by a panel of experts. The first criteria for economic development for these experts was political stability (p. A8).

3. This diagram depicting a dialectical process has been widely used in economics. Professor Paul Streeten (1967) used it to show economic development. Although he pioneered in his effort to include many sociocultural variables in the income-decreasing force, he did not include factors of political violence in his expanded paradigm. Similar diagrams have been used widely, from analysis of business cycles (Kaldor, 1940) to the analysis of mutual causation between white prejudices and the consequent black standard of living (Swan, 1962).

10

Summary and Policy Implications

Injustice is tolerable only when it is necessary to avoid an even greater injustice.

John Rawls[1]

SUMMARY

The presence of political violence poses a serious threat to the pursuit of peace and prosperity of a nation. With technological progress this threat becomes serious as the potential for disruption of normal life by a dissident group becomes increasingly possible. From a hijacking of an airplane to a nuclear detonation in a crowded city, the list of possibilities looks ominous indeed. The successful management of violent political conflict requires a thorough understanding of their causes. Therefore, in this study we started with an effort to understand the motivations of the potential participants in the acts of political violence.

The Logic of Participatory Behavior

Standard economic theory assumes that an individual's actions are guided by his attempts to maximize his own utility. However, in contrast to this one-dimensional view of human behavior, we have posited the hypothesis that a person's perception of himself consists of his own self as an individual separate from everyone else as well as a member of the social group to which he belongs, either by birth or by choice. This hypothesis implies that an individual maximizes his utility, which is composed of both his individual and collective utility. His quest for the maximization of individual utility compels him to engage in economic activities, whereas his desire to maximize group utility prompts him to take part in actions designed to achieve collective goods. In the recent development of the theory of sociopsychology (Gurr, 1970), it has been argued that a person takes part in a rebellion out of his feeling of relative deprivation. However, in effect, in this study we attempt to refine this hypothesis to include frustration or "relative deprivation" with respect to an individual's collective goal. We posit that it is not *just* the frustration that one feels as an individual that prompts one to take part in acts of political dissidence. Personal frustration caused by an individual's inability to attain something he feels is rightfully his either will lead to actions within the limits of the law (such as a litigation) or will lead to some other acts of deviation, which can vary from criminal activity to various kinds of psychotic or sociopathic behavior.

However, if the frustration that one feels is linked to a group to which he belongs, the best course of action for him may be to take part in a political movement. The intensity of passion with which an individual is likely to pursue his group utility is going to be linked directly to one's perception of the closeness of association with the group and, of course, the intensity of frustration. We argue that the former is the product of one's ideology, and the latter, his environment. The term *ideology* has many different connotations; however, we define ideology as simply the preference for collective good. We hypothesize that behaviorally ideological preferences are influenced by, among others, cultural ethos, education, and the efficacy of opposition leadership. Given the state of an individual's group identity, the structural (or environmental) factors determine his choice of political participation. For example, the state of unemployment for an individual lowers the opportunity cost of participation in political activities. But the state of unemployment of an individual will not automatically lead to political participation unless the cause of his misery can be linked to his group membership through the ideological filtering provided by the opposition leadership. That is, if this unemployed individual (who may already be susceptible to dissident ideology because of his lowered opportunity cost) is convinced that his state of being is caused by either his ethnic origin or his economic class membership, he is more apt to take part in an act of political dissidence.

Therefore, we argue that the participation of an individual in acts of political violence will be the outcome of a dialectical interaction between the sets of push and pull factors shaped by the actions of the political authorities and the opposition leadership (with random shocks provided by the antecedent events). The ruling authorities attempt to lessen the feeling of collective frustration by attempting to promulgate political legitimacy or the feeling that the present political and economic structure is the one that is best suited for the achievement of individual as well as collective goals. This can be done either by providing better economic and political opportunities for the potential participants, by lowering the cost of minority group membership by the passage and enforcement of laws prohibiting discrimination, or by raising the cost of political activities by enforcing coercive measures. The dissident leadership, on the other hand, offers ideological justification and, given enough power, attempts to apply its own version of coercion.   The relative strengths of these two sets of carrots and sticks prompt actions by ordinary individuals, which, in the aggregate, determine the level of political stability of a nation.

Therefore, our behavioral model attempts to demonstrate the process of political participation by classifying the factors of individual motivation into two broad categories: factors of individual utility and factors of group or collective utility. The factor of individual utility is shaped by what an individual is able, or hopes to achieve within the status quo.   The factors of collective utility, on the other hand, constitute the promise of what one can hope to achieve as an individual as well as a member of a dissident group resulting from the successful conclusion of a political movement. We have called the first category of collective good *excludable* collective goods, and the second category, we have called *nonexcludable* or pure public goods. We further hypothesize that the excludable public goods are achieved largely through individual effort (by taking an active part in a political action) whereas nonexcludable public goods are distributed among the group members irrespective of their effort.

Hence, we may safely conclude that to understand the causes of political participation is to understand the psychology of group formation and the dynamics of their evolution.   Looking at the formation of group identity, we divided it into two categories: *ascriptive* and *adoptive*. An ascriptive group is based upon birth. Thus, divisions along the lines of ethnicity, language, or even religion can be classified as ascriptive groupings. The membership in these groups are involuntary and are virtually impossible to renounce.

In contrast, groups can also be formed according to tastes, preference, or economic achievement. Thus, one may want to join a radical environmental group such as Green Peace, or an animal-rights activist group. These groups can be called adoptive groups. We can even classify membership in economic class in the same category.

This hypothesis leads to some interesting conclusions regarding the participatory behavior in acts of political violence. The individual participatory decisions in actions against a political system are affected by the social, political, and economic environment, which reinforce the feeling of a group identity.   Thus, the effects of discrimination facilitates the growth of perception as a member of an aggrieved group and the proliferation of dissident ideology. The lack of political freedom in a strict authoritarian rule, for example, helps spread the notion of a division between those who are in and those who are out of the political system. This feeling of a schism helps to identify the ruling group as the source of most of these frustrations and hence the proliferation of ideology of collective identity.

Our analysis suggests that factors of economic deprivation, such as unemployment or poverty, by themselves may not cause political turmoil unless combined with some kind of a group identity.

In other words, being unemployed or being poor will only lower a person's opportunity cost of taking part in political activities. Widespread unemployment and poverty will create trouble for the regime if this state of being is associated with a group. Especially if the line of poverty cuts along the line of ethnic identity or some other line of ascriptive group identity, it will deepen the sense of frustration within the group. Thus, the concentration of poverty and unemployment, for example, has contributed to Catholic grievances in northern Ireland. In contrast, we find that even during the height of the Great Depression in the United States, the spread of radicalism and acts of violent political activities were relatively limited. This lack of political activism was the result of the pervasiveness of the individualistic ideology in the American psyche. Therefore, those who were affected by the Great Depression either blamed themselves for their misery, or the sense of their group identity was limited to job actions or union activities. We can also conjecture that for the vast majority of the United States population suffering from the devastation of the economic chaos, the actions of President Franklin D. Roosevelt were perceived to be closely related to their own as well as collective interests. This perception may have reduced the sense of alienation and did not reinforce the feeling of separation between the haves and the have-nots.[2] Along the same line of reasoning, we can explore the reasons behind the lack of violent black political actions during the late 1970s and 1980s. Even in the face of cuts in the programs that benefitted blacks and the other minorities the most during the years of the Reagan administration[3], the sense of black identity was diluted in the aftermath of the passage of civil rights legislation. A large portion of the black population took advantage of the new openness in the system and joined the ranks of the middle class and stopped associating with the larger "black cause." The healthy growth in the overall economy during this time period was also able to include in its burgeoning middle class its newest members from the black community without much overt conflict or controversy. Therefore, the significant improvement in race relations during the last 20 years since the days when the Kerner Commission report predicted a race civil war can be attributed to the social mobility offered by the American society, causing a lowering of group identity within the black community. The death of Martin Luther King Jr. and the failure of the rest of the civil rights leaders to assume the same leadership role, as well as a technologically superior surveillance by the Federal Bureau of Investigation (FBI), inflicted a severe blow to the black political movement. Finally, one may conjecture whether in the ghetto economies, where the blacks have experienced no real advancement in the quality of life, the appetite for participating in dissident political actions was not tempered by the lure of easy money due to the proliferation of the drug trade. By following the logic of our behavioral model, we can argue that the infusion of a large quantity of money has lowered people's appetite for political action, as their

254 The Economics of Political Violence

opportunity cost of time for political activities has risen. Therefore, by using our model, we can say that the lessening of group identity in the black community owing to the increased level of social mobility and the overall improvement in the economy, the lack of ideological leadership, the swift apprehension and severity of punishment for dissident activities, and alternate source of economic well-being, drug money, have all contributed to the falsification of the dire predictions of the Kerner Commission.

Political Instability and the Aggregate Economy

Having analyzed the factors of individual participation in collective actions in the second part of the book, we turned our attention to the effects of political instability on the economic growth of a nation. If from the standpoint of an individual the decision to participate causes a profound effect upon his personal life, the impact of their collective decisions on the welfare of the aggregate economy is no less telling. The presence of political instability affects the economic performance of a nation in two different ways. First, it introduces an additional dose of environmental uncertainty to a naturally jittery market. This additional uncertainty impacts the economic behavior of an individual, who, in his quest for certainty of pecuniary returns, turns toward those assets that he perceives to be free of political risks. Typically, these assets turn out to be the ones which are hoarded under the proverbial "mattress" outside of the economic income stream, or are sent outside the country to a safer haven. In any case, they represent a net loss to the income flow of a national economy.

Second, political instability interferes directly with the production process itself. For instance, as a result of political instability, mines and factories are often shut down because of strikes or sabotage. In the agricultural sector, farmers often fall victim to political turmoil as the two opposing sides vie for their willing or unwilling support. The guerrillas attempt to impose their political and economic system and either recruit the able-bodied peasants to their cause or attempt to impose heavy costs for noncompliance. The government, on their part, often imposes harsh penalties for cooperating with the rebel forces. As a part of a "pacification program" the authorities may even relocate those peasants who are in geographic proximity to the area of violent conflict. The ranks of the peasants cultivating the land also dwindle as the government starts to conscript them to fight off the insurrection. Further, prolonged political strife takes a tremendous toll on the stock of human capital as the intellectuals and the skilled laborers start leaving the country in search of a safer environment.

Therefore, political instability can indeed exact a heavy toll on the economic performance of a nation. In our simulation game, we have shown the devastating effects of prolonged political instability on economic development. We have demonstrated that even the presence of an average amount of political instability can set back a nation in its developmental path by decades. This result points to the predicaments of the politically unstable developing nations, many of which have earned the informal title of "undevelopable." Indeed, one may argue that the cause of their economic underdevelopment lies not in the lack of investible capital, as has been argued in traditional economics; to a large extent, their effort to catch up with the developed world is being frustrated by their inability to achieve political stability.

In fact, along the same line one may conjecture that the experiences of the three North American giants - the United States, Canada, and Mexico - demonstrate the role of political stability as a necessary condition for economic development. During the last 150 years, since the independence of Mexico, Mexico has consistently failed to keep pace with its neighbors in the north. One may wonder how much of this divergence can be explained by its lack of political stability and failure of the Mexican political elites to promote faith in the integrity of their political institutions.

At this time, we must point out, however, that our advocacy of political stability does not automatically extend toward the maintenance of the status quo regardless of the type of political regime and economic injustice. Our analysis simply points to the significant cost factor of prolonged political instability within a nation. To be sure, much of the political development of the Western world has been achieved through bloodshed and revolution. From the Magna Carta to the U.S. Constitution, most movements for political reform and independence have been the products of violent upheavals. Similarly, around the world, few social changes for equality and freedom have been introduced by the privileged class on their own accord without conflict. In fact, while many revolutions for economic equality have had dubious success, many of the successful revolutions for political reform have been able to achieve their stated goals. In such cases the conditions of economic reversal have been temporary, as the introduction of democracy, with the accompanying political and economic freedom, has been able to unlock the true potential of national economic development through the expansion of the market and a calmer, more stable political system providing the necessary condition for economic growth. The economic expansion of the postcolonial United States, Japan after the Meiji Restoration, and the Turkish experience after Ataturk's overthrow of the old order should dispel any notion of a long-term ill effect of a revolutionary movement in pursuit of political reform.

The simulation games based on the estimated simultaneous equation system yielded interesting results with regard to some of the institutional and economic factors affecting the growth of an economy. The first institutional factor that seems to have a strong effect on the economic development of a nation is the form of government. In a romantic Rousseauvistic world of conformity of "popular will," it is indeed conceivable that individual preference will be perfectly matched by group preferences, which will, in turn, follow the national preference. In such a case, we can expect a unified national character capable of producing economic miracles. However, the sustenance of this political stability, cohesion of purpose, and economic performance will depend on the continuation of meshing of preferences, and the lure of an unbroken economic prosperity. Let us explain.

The meshing of preferences means a convergence between individual preference and ideologically oriented group preference. In such a case an individual will be willing to forgo his own aspirations for the sake of the larger entity, the nation. This level of nationalistic fervor can be preserved by resorting to a strong sense of national identification, the cause of which is greatly helped by the existence of cultural heritage, the prospect of economic prosperity, or the perceived existence of an external threat. Thus, in the case of Japan, we see the forging of extremely strong nationalistic feeling brought about by a cohesion of purpose and political stability despite the lack of democratic values, as understood in the Western context (C. Johnson, 1988). The systematic rejection of individual self-interested behavior in favor of duty, loyalty, and goodwill, which Michio Morishima (1982) calls "the Japanese ethos," provides a vivid example of a fusion between individual and group preferences at a national level.

The cohesion of purpose and the extreme sense of national identity, however, is easily maintained as long as the threat of an external enemy and/or the prospect of continual economic prosperity resulting from political stability remains alive. But as is demonstrated in the case of South Korea, with the military and political threat from the north dwindling in the minds of a significant segment of the population, the demand for a change in their form of government is becoming increasingly intense. This feeling for the need for a change has been further reinforced by the relatively lackluster economic performance of the South Korean economy in the early 1980s, which caused many of the young students become doubtful of their future in the South Korean economy (C. Johnson, 1988).

However, such forging of individual and collective preference is more of an exception in the world scene. In fact, it is more of a rule to associate democracy with political legitimacy. Therefore, in our simulation games we find distinct evidence toward the hypothesis that in the long run democracy is much better suited for economic growth. In the social sciences a debate has been going on for a considerable period of time as to whether democracy is the natural outcome of economic prosperity. In fact, in Western social sciences there is a broad range of convergence of opinion that democracy, economic growth, and the development of middle class go hand in hand.[4] Our simulation games do not shed any direct light on the question of whether economic development brings about democracy. However, they do point to the fact that, in general, democracy and the growth of the middle class are closely linked with political stability and therefore, in turn, to economic development.

Although our empirical model provides no evidence, in light of
our previous discussion, however, the broad convergence of opinion
causally linking economic growth to democracy makes eminent sense.
We have seen from our empirical results that the growth of the middle
class (the income share of the middle 40 percent of the population) is
positively correlated with the growth of per capita income. Therefore,
it seems logical to argue that since a burgeoning middle class requires
an increased level of social mobility, in a highly stratified society
economic progress will sow the seeds of demand for political reform.
At the same time, our model would suggest that this demand for
political reform will not come automatically.   As long as the
nondemocratic regime is able to provide a national consensus based on
ideology and/or continuing economic progress, the nation will remain
politically stable.

WHAT IS *NOT* TO BE DONE: SOME POLICY IMPLICATIONS

In the previous section we made it clear that we do not pass any
value judgment regarding the morality of acts of political dissidence per
se or the government's attempts to coerce the opposition into
submission. In this spirit, we would like to discuss issues of public
policy. Our discussion will be based on the assessment of the costs
and benefits for the nation as a whole as well as for the parties engaged
in political strife. The implication of our analysis is that besides the
sense of justice and fairness on the part of the powerful, if peace,
harmony, and cooperation prevail over conflict, they can be brought
about by appealing to the self-interest of those who are presently
holding the positions of privilege within the society. Brennan (1973),
for example, has argued that when individual endowments and claims
differ greatly, redistribution policies may emerge from the self-interest
of the participants from the fear of those who hold large assets. They
may agree to allow fiscal redistribution, within limits, because they
may thus protect their own asset holdings against violence, revolution,
and political uncertainty.

In other words, our study points to the fact that resolution of
conflict may be achieved not because of any sudden change of heart or
an overflowing of a feeling of "brotherhood among men" but because
of the desires of the contestants to maximize their own long-term self-
interests. In this spirit, we may propose a few political strategies for
the analysis of political conflicts and their ultimate resolution.

As a political activist, Lenin could boast of knowing what had
to be done to bring about a communist revolution. As social scientists,
our motivation is different. Therefore, we may point out some of the
pitfalls of political strategy under the heading: what is *not* to be done.
With the aid of our analysis, we may point out that one must not:

1. Assume universality of motives of participation and intensity of passion
2. Ignore factors of group identity
3. Underestimate the costs of action

The Assumption of Universality of Motives and Intensity of Passion

The success of political rhetoric in inciting people to take part in an act of collective violence often depends on the simplicity of the message. The most sweeping generalization in identifying the enemy results in the elimination of distinction among competing motivations of the individuals of the opposition. Our model points to the fact that during the course of a political movement the participants vary in almost every aspect of their behavioral profile. This variation gets reflected in their level of participation as well as their choice of acts of rebellion. However, strategists on the sides of both the rebel and the established political elite tend to make this erroneous assumption, often with catastrophic consequences. For instance, we see that several Marxist strategists[5] have operated under the mistaken assumption that there already exists a strong revolutionary fervor among the oppressed; as soon as these hapless, frustrated individuals are shown the revolutionary way, - usually by staging an attack against a well-recognized symbol of oppression - this will prove to be the "spark that ignites the prairie fire." However, in reality, even the most "oppressed" have variations of motivations and opportunities. The sudden killing of a landlord or an isolated incidence of an armed insurrection against the established political system may not turn out to be of much incendiary capability. This is because the link between the demonstration of the success of a revolutionary act and a wide scale popular participation in an uprising is not a matter of automatic mutatis mutandis and, in fact, is part of a vastly complicated process. For example, a demonstrated act of revolt, such as killing a hated village money lender or landlord, or staging a guertilla attack on a government position, may not ignite class hatred as an automatic response, as each potential participant will evaluate his benefits and costs filtered through the myriad vignettes of ideology, fear, and other personal factors of motivation.

The assumption of the existence of such ready-made revolutionary zeal has almost always been proved fatal to the provocateur. In contrast to the Latin American communist strategists, who tend to believe that a quick military action is the medicine to awake people's "natural instinct for class hatred," Mao, in his essay "On Correcting Mistaken Ideas in the Party," (1972a) pointed out :

Some comrades suffer from the malady of revolutionary impetuosity; they will not take pains to do minute and detailed work among the masses, but, riddled with illusions, want to do big things (p.55).

To Mao, (and to Lenin) a successful revolution would require the politicization of the masses before any military action is undertaken. The primary task of this politicization is of course to inject a strong ideological preference within the masses and conclusively demonstrate the impotence of the established regime to provide them with conditions for achieving what they think they ought to achieve.

Such an assumption of universality of revolutionary profile is certainly not confined to the overtly romantic communist revolutionary strategists; it has also guided some U.S. foreign policies with disastrous consequences. A primary example of such an assumption can be found in the planning of the Bay of Pigs invasion. The CIA-inspired coup attempt in Cuba was based on the assumption that the people of Cuba were ready for a counterrevolution and were waiting for the single signal from the United States that liberation was on the way. Similar erroneous assessments of revolutionary motivations have plagued the U.S. involvement in Vietnam, and are presently playing an important role in the formulation of policy against Nicaragua's Sandanista regime.

Factors of Group Identity

In our formulation of a behavioral hypothesis on the motivation to join the forces of opposition, we noted the importance of ideology, which we defined as the preference for collective goods for the group in which the potential participant belongs. From this premise, we can deduce that the intensity of ideological fervor is likely to deepen with the recognition of one's group identity.

The understanding of this group membership is important in the management of conflict. Thus, conflict based on ascriptive group membership is likely to be protractive in nature. In contrast, since adoptive group membership, by definition, cannot be bequeathed automatically, conflicts based on adoptive differences can have a finite life span.

Therefore, government's policy must be directed toward the reduction of factors that reinforce divisive group identities and toward building national rather than sectoral identities. Where factional group identities are based on obvious racial, linguistic, or ethnic characteristics, the reduction of group identity becomes more problematic. In such cases policies promoting equal opportunity and other civil rights and the outlawing of discriminatory practices offer the only way out. When group identities are not based on obvious characteristics, the minority groups sense of isolation may be reduced by prohibition of questions with regard to religion or parental lineage for application for employment or admission into schools or social clubs. In other words the breaking down of divisive group identities requires the guarantee of social justice. We will have occasion to say a few words about social justice shortly.

Underestimate the Costs of Confrontation: To Crush or to Kiss the Enemy Is the Question

Niccolo Machiavelli had advised his young ward either to crush or to kiss the enemy but never to choose the middle ground of hesitation and halfhearted measures. Some 500 years since his writing, policymakers still face the same age-old dilemma. It is of course not possible to provide a specific answer to the question of the relative efficacy of the two options, even though the basic wisdom of the advice is beyond question. In this brief sketch, we may chalk out conditions under which one or the other would be advisable.

However, before attempting to deal with the issue at hand, it is useful to recognize the reason why most political authorities facing the choice between the two will tend to choose the option to crush. Plainly the logic for this choice lies in the fact that the option to coerce seems more cost-effective than cooption. Coercion appears to be more cost-effective for several reasons. First, the option to coopt involves sharing - sharing of power, privilege, and wealth - which up until now has been the sole domain of the dominant group. Therefore, the prospect of sharing is likely to be viewed dimly in many corners of the political elite group and may promote right-wing extremism. For example, the acceptance of universal suffrage based on one man one vote can mean a tremendous loss to the minority group of white South Africans. Similarly, the concept of a hostile Palestinian state within earshot is viewed with extreme apprehension by many Israelis. Second, having already possessed a ready force of military and internal security, the results of coercion seem to be without a great deal of cost and to provide immediate results. Men and women in politics are typically short-term utility maximizers. The long-term solutions, unless pushed to a corner, are inevitably greeted with little enthusiasm. Finally, psychologically we all want a clear-cut military victory. The tremendous surge of popularity of Ronald Reagan after the successful invasion of Granada, Margaret Thatcher after the Falklands War, and Indira Gandhi after the 1972 war with Pakistan testifies to the politicians' need for a clear-cut military victory.

However, on the other side of the coin is the system's capability to maintain a high level of coercion. As we have noted, there is reason to believe that the relationship between coercion and participation in dissident activity, at least for the nondemocratic nations, resembles an inverted U; at the initial stage the use of force is seen primarily as an act of provocation prompting yet more acts of defiance. The level of hostile political participation, however, can be brought down only after a considerable amount of show of force. Before embarking on a course of coercion, the political authorities would do well to scrutinize their ability to sustain a high level of coercion for a considerable period of time, if needed. This is because the path to coercion is like riding a tiger; there is no comfortable way of dismounting without killing the animal first.

Therefore, before embarking on the course of coercion, the political leadership will be well advised to evaluate the limitations or constraints of their coercive capabilities. What constitutes the constraints of coercive capability? The constraints can be classified in four categories: organizational, technological, legal, and political. The organizational capability refers to the capacity of the governmental bureaucracy to deliver punishment by apprehending the perpetrators. If a government has limited organizational capability, it will simply fail to deliver the desired dose of punishment. For example, toward the end, in Czarist Russia the police department was besieged by inefficiency and lack of morale. In fact, when Lenin was caught by the Russian police, he had fully expected not to live and was extremely surprised when he was let go (Smelser, 1963). Similarly, Green (1986) has argued that the primary reason for the collapse of the Shah's regime can be traced to the organizational weakness of his state organizations to deliver coercion. Because of the pressure from the various human rights movements and the Carter administration in Washington, he had to restraint his level of repression. Also, Green speculates that toward the end of his reign the Shah was preoccupied with his desire to secure the Peacock Throne for his son. As a futile attempt to gain support from his subjects, the Shah decided to adopt a softer course, which of course backfired, paving the way for a full-fledged revolution led by Ayatollah Khomeini.

The constraint to apply coercion can also be of technological origin. Many developing nations are handicapped in their efforts to enforce strict surveillance and to monitor the movements of dissident groups. On the other hand, owing to the ever-increasing technological capability to keep people under surveillance, most of the radical dissident movements suffer military defeats in the relatively more technologically advanced parts of the world. Therefore, unless the movement is located in a technologically backward nation, the prospect of a classical communist-type mass uprising culminating in Long March seems remote indeed. As a result, in the more developed nations, political frustrations must find expression through the works of small revolutionary cells carrying out desperate acts of "propaganda by deed."

Also, besides the technology of instruments of communication and transportation, the security forces in developed nations have become experts in counter-revolutionary tactics, which can include the use of misinformation campaigns, agent provocateurs, and in some cases, even political executions (G. T. Marx, 1982). In the face of such expert assault, inexperienced political movements, unless backed by massive popular support, often do not even have the chance to pose a minimal threat to a national government.

At the same time, in contrast to many of the less developed, nondemocratic nations, the economically developed democratic nations, owing to their pluralistic political structures and well-established legal systems often find it difficult to dole out too much repression without severely compromising their constitutionally guaranteed fundamental rights. The presence of powerful tort laws and a well-defined constitutional guarantee of fundamental rights may force the authorities to walk a fine line and thereby severely diminish their capability to inflict punishment on the dissident groups. Indeed, as our empirical findings suggest, within a democratic system a true solution of peace and stability has to be a political, and not a military one.

The political constraint toward the use of force to suppress a dissent movement includes the weight of public opinion, both domestic and international. In today's world the power of the media is undeniable. This is especially true of television journalism, which inevitably draws the wrath of the authorities bent on preserving law and order at any cost. Therefore, it is no surprise that the relationship between the authorities and the reporters quickly takes on an adversarial character in an area of intense political strife. As a matter of fact, the first casualty of a conflict situation has historically been the freedom of the press.

Besides reaching the limits of power in attempting to coerce a political movement, a successful policy of deterrence based on the use of force alone can have another problem. If the authorities are successful in systematically eliminating the leaders of the opposition without addressing the causes of political unrest, they run the risk of creating chaos in the opposition movement. This chaos can lead to extreme factionalization of a political movement, which can leave the authorities with no effective leader in the opposition with whom to deal. Analogous to the slaying of Hydra, the destruction of the mainstream dissident leadership can promote truly violent cells with strong ideological attachment but little organizational or mobilization capabilities. This can surely lead to more daring acts of propaganda by deed, destruction of innocent lives and property, and protraction and gradual deepening of hostility.

The previous discussion must not imply that a policy of deterrence is always self-defeating. Rather, a true policy of deterrence must recognize the differences in the motives among the members of the dissident group. Therefore, a policy that physically (through restraints) as well as politically isolates the dissident activists, and through a selective reward and punishment system reinforces the legitimacy of the political elites, is likely to bring about a long-term peace. The lessons of history support no example of any dominant group being able to impose its will on its subject group forever. Therefore, it seems reasonable enough to assume that if in the old days it was difficult to enslave a group of people for a considerable period of time without their revolting, with the acceptance of certain human values and the ever-quickening pace of flow of information, it will be almost impossible to accomplish the same feat in the modern world. Hence, by combining Machiavelli's wisdom with our analysis, we can state that if the enemy can be clearly identified and can be isolated from the larger segment of the population (by demonstrating that the group's philosophy is considerably distant from the prevalent position of the larger dissident group in question), the authorities can indeed successfully "crush" him. If, on the other hand, the enemy has a wide political base, it is best to come to a compromise by promoting the moderates within the opposition.

The careful evaluation of the costs of action is also a must for the dissident groups. The basic reason why a political action is undertaken is to gain support for the movement. However, while some actions help crystallize public opinion in favor of a movement, some others, if perceived to be out of step with the feelings of the potential group of participants, can backfire and deal a severe blow to the success of a political movement. Thus, the decision to disobey the "salt law" by Gandhi, a symbolic action at best, was a clear turning point in the Indian political movement for independence. The civil rights marches staged by Martin Luther King and his followers are also examples of a successful strategy of political action. Similarly, the spontaneous Arab uprising in the Israeli West Bank area, the so-called *intefada* , at the time of this writing seems to be achieving its goal of gaining world attention to the Arab cause in the occupied territories. On the other hand, there are plenty of examples where a premature or otherwise out-of-step action has set back the cause of a dissident movement by swaying public opinion against the movement.[6]

THE COSTS OF POLITICAL INSTABILITY: A TRADE-OFF BETWEEN ETHICS AND EFFICIENCY?

In the study of public economics the existence of a trade-off between ethics and efficiency is taken for granted. Policy measures are debated by keeping this ubiquitous assumption as a self-evident truth. The arguments in favor of this trade-off assumption can be elaborated with the help of an illustrative example. Suppose the fabled island of Robinson Crusoe is inhabited by two persons: Crusoe himelf and Friday. The total wealth of the island is distributed between these two individuals. Now, suppose the economic affluence of the island is measured in terms of the amount of goods and services that Crusoe and Friday can obtain from the neighboring island by trading the surplus (amount above their personal consumption) fish that they can catch. Therefore, in such a situation the greater the surplus for trading, the higher the measure of economic well-being. The rate of increase in the measure of economic well-being is called efficiency. From this scenario, it seems obvious that the island's capacity to generate surplus for trade goes up as the distribution of fish becomes more skewed in favor of one person, as there exists a finite capacity for each individual to consume fish. On the other hand, an attempt to distribute fish equally between the two inhabitants is likely to lower the surplus for trade, as both of them together will consume a large part of the catch. Therefore, under the standard Keynesian assumption of a positive relationship between income, on one hand, and saving and investment, on the other, the trade-off between ethics (an equal distribution of wealth) and efficiency (rate of growth of income) becomes self-evident.

The argument in favor of this trade-off becomes even more convincing when the government bureaucracy as the redistributive agent is taken into account. In such a case, not only economic efficiency suffers as the aggregate savings and investment goes down, but also the need to support an unproductive bureaucracy turns out to be another source of leakage. Therefore, the logical outcome of this scenario is the policy prescription of a greater concentration of income to increase the aggregate level of efficiency. It is further argued that by so doing the poor may suffer in the short run, but in the long run, when the size of the pie increases, the absolute size of the share of the poor will increase, making them economically better off. This is the cornerstone of the trickle down theory, which implores the developing nations not to worry about economic inequality during the transitional period (Kuznets, 1955). The empirical results of Chapter 9 disputes the universality of the trade-off between ethics and efficiency. The outcomes of our simulation game point to the interesting conclusion that even though a redistribution in favor of the wealthy class has the immediate impact of an increased level of national investment (gross capital formation), the income-enhancing force emanating from the increased investment may be washed away by the income-decreasing effect resulting from an increased level of political violence caused by the maldistribution of income. Thus, in our example, Friday may not take the prospect of a redistribution of wealth to Crusoe for the sake of increase in the level of efficiency too kindly. If he decides to take violent political actions against Crusoe, the resulting disruption in the production process will surely reduce the absolute levels of share for both parties. Or, viewed from a different angle, if there existed an extremely unequal distribution of income such that Friday was weak and unmotivated from lack of nutrition, education, or economic opportunities, a redistribution of income from Crusoe to Friday may in fact, create a condition of a higher level of economic efficiency.

In order to ascertain this trade-off between ethics and efficiency we conducted simulation games on the basis of our estimated system of simultaneous equations. From the results we can see a far more complex relationship between the two than is espoused by the ubiquitous downward-sloping curve depicted in almost all the textbooks dealing with public sector economics and the theories of economic development. Our simulation results, while supporting a relative loss of efficiency as a result of a redistribution of income in favor of the poorest segments of the population, also point out a similar relationship with respect to an income transfer to the wealthy. In fact, the model is unequivocal in the efficiency of a redistribution in favor of the middle class of the society.

However, in this context, it is needless to say that while it is relatively simple to define efficiency, it is not possible to define exactly what is meant by ethics. Certainly the term ethics in the national policy context contains connotations of distributive justice. But a quick glance at the literature will surely discourage even the boldest in making any kind of a categorical statement. Yet the entire notion of the causes of participation in political violence to attain collective goods is so closely connected to the question of justice and fairness that it will be inappropriate to close the book without mentioning a few words about social justice.

In his seminal work *On Economic Inequality*, (1973) economist Amartya K. Sen has demonstrated the quagmire of the concept of distributive justice. Since distributive fairness cannot be separated from the question of "just desserts," we are unable to provide a generalized rule of distributive justice. Yet, the importance of the concept of justice in determining political stability of a nation is so obvious that philosopher David Hume (1902) pointed out that justice is the bond of society, and without it no association of human individuals could subsist.

While we may not come to any conclusion regarding the fairness of distributive justice, as political scientist Robert Lane (1986) points out, within the context of our discussion the understanding of procedural justice can prove to be fruitful. Procedural justice does not guarantee the end result of a distributive game but ensures the basic fairness of the process of distribution. To give an example, the participants in a winner-take-all lottery will not complain about the outcome as long as they are willing participants and are assured of the impartiality of the draw. In such a case, even an extreme distribution of income in the hands of one person will be considered "fair" as long as everybody in the group had an equal chance to win.[7]

Based on the work of Robert Lane (1986), we can point out four aspects of procedural justice: dignity, relief from procedural pain, uniformity of standard of justice, and the outcome of justice itself. The dignity aspect of procedural justice has three components: the recognition, protection, and preservation of self-esteem of every individual in the society; a sense of controlling one's own destiny; and an understanding of the justice process. If an individual is stripped of his dignity, even the most equal distribution of wealth will seem oppressive, arbitrary, and capricious. The second aspect of procedural justice is the relief from the procedural pain by which every individual is assured of a speedy disbursement of justice without a great deal of cost of justice procedure. If the process of seeking legal justice is cumbersome and time-consuming, justice cannot be preserved. The third aspect of procedural justice is the resonance between the standards of justice of the judge and the judged. If one is being judged by a standard that is completely alien to him, he cannot accept the verdict as just. The sense of justice, therefore, must include the convergence of value and the notion of ethical standard. The final aspect of procedural justice refers to the actual justice itself, or the provision of some minimum economic safety net. This aspect of procedural justice may come close to the Rawlsian (Rawls, 1971) concept of distributive justice, which maintains that the ethics of income distribution in a society should be judged by the well-being of its poorest members. Since it is hard to convince a starving individual of the fairness of the distributive process, the notion of procedural justice must include some minimum guarantee of economic well-being.

Despite the problems of defining ethics or social justice, our model makes a strong statement toward the expansion of the horizon for traditional neoclassical economics. Traditional economics has built an unbridgeable gap between positive and normative aspects of policy-making. The faith in the equilibrating capability of the market has permitted the economists to ignore matters of normative judgment with the assumption that these problems are but temporary in nature and that they would be taken care of by the inevitability of economic prosperity. However, as in many times in history, reality may force social science, in general, and economics, in particular, to pay attention to such thorny questions.

In fact, looking at the world today, contrary to the optimistic predictions of Kuznets (1965) and Zimmerman (1965), economic prosperity has not provided a trend toward a greater equalization of income. There is evidence that the relative economic condition of the poor in developing countries has deteriorated significantly over the last couple of decades (Jain, 1976; Paukert, 1973). Even in the United States some evidence is surfacing pointing toward the separation of the "great American middle class" into rich and poor. These disturbing tendencies, if they continue, may indicate an increasing level of economic and, consequently, political polarization.

In the area of employment we find a similarly bleak picture. Morawetz (1978) observes that during the deacades of the 1960s and 1970s, while the rate of growth of output increased significantly in many of the Third World countries, the rate of growth of employment was minimal. Coupled with a high rate of growth of population, this spells an explosion of unemployment, which continues to spill over into the developed countries in terms of legal and illegal immigration at an alarming rate. The rapid rate of growth of population in the Third World nations has also produced a disproportionate number of unemployed youths with little to show and even less to look forward to.

The spread of technological innovations in the areas of communication and transportation, has done a great deal to increase peoples' awareness of the rest of the world and, in the process, has heightened their expectations. Increasingly, questions are being raised by those who until now have been accepting of their situation about the ethics of economic inequality and the concentration of political power.

Consequently, in view of what appears to be an increasing trend toward political instability, it is imperative that a greater energy be devoted to the understanding and management of social conflict. It is especially important that we understand the parameters of a trade-off between ethics and efficiency in formulating national policies. Thus, a policy that concentrates income in the hands of a few wealthy investors may indeed generate an increased level of investment and hence help economic growth. However, if this act is perceived to be unethical by a significant portion of the populace, it might generate political instability, which, in turn, might stand in the way of attaining the desired growth path. History is full of examples of such imprudent decisions, where the pursuit of ephemeral efficiency has led to less-than-optimal decisions in the long run. Thus, in the case of Pakistan, it made eminent economic sense to divert a larger part of the economic resources to the western part of the country, which had certain locational advantages (Sen Gupta, 1972; Papanek, 1977). However, this ran contrary to the aspirations of the Pakistanis living in the eastern part of the country, and ultimately it contributed to the dismemberment of the nation.

Another example of using only an economic rationale was evident in India's Second 5-Year Plan. Following the logic that the sacrifice of present consumption and employment was beneficial for long-run economic growth, the Second 5-Year Plan emphasized investment in the capital-intensive sectors, ignoring the less productive but more labor-intensive sectors (Bhagwati and Chakravarty, 1969). More recent Indian plans have attempted to balance the need for employment in a labor surplus economy with the need for a high rate of growth.[8] However, even in the attempt at balancing this conflicting need, owing to the lack of a compelling theory, efforts such as these are conducted in an ad hoc fashion. We advance the proposition that if greater attention is directed toward understanding of the nature of the trade-off through study of the motivations for participation in political violence, it may provide us with a more fruitful avenue for analysis of public policy.

In this study, we have attempted to look for the motivations of participation in acts of political violence. We have also tried to demonstrate the cost of political instability. We believe that it is important that policymakers on all sides become more aware of the *true* costs of social injustice which go far beyond the headline-grabbing news reports of death, kidnapping, and macabre violence. The social costs include the destruction of the social fabric, the brutalization of the participants, and the imposition of severe economic costs to everyone in the nation. Needless to say, the total costs of all these factors are incalculable. Hence, it seems appropriate to end this book by remembering a famous quip from Mohandas Gandhi: "The policy of a tooth for a tooth and an eye for an eye leaves both the contenders toothless and blind."

NOTES

1. Rawls (1971, p. 4).

2. The misery of economic hardship led an increased level of suicide rate but not radical political activism.

3. National Economic Council in a recent report (1989) on the economic achievements of the black community in the United States provided a mixed evaluation. They concluded:

· The greatest economic gains for blacks occurred in the 1940s and 1960s. Since the early 1970s, the economic status of blacks relative to whites has, on average, stagnated or deteriorated.

· The political, educational, health, and cultural statuses of blacks showed important gains from the 1940s through the 1960s. In addition, some important indicators continued to improve after the early after the early 1970s.

· Among blacks, the experiences of various groups have differed, and status differences among those groups have increased. Some blacks have attained high-status occupations, income, education, and political positions, but a substantial minority remain in disadvantaged circumstances [p. 6].

4. Thus, Barrington Moore (1966) is emphatic in stating: " We may simply register strong agreement with the Marxist thesis that a vigorous and independent class of town dwellers has been an indispensable element in the growth of parliamentary democracy. No bourgeois, no democracy" (p. 418).

5. Examples are Che Guevara, Carlos Marighela, or Charu Mazumder, leader of the Naxalite movement in West Bengal, India.

6. While the sniping attacks on British soldiers stationed in northern Ireland have given some measure of success to the IRA, the use of indiscriminate terror against the civilian population has often done the opposite for the rebel group. A prime example of this kind of failed campaign can be found in their bombing tactics before the World War II. In January 1939, the IRA started a bombing campaign against civilian targets. Until the mid-1940, bombs exploded in the the railroad stations, post offices, and movie theaters with the inevitable consequence of killing and injuring unsuspecting bystanders. In its worst incident, in August 1939, five people were killed in Broadgate in Coventry. Unfortunately for the IRA, the timing of their campaign

was just as ill chosen as their targets. Facing the Nazi menace, the British government, as well as the public was totally absorbed with Europe. The fear of an external foe squarely crystallized public opinion against the IRA and helped the government to launch one of its most successful police operations against the organization (Coogan, 1970: 150-73).

7. For a brilliant discussion of ethics and economics, see Sen (1987).

8. I am grateful to Professor Paul Streeten for making these points.

Appendix:
Index for Political Instability

[The Discriminant Scores]*

Year	United States	Canada	Haiti	Domini-can Rep.	Jamaica	Trinidad	Barbados	Mexico	Guate-mala	Hondu-ras
1948	.002	.005	1.054	.938	.931	.925	.924	.131	0.0	1.054
1949	.044	0.0	.941	.925	.925	.924	.924	0.0	.266	.924
1950	.063	.012	2.335	.924	.953	.924	.924	.070	.064	1.188
1951	.080	.002	.924	.924	.930	.924	.924	.037	.044	.924
1952	.022	.010	.924	.924	.953	.924	.924	.278	.021	.924
1953	.027	.011	.924	.924	.925	.924	.924	.016	.298	.924
1954	.093	0.0	.924	.924	.929	.925	.924	.075	3.888	2.335
1955	.009	0.0	.924	.924	.924	.953	.924	.006	1.218	.925
1956	.088	.007	2.337	.924	.924	.958	.924	.054	.948	2.605
1957	.158	0.0	4.508	.924	.925	.925	.924	.049	2.457	1.194
1958	.156	.011	1.599	.924	.925	.924	.924	.296	.933	.933
1959	.107	.006	1.212	.938	.926	.924	.924	.749	.952	1.478
1960	.307	.015	1.467	1.200	.927	.925	.924	.079	1.231	.926
1961	.389	0.0	.962	1.368	.938	.924	.924	.394	.932	.924
1962	.188	.058	.924	3.852	.948	.924	.924	.306	1.151	.926
1963	.499	.031	1.231	2.379	.002	.001	.924	.018	2.323	2.315
1964	.554	.043	3.154	.982	0.0	0.0	.924	.010	.929	.924
1965	.583	.022	.924	3.157	0.0	0.0	.924	.022	1.197	.927
1966	.800	.026	1.503	1.379	.008	0.0	.924	.015	1.048	.924
1967	1.154	.003	1.133	.941	.006	0.0	0.0	.041	1.340	.924
1968	.528	.012	.928	.929	.005	0.0	0.0	.172	1.060	.924
1969	.366	.031	.927	.935	.001	0.0	0.0	.019	1.190	.944
1970	1.066	.153	.925	1.079	0.0	.275	0.0	.007	2.243	.924
1971	.368	.014	.924	1.057	0.0	.009	0.0	.017	1.195	.924
1972	.327	.142	.924	.925	0.0	0.0	0.0	.011	1.576	2.311
1973	.233	.001	.926	.926	0.0	0.0	0.0	.012	1.061	.924
1974	.141	0.0	.924	1.187	0.0	0.0	0.0	.170	1.081	.924
1975	.112	.007	.924	.925	0.0	0.0	0.0	.282	.926	2.320
1976	.059	.032	.925	.924	.029	0.0	0.0	.023	.927	.925
1977	.080	.001	.924	.929	.135	0.0	0.0	.061	1.056	.924
1978	.260	.001	.924	.930	.001	0.0	0.0	.016	1.214	2.312
1979	.467	.013	.928	.924	.035	0.0	0.0	.001	1.447	.925
1980	.652	.003	.926	.933	.050	0.0	0.0	.003	1.090	.926
1981	.420	.004	.926	.934	.001	0.0	0.0	.001	.964	.931
1982	.289	.012	1.190	.935	0.0	0.0	0.0	.001	2.372	.936

* The Scores were calculated by using Equation (7.2).
   A Country is considered democratic if had a democratic form of government during the last 5 years.

Political Instability Quotient

Year	El Sal-vador	Nicara-gua	Costa Rica	Panama	Colom-bia	Vene-zuela	Ecuador	Peru	Bolivia	Brazil
1948	2.316	.926	.993	1.216	.425	2.335	.002	2.620	.001	.003
1949	1.188	.925	1.191	2.642	.198	.937	.264	2.312	.081	0.0
1950	.924	1.193	1.193	.924	.019	1.326	.265	.944	1.366	.012
1951	.924	.924	.932	2.387	.352	1.457	.002	1.189	2.897	.063
1952	.925	.924	.925	.939	.965	2.716	.552	.924	2.341	.071
1953	.924	.924	.924	.930	2.361	.952	.034	.924	1.483	.038
1954	.924	1.320	.003	..933	.991	.925	.266	1.188	.924	1.463
1955	.924	.924	.284	1.318	.947	1.054	.023	.948	.925	1.388
1956	0.0	1.054	0.0	.964	.970	.998	.572	1.220	1.103	.148
1957	0.0	.924	0.0	.924	2.849	.940	.009	.933	.954	.131
1958	.001	.949	.001	1.042	1.658	4.071	.014	.967	1.221	.067
1959	0.0	4.381	0.0	.996	3.310	.970	.098	.951	.986	.113
1960	2.844	1.456	.002	.927	.935	2.343	.008	.924	.987	.062
1961	2.312	.926	0.0	.925	1.280	1.573	2.283	.941	1.092	.043
1962	.926	.929	0.0	.922	.947	1.581	.309	2.379	.939	.798
1963	.924	.954	0.0	.924	1.026	1.252	2.314	2.322	.933	.942
1964	.924	1.189	0.0	1.189	.951	1.151	.929	.951	2.650	2.391
1965	.924	.924	0.0	.953	1.008	.996	1.242	.976	1.559	.945
1966	.924	.924	0.0	.965	.961	1.210	2.393	.930	.924	1.180
1967	.925	.943	0.0	.925	.934	1.068	.937	.972	.954	.934
1968	.924	.924	0.0	3.878	1.388	.932	.929	2.334	1.223	1.104
1969	.925	.925	.005	1.188	.011	.938	.933	.933	2.443	1.200
1970	.924	.928	.005	1.054	.008	.925	2.318	.934	2.609	.967
1971	.924	.924	.001	.924	.028	.932	1.189	.934	2.718	.929
1972	1.189	.925	0.0	.924	.145	1.327	2.311	.933	.942	.929
1973	.924	.924	0.0	.924	.010	.945	.925	.974	1.192	.927
1974	.925	.925	0.0	.924	.005	.924	.924	.959	1.498	.999
1975	.930	.925	.003	.931	.166	.926	1.203	2.340	.950	.946
1976	.924	.926	.029	.933	.317	.928	2.359	1.263	1.017	.926
1977	1.199	.929	0.0	.935	.179	.925	.956	1.014	1.188	.968
1978	.924	1.881	0.0	.931	.045	.924	1.057	1.003	4.535	.933
1979	1.061	2.704	.022	.954	.002	.924	.924	.942	2.629	.933
1980	1.382	.936	.009	.930	.327	.926	.934	.955	2.624	.924
1981	1.042	.937	.015	.925	.009	.924	.924	.939	2.598	.937
1982	2.826	.942	.003.29	.924	.016	.925	.933	1.073	1.198	.924

Political Instability Quotient

Year	Para-guay	Chile	Argen-tina	Uruguay	United King-dom	Ireland	Nether-lands	Belgium	Luxem-bourg	France
1948	4.018	.265	.018	.929	0.0	.025	.013	.046	.001	.289
1949	5.085	.080	.002	.924	.020	.001	0.0	.020	0.0	.026
1950	1.188	.074	.007	.925	.088	0.0	.001	.484	0.0	.227
1951	.924	.061	.340	.934	.047	.010	0.0	.007	0.0	.082
1952	.924	.069	.080	.924	.007	.005	0.0	.016	0.0	.055
1953	.924	0.0	.035	.924	0.0	.001	.001	.001	0.0	.047
1954	2.313	.019	.027	.924	.001	.001	0.0	0.0	0.0	.008
1955	1.459	.024	4.582	.924	.002	.0012	0.0	.050	0.0	.137
1956	.948	.009	1.455	.924	0.0	.003	.006	.005	0.0	.263
1957	.924	.084	1.029	.925	.006	.010	0.0	.001	0.0	.024
1958	1.206	.037	1.247	.924	.081	.009	0.0	.001	0.0	1.510
1959	1.492	0.0	1.368	.929	.055	.003	0.0	.005	0.0	.050
1960	.924	.036	2.008	1.064	.050	.001	0.0	.111	0.0	.135
1961	.925	.042	1.258	.939	.032	.007	0.0	.097	0.0	.409
1962	.924	.009	4.117	.934	.112	0.0	0.0	.015	0.0	.354
1963	.934	0.0	1.211	.924	.019	0.0	0.0	.022	0.0	.023
1964	.924	.001	.978	1.238	.013	0.0	0.0	0.0	0.0	.021
1965	.924	.042	1.148	.946	.021	.007	.001	.006	0.0	.003
1966	.924	.064	2.511	.925	.022	.013	.013	.024	0.0	0.0
1967	.924	.025	.933	.952	.035	.008	.006	.002	0.0	.038
1968	.928	.032	.992	.998	.132	.001	.002	.028	0.0	.185
1969	.924	.301	1.368	1.072	.259	.004	0.0	.001	0.0	.069
1970	.925	.436	2.564	1.069	.325	.005	.001	.001	0.0	.088
1971	.924	.179	2.610	.928	.669	.001	.002	.001	.001	.061
1972	.924	.259	1.262	1.587	1.777	.095	0.0	.003	0.0	.094
1973	.925	4.522	2.280	5.163	5.909	.144	.001	.001	0.0	.179
1974	.924	.975	2.548	.925	1.742	.158	.015	.002	0.0	.336
1975	.924	.944	3.813	.929	.829	.013	.005	.004	0.0	.254
1976	.926	.924	4.442	2.312	.667	.153	0.0	.001	0.0	.414
1977	.924	.925	1.219	.927	.402	.010	.022	0.0	0.0	.095
1978	.925	.949	1.191	.924	1.039	.001	.005	.002	0.0	.023
1979	.924	.937	.936	.924	1.148	.269	.134	.018	0.0	1.196
1980	1.184	1.205	.925	.925	1.095	.003	.028	.010	0.0	.585
1981	.924	.937	.995	.924	2.144	.009	.002	.032	0.0	.192
1982	.924	.930	1.089	.924	2.606	.002	.004	.015	.009	.270

Political Instability Quotient

Year	Switzer-land	Spain	Portugal	W.Germ-any	Austria	Italy	Malta	Yugo-slavia	Greece	Cyprus
1948	.006	.942	.925	.109	.004	.476	0.0	1.100	3.753	.926
1949	0.0	.966	.924	.010	.011	.493	.024	.925	1.292	.924
1950	0.0	1.055	.924	.098	.122	.387	0.0	.933	.008	.934
1951	0.0	1.044	.924	.096	.013	.117	0.0	.931	.053	.925
1952	0.0	.970	.929	.116	.045	.114	.009	.926	.022	.924
1953	0.0	.924	.924	.317	.001	.209	0.0	1.009	.002	.928
1954	0.0	.960	.924	.090	.007	.191	.006	.925	.126	.957
1955	.001	.925	.924	.028	0.0	.026	.005	.924	.007	1.296
1956	0.0	1.004	.924	.005	0.0	.055	0	.924	.002	1.395
1957	.002	1.145	.924	0.0	.001	.014	.005	.924	.009	1.178
1958	.001	.949	1.018	.008	0.0	.035	.075	.009	0.0	1.263
1959	.013	.941	.924	.006	.073	.088	.022	.002	0.0	1.001
1960	0.0	.942	.924	.010	.013	.212	.005	0.0	.005	.955
1961	.005	.925	.927	.029	.013	.098	.029	.013	.004	.933
1962	0.0	.999	1.322	.062	.013	.164	.024	.003	.010	1.202
1963	0.0	.942	.929	.009	.001	.086	0.0	0.0	.012	.972
1964	.006	.943	.930	.006	0.0	.041	.029	0.0	.006	2.648
1965	0.0	.964	1.063	.041	.006	.014	0.0	0.0	.126	.944
1966	0.0	.982	.924	.011	0.0	.046	0.0	.011	.016	.961
1967	.001	1.169	.928	.060	0.0	.024	0.0	.140	2.600	.946
1968	.002	.996	.953	.135	0.0	.104	0.0	.024	.933	.939
1969	.001	.947	.975	.088	.002	.217	.001	.001	.956	.930
1970	.003	.988	.937	.048	0.0	.189	.009	.001	.927	1.061
1971	0.0	.929	.936	.140	0.0	.313	0.0	.025	.936	.930
1972	.008	1.044	.927	.010	.001	.137	0.0	1.158	1.046	.940
1973	.006	1.119	.939	.016	.002	.058	0.0	.001	4.227	1.523
1974	.003	1.143	2.826	.160	0.0	.141	0.0	0.0	.999	2.663
1975	.010	1.933	2.393	.012	.132	.199	0.0	.004	1.130	.960
1976	.003	1.762	1.063	.150	.001	.449	0.0	.001	.977	.943
1977	.001	1.652	.960	.143	.001	.482	0.0	.001	.956	.925
1978	.001	1.438	.956	.028	0.0	.892	0.0	0.0	.981	1.058
1979	.001	1.908	.926	.025	0.0	1.888	.002	0.0	1.057	.924
1980	.014	1.271	.948	.033	.001	2.550	0.0	.001	.400	.924
1981	.007	1.419	.924	.384	.003	.157	.005	.018	.037	.925
1982	.008	1.127	.938	.041	.002	.168	0.0	.006	.018	.924

Political Instability Quotient

Year	Finland	Sweden	Norway	Den-mark	Iceland	Gambia	Mali	Senegal	Mauri-tania	Niger
1948	.110	0.0	0.0	0.0	0.0	.924	.924	.924	.924	.924
1949	.168	0.0	.004	.001	.001	.924	.924	.924	.924	.924
1950	.001	.024	0.0	.010	0.0	.924	.924	.924	.924	.924
1951	.017	0.0	.002	.002	0.0	.924	.924	.924	.924	.924
1952	0.0	.001	0.0	.009	0.0	.924	.924	.924	.924	.924
1953	0.0	0.0	0.0	.030	0.0	.924	.924	.924	.924	.924
1954	0.0	0.0	0.0	0.0	0.0	.924	.924	.924	.924	.924
1955	0.0	0.0	.001	0.0	0.0	.924	.924	.924	.924	.924
1956	0.0	0.0	0.0	.001	0.0	.924	.924	.924	.924	.924
1957	0.0	0.0	0.0	0.0	0.0	.924	.924	.924	.924	.924
1958	.001	0.0	0.0	.001	0.0	.924	.924	.929	.924	.924
1959	0.0	0.0	0.0	0.0	0.0	.924	1.229	.978	.924	.924
1960	.001	0.0	0.0	.003	0.0	.924	.924	.924	.924	.924
1961	0.0	0.0	.001	.002	.001	.924	.924	.930	.924	.924
1962	.002	0.0	0.0	.005	0.0	.924	.937	1.458	.935	.924
1963	0.0	0.0	0.0	0.0	.001	.924	.925	1.247	.924	1.185
1964	0.0	0.0	0.0	0.0	0.0	.924	.925	.924	.924	1.219
1965	0.0	.024	0.0	0.0	0.0	.924	.924	.924	.924	1.054
1966	0.0	.009	.008	.001	0.0	.933	.924	.968	.934	.924
1967	0.0	.001	.002	0.0	0.0	.924	.925	1.187	.942	.924
1968	0.0	.006	0.0	.005	.009	.924	2.311	.998	.924	.924
1969	0.0	0.0	0.0	.001	0.0	.924	2.311	.952	.924	.924
1970	0.0	.006	.009	.001	0.0	.924	.924	.924	.924	.924
1971	0.0	.140	0.0	0.0	0.0	.924	.924	.924	.924	.924
1972	.001	.003	0.0	0.0	.001	.924	.924	.924	.933	.925
1973	0.0	.001	.001	0.0	.001	.924	.924	.958	.924	.933
1974	0.0	.002	.005	.020	0.0	.924	.924	.924	.924	2.313
1975	.001	.002	.001	0.0	0.0	.924	.924	.924	.924	.924
1976	0.0	.001	0.0	.009	0.0	.924	.924	.924	.925	1.211
1977	0.0	.006	.001	.001	.009	.924	.941	.924	.926	.924
1978	0.0	0.0	0.0	0.0	0.0	.924	.924	.925	2.312	.924
1979	0.0	0.0	.001	0.0	.001	.924	.924	.924	.925	.924
1980	0.0	.009	0.0	.001	0.0	.924	.946	.933	2.311	.925
1981	0.0	.001	.002	.001	0.0	1.190	.924	.924	1.188	.924
1982	0.0	.001	0.0	.001	0.0	.924	.924	.924	.924	.924

Political Instability Quotient

Year	Ivory Coast	Upper Volta	Liberia	Sierra Leone	Ghana	Togo	Cameroon	Nigeria	Gabon	Central Africa
1948	.924 ·	.924	.924	.924	.989	.924	.924	.924	.924	.924
1949	.924	.924	.924	.924	.924	.924	.924	1.016	.924	.924
1950	.924	.924	.924	.924	.983	.924	.924	.924	.924	.924
1951	.924	.924	.924	.924	.925	.928	.924	.924	.924	.924
1952	.924	.924	.924	.924	.925	.924	.924	.929	.924	.924
1953	.924	.924	.924	.924	.948	.924	.924	.987	.924	.924
1954	.924	.924	.924	.925	.925	.924	.924	.929	.924	.924
1955	.924	.924	.924	.924	.924	.924	1.028	.924	.924	.924
1956	.924	.929	.924	.924	.930	.924	.924	.924	.924	.924
1957	.924	.924	.924	.924	.934	.924	.950	.924	.924	.924
1958	.924	.924	.924	.924	.930	.930	.974	.949	.924	.924
1959	.924	.948	.924	.924	.948	.924	.990	.948	.924	.924
1960	.924	.929	.924	.928	.925	1.054	.941	.971	.924	.924
1961	.924	.924	.937	.924	.951	.924	.935	.940	.924	.924
1962	.924	.924	.924	.924	.936	.924	.924	.934	.948	.924
1963	.924	.924	.925	.924	.924	2.466	.924	.930	.924	.924
1964	.924	.924	.924	.924	.924	.924	.927	1.225	4.011	.924
1965	.924	.924	.924	.924	.925	.924	.924	1.117	.924	.924
1966	.933	.929	.924	.924	2.340	1.190	.924	3.676	.924	2.311
1967	.924	.924	.924	2.604	1.205	2.441	.924	1.144	.924	.924
1968	.924	.924	.924	2.317	.937	.924	.925	5.219	.924	.924
1969	.937	.924	.924	.924	.942	2.311	.924	5.066	.924	.924
1970	.925	.937	.924	.929	.933	.924	.925	1.188	.924	.924
1971	.933	1.122	.924	1.465	.933	.924	.931	.969	.924	.924
1972	.924	.924	.924	.924	2.575	.924	.924	.937	.924	.947
1973	.924	1.185	.924	.924	.924	.924	.924	.938	.924	.924
1974	.924	.924	.933	.925	.929	.924	.937	.954	.924	.924
1975	.924	.924	.924	.950	.929	.924	.924	2.460	.924	.924
1976	.924	.924	.924	1.188	.924	.924	.924	1.472	.925	1.188
1977	.924	.924	.925	.930	.955	.924	.924	.930	.924	.924
1978	.924	.924	.924	.924	1.010	.924	.924	.959	.924	.924
1979	.924	.924	.934	.925	2.637	.924	.925	.933	.924	2.379
1980	.924	.924	2.631	.943	.946	.924	.924	.929	.924	.924
1981	.933	.924	.992	.955	.966	.924	.924	.952	.930	2.345
1982	.924	.924	.933	.924	2.576	.924	.924	.945	.924	1.452

Political Instability Quotient

Year	Chad	Zaire	Uganda	Kenya	Tan-zania	Ethio-pia	Zambia	Zimba-bwe	Malawi	South Africa
1948	.924	.924	.924	.925	.924	.925	.924	.924	.924	.017
1949	.924	.924	.924	.929	.924	1.059	.924	.924	.924	.079
1950	.924	.924	.924	.930	.924	1.257	.924	.929	.924	.079
1951	.924	.924	.924	.924	.924	.926	.924	.929	.924	.026
1952	.924	.924	.925	1.605	.924	.924	.924	.949	.924	.155
1953	.924	.924	.927	3.555	.928	.926	.924	.924	.924	.055
1954	.924	.924	.926	2.657	.928	.924	.924	.924	.924	.016
1955	.924	.924	.925	1.429	.924	.924	.924	.924	.924	.014
1956	.924	.924	.930	1.226	.924	.924	.924	.924	.924	.125
1957	.925	.924	.925	1.042	.924	.925	.924	.924	.924	.174
1958	.924	.929	.930	.930	.929	.924	.929	.924	.924	.021
1959	.925	1.055	.943	.945	.924	.924	.934	.924	.924	.169
1960	.924	.924	.997	.958	.925	3.677	1.136	.924	1.425	.715
1961	1.054	.924	.926	.943	.979	.931	.989	.924	.980	.092
1962	.924	.953	1.071	1.020	.924	.949	1.096	.924	.927	.056
1963	.949	2.381	1.188	1.232	.933	.924	1.024	.924	.924	.059
1964	.924	.973	1.200	.978	.958	1.054	1.013	.924	.925	.051
1965	.978	2.500	.943	1.086	.925	.924	2.410	.924	1.126	.013
1966	.924	1.195	2.369	.939	.925	.925	1.042	.924	.937	.144
1967	.925	.924	.924	.925	.924	1.077	.937	.925	.927	.007
1968	.925	3.982	.924	.910	.925	.930	1.078	.924	.927	.031
1969	.935	1.188	.925	1.093	1.199	.926	.925	.924	.924	.010
1970	.933	1.200	1.185	.924	.924	.925	.934	.924	.950	.055
1971	1.192	.942	5.095	.925	.924	.927	.929	.924	.924	.039
1972	.931	1.207	1.220	.924	1.184	.926	.955	.924	.924	.042
1973	.927	.926	.979	.924	.924	.929	.972	.924	.925	.076
1974	.924	.924	1.505	.929	.924	7.543	.940	.925	.924	.071
1975	2.317	.924	.956	1.089	.926	1.753	.932	.924	.924	.008
1976	.924	.924	2.288	.925	.924	1.583	.970	.924	.924	.359
1977	1.202	2.595	1.876	.924	.933	2.297	.986	.924	.924	.204
1978	.939	.957	.924	.924	.937	.966	1.018	.924	.924	.032
1979	1.195	.924	2.354	.924	.924	.933	.949	.924	.924	.028
1980	.930	.924	2.319	.926	1.197	1.261	1.065	.924	.924	.173
1981	.928	.924	.938	.929	.924	3.677	.937	.924	.924	.079
1982	2.319	.924	.926	1.189	.925	.924	1.078	.924	.924	.028

Political Instability Quotient

Year	Botswa-na	Morocco	Algeria	Tunisia	Libya	Sudan	Iran	Turkey	Iraq	Egypt
1948	.924	1.113	.924	.925	.953	.979	1.061	0.0	.984	1.692
1949	.924	.924	.924	.924	.996	.924	1.087	0.0	.934	1.193
1950	.924	.928	.926	.928	.925	.925	1.083	0.0	1.197	.942
1951	.924	.960	.929	.933	.930	.947	1.441	0.0	.929	1.235
1952	.924	1.271	.939	3.136	.933	.924	1.213	0.0	.985	3.815
1953	.924	2.419	.924	1.978	.924	.924	3.168	0.0	.948	1.275
1954	.924	2.033	.975	1.123	1.058	.950	1.025	0.0	.929	3.816
1955	.924	3.388	1.240	.953	.927	1.299	.944	.052	.924	.931
1956	.924	1.359	2.331	1.332	.925	.979	.955	.009	1.047	.941
1957	.924	1.201	1.813	.942	.924	1.315	.956	.034	.924	1.094
1958	.924	1.013	2.944	1.057	.924	2.575	.939	.007	3.607	.924
1959	.924	.958	1.796	.951	.949	1.469	.927	.022	2.965	.927
1960	.924	.951	1.925	.933	.925	.928	.951	2.370	.961	.924
1961	.924	.933	5.908	.956	.924	.939	1.019	.954	.966	.939
1962	.924	.951	2.191	.924	.924	.924	1.093	1.197	.988	.934
1963	.924	.926	1.090	.924	.924	.948	1.047	1.197	6.420	.924
1964	.924	.938	1.149	.925	.953	3.855	.944	.931	1.207	.929
1965	.924	1.019	2.361	.926	.939	1.090	1.208	.929	1.225	1.192
1966	.924	.949	.968	.925	.924	1.194	.925	.943	1.601	.937
1967	.924	.938	1.198	.978	.946	.924	.924	.944	.932	1.188
1968	.924	.941	.925	.924	.924	.949	.925	.941	5.238	.958
1969	.924	.946	.924	.924	2.575	2.312	.935	.982	1.143	.924
1970	.924	.937	.929	.926	1.189	.942	1.056	.962	1.421	.934
1971	.924	1.232	.924	1.054	.924	3.745	.984	1.408	.928	1.063
1972	.924	1.229	.924	.934	.929	.924	.980	.024	.938	.953
1973	.924	1.243	.924	.924	.934	1.190	1.102	.003	1.815	1.223
1974	.924	1.005	.925	.930	.924	.929	.924	.007	1.121	1.194
1975	.924	1.054	.924	.924	1.189	1.191	1.224	.082	1.222	.942
1976	.924	.924	1.054	.924	.929	1.312	1.261	.50	.929	.940
1977	.924	.924	.924	.925	1.164	.925	.936	.034	1.421	1.069
1978	.924	.933	.925	.967	.924	.924	1.454	.452	1.257	.941
1979	.924	.924	.924	.925	.927	.930	3.026	.455	1.007	.924
1980	.924	.924	.947	.968	.927	.929	1.625	2.960	.931	.926
1981	.924	.938	.932	.925	1.188	.930	9.445	.005	.924	1.122
1982	.924	.925	.925	.942	.924	.948	2.033	.006	.925	.945

Political Instability Quotient

Year	Syria	Lebanon	Jordan	Israel	Saudi Arabia	North Yemen	Kuwait	Afghan-istan	Japan	India
1948	1.048	.925	.924	.293	.924	4.230	.924	.924	.109	.322
1949	5.151	1.224	1.054	.010	.924	1.694	.924	.925	.208	.240
1950	3.423	1.187	.929	.005	.924	.924	.929	.924	.101	.334
1951	3.845	1.116	1.067	.065	.924	.924	.924	.924	.025	.016
1952	.969	1.006	.946	.151	.924	.924	.924	.924	.204	.082
1953	1.189	1.197	.929	.005	.937	.927	.924	.925	.018	.116
1954	2.598	.974	.945	.006	.924	.924	.924	.924	.057	.040
1955	1.336	.933	1.009	.015	.924	3.724	.924	.934	.017	.104
1956	1.271	.964	1.015	.032	.924	.924	.946	.924	.051	.515
1957	1.081	1.083	1.291	.146	.924	.924	.925	.924	.016	.079
1958	.928	1.955	1.480	.016	.927	.924	.924	.924	.036	.072
1959	.929	1.128	.924	.060	.924	.946	1.189	.957	.017	1.622
1960	.927	.944	2.356	0.0	.924	.925	.924	.928	.345	3.226
1961	2.331	.934	.937	.047	.924	.931	.924	.924	.051	.662
1962	2.640	1.199	.924	.004	.924	3.844	.924	.924	.057	1.565
1963	3.024	.955	.952	.044	.924	1.244	.924	.924	.012	1.535
1964	1.358	.931	.924	0.0	.924	1.078	.924	.924	.001	1.201
1965	1.219	.929	.931	.009	.924	3.845	.924	.948	.001	3.226
1966	2.732	1.068	.979	.037	.925	1.375	.924	.924	.013	.662
1967	.970	.960	.929	.015	.988	2.806	.924	.924	.062	1.605
1968	.928	.997	.928	.005	.924	1.018	.924	.933	.096	.239
1969	2.311	1.042	.937	.011	1.023	1.063	.933	.925	.098	.293
1970	2.326	.986	1.073	.009	.925	.938	.924	.925	.034	.226
1971	.924	1.094	1.012	.036	.924	.925	1.054	.924	.033	.094
1972	1.054	1.096	.929	.016	.924	.951	.933	.924	.013	.064
1973	1.341	1.002	.924	.018	.924	1.181	.924	2.413	.002	.179
1974	.926	1.456	.933	.063	.924	2.311	.925	.924	.027	2.128
1975	.927	3.159	.924	.028	1.057	1.188	.933	.924	.020	.192
1976	1.334	2.542	.929	.070	.924	.924	.925	.924	.010	.022
1977	1.336	1.353	.924	.051	.924	1.324	.925	1.055	.008	.066
1978	.924	.971	.924	.047	.924	1.358	.924	2.443	.036	.096
1979	1.324	.952	.924	.132	.938	.924	.930	12.512	.002	.260
1980	1.076	1.122	.924	.225	1.132	.925	.926	2.680	.003	.499
1981	.928	1.108	.924	.278	.926	1.387	.924	1.455	.004	.129
1982	1.274	1.252	.929	.306	.934	.927	.926	.970	.004	.260

Political Instability Quotient

Year	Paki-stan	Burma	Sri Lanka	Nepal	Thai-land	Cam-bodia	Laos	S.Viet-nam	Malay-sia	Singa-pore
1948	.928	1.162	.005	.924	1.709	.924	.924	.936	1.304	.039
1949	.924	.363	0.0	.924	.950	.924	.924	.960	1.833	.024
1950	.934	.323	0.0	2.347	.924	1.184	.924	1.259	1.508	.056
1951	.924	.376	0.0	.930	2.597	1.054	.924	1.364	1.531	.003
1952	.974	.098	.001	1.196	.925	.927	.924	1.203	1.490	.019
1953	1.027	.052	.098	.930	.924	2.471	.925	1.074	1.746	.009
1954	1.060	.023	0.0	.961	.925	.944	1.330	.953	1.010	.029
1955	.928	.159	.009	.924	.939	.926	.979	5.223	2.388	.143
1956	.949	.015	.049	.924	.937	.924	.935	1.069	1.437	.077
1957	.930	.009	.076	.954	2.313	.924	.924	.927	1.654	0.0
1958	2.469	1.409	.216	.924	2.311	.924	.928	.936	1.435	.024
1959	.925	.003	.139	.924	.927	.924	1.001	130.93	1.430	0.0
1960	.924	.008	0.0	2.314	.924	.941	8.293	131.36	1.221	0.0
1961	.949	.958	.050	.945	.937	.924	1.006	1.044	.926	0.0
1962	1.114	2.342	.269	1.000	.926	.924	.949	1.147	.924	.001
1963	1.094	.930	0.0	.924	.924	.924	1.633	2.974	.940	.010
1964	1.152	.966	.043	.950	.925	.924	2.491	6.188	1.108	0.0
1965	1.150	.941	.010	.955	.933	.929	1.477	5.912	.938	0.0
1966	1.039	.925	.038	.924	.927	.927	1.212	2.503	.963	.005
1967	.945	1.094	0.0	.930	.947	.930	.942	1.833	1.028	.001
1968	1.305	1.062	0.0	.929	.934	.930	.953	3.201	.930	.007
1969	3.955	.931	.009	.939	.934	.928	.945	4.384	1.060	.004
1970	.962	.933	.010	.925	.930	3.033	.944	2.076	.943	.007
1971	5.638	.926	.052	.925	2.314	1.152	1.243	2.778	.927	.001
1972	1.312	.926	.003	.947	.938	2.401	1.032	2.702	.924	.001
1973	1.093	.929	0.0	.925	2.325	1.653	1.214	2.042	.924	0.0
1974	1.227	.945	0.0	.926	.949	1.122	.932	1.634	1.062	.001
1975	1.161	.984	.131	.924	1.049	3.515	6.660	1.518	.932	0.0
1976	1.159	1.196	.006	.924	2.490	1.584	.931	.924	.935	0.0
1977	2.624	.937	.039	.930	2.603	1.089	.926	.924	.924	0.0
1978	1.012	.927	.001	.924	.934	1.188	.925	.924	.924	0.0
1979	1.008	.925	0.0	.997	1.191	2.577	.924	.924	.926	0.0
1980	.930	.926	.009	.943	.939	.924	.924	.924	.924	0.0
1981	.958	.924	.017	.925	1.196	.926	.924	.924	.924	0.0
1982	.971	.926	.011	.924	.927	.926	.925	.924	.925	0.0

Political Instability Quotient

Year	Phili- ppines	Indo- nesia	Aus- tralia	New Zealand
1948	.960	2.368	.001	0.0
1949	.991	.980	.015	.001
1950	1.054	1.497	.096	0.0
1951	2.425	1.100	.010	.009
1952	1.507	.951	0.0	0.0
1953	1.489	.971	.001	0.0
1954	.939	.946	0.0	0.0
1955	1.076	6.806	.005	0.0
1956	.927	.995	0.0	0.0
1957	.951	.980	0.0	0.0
1958	.927	1.348	0.0	0.0
1959	.955	1.045	0.0	0.0
1960	1.059	.988	.005	0.0
1961	.938	.930	0.0	0.0
1962	1.057	.959	0.0	0.0
1963	1.058	1.038	0.0	0.0
1964	.930	.960	0.0	0.0
1965	.933	1.796	.001	0.0
1966	1.074	4.702	.017	.001
1967	1.049	.985	.005	.009
1968	1.476	.960	.019	.001
1969	1.087	1.195	.007	0.0
1970	.998	.930	.023	.002
1971	1.115	.925	.012	.001
1972	.970	.929	.006	0.0
1973	.972	.929	.002	0.0
1974	.947	.939	.006	.005
1975	1.077	.924	.012	.001
1976	.940	.924	.005	.001
1977	.947	.924	.004	0.0
1978	1.066	.926	.001	0.0
1979	.934	.924	.009	0.0
1980	1.096	.925	.130	.005
1981	.949	.930	.002	0.0
1982	.944	.930	.004	.001

Bibliography

Abrahamian, E. (1986). "Structural Causes of the Iranian Revolution" in J. A. Goldstone. (ed.) *Revolutions: Theoretical, Comparative, and Historical Studies*, pp. 119-126. San Diego: Harcourt Brace Jovanovich, Publishers.

Adelman, I., and C. T. Morris. (1967). *Society, Politics, and Economic Development: A Quantitative Approach.* Baltimore: Johns Hopkins University Press.

Adelman, I., and C. T. Morris. (1968). "Performance Criteria for Evaluating Economic Development Potentials: An Operational Approach" *Quarterly Journal of Economics* 62.

Adelman, I., and C. T. Morris. (1973). *Economic Growth and Social Equality in Developing Countries.* Stanford: University Press.

Ahluwalia, M. (1974). "Income Inequality, Some Dimensions of the Problem." In *Redistribution with Growth*, pp. 3-37. Cheney et al. (eds.) New York: Oxford University Press.

Ahluwalia, M. (1976a). "Income Distribution and Development: Some Stylized Facts." *American Economic Review* 66: 128-35.

Ahluwalia, M. (1976b). "Inequality, Poverty and Development." *Journal of Development Economics* 3: 307 - 42.

Akbar, M. J. (1985). *India: The Siege Within: Challenges to a Nation's Unity.* Middlesex, England: Penguin Books.

Akerlof, G. A. (1984) "Loyalty Filters." *American Economic Review* 73.

Alexander, F. (1941). "The Psychiatric Aspects of War and Peace." *American Journal of Sociology* 66: 504 - 20.

Alexander, J. (1985). *Neofunctionalism.* Beverly Hills, Calif: Sage Publications.

Allais, M. (1952). "The Foundations of a Positive Theory of Choice Involving Risk, and a Criticism of the Postulates and Axioms of the American School" (Translation of " Fondements d'une théorie des choix comportant un risque et critique des postulates et axiomes de l'eloce Americane," Paris, CNRS). In M. Allais and O. Hagen (eds.). (1979). *Expected Utility Hypotheses and the Allais Paradox: Contemporary Discussions of Decisions under Uncertainty with Allais' Rejoinder.* Dorchet, Holland: D. Reidel.

Almon, S. (1968)."The Distributed Lag between Capital Appropriation and Expectation" *Econometrica* 33: 178- 96.

Almond, G., and S. Powell. (1977). *Comparative Politics: System, Process and   Policy.* Boston: Little, Brown & Co.

Almond, G., S. Flanigan, and R. Mundt, (1973). *Crisis Choice and Change.* Boston: Little, Brown & Co.

Almond, G. and S. Verba. (1963). *The Civic Culture: Political Attitudes and Democracy in Five Nations.* Princeton, N. J.: Princeton University Press.

Almond, G., and S. Verba. (1965). *The Civic Culture,* Boston: Little, Brown & Co.

Amemiya, T. (1981). "Qualitative Response Models: A Survey." *Journal of Economic Literature* 19: 1483 - 1536.

Aronfreed, J. and V. Paskal (1968). "Altruism, Empathy and the Conditioning of Positive Affect." In J. Aronfreed (ed.), *Conduct and Conscience.* New York: Academic Press.

Arrow, K. J. (1951). *Social Choice and Individual Values.* New York: John Wiley & Sons.

Arrow, K. J. (1972). "Gifts and Exchanges." *Philosophy and Public Affairs.* 1: 343 - 62.

Arrow, K. J. (1979). "Values and Collective Decision Making." In F. Hahn and M. Hollis (eds.) *Philosophy and Economic Theory.* New York: Oxford University Press.

Astin, A. W., and A. E. Bayer. (1971). "Antecedents and Consequences of Disruptive Campus Protests." *Measurements and Evaluations in Guidance.* 4: 18 - 30.

Aubrey, J. (1898). *Brief Lives.* In A. Clark (ed.) Oxford: Clarendon Press.

Avinery, S. (1969). *Karl Marx on Colonialism and Modernization.* New York: Doubleday.

Axelrod, R. (1970). *Conflict of Interest: A Theory of Divergent Goals with Applications to Politics.* Chicago: University of Chicago Press.

Axelrod, R. (1981). "The Emergence of Cooperation among Igoists." *American Political Science Review* 75: 306 - 18.

Axelrod, R. (1986). "An Evolutionary Approach to Norms", *American Political Science Review* 80: 1095-1112.

Ayers, C. (1952). *The Industrial Economy.* Boston: Houghton Mifflin.

Ayers, C. (1961). *Toward a Reasonable Society.* Austin: University of Texas Press.

Bacciocco, E. J. (1974). *The New Left in America: Reform to Revolution 1956 to 1970.* Hoover Institute, Stanford: Stanford University Press.

Bandura, A. (1973). *Aggression: A Social Learning Analysis.* Englewood Cliffs, N. J.: Prentice-Hall.

Bandura, A., and R. H. Walters. (1963). *Social Learning and Personality Development.* New York: Holt, Reinhart, and Winston.

Banerjee, S. (1980). *In The Wake of Naxalbari: A History of The Naxalite Movement in India.* Calcutta: Subarnarekha.

Banfield, E. C. (1968). *The Un-Heavenly City: The Nature and the Future of Our Urban Crisis.* Boston: Little, Brown.

Banks, A. (1971). *Cross-Polity Time Series Data*. Cambridge: MIT Press.

Barry, B. (1978) *Sociologists, Economists and Democracy*. Chicago: University of Chicago Press.

Bartzel, Y., and E. Silberberg. (1973).   "Is the Act of Voting Rational?" *Public Choice* 16: 51 - 8.

Batra, R. (1987). *The Great Depression of 1990*. New York: Simon and Schuster.

Becker, G. S. (1968). "Crime and Punishment: An Economic Application." *Journal of Political Economy* 76: 169 - 72.

Becker, G. S. (1974). "A Theory of Social Interactions." *Journal of Political Economy* 82: 1063 - 093.

Becker, G. S. (1976a). "Altruism, Egoism, and Genetic Fitness." *Journal of Economic Literature* 14: 817 - 26.

Becker, G. S. (1976,b). *Economic Approach to Human Behavior*. Chicago: University of Chicago Press.

Bell, D. (ed). (1964). *The Radical Right*. Garden City, N.Y.: Doubleday-Anchor Books.

Bell, D., and I. Kristol. (1981). *The Crisis in Economic Theory*. New York: Basic Books.

Bendix, R. A., and S. Lipset (eds.). (1966). *Class, Status, and Power*. New York: The Free Press.

Bentham, J. (1963) *An Introduction to the Principles of Morals and Legislations*. New York: Hafner.

Berkowitz, L. (1968). *The Roots of Aggression: A Re-examination of the Frustration-Aggression Hypothesis*. New York: Atherton Press.

Berkowitz, L., and W. H. Connor. (1966). "Success, Failure, and Social Responsibility." *Journal of Personality and Social Psychology* 4: 664 - 69.

Berkson, J. (1965). "Application of the Logistic Function to Bio-Assay." *Journal of the American Statistical Association* 39: 357-365.

Bettelheim, C. (1961). *Studies in the Theory of Planning* New York: Casis Publishing House.

Bhagwati, J., and S. Chakravarty. (1969). "Survey of National Economic Policy Issues and Policy Research." In *American Economic Review* suppl. Sept. pp. 1 - 118.

Black, D. (1958). *The Theory of Committees and Elections.* Cambridge: Cambridge University Press.

Blair, D. and R. Pollack. (1979). "Collective Rationality and Dictatorship: The Scope of Arrow's Theorem." *Journal of Economic Theory* 21.

Blake, R. H., L. Berkowitz, R. Belamy, and J. Mouton. (1956). "Volunteering as an Avoiding Act." *Journal of Abnormal and Social Psychology* 53: 154 - 56.

Blake, R. H., M. Rosenbaum, and R. Duryea. (1955). "Gift-giving as a Function of Group Standards." *Human Relations* 8: 61 - 73.

Blaug, M. (1968). *Economic Theory in Retrospect.* Homewood, Ill: Richard D. Irwin.

Blauner, R. (1972) "Whitewash over Watts." In *Radical Oppression in America.* New York: Harper & Row, pp. 194 - 217.

Blaug, M. (1980). *The Methodology of Economics.* Cambridge: Cambridge University Press.

Block, J; N. Haan; and M. B. Smith. (1969) "Socialization Correlates of Student Activism." *The Journal of Social Issues* 25 (4): 143 - 77.

Blumberg, P. (1973). Industrial Democracy: *The Sociology of Participation.* New York: Schocken Books.

Blumer, H. (1951). "Collective Behavior." In Lee, A.M. (ed.), *Outline of the Principles of Sociology.* New York: Barnes and Noble, pp. 166 - 222.

Blumer, H. (1978). "Social Unrest and Collective Protest." In N. K. Danzin (ed.), *Studies in Symbolic Interaction.* 1: pp. 1 - 54.

Bottomore, T. B. and M. Rubel (eds.), (1964). *Karl Marx: Selected Writings in Sociology and Social Philosophy.* New York: McGraw-Hill.

Boulding, K. (1962). *Conflict and Defiance*. New York: Harper & Row.

Boulding, K. (1966). "Conflict Management as a Learning Process." In de Rench, A.(ed.), *Conflict and Society*. Boston: Little, Brown.

Boulding, K. (1970). *A Primer on Social Dynamics: History as Dialectics and Development*. New York: The Free Press.

Bowels, S. and H. Gintis. (1976). *Schooling in Capitalist America*. New York: Basic Books.

Branson, W. H. (1979). *Macroeconomic Theory and Policy*. 2nd ed. New York: Harper & Row.

Brennan, G. (1973). "Pareto Desirable Redistribution: The Nonaltruistic Dimension." *Public Choice* Spring, pp. 43 - 68.

Brennan, G., and J. M. Buchanan. (1982). "Voter Choice and the Evaluation of Political Alternatives: A Critique of Public Choice." Unpublished Paper. Center for the Study of Public Choice, Viriginia Polytechnic Institute and State University.

Brodbeck, M. (1973). Methodological Individualism: Definition and Reduction. In J. O'Neill (ed.), *Modes of Individualism and Collectivism*. London: Heinemann, pp. 287 - 311.

Brown, M., and A. Godin. (1973). *Collective Behavior: A Review and Reinterpretation of the Literature*. Pacific Palasade, Calif: Goodyear.

Brown, R. (1954). "Mass Phenomena." In Lindzey, G. (ed.) *Handbook of Social Psychology*. Cambridge: Addison-Wesley. 2: 833 - 76.

Bryan, J. H. and M. A. Test. (1967) "Models and Helping: Naturalistic Studies in Aiding Behavior." *Journal of Personality and Social Psychology* 6: 400 - 07.

Bryson, G. (1945). *Man and Society: The Scottish Inquiry of the Eighteenth Century*. Princeton: Princeton University Press.

Buchanan, J. and G. Tullock. (1962). *The Calculus of Consent*. Ann Arbor: University of Michigan Press.

Bwy, D. (1968a). "Dimensions of Social Conflict in Latin America." *American Behavioral Scientist* March-April, pp. 38 - 50.

Bwy, D., (1968b). "Political Instability in Latin America: The Cross-Cultural Test of a Causal Model." *Latin American Research Review*. 3: 17 - 66.

Campbell, D., and D. Fiske. (1959). "Convergent and Discriminant Validation by the Multitrait-Multimethod Matrix." *Psychological Bulletin* 56: 81 - 105.

Caplan, N. (1970) "The New Ghetto Man: A Review of Recent Empirical Findings." *Journal of Social Issues*. 26: 59 - 73.

Caplan, N., and J. M. Paige. (1968). "A Study of Ghetto Rioters" *Scientific American* 219 (2): 15 - 22.

Chalmers, J. A., and R. B. Shelton. (1975). "An Economic Analysis of Riot Participation." *Economic Inquiry* 13: 322 - 336.

Chamberlin, J. (1974). "Provision of Collective Goods as a Function of Group Size." *American Political Science Review* 68: 707 - 715.

Chomsky, N. (1968). *Language and Mind*. New York: Harcourt, Brace, and World.

Cohen, J. L. (1981). "Can Human Irrationality Be Experimentally Demonstrated?" *The Behavioral and Brain Sciences* 4: 317-370.

Coleman, J. S. (1968). "The Mathematical Study of Change." In H. M. Blalock and A. B. Blalock (eds.), *Methodology in Social Research*, pp. 428-478. New York: McGraw-Hill.

Coleman, J. S. (ed.), (1968). *Education and Political Development*. Princeton: Princeton University Press.

Collard, D. A. (1978). *Altruism and Economy*. Oxford: Martin Robinson.

Collard, D. A. (1983). Economics of Philanthrophy: A Comment. *Economic Journal* 93: 637 - 8.

Commons, J. R. (1943). *Institutional Economics*. New York: Macmillan.

Commons, J. R. (1950). *The Economics of Collective Action*. New York: Macmillan.

Coogan, T. P. (1970). *The IRA* . London: Pall Mall.

Cordes, B., B. Jenkins, and K. Kellen. (1985). *A Conceptual Framework for Analyzing Terrorist Groups*. Santa Monica: Rand Corporation.

Cornelius, W. A., Jr. (1969). "Urbanization as an Agent of in Latin American Political Instability: The Case of Mexico." *American Political Science Review* 63 (3): 833 - 57.

Coser, L. A. (1956). *The Functions of Social Conflict*. Glencoe, Ill: Free Press.

Coser, L. A. (1965). *Men of Ideas*. New York: Free Press.

Coser, L. A. (1968). *Continuities in the Study of Social Conflict*, New York: Free Press.

Cox, D. R. (1970). *Analysis of Binary Data*. London: Methuen.

Crawley, A. (1956). *Escape from Germany*. London: Colliar Publishing.

Crook, J. (1980). *The Evolution of Human Consciousness*. Oxford: Oxford University Press.

Crosby, F. (1979). "Relative Deprivation Revisited: A Response to Miller, Bolce, and Halligan." *American Political Science Review* 73: 103 - 12.

Cutright, P. (1968). "National Political Development: Measurement and Analysis." *American Sociological Review* 28: 253-264.

Dahrendorf, R. (1958). "Toward a Theory of Conflict." *Journal of Conflict Resolution* 2: 69 - 105.

Darley, J. M., and B. Latane, (1968). "Bystander Intervention in Emergencies: Diffusion of Responsibility." *Journal of Personality and Social Psychology* 8: 377 - 83.

Das Gupta, A. K. (1985). *Epochs of Economic Theory*. Oxford: Basil Blackwell.

Davidson, D. (1976). "Psychology as Philosophy." In J. Glover (ed) *The Philosophy of Mind*. Oxford: Oxford University Press.

Davidson, D. (1982). *Essays on Actions and Events*. Oxford: Clarendon Press.

Davies, J. C. (1962). "Toward A Theory of Revolution." *American Sociological Review* 27: 5 - 19.

Davies, J. C. (1969). "The J-Curve of Rising and Declining Satisfaction as a   Cause of Some Great Revolutions and a Contained Rebellion." In H. D. Graham, and T. Gurr (eds.), *The History of Violence in America*. New York: Praeger, pp. 690 - 730.

Davis, J. A. (1959). "A Formal Interpretation of the Theory of Relative Deprivation." *Sociometry* 20: 280 - 96.

Davis, J. H., N. L. Kerr, R. L. Atkins, R. Holt, and D. Meek., (1976). "The Decision Process of 6-and 12-Person Mock Juries Assigned Unanimous and Two-thirds Majority Rules," *Journal of Personality and Social Psychology* 32: 1 - 14.

Dawkins, R. (1976). *The Selfish Gene*. New York: Oxford University Press.

Deaux, K., and L. Wrightsman. (1984). *Social Psychology in the 80's*. 4th ed. Monterey, Calif: Brooks/Cole.

Debreu, G. (1959). *Theory of Value*. New York: Wiley.

de Mesquito, B. B. and D. Lalman. (1986). "Reason and War." *American Political Science Review* 80 (4): 1113 - 30.

DeNardo, J. (1986) *Power in Numbers*. Princeton: Princeton University Press.

de Tocqueville, A. (1955). *The Old Regime and the French Revolution*, (trans.: S. Gilbert; original publication, 1856), Garden City, N. Y.: Doubleday.

Dickson, P., and K. Roelisberger. (1939). *Management and the Worker*. Cambridge: Harvard University Press.

Dollard, J. et al. (1939). *Frustration and Aggression*. New Haven: Yale University Press.

Dowes, R. et al. (1986). Organizing Groups for Collective Action.
    American Political Science Review, 80: 1171-1186.

Downes, B. (1968). "Social and Political Characteristics of Riot
    Cities: A Comparative Study," *Social Science Quarterly*. 49:
    504 - 20.

Downes, B. (1970). "A Critical Reexamination of the Social and
    Political Characteristics of Riot Cities."*Social Science Quarterly*
    51: 349 - 360.

Downs, A. (1957). *An Economic Theory of Democracy*. New York:
    Harper and Row.

Duff, E. A., and J. F. McCamant. (1968). "Measuring Social and
    Political Requirements for System Stability in Latin America."
    American Political Science Review 62 (4): 1125 - 43.

Dunlap, R. (1970). "A Comment on Multiversity, University Size,
    University Quality, and Student Protest: An Empirical Study."
    American Sociological Review 35: 383 - 400.

Dyke, C. (1981). *Philosophy of Economics*. Englewood Cliffs, N.
    J.: Prentice-Hall.

Eckstein, H. (1970). "On the Causes of Internal Wars." In Eric
    Nordlinger, (ed) *Politics and Society*, Englewood Cliffs, N.J.:
    Prentice-Hall.

Eckstein, R. (1972). "The Facilitation of Positive Human Qualities."
    Journal of Social Issues 28: 71 - 85.

Ehrlich, I. (1973). "Participation in Illegal Activities: A Theoretical
    and Empirical Investigation." *Journal of Political Economy*
    81: 521 - 65.

Eisinger, P. K. (1973). "The Conditions of Protest Behavior in
    American Cities." *American Political Science Review* 62: 11 -
    28.

Eliott, J. E. (1984). "Karl Marx on Late Stage of Capitalism," *Journal
    of Economic Issues* 18.

Elster, J. (1979 a) "Anomalies of Rationality: Some Unresolved
    Problems in the Theory of Rational Behavior." In L. Levy-
    Garboua (ed.) *Sociological Economics*. London: Sage
    Publications.

Elster, J. (1979 b). *Ulysses and the Syrens. Studies in Rationality and Irrationality.* Cambridge: Cambridge University Press.

Elster, J. (1983). *Sour Grapes.* Cambridge: Cambridge University Press.

Erikson, E. (1968). *Identity, Youth, and Crisis.* New York: W.W. Norton.

Etzioni, A. (1983). "Toward A Political Psychology of Economics." *Political Psychology* 4: 77 - 86.

Eyck, E. (1963). *History of the Weimer Republic.* (Trans. H. P. Hension and R. G. L. Waite) Cambridge: Harvard University Press.

Fanon, F. (1968). *The Wretched of the Earth.* (Trans. C. Farrington) New York: Grove Press.

Feagin, J. R., and H. Hahn. (1973). *Ghetto Revolts: The Politics of Violence in America.* New York: Macmillan & Co.

Feeny, D. (1983). "The Moral or the Rational Peasant? Competing Hypotheses of Collective Action." *Journal of Asian Studies* 62 (4): 769 - 789.

Feierabend, I., R. Feierabend, and B. Nesvold. (1969). "Social Change and Political Violence: Cross National Patterns," in Hugh D. Graham and T. Gurr (eds.) *Violence in America: Historical and Comparative Perspectives*, A Report to the National Commission on the Causes and Prevention of Violence, New York: Signet Books.

Ferejohn, J. and Fiorina, M. (1974). "The Paradox of Not Voting: A Decision Theoretic Analysis." *American Political Science Review* 68 (2): 525 - 36.

Fernbach, D. (ed.). (1974). *Karl Marx: The Revolution of 1848.* New York: Vintage Books.

Feuer, L. A. (1959). *Marx and Engels: Basic Writings on Politics and Philosophy.* New York: Anchor Books.

Feuer, L. A. (1969). *The Conflict of Generations.* New York: Basic Books.

Fine, B. (1984). *Marx's Capital.* London: Macmillan.

Fitzgibbon, R. 1969. "Measuring Democratic Change in Latin America." *The Journal of Politics* 29: 129-66.

Flacks, R. (1967). "The Liberated Generation: An Exploration of the Roots of Student Protest." *The Journal of Social Issues* 23: 52 - 75.

Flanigan, W., and E. Fogelman. (1970). "Patterns of Political Violence in Comparative Historical Perspective." *Comparative Politics* 3(1): 1 - 20.

Fogelson, R. (1971). *Violence as Protest*. Garden City, N. Y.: Doubleday.

Ford, W. F., and Moore (1970) "Additional Evidence on the Social and Political Characteristics of Riot Cities," *Social Science Quarterly*. 51: 339 - 348.

Franda, F. M. (1971). *Radical Politics in West Bengal*. London: M. I. T. Press.

Frank, J. (1968). *Sanity and Survival: Psychological Aspects of War and Peace*. New York: Vintage Books.

Franke, R. H., and J. D. Kaul. (1978) "The Hawthorne Experiment: First Statistical Interpretation." *American Sociological Review* 43 (5): 623 - 42.

Freud, S. (1930). *Civilization and Its Discontents*. (Trans. J. Reviere) London: Hogarth Press.

Friedman, M. (1953). *Essays in Positive Economics*. Chicago: University of Chicago Press.

Frohlic, N., and J. Oppenheimer. (1970). "I Get By with a Little Help from My Friends." *World Politics* 23: 104 - 120.

Frohlic, N., and J. Oppenheimer. (1974). "Self Interest or Altruism, What Difference?" *Journal of Conflict Resolution* 18: 55 - 73.

Frohlic, N.; T. Hunt; and J. Oppenheimer, (1975) "Individual Contributions for Collective Goods: Alternative Models." *Journal of Conflict Resolution* 19: 310 - 29.

Galbraith, J. K. (1958). *The Affluent Society*. Boston: Houghton Mifflin.

Galbraith, J. K. (1977). *The Age of Uncertainty*. Boston: Houghton-Mifflin.

Galtung, A. (1964). "A Structural Theory of Aggression." *Journal of Peace Research* 1(2): 94 - 119.

Gamson, W. A. (1974). *The Strategy of Social Protest*. Homewood, Ill.: Dorsey Press.

Garfinkel, H. (1967). Studies in Ethnomethodology. New York: Prentice-Hall.

Geertz, C. (1967). "The Integrative Revolution: Primordial Sentiments and Civil Politics in New States." In C. Welch (ed.) *Political Mobilization*. Belmont, Calif: Wadsworth Publishing Co., pp. 167-187.

Georgescu-Roegan, N. (1979). Methods in Economic Science. *Journal of Economic Issues*   13: 317 - 28.

Geshwender, J. A. (1964). "Social Structure and the Negro Revolt: An   Examination of Some Hypotheses." *Social Forces* . 42: 248 - 256.

Geshwender, J. A. (1968). "Civil Rights Protests and Riots: A Disappearing Distinction." *Social Science Quarterly*. 49: 479 - 493.

Ghosh, S. (1975). *The Naxalite Movement: A Maoist Experiment*. Calcutta: Firma K. L. Mukhopadhyay.

Gilman, J. (1958). *The Falling Rate of Profit*. New York: Cameron Associates.

Gintis, H. (1970). "The New Working Class and Revolutionary Youth." *Continuum* Spring-Summer, pp. 151 - 174.

Goffman, E. (1963). *Behavior in Public Places*. New York: The Free Press.

Goodman, P. (1965). "Thoughts on Berkeley." *New York Review of Books*. 3 (11): 5 - 6.

Goodspeed, D. J. (1962). *The Conspirators: A Study of the Coup d'État*. New York: The Viking Press.

Gordon, R. (1971). "Rigor and Relevance in a Changing Institutional Setting." *American Economic Review* 61: 1 - 7.

Gordon, R. (1984) *Macroeconomics*. (3rd ed.) Boston: Little Brown.

Gouldner, A. (1970) *The Coming Crisis of Western Sociology*. New York: Equinox Books.

Green, J. D. (1986). "Counter-mobilization in the Iranian Revolution." In J. A. Goldstone (ed) *Revolutions: Theoretical, Comparative and Historical Studies* . San Diego: Harcourt Brace Jovanovich.

Gruchy, A. (1971). *Contemporary Economic Thought*. Clifton, N. J.: Augustus M. Kelly.

Guevara, C. (1985).   Guerrilla Warfare (2nd ed.) Lincoln: University of Nebraska Press.

Gunning, P. (1972).   "An Economic Approach to Riot Analysis." *Public Choice* 13: 31 - 46.

Gupta, D. K. (1977). *Socio-Economic Costs of Unemployment and Income Inequality: A Cross National Study, 1948-67*. Unpublished Ph.D dissertation, University of Pittsburgh.

Gupta, D. K. (1984). "Assessing Risk in Planning: Sociopolitical Violence, Economic Development, and the Implications of an Integrated Model." *Managing International Development* March/April: 47-61.

Gupta, D. K. (1987a). "Political Psychology and Neoclassical Theory of Economic Growth: The Possibilities and Implications of an Attempted Resynthesis." *Political Psychology* 8(4): 637 - 666.

Gupta, D. K. (1987b). "Economic Behavior and Violent Collective Behavior." *Journal of Behavioral Economics* 15:33-46.

Gupta, D. K., and H. Singh. (1988).   "Rational Expectation and Participation In   Collective Violent Political Action: A Theoretical Overview." Department of Public Administration, San Diego State University.

Gupta, D. K. and Y.P. Venieris. (1981). "Introducing New Dimensions in Macro Models: The Sociopolitical and

Institutional Environments." *Economic Development and Cultural Change*. 29: 31 - 58.

Gurr, T. R. (1968). "A Causal Model of Civil Strife: A Comparative Analysis Using New Indices." *American Political Science Review* 42: 1104 - 24.

Gurr, T. R. (1970). *Why Men Rebel*. Princeton: Princeton University Press.

Gurr, T. R. and C. Ruttenburg. (1967). "The Conditions of Civil Strife: First Tests of a Causal Model." Research Monograph no. 28. Center of International Studies, Princeton University, April.

Guttman, J. M. (1978). "Understanding Collective Action." *American Economic Review*. Papers and Proceedings. 68: 251-5.

Habermas, J. (1988). *On the Logic of Social Sciences*. S. Nicholsen and J. A. Stark (translated) Cambridge: The MIT Press.

Habermas, J. (1970). *Toward a Rational Society: Student Protest, Science, and Politics*. (Trans. J. J. Shapiro) Boston: Beacon Press.

Hahn, F.H. (1970). "Some Adjustment Problems." *Econometrica* 38: 1 -17.

Hahn, F. H. and M. Hollis. (eds.) (1979). *Philosophy and Economic Theory*. Oxford: Oxford University Press.

Halebsky, S. (1976). *Mass Society and Political Conflict*. London: Cambridge University Press.

Hamilton, W. D. (1964) "Genetic Evolution of Social Behavior, I and II." *Journal of Theoretical Biology* 7: 1 - 52.

Hardin, R. (1978). "Groups in the Regulation of Collective Bads." Paper presented at the annual meeting of the Public Choice Society, New Orleans, La.

Hardy, M. (1979). "Economic Growth, Distributional Inequality, and Political Conflict in Industrial Societies." *Journal of Political and Military Sociology* 5: 209 - 27.

Harsanyi, J. C. (1980). "Rule Utilitarianism, Rights, Obligations and the Theory of Rational Behavior." *Theory and Decision* 12: 115-33.

Hartman, J., and W. Hsiao. (1988). "On Democracy, Economic Development, and Income Inequality." *American Sociological Review* 53: 794 - 99.

Hatfield, E., G. W. Walster, and J. Piliavin. "Equity Theory and Helping Relationships." In L. Wispe (ed.) *Altruism, Sympathy, and Helping* New York: Academic Press.

Hauser, P. M. (1963) "The Social, Economic, and Technological Problems of Rapid Urbanization." in B. F. Hoselitz and W. F. Moore (eds.) *Industrialization and Society*. The Hague: UNESCO.

Heller, J. A. (1983). *Mexico in Crisis*. (2nd ed.) New York: Holmes and Meier Publishers.

Heller, W. (1975). "What's Right with Economics?" *American Economic Review* 65: 1-26.

Helm, D. (1984). "Predictions and Causes: A Comparison of Friedman and Hicks on Methods." *Oxford Economic Papers* vol. 36.

Helm, D. (1986). *Enforced Maximization*. Oxford: Clarendon Press.

Hibbert, C. (1978). *The Great Mutiny: India 1857*. New York: The Viking Press.

Hibbs, D. P., Jr. (1973). *Mass Political Violence: A Cross-National Causal Analysis*. New York: Wiley.

Hibbs, D. P. Jr. (1976). "Industrial Conflict in Advanced Industrial Countries." *American Political Science Review* 70: 1033-1058.

Hicks, J. R. (1937). "Mr. Keynes and the 'Classics': A Suggested Interpretation." *Econometrica* 5: 147 - 59.

Hicks, J. R. (1983). A Discipline and not a Science." In J. R. Hicks (ed.) *Classics and Moderns*. Oxford: Basil Blackwell.

Hidaka, R. (1988) "Personal Perspectives." In G. McCormack and Y. Sugimoto (eds.) *Democracy in Contemporary Japan*. Armonk, N. Y.: M.E. Sharpe, pp. 228 - 46.

Himmelweit, H. T. (1950). "Frustration and Aggression: A Review of Recent Experimental Work." In T. H. Pear (ed.) *Psychological Factors in War and Peace.* London: Hutchinson.

Hirschleifer, J. (1977). "Economics from a Biological Viewpoint." *Journal of Law and Economics* 20.

Hirschleifer, J. (1978). "Competition, Cooperation, and Conflict in Economics and Biology." *American Economic Review Proceedings* 68: 238 - 43.

Hirschleifer, J. (1985). "The Expanding Domain of Economics." *American Economic Review* 75.

Hirschman, A. O. (1970). *Exit, Voice and Loyalty.* Cambridge: Harvard University Press.

Hirschman, A. O. (1981). *On Trespassing: Economics, Politics and Beyond.* Cambridge: Cambridge University Press.

Hoffer, E. (1951). *The True Believer: Thoughts and the Nature of Mass Movements.* New York: Harper & Row.

Holloway, R. (1968). "Human Aggression: The Need for a Species-Specific Framework." In F. Morton et al. (eds.) *The Anthology of Armed Conflict and Aggression.* New York: Natural History Press.

Hornstein, H. A., E. Fisch, and M. Holms. (1968). "The Influence of a Model's Feelings about His Behavior and His Relevance as a Comparison Other on Observer's Behavior." *Journal of Personality and Social Psychology* 10: 222 - 6.

Hoselitz, B. F. (1968). "Investment in Education and Its Political Impact." In J. A. Coleman (ed.) *Education and Political Development.* Princeton.: Princeton University Press.

Hoyt, E. E. (1951). "Want Development in Underdeveloped Areas." *Journal of Political Economy* 194-202.

Hume, D. (1902). *An Enquiry Concerning the Principles of Morals.* L. A. Selby-Bigge (ed.). Oxford: Oxford University Press.

Huntington, S. P. (1961). "Patterns of Violence in World Politics." In S. P. Huntington (ed.), *Changing Patterns of Military Politics.* New York: Free Press.

Huntington, S. P. (1965).   "Political Development and Political Decay." *World Politics* 17 (3): 386 - 430.

Huntington, S. P. (1968). *Political Order in Changing Societies*. New Haven: Yale University Press.

Huntington, S. P., and J. M. Nelson. (1978). *No Easy Choice: Political Participation in Developing Countries*. Cambridge: Harvard University Press.

Ireland, T. (1976).   "The Rationale of Revolt." *Papers in Non-Market Decision Making* 3: 49 - 66.

Jain, S. (1976).   *Size Distribution of Income*. Washington D. C.: World Bank Study.

Jambu, M., and M. O. Lebeaux. (1983). *Cluster Analysis and Data Analysis*. Amsterdam: North Holland.

Johnson, B. (1987). *The Four Days of Courage: The Untold Story of the People Who brought Marcos Down*. New York: Free Press.

Johnson. C. (1966). *Revolutionary Change* (2nd ed. 1982). Hoover Institute, Stanford: Stanford University Press.

Johnson, C. (1988).   "The Democratization of South Korea: What Role Does Development Play ?"   Paper presented at the Second Ilhae-Carnegie Conference on Democracy and Political Institutions. The Ilhae Institute, Seoul, Korea, July 8-9.

Johnson, H. (1971). "Keynesian Revolution and Monetarist Counter-Revolution." *American Economic Review* 61: 1 - 14.

Johnson, P (1983). *Modern Times: The World from the Twenties to the Eighties*. New York: Harper & Row.

Kahneman, D., and A. Tversky. (1972). "Subjective Probability: A Judgement of Representativeness." *Cognitive Psychology* 3: 207 - 32.

Kahneman, D., and A. Tversky. (1973). "Availability: A Heuristic for Judging Frequency and Probability." *Cognitive Psychology* 2: 207 - 32.

Kahneman, D., and A. Tversky. (1979).   "Prospect Theory: An Analysis of Decision Under Risk." *Econometrica* 263-291.

Kaldor, N. (1940). "A Model of the Trade Cycle." *Economic Journal* 78 - 92.

Kalt, J. P. (1981) *The Economics and Politics of Oil Price Regulation.* Cambridge: Cambridge University Press.

Kalt, J. P., and M. A. Zupan. (1984). "Capture and Ideology in the Economic Theory of Politics." *American Economic Review* 74: 279 - 300.

Kau, J. B., and P. H. Rubin. (1979). "Self-Interest, Ideology, and Logrolling in Congressional Voting." *Journal of Law and Economics* 22: 365-384.

Keddie, N. (1981). *The Roots of Revolution: An Interpretative History of Modern Iran.* New Haven: Yale University Press.

Kellen, K. (1979). *Terrorists--What Are They Like? How Some Terrorists Describe Their World and Action.* Santa Monica: Rand Corporation Study No. N-1300-SL.

Keniston, K. (1968). *Young Radicals.* New York: Harcourt, Brace, and World.

Kerner, O. (1968). *Report of the National Advisory Commission on Civil Disorders.* Washington, D. C.: U.S. Government Printing Office.

Kerr, C. (1964). *The Uses of the University.* Cambridge: Harvard University Press.

Kerr, C.; J. T. Dunlop; F. H. Harbison; and C. A. Myers. (1960). *Industrialism and Industrial Man.* Cambridge: Harvard University Press.

Keynes, J. M., (1936). *The General Theory of Employment, Interest, and Money.* London: Macmillan.

Kogan, E. (1950). *The Theory and Practice of Hell.* London: Secker and Warburg.

Kornai, J. (1971). *Anti-Equilibrium.* Amsterdam: North Holland.

Kornai, J. (1985). *Contradictions and Dilemmas.* Cambridge: Cambridge University Press.

Kornhauser, W. (1959). *The Politics of Mass Society.* New York: The Free Press.

Krebs, D. (1970). "Altruism: An Examination of the Concept and a Review of the Literature." *Psychological Bulletin* 73: 258 - 302.

Krebs, D. (1975). "Empathy and Altruism." *Journal of Personality and Social Psychology* 32: 1124 - 46.

Krebs, D. (1978). "A Cognitive -developmental Approach to Altruism." In L. Wispe (ed.) *Altruism, Sympathy, and Helping.* New York: Academic Press.

Kuh, E. (1959). "The Validity of Cross-sectionally Estimated Behavioral Equations in Time Series Applications," *Econometrica* 27: 197-214.

Kuh, E., and J. R. Meyer. (1957). "How Extraneous are Extraneous Estimates?" *The Review of Economics and Statistics.* 39: 380 -393.

Kuhn, T. (1970). *The Structure of Scientific Revolutions.* Chicago:University of Chicago Press.

Kuran, T. (1988) *Sparks and Pairie Fires: A Theory of Unanticipated Political Revolution.* MRG Working Paper # M8808. Department of Economics, University of Southern California.

Kuznets, S. (1955). Economic Growth and Economic Inequality. *American Economic Review* 45: 1 - 28.

Kuznets, S. (1963). "The Contribution of Wesley Mitchell." In Ayres, C.E., et al. (eds.) *Institutional Economics: Veblen, Commons and Mitchell Reconsidered.* Berkeley: University of California Press.

Kuznets, S. (1965). "Economic Growth and Economic Inequality." *American Economic Review* 65.

Laffont, J. J. (1975). "Macroeconomic Constraints, Economic Efficiency and Ethics: An Introduction to Kantian Economics." *Economica* 42: 430 - 7.

Lane, R. (1986). "Procedural Justice: How One Is Treated vs. What One Gets." Paper Presented at the Annual Meeting of the

International Society of Political Psychology, June 29 - July 3. Amsterdam.

Laquer, W. (1977). *Terrorism*. Boston: Little, Brown & Co.

Lasswell, H., and Kaplan, A. (1950). *Power And Society: A Framework For Political Inquiry*. New Haven: Yale University Press.

Latane, B., and J. Rodin. (1969). "A Lady in Distress: Inhibiting Effects of Friends and Strangers on Bystander Intervention," *Journal of Experimental and Social Psychology*. 5: 189 - 202.

Latsis, S. J., (ed.) (1976). *Methods and Appraisal in Economics*. Cambridge: Cambridge University Press.

Le Bon, G. (1895). *Psychologie des Foules*. Translation as *The Crowd*. New York: Viking Press, Compass Edition, 1960.

Lehman-Wilzig, S. (1990). *Stiff-Necked Peaple, Bottle-Necked System: The Evolution and Roots of Israeli Public Protest, 1949-1986*. Indiana University Press (forthcomimg).

Lenin, V. I. (1969). *What Is To Be Done?* Originally published in 1902, New York: International Publishers.

Lerner, D. (1958). *The Passing of Traditional Society*. New York: The Free Press.

Lerner, D. (1963). *Toward a Communication Theory of Modernization: A Set of Considerations and Political Development*. Princeton: Princeton University Press.

Lewis, A. (1968). *Theory of Economic Growth*. New York: Harper & Row. New York.

Lieberson, S., and A. Silverman. (1965). "The Preciptants and Underlying Conditions of Race Riots." *American Sociological Review* 30: 887-898.

Lieske, J. A., (1978). "The Conditions of of Racial Violence in American Cities: A Developmental Synthesis." *American Political Science Review* 72:1324-1340.

Lieske, J. A., (1979). "Inadvertent Empirical Theory: A Crtitique of 'The J-Curve Theory and Black Urban Riots.'" *Political Methodology* 6: 29-62.

Lipset, S. M. (1959). "Some Social Perquisites of Democracy: Economic Development and Political Legitimacy." *American Political Science Review* 53: 69-105.

Lipset, S. M. (1963). *Political Man.* New York: Doubleday.

Lipset, S. M. (1976). *Rebellion in the University.* Chicago: University of Chicago Press. Originally published in 1971.

Lipset, S. M., and E. Raab (1970). *The Politics of Unreason: The Right-Wing Extremism in America, 1790-1970.* New York: Harper & Row.

Lipset, S. M., and S. Wolin. (eds.) (1965). *The Burkeley Student Revolt.* Garden City, N. Y.: Anchor Books.

Lipskey, M. (1968). "Protest as a Political Resource." *American Political Science Review* 62: 1135-1137.

Lorenz, K. (1966). *On Aggression.* New York: Harcourt, Brace and World.

Losco, J. (1986). "Understanding Altruism: A Critique and Proposal for Integrating Various Approaches." *Political Psychology* 7: 323-348.

Lupsha, P. (1969). "Explanation of Political Violence: Some Psychological Theories Versus Indignation." *Politics and Society* 2: 80-104.

Lyonns, G. (1965). "The Police Car Demonstration: A Survey of Participants." In S. M. Lipset and S. Wolin (eds.) *The Berkeley Student Revolt.* Garden City, N. Y.: Anchor Books, pp. 519-530.

McCarthy, J. D., and M. N. Zald. (1973). *The Trends of Social Movements in America: Professionalization and Resource Mobilization.* Morristown, N. J.: General Learning Press.

McCarthy, J. D., and M. N. Zald. (1977). "Resource Mobilization in Social Movements: A Partial Theory." *American Journal of Sociology* 82: 1212 - 39.

McClosky, D. N. (1983). "The Rhetoric of Economics." *Journal of Economic Literature.*

McClosky, D. N. (1985). *The Rhetoric of Economics.* Madison: The University of Wisconsin Press.

McCone, J. (1969). *Violence in the City: An End or a Beginning? A Report by the Governor's Commission on the Los Angelos Riots* (December 2). Sacramento, State of California.

McFarland, A. S. (1969). *Power and Leadership in Pluralist System.* Stanford: Stanford University Press.

McPhail, C. (1971). Civil Disorder Participation: A Critical Examination of Recent Research. *American Sociological Review*, 36: 1058 - 73.

Machina, M. (1983). "Generalized Expected Utility Analysis and the Nature of Observed Violations of the Independence Axiom." In B. P. Stigum and F. Wenstop (eds) *Foundations of Utility and Risk Theory with Applications.* Holland: D. Reidel Publishing.

Mao Tse-tung. (1972a). "A Selected Spark Can Start A Prairie Fire." *Selected Military Writings of Mao Tse Tung.* Peking: Foreign Language Press.

Mao Tse-tung. (1972b). "On Correcting Mistaken Ideas in the Party." *Selected Military Writings of Mao Tse Tung.* Peking: Foreign Language Press.

Mao Tse-tung, and C. Guevara, (1961). *The Guerrilla Warfare.* London: Cassell.

Marcuse, H. (1969). *One Dimensional Man: Studies in the Ideology of Advanced Industrial Society.* Boston: Beacon Press.

Margolis, H. (1982). *Selfishness, Altruism and Rationality.* Cambridge: Cambridge University Press.

Marx, G. T. (1974). "Thoughts on a Neglected Category of Social Movement Participant: The Agent Provocateur and the Informant." *American Journal of Sociology.* 80: 402 - 442.

Marx, G. T. (1982). "External Efforts to Damage or Facilitate Social Movements: Some Patterns, Explanations, Outcomes, and Complications," In J. Wood and M. Jackson (eds) *Social Movements: Development, Participation, and Dynamics*, pp. 181-200. Belmont, Calif: Wadsworth Publishing.

Marx, G. T., and J. Wood (1975) "Strands of Theory of Research in Collective Behavior," *Annual Review of Sociology.* 1: 363 - 428.

Marx, K. (1906). *Capital.* New York: The Modern Library, Random House. Originally published in 1859.

Marx, K. (1961). "Economic and Philosophical Manuscripts." (T. B. Bottomore, Trans.). In Erich Fromm, *Marx's Concept of Man*, pp. 85 - 196. Frederick Unger Publishers. Originally published in 1884.

Maslow, A. (1962). *Toward A Psychology of Being.* Princeton: Van Nostrand Reinhold Co.

Mason, T. D. (1984). "Individual Participation in Collective Radical Violence: A Rational Choice Perspective." *American Political Science Review* 78: 1040-56.

Mason, T. D., and J. A. Murtagh, (1985). "An Empirical Examination of the 'Urban Black' versus the Social Marginality Hypotheses." *Political Behavior* 7(4): 352 - 74.

Masters, R. (1983). "The Biological Nature of the State." *World Politics* 35: 161 - 193.

Matthews, R. C. O. (1984). "Darwininsm and Economic Change." *Oxford Economic Papers* 36.

Mattick, P. (1969). *Marx and Keynes: The Limits of the Mixed Economy.* London: Merlin Press.

Mayr, E. (1965). "Cause and Effect in Biology," in D. Lerner (ed.) *Cause and Effect.* New York: Free Press.

McCarthy, J. D., and M. N. Zald. (1973). *The Trends of Social Movements in America: Professionalization and Resource Mobilization.* Morristown, N. J.: General Learning Press.

McCarthy, J. D., and M. N. Zald. (1977). "Resource Mobilization in Social Movements: A Partial Theory." *American Journal of Sociology.* 82: 1212 - 39.

McClosky, D. N. (1983). "The Rhetoric of Economics." *Journal of Economic Literature.*

McClosky, D. N. (1985). *The Rhetoric of Economics.*   Madison: The University of Wisconsin Press.

McCone, J. (1969). *Violence in the City: An End or a Beginning? A Report by the Governor's Commission on the Los Angelos Riots* (December 2). Sacramento, State of California.

McFarland, A. S. (1969). *Power and Leadership in Pluralist System.* Stanford: Stanford University Press.

McPhail, C. (1971).   Civil Disorder Participation: A Critical Examination of   Recent Research. *American Sociological Review* 36: 1058 - 73.

Mehmet, O. (1978). *Economic Planning and Social Justice in Developing Countries*, New York: St. Martin's Press.

Meier, N. C.; G. H. Mennenga; and H. J. Stoltz. (1941).   "An Experimental Approach to the Study of Mob Behavior." *Journal of Abnormal and Social Psychology* 48: 364 - 6.

Melvin M., and M. Cherkaouri. (1988).   "Gold Prices and Political Crisis: The Link Between Mid-East Oil and Gold." Paper presented at the Fourth Annual Conference of the Society of American Behavioral Economics, San Diego State University, San Diego, California.

Merton, R. K. (1957). *Social Theory and Social Structure.* Revised edition. London: Free Press of Glencoe.

"Mexico's Capital Flight Still Racks Economy, Despite Brady Plan: In a Nation Starved for Cash The Rich Buy Condos, Art In U.S. to Shelter Money." *The Wall Street Journal.* (September 25, 1989, p. 1).

Midlarsky, E., and Suda, W. (1978). "Some Antecedents of Altruism In Children: Theoretical And Empirical Perspectives." *Psychological Report* 43: 187-208.

Midlarsky, M. (1972). "Analyzing Diffusion and Contagion Effects: The Urban Disorders of the 1960." *American Political Science Review* 72: 996 - 1009.

Mill, J. S. (1884). *Principles of Political Economy.* New York: Appleton.

Miller, A., L. Bolce, and M. R. Halligan. (1977). "The J-Curve Theory and the Black Urban Riots: An Empirical Test of Progressive Relative Deprivation Theory. *American Political Science Review* 71: 964-82.

Miller, N. E. et al. (1941). "The Frustration-Aggression Hypothesis," *Psychological Review* 48: 337 - 42.

Mitchell, E. J. (1979). "The Basis of Congressional Energy Policy," *Texas Law Review* 57: 591 - 630.

Mitchell, W. C. (1910). "The Rationality of Economic Activity." *Journal of Political Economy* February, March: 97-113 and 197-216, respectively.

Moore, B. (1968). *Injustice: The Social Bases for Obedience and Revolt*. Whit Plains, N. Y.: M. E. Sharpe, Inc.

Moore, B. (1966). *Social Origins of Dictatorship and Democracy*. Boston: Beacon Press.

Morawetz, D. (1978). *Employment Implications of Industrialization in Developing Countries: A Survey. Economic Planning and Social Justice in Developing Countries*. New York: St. Martin's Press.

Morgan, R. J., and T. Clarke, (1970). "The Causes of Radical Disorder: A Grievance Level Explanation." *American Sociological Review*, 38: 611 - 24.

Morishima, M. (1982). *Why Has Japan 'Succeeded?' Western Technology, Japanese Ethos*. Cambridge: Cambridge University Press.

Moss, R. (1971). "Urban Guerrilla Warfare." Adelphi Papers, number Seventy Nine, London: The International Institute for Strategic Studies.

Mueller, D. (1979). *Public Choice*. New York: Cambridge University Press.

Mukherjee, K., and R. S. Yadav. (1980) *Bhojpur: Naxalism in the Plains of Bihar*. New Delhi, India: Radha Krishna Prakashan.

Muller, E. N. (1985) "Income Inequality, Regime Repressiveness, and Political Violence." *American Sociological Review* 50 (1): 47 - 61.

Muller, E. N. (1988). "Inequality, Repression, and Violence: Issues of Theory and Research Design." *American Sociological Review* 53 (5): 800 - 06.

Muller, E. N., and K. Opp. (1986). "Rational Choice and Rebellious Collective Action." *American Political Science Review* 80: 471 -87.

Musgrave, A. (1981). "Unreal Assumptions in Economic Theory: The F-Twist Untwisted." *KYKLOS* . 34: 377-378.

Musgrave R., and P. Musgrave. (1980). *Public Finance in Theory and Practice*. New York: McGraw-Hill.

Muth, J. F. (1961). "Rational Expectations and Theory of Price Movements," *Econometrica* , pp. 413 - 29.

Myrdal, G. (1968). *Asian Drama, An Inquiry into the Poverty of Nations*. New York: Pantheon Books.

Nagel, J. (1974). "Inequality and Discontent: A Non-Linear Hypothesis." *World Politics* 453-477.

Nash, P. (1937). "The Place of Religious Revitalism in the Formation of the Intercultural Community on Kalamath Reservation." In Eggan, F. (ed.) *Social Anthropology of North American Tribes*. Chicago: University of Chicago Press.

Nelson, R. R., and S. G. Winter. (1982). *An Evolutionary Theory of Economic Change*. Cambridge: Harvard University Press.

Nieburg, H. L. (1962). "The Threat of Violence and Social Change." *American Political Science Review* 35: 865 - 73.

Nisbet, R. E., and E. Borgida. (1975). "Attribution and the Psychology of Prediction." *Journal of Personal and Social Psychology* 32: 932 - 43.

Oberschall, A. (1973). *Social Conflict and Social Movements*. Englewood Cliffs, N.J: Prentice-Hall.

Olson, M. (1968). "Rapid Growth as Destabilizing Force." *Journal of Economic History* 23: 529 - 52.

Olson, M. (1971). *The Logic of Collective Action*. Cambridge: Harvard University Press.

Opp, K. (1986). "Soft Incentives and Collective Action." *British Journal of Political Science* 16: 87 - 112.

Palmer, J. L., and I. V. Sawhill. (eds.) (1984). *The Reagan Record: An Assessment of America's Changing Domestic Priorities.* An Urban Institute Study. Cambridge: Ballinger Publishing Co.

Papanek, G. F. (1977). *Pakistan's Development..* Cambridge: Harvard University Press.

Papanek, G. F. (1978). Economic Growth, Income Distribution and The Political Process in LDC's." In *Income Distribution and Economic Inequality.* Z. Griliches et al. (eds.) Campus Verlag-Halstead Press, Frankfurt-New York. pp. 259-273.

Park, R. E. and Burgers, E.W. (1924). *Introduction to the Science of Sociology* Chicago: University of Chicago Press.

Parsons, H. M. (1978). "What Caused the Hawthorne Effect?" *Administration and Society* 10 (4): 259 - 84.

Parsons, T. (1949). *The Structure of Social Action.* Glencoe: Free Press.

Parsons, T. (1951). *The Social System.* New York: Free Press of Glencoe.

Parsons, T., and N. Smelser. (1956). *Economy and Society: A Study in the Integration of Economic and Social Theory.* New York: Free Press.

Patchen, R. (1961). *The Choice of Wage Comparisons.* Englewood Cliffs, N. J.: Prentice-Hall.

Patten, S. N. (1912). *The New Basics of Civilization.* New York: McMillan.

Paukert, F. (1973). "Income Distributions At Different Levels Of Development." *International Labour Review* 108: 97 - 125.

Peltzman, S. (1976). "Toward A More General Theory of Regulation," *Journal of Law and Economics* 19: 211 - 40.

Peltzman, S. (1982). "Constituent Interest and Congressional Voting," Unpublished, University of Chicago Economic and Legal Organization Workshop, February.

Pettigrew, T. F. (1967). "Social Evaluation Theory" in D. Levine (ed.) Nebraska Symposium on Motivation. vol. 15, Lincoln: University of Nebraska Press.

Phelps-Brown, E. (1972). "The Underdevelopment of Economics." *Economic Journal* 82: 73-86.

Pigou, A. C. (1943). "The Classical Stationary State." *Economic Journal* 53: 343-351.

Pinard, M. (1971). *The Rise of a Third Party*. Englewood Cliffs, N. J.: Prentice-Hall.

Pindyck, R., and D. Rubinfeld. (1981). *Econometric Models and Econometric Forecasts*. New York: McGraw-Hill.

Pitt, J. C. (ed.) (1981). *Philosophy in Economics*. Dordrecht: Reidel.

Piven, F. (1976). "The Social Structuring of Political Protest." *Politics and Society* 6: 297-326.

Plekhanov, G. (1929). *Fundamental Problems of Marxism*. (ed.) D. Ryaznov London: Martin Lawrence.

Plekhanov, G. (1950). *The Role of the Individual in History*. London: Lawrence and Wishart.

Popkin, S. (1979). *The Rational Peasant*. Berkeley: University of California Press.

Popper, K. (1960). *The Poverty of Historicism*. Boston: Beacon Press.

Popper, K. (1988). "Popper on Democracy." *The Economist*. London. April 23. pp. 19-22.

Powell, G. P., and Steifbold, R. P. (1977). "Anger, Bargaining and Mobilization as a Middle-Range Theories of Elite Conflict Behavior." *Comparative Politics* : 379-399.

Pye, L. (1966). *Aspects of Political Development*. Boston: Little Brown.

Radnitzki, G. (1970). *Contemporary Schools of Metascience*. New York: Humanities Press.

Ransford, H. E. (1968). "Isolation, Powerlessness, and Violence: A Study of Attitudes and Participation in the Watts Riot." *American Journal of Sociology* 73: 581 - 91.

Rawls, J. (1971). *A Theory of Justice* . Cambridge, Mass: Harvard University Press.

Reitzler, K. (1943). "On the Psychology of Modern Revolution." *Social Research* 10: 320 - 36.

Richter, M. K. (1971). "Rational Choice." In J. S.Chipman, L. L. Hurwicz, L. M. K. Richter, and H. F.Sonnenschein. (eds.) *Preference, Utility and Demand.* New York: Harcourt.

Riker, W., and P. C. Ordeshook. (1972). *Positive Political Theory.* Englewood Cliffs, N.J: Prentice-Hall.

Robinson, J. (1962). *Economic Philosophy.* London: Watts.

Roeder, P. G. (1982). "Rational Revolution: Extensions of the 'By-product' Model of Revolutionary Involvement." *Western Political Quarterly* 35: 5 - 23.

Rogin, M. P. (1967). *The Intellectuals and McCarthy.* Cambridge: The MIT Press.

Rosenhan, D. (1969). "Studies in Altruistic Behavior: Developmental and Naturalistic Variabels Associated with Charitability." Paper presented at the meeting of The Society for Research in Child Development.

Rosett, R. (1971). "Weak Experimental Verification of the Expected Utility Hypothesis." *Review of Economic Studies* 38: 481 - 492.

Rude, G. (1960). *The Crowd in French Revolution.* Oxford: Oxford University Press.

Rude, G. (1964). *The Crowd in History.* New York: John Wiley & Sons.

Rudra, A. (1974). "Usefulness of Plan Models: An Assessment Based on Indian Experience." In A. Mitra (ed.) *Economic Theory and Planning: Essays in Honour of A. K. Das Gupta.* Calcutta, India: Oxford University Press.

Rummel, R. (1963). "Dimensions of Conflict Behavior Within and Between Nations." *Yearbook of the Society for General Systems Research.* 8: 1 - 49.

Runciman, W. G. (1966). *Relative Deprivation and Social Justice: A Study of Attitudes to Social Inequality in Twentieth Century England.* Berkeley: University of California Press.

Russett, B. (1964). Inequality and Instability: The Relation of Land Tenure to Politics." *World Politics* 16:442-454.

Salert, B. (1976). *Revolutions and the Revolutionaries.* New York: Elsevier.

Sama Shastri, R. (1967). *Kautilya's Arthasastra.* Mysore, India: Mysore Printing and Publishing House.

Samuelson, P.   (1948). *Foundations of Economic Analysis.* Cambridg: Harvard University Press.

Samuelson, P.   (1954). "The Pure Theory of Public Expenditure," *Review of Economics and Statistics* 36: 387 - 89.

Samuelson, P. (1955). "Diagramatic Exposition of a Theory of Public Expenditure." *Review of Economics and Statistics* 37 (4): 350 -6.

Sandmo, A. (1969).   "Capital Risk, Consumption, and Portfolio Choice." *Econometrica* 37: 586 - 99.

Saranson, I., R. E. Smith; and E. Diener.   (1975).   "Personality Research: Components of Variance Attributable to the Person and the Situation." *Journal of Social Issues* 28: 71 - 85.

Savio, M. (1965). "An End to History." In S. M. Lipset and S. S. Wolin (eds.) *The Barkeley Student Revolt.* pp. 216 - 19. Garden City, N. Y.: Doubleday Anchor Books.

Schelling, T. C. (1960). *The Strategy of Conflict.* Cambridge: Harvard University Press.

Schelling, T. C. (1978). *Micromotives and Macrobehavior.* New York: Norton.

Schmidt, P., and R. P. Strauss. (1975). "The Prediction of Occupation Using Multiple Logit Models." *International Economic Review* 16 (2): 471-486.

Schoemaker, P. (1982). "The Expected Utility Model: Its Variants, Purposes, Evidence, and Limitations." *Journal of Economic Literature* 529-564.

Schumpeter, J. (1955). *The Theory of Economic Development.* Cambridge: Harvard University Press.

Schwab, J. J. (1969). *College Curricula and Student Protest.* Chicago: University of Chicago Press.

Schwartz, R. A. (1976). "Personal Philanthropic Contributions," *Journal of Political Economy* 78: 1264 - 91.

Scott, J. W., and M. El-Assal. (1969). "Multiversity, University Size, University Quality and Student Protest: An Empirical Study." *American Sociological Review* 34: 702 - 9.

Sears D. O., and J. B. McConahey. (1973). *The Politics of Violence: The New Urban Black and the Watts Riot.* Boston: Houghton Mifflin.

Sen, A. K. (1967). "Isolation, Assurance and Social Rate of Discount." *Quarterly Journal of Economics* 81: 112-24.

Sen, A. K. (1970). *Growth Economics.* Middlesex: Penguin Books.

Sen, A. K. (1973) *On Economic Inequality.* New York: W. W. Norton Co.

Sen, A. K. (1977). "Rational Fools: A Critique of the Behavioral Foundation of Economic Theory." *Philosophy and Public Affairs* 6: 317-344. Reprinted in F. Hahn and M. Hollis, (eds.) *Philosophy and Economic Theory.* New York: Oxford University Press.

Sen, A. K. (1987). *On Ethics and Economics.* Oxford: Basil Blackwell.

Sen Gupta, A. (1972). "Regional Disparity and Economic Development of Pakistan." In V. K. R. V. Rao (ed), *Bangladesh Economy Problems & Perspectives, Institute of Economic Growth.* pp. 15 -55. New Delhi, India: Vikash Publications.

Shaw, M. E. (1978). "Communications Networks Fourteen Years Later." In L. Berkowitz (ed.) *Group Processes.* New York: Academic Press.

Sherman, H. J., and Wood, J. L. (1979). *Sociology: Traditional and Radical Perspectives*. New York: Harper & Row.

Shorter, E., and C. Tilly. (1974). *Strikes in France, 1830-1968.* New York: Cambridge University Press.

Siegelman, L. and M. Simpson. (1977). "A Cross-National Test of the Linkages Between Economic Inequality and Political Violence." *Journal of Conflict Resolution* 10: 41 - 64.

Silver, M. (1974). "Political Revolution and Reforming: An Economic Approach." *Public Choice* 17: 63 - 71.

Simon, H. A. (1979). "Human Nature in Politics: The Dialogue of Psychology with Political Science," *American Political Science Review*: 79 (2): 293-304.

Singh, H. (1986). "When are Expectations Rational? Some Vexing Questions and Behavioral Clues." *Journal of Behavioral Economics* 15: 191 - 210.

Skolnick, J. H. (1969). *The Politics of Protest.* New York: Ballentine.

Slovic, P. (1966). "Value As A Determiner of Subjective Probability: IEEE." *Transactions On Human Factors In Electronics.* 1: 22-28.

Slovic, P., and S. Lichtenstein. (1968) "Relative Importance of Probabilites and Payoffs in Risk Taking," *Journal of Experimental Psychology.* 78: 1 - 18.

Smelser, N. J. (1963). *Theory of Collective Behavior*, New York: The Free Press of Glencoe.

Smelser, N. J. (1972). "Some Additional Thoughts on Collective Behavior." *Sociological Inquiry* 42: 97 - 101.

Smelser, N. J.   (ed). (1973). *Karl Marx on Society and Social Change.* Chicago: University of Chicago Press.

Smelser, N. J. (1974). "Growth, Structural Change, and Conflict in California Higher Education, 1950 - 1970." In N. J. Smelser and G. Almond (eds.) *Public Higher Education in California.* pp. 9 - 141. Berkeley: University of California Press.

Smelser, N. J., and S. Lipset. (1966). *Social Structure and Mobility in Economic Development*. Chicago: Aldine Press.

Smith, D. N. (1974). *Who Rules the Universities?* New York: Monthly Review Press.

Snyder, D. (1975). "Institutional Setting and Industrial Conflict." *American Sociological Review* 40: 395 - 405.

Snyder, D. (1978). "Collective Violence: A Research Agenda and Some Strategic Considerations." *Journal of Conflict Resolution* 22: 499 - 535.

Snyder, D., and C. Tilley. (1972). "On Debating and Falsifying Theories of Collective Violence." *American Sociological Review* 39: 610 - 3.

Snyder, D., and C. Tilley. (1974). "Hardship and Collective Violence in France, 1830 - 1960." *American Sociological Review* 37: 520 - 30.

Solow, R. E. (1986). "Economics, Is Something Missing?" In W. N. Parker (ed.) *Economic History and Modern Economist*, pp. 21 -29. Oxford: Basil Blackwell.

Somers R. H. (1965). "The Mainsprings of Rebellion: A Survey of Berkeley Students in November, 1964." In S. M. Lipset and S. S. Wolin (eds.) *The Berkeley Student Revolt*, pp. 530-557. Garden City, N. Y.: Anchor Books.

Somers, R. H. (1969). "The Berkeley Campus in the Twilight of the Free Speech Movement: Hope or Futility?" In J. McEvoy and Abraham Miller (eds) *Black Power and Student Rebellion*, pp. 419-440. Belmont, Calif.: Wadsworth.

Sommers, P., and D. Suits. (1971). "A Cross-Section, Model of Economic Growth." *Review of Economics and Statistics*. 8: 121-28.

Spencer, H. (1967). *The Evolution of Society: Selections from Herbert Spencer's Principles of Sociology*. Chicago: University of Chicago Press.

Spencer, R. (1965). "Nature and Value of Functionalism in Anthropology." In D. Martindale (ed) *Functionalism in Social Sciences*. Phiadelphia: American Academy of Political and Social Sciences.

Spilerman, S. (1970). "The Causes of Racial Disturbances: A Comparison of Alternative Explanantions." *American Sociological Review.* 35, pp. 627-649.

Spilerman S. (1971). "The Causes of Racial Disturbances: Tests of an Explanation." *American Sociological Review* 36: 427-42.

Spilerman, S. (1976). "Structural Characteristics of Cities and the Severity of Racial Disorders. *American Sociological Review* 41: 771 - 93.

Stallings, R. (1973). "Patterns of Belief in Social Movements: Clarifications from an Analysis of Environmental Groups." *Sociological Quarterly* 14: 465 - 80.

Stark, R. (1972). *Police Riots.* Belmont: California: Wadsworth.

Steedman, I. (1977). *Marx after Sraffa.* London: Unwin Brothers.

Steedman, I., and U. Kraus. (1986). "Goethe's Faust, Arrow's Possibility Theorem and the Individual Decision Taker." In J. Elster (ed.) *The Multiple Self.* Cambridge: Cambridge University Press.

Steiner, J. F. (1969). *Treblinka.* London: Corgibooks.

Stewart, D., and Y. P. Venieris. (1985). "Sociopolitical Instability and the Behavior of Savings in the Less Developed Countries." *Review of Economics and Statistics.* 67: 557-63.

Stigler, J. (1958). "Ricardo and the 93% Labor of Value." *American Economic Review* 48: 357-67.

Stigler, J. (1971). "The Economic Theory of Regulation." *Bell Journal of Economics* 2: 3 - 21.

Stigler, J. (1981). "Economics of Ethics?" In S. McMurrin (ed.) *Tanner Lectures on Human Values*, vol II. Cambridge: Cambridge University Press.

Stiglitz, J. E. (1988). *Economics of the Public Sector.* 2nd ed. New York: W. W. Norton & Co.

Streeten, P. (1967). "The Use and Abuse of Models in Development Planning." In Martin, K. and Knapp, J. (eds.) *The Teaching and Development Economics: Its Position in the Present State of Knowledge.* London: Frank Cass.

Stouffer, S. A., et al. (1949). *The American Soldier: Adjustment During Army Life*. Princeton: Princeton University Press.

Sugden, R. (1984). "Reciprocity: The Supply of Public Goods Through Voluntary Contributions." *Economic Journal* 94: 772-787.

Swan, T. (1962). "Circular Causation." *Economic Record* : 421-26.

Sweezy, P. (1981). *Four Lectures on Marxism*. New York: Monthly Review Press.

Tanter, R. (1966). "Dimensions of Conflict Behavior Within and Between Nations, 1958-60," *Journal of Conflict Resolution* 10: 41 - 64.

Taylor, C. and M. Hudson (1972). *World Handbook of Political and Social Indicators*. 2nd ed. New Haven: Yale University Press.

Taylor, C., and M. Jodice. (1982). *Annual Events Data*. Inter University Consortium.

Tilly, C. (1964). *The Vendee*. Cambridge: Harvard University Press.

Tilly, C. (1969a). "Collective Violence in European Perspective," in H. D. Graham and T. R. Gurr (eds.) *The History of Violence in America*, pp. 4 - 45. New York: Praeger.

Tilly, C. (1969b). "Collective Violence in European Perspective," in H. D. Graham and T. R. Gurr (eds.) *Violence in America: Historical and Comparative Perspectives*, pp. 4-42. A report to the National Commission on the Causes and Prevention of Violence, June 1969. New York: Signet Books.

Tilly, C. (1974). "The Chaos of the Living City." In C. Tilly (ed.) *An Urban World*. Boston: Little Brown.

Tilly, C. 1978. *From Mobilization to Revolution*. Boston: Addison and Wesley.

Trimberger, E. K. (1986). "A Theory of Elite Revolutions." In J. A. Goldstone (ed.) *Revolutions: Theoretical, Comparative, and Historical Studies*, pp. 159 - 172. San Diego, Ca.: Harcourt Brace and Jovanovich.

Trivers, R. L. (1971). "The Evolution of Resiprocal Altruism." *Quarterly Review of Biology* 46: 35 - 37.

Trotsky, L. (1932). *The History of Russian Revolution*. Garden City, N. Y.: Doubleday.

Tsaklouglou, P. (1988). "Development and Inequality Revisite." *Applied Economics* 20 (4): 509 - 32.`

Tucker, G. S. L. (1961). "Ricardo and Marx." *Economica* 28: 252-269.

Tugwell, R. G. (1924). "Experimental Economics." In Tugwell, R.G. (ed.) *The Trend of Economics*. New York: Alfred A. Knopf.

Tullock, G. (1971). The Paradox of Revolution. *Public Choice* 11: 89 -99.

Tullock, G. (1974). "Does Punishment Deter Crime?" *The Public Interest.*

Tully, M., and S. Jacob. (1985). *Amritsar: Mrs. Gandhi's Last Battle*. Calcutta, India: Rupa & Co. By arrangement with Pan Books Ltd. London.

Turner, R. H., and L. M. Killian (1957). *Collective Behavior*. 2nd ed published in 1972. Englewood Cliffs, N. J.: Prentice-Hall.

Veblen, T. (1899). *The Theory of the Leisure Clan: An Economic Study of the Evolution of Institutions*. New York: Macmillan Co.

Venieris, Y. P., and D. K. Gupta. (1983). "Sociopolitical and Economic Dimensions of Development: A Cross-Sectional Model," *Economic Development of Cultural Change* 31: 727 - 57.

Venieris, Y. P., and D. K. Gupta. (1985). "Macro Interactions in a Social System: A Case Study of Great Britain." *Southern Economic Journal* January: 681-696.

Venieris, Y.P., and D. K. Gupta. (1986). "Income Distribution and Sociopolitical Instability as Determinants of Savings: A Cross-Sectional Model." *Journal of Political Economy* 94: 873 - 84.

Volkan, V. D. (1988). *The Need to Have Enemies & Allies: From Clinical Practice to International Relations*. Dunmore, Penn.: Jason Aronson.

Vraa, C. W. (1974).   "Emotional Climate As A Function Of Group Composition." *Small Group Behavior* 5: 105 - 20.

"A Year of Violence Divides, Yet Unites a West Bank Family. After 4 Months in Desert Jail, "Good Arab" Father Now Sides with a Radical Son." (1988). *The Wall Street Journal,* December 12, p. 1.

Wallace, J., and E. Sadalla,   (1966). "Behavioral Concequences of Transgression: The Effect of Social Recognition." *Journal of Experimental Research in Personality* 46: 35 - 37.

Ward, B. (1972). *What's Wrong with Economics?*   London: Macmillan.

Watkins, M. W. (1958). "Veblen's View of Cultural Evolution." In D. F. Dowd (ed) *Thostein Veblen: A Critical Reappraisal.* Ithaca, N. Y.: Cornell University Press.

Weede, E. (1981).   "Income Inequality, Average Income, and Domestic Violence." *Journal of Conflict Resolution* 25: 304 - 14.

Weisskopf, W. (1949).   "Psychological Aspects of Economic Thought." *Journal of Political Economy* 62: 304 - 14.

Welldon, J. E. C. (1883).   Translated in 1905. *The Politics of Aristotle.* New York: Macmillan.

Wilkinson, P. (1979). "Social Scientific Theory and Civil Violence." In Y. Alexander; D. Carlton; and P. Wilkinson (eds.) *Terrorism: Theory and Practice.* Boulder, Colo.: Westview Press. 45 -72.

Willhoite, F., Jr. (1980). "Reciprocity, Political Origins and Legitimacy." Paper presented at American Political Science Association Annual Meeting, Washington D. C.

Wilson, D. S. (1980). *The Natural Selections of Populations and Communities.* Menlo Park, Calif.: Benjamin Cummings.

Wilson, E. O. (1975). *Sociobiology,   The New Synthesis.* Cambridge.: Belknap.

Wilson, J. (1961).   "The Strategy of Protest." *Journal of Conflict Resolution* 3: 291 - 303.

Wilson, J. (1973). *Introduction to Social Movements*. New York: Basic Books.

Wirth, L. (1957). "Urbanism as a Way of Life." in P. K. Hatt and A. J. Reiss (eds.) *Cities and Society*. New York: The Free Press of Glencoe.

Wispe, L. (1978). *Altruism, Sympathy, and Helping*. New York: Academic Press.

Wolf, E. R. (1986) "Peasant Rebellion and Revolution." In J. A. Goldstone (ed) *Revolutions: Theoretical, Comparative, and Historical Studies*, pp. 173 - 81. San Diego, California: Harcourt, Brace, Jovanovich.

Wolfe, K. (1939). *Dachau: The Nazi Hell*. London: Aldor Publishing.

Wolfenstein, E. (1967). *The Revolutionary Personality: Lenin, Trotsky, and Gandhi*. Princeton: Princeton University Press.

Woo, H. K. H. (1986). *What's Wrong With Formalization in Economics?* Newark, Calif.: Victoria Press.

Wood, J. L. (1974). *The Sources of American Student Activism*. Lexington, Mass.: Lexington Books.

Wood, J. L. (1975).   "New Left Ideology: Its Dimensions, and Development." Sage Professional Paper in American Politics Series, Vol. 2, no. 04-022. Beverly Hills and London: Sage Publications.

Wood, J. L., and P. T. Gay. (1978). *Empirical Tests of Paradigms and Theories for Module in Social Movements*. Washington D. C.: The American Political Science Association. (August).

Wood, J. L., and W. Ng. (1980).   "Socialization and Student Activism: Examination of a Relationship. *Research in Social Movements, Conflict and Change*. 3: 21 - 43.

Wood, J. L., and M. Jackson. (1982). *Social Movements: Development, Participation, and Dynamics*. Belmont, California: Wadsworth.

Wyden, P. (1979). *Bay of Pigs: The Untold Story*. New York: Simon and Schuster.

Yoo, J. (1985). "Does Korea Trace Japan's Footsteps? A Macroeconomic Appraisal." *KYKLOS* 38: 578-598.

Yotopoulos, P. and Nugent, J. B. (1976). *Economics of Development: Empirical Investigations*. New York: Harper & Row.

Zellner, A., and T. H. Lee. (1964). "Joint Estimation of Relationship Involving Discrete Random Variables." *Econometrica* 33: 382 -94.

Ziegenhagen, E. A. (1986). *The Regulation of Political Conflict*. New York: Praeger.

Zimmerman, J. (1965). *Poor Lands, Rich Lands: The Widening Gap*. New York: Random House.

Index

About the Author

Dipak K. Gupta is a Professor in the School of Public Administration and Urban Studies and Co-Director of the Institute for International Security and Conflict Resolution at San Diego State University. Professor Gupta received Master's degrees in Economics from Visva Bharati University, Santiniketan, India, and the University of Pittsburgh. He earned his Ph.D. in the area of Economic and Social Development from the Graduate School of Public and International Affairs at the University of Pittsburgh. He received a post-doctoral fellowship at the Institute for International Politics and Economics in Belgrade, Yugoslavia. He has also been a visiting scholar at St. Anthony's College, Oxford University, and El Colegio de Mexico in Mexico City.

Professor Gupta has published articles in journals such as *Journal of Political Economy, Economic Development and Cultural Change, Southern Economic Journal, Urban Affairs Quarterly, Columbia Journal of World Business, Political Psychology, Fordham Urban Law Journal, Public Administration Quarterly,* and *Journal of Behavioral Economics.*